The Screen of Change

Lives made over by the moving image

Peter Hopkinson

Introduction by Kevin Brownlow

'A real contribution to the literature of film in the 20th century.'

Raymond Fielding
(Dean and Professor, School of Motion Picture
Television and Recording Arts, Florida State University)

'A history of the moving image told from the perspective of somebody who has experienced many of the major developments in the industry at first hand.'

Melvyn Bragg
(Controller Arts, London Weekend Television)

UKA PRESS
Published by UKA Press
UKA Press, 55 Elmsdale Road, Walthamstow, London, E17 6PN, UK
UKA Press Europe, Olympiaweg 102-hs, 1076 XG, Amsterdam, Holland
UKA Press, Anders YCCreative, Yajimaya, 2-1-8 Yaizu 425, Japan

First published in Great Britain in 2008 by UKA Press

A CIP catalogue record for this book is available from the British Library

ISBN: 978-1-905796-12-0
[1-905-796-12-9]

Cover photograph © Peter Hopkinson

Printed in the United Kingdom

'Documentaries are for disappointed feature film-makers or out of work poets.'

Michael Powell

'More remains to be done in the field of documentary and didactic films than in fiction cinema.'

Eric Rohmer

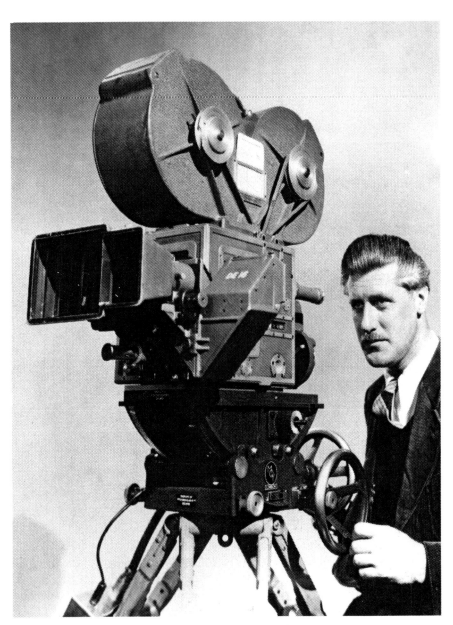

Technicolor three-strip camera

To

Basil Wright

Contents

Introduction

I began my career as a film editor with Peter Hopkinson in the 1950s. I liked working with him. He was an enthusiast, dedicated to his craft. He was also the strong, silent type, the sort of man you would choose to go into the jungle with. I only wish I had done so; he would have enhanced the experience with his curiosity and knowledge. But he was just as impressive in ordinary life. When something serious occurred on a film we were both working on, and he was unjustly accused by the management, it never occurred to him to make excuses. He simply sat, shouldering the blame and keeping it away from the rest of us.

He was a lover of cinema from an early age. He had his own projector and collection of films when he was a boy. We shared a fascination with American films, and he was old enough to have seen them when they were silent. His enthusiasm for the director King Vidor sent me in search of his films – which were every bit as brilliant as he said they were – and then in search of the man. Hopkinson had this effect on you. His description in this book of Vidor's *The Citadel* will have you searching for the DVD[1].

Peter also loved music, and he had a special fondness for Elgar, from the days when the name was frowned upon by the high-tone critics. His politics were left-wing, and his influences were Picture Post, the Crown Film Unit, the Academy cinema...

But he was a far more glamorous figure than this prosaic list suggests, for he had shot footage under fire, he had worked for Cinerama, he had photographed and directed for *March of Time*...

Ah, the *March of Time*! Working with Peter and recalling this marvellous series led me to include a fake German newsreel in my film *It Happened Here*, the story of the Nazi occupation of England, a homage in its turn to Orson Welles, who had included *News on the March!* in *Citizen Kane*.

1. In fact at time of writing *The Citadel* (1938) does not seem to be available in any format, DVD or otherwise, which is a great pity.

I had always wanted to be a newsreel cameraman, and with the Hopkinson example so close at hand, I took a l6mm camera to Prague in 1968, just after the Russians had invaded, getting arrested for my trouble by the Soviet Army. But this paled into insignificance against the real thing, and I always acknowledged the courage it took to film real warfare, as Peter had done so often. Strange as it may sound, one of his most courageous deeds involved *not* filming that warfare. Peter was confronted by a cameraman's dream come true when a parachute drop in wartime Greece took place directly on top of him. But a gale caused chaos; when soldiers landed in the sea and were dragged into danger, he put his camera aside and rushed to the rescue.

Peter was born in Harrow, Middlesex in 1920, and remembered seeing *Metropolis* at the Harrow Coliseum, a cinema that was far more a temple of worship to him than the church on the hill. When talkies came in, a cousin gave him his silent 35mm projector, which filled his bedroom. He spent all his pocket money on films. He became too devoted; exams were looming and instead of spending his last day revising, he rushed to the West End to see *The Tunnel* with Richard Dix. He failed the exam and his father restricted his film-going.

Stunned by the impact of *Things to Come,* the sixteen-year-old Hopkinson wrote to its producer, Korda – no vacancies. He tried Ealing, and got a job as clapper boy on George Formby comedies. When Ealing laid him off, his father demanded that he got a safe job in a bank. 'I bet you five shillings', said the defiant Peter, 'that within a week I will get another job at another studio'.

And he did – at Denham, home of Korda. A high point of his life, as you will read in this book, was working with the great American director King Vidor on *The Citadel*, A J Cronin's story of an idealistic young doctor in a Welsh mining village and his struggle against the corrupt medical profession in London. Vidor, friendly and democratic, told him all about early Hollywood. 'I was in the clouds', wrote Hopkinson in *Split Focus*, 'and I lived that film just as intensely, I'm certain, as did its director'. But after *The Citadel*, everything was an anti-climax, although he did travel briefly on a flying carpet for *The Thief of Bagdad*

9

(1940). In 1939, he was called up and had to bid farewell both to Denham and to his ambitions.

During the phoney war, he showed his fellow soldiers Eisenstein's *Battleship Potemkin* only to discover that they far preferred westerns. When Hitler invaded Russia, he volunteered for service overseas and was accepted, but at the last minute he heard he'd been selected as a cameraman. It was December 1941 and he was 21.

While he was trying to get *Split Focus* published, he was lucky enough to find a sympathetic agent, Hope Leresche. With unusual generosity, he told her about my film *It Happened Here* – and one unforgettable lunchtime she commissioned a book about it. *How It Happened Here* was published in 1968. David Gardiner republished it at UKA Press in 2005 – and when I showed him *The Screen of Change* in 2007 he decided that that should be published too. I only wish Peter could have seen the result. He checked some of the text and was able to make corrections to Part One, but he fell ill and died before he could correct Part Two. If there was anything he would have wanted after he had gone, however, it was for this book to be made available.

The Screen of Change is almost an autobiography. It was first written in the 1970s and updated in 2001. It would benefit from being updated again, so rapid has been the advance of the electronic image, but this would require rewriting. David Gardiner and I decided to keep the text just as Peter completed it. It might benefit from further editing, but we have not tampered with its integrity. His was a unique voice and we present this memoir precisely as he wrote it. Its value can only increase with time.

Kevin Brownlow
London, 2007.

Part One

1. BACK TO SCHOOL IN POONA

'Teaching – what a wonderful thing that would be. How I'd love to be a teacher.'

Orson Welles

Shantaram directs at his old Prabhat studios

You came from Singapore, Indonesia, Thailand, Nepal, Sri Lanka and India.

You could just as easily have come from Florida or California; Beaconsfield or Brixton; Senegal, Cairo, Krakow or Central or South America.

You wanted to make films. You asked questions:

'Why do we have to write a script?'

'Why can't we make an experimental film?'

'Isn't the tradition of the Director elitist?'

'Why can't we film as a group?'

'What's the point of history? History is what we make and do now.'

You were student film-makers. I was your temporary teacher, thrust into this novel position by years of filmmaking myself, the publication of a book of my first thirty years adventure with a movie camera, and a letter which had followed soon after:

'The Film Institute of India, in collaboration with UNESCO, is organising its second regional training course in documentary, short-film script writing – the object of the course is to provide practising Asian film-makers with an opportunity of seeing and developing new styles and techniques of short subject film making for screen and television in order to improve the quality and effectiveness of documentary production in the region.'

'Would you,' the writer of this letter went on to ask me, 'be interested in participating at this course as a short term UNESCO consultant? Your primary task would be to provide guidance and teaching support in the field of documentary, short-film production for use by television. Mr Basil Wright, who has agreed to participate as the other consultant will confine his contribution to the documentary film in its traditional screen role'.

UNESCO, I knew, meant the United Nations Educational Scientific and Cultural Organisation. Brought into being primarily by British initiative soon after the Second World War, in the belief that since wars begin in the minds of men, it is in the minds of men that the defences of peace must be constructed. And Basil Wright – the first of the young *cinéastes* fresh down from Cambridge to join John Grierson in the creation of the Brit-

13

ish Documentary Film Movement in the 1930s. Maker himself of such classics of the time as *Song of Ceylon* and, with Harry Watt, *Night Mail*.

My response to this personal appeal by UNESCO had been an immediate and unqualified 'yes'. In the formal speech which I was called upon to make at the inauguration of the course I gave my reason:

'It is now twenty years since I was last in India. More than twenty years, in fact, for I arrived with a film camera hard on the heels of independence (in 1947). My task then was to film and chronicle those first two tremendous, and turbulent, years of freedom. To me then – at much the same age of most of you in this hall now – that was the most exciting and worthwhile assignment of a young lifetime ... As a Cameraman/Reporter I travelled and filmed the length and breadth of this great country, and when I finally flew off to Japan from Calcutta, left a large part of my heart here behind me. Now, twenty years later, I am back once again, and people are asking me what changes I note, what developments I observe. Well, *you* are the great change, *the* great development.'

Who were they, this cross-section of a new generation of Indian and Asian film-makers, for whom I had been chosen to be some sort of guru? Some had graduated from this same Film and now Television Institute of India a few years before. Others had found their own way into commercial production. Nearly half the twenty-two assembled for our own special course (while the Institute's regular students now went on holiday) were from countries other than India: from Nepal, in the far north in the foothills of Tibet; from Thailand, with its gently tinkling tolerance of temples; Indonesia, that great group of islands and home of more than two hundred million; Singapore, originator of gin slings and now aggressive capitalism; Sri Lanka, formerly Ceylon, then still serene in its Buddhist certainties, and the location as well as subject of my companion Basil Wright's own most personal film.

Students at work at the Film Institute of India

Representing all of these countries, cultures and peoples, every one of these challenging young faces now sizing me up was already a film-maker. Like Ananda Berera from Singapore, heading up and producing a current affairs programme for his city-state's television service; Tissa Liyanasuriya, bringing with him *Deepthi*, his film of the culture behind the lives of four students at Sri Lanka's university; Sai Paranjype, the only woman, whose grandfather had been the subject of India's first newsreel when, back in 1901, he had returned in glory to Bombay after winning unique distinction in mathematics at Cambridge. Now his grand-daughter was going to write one of our best scripts.

They were me, as I had been them, a generation back. And I was them, but for the geographic and historic accident of birth, somewhere else, away in Europe, just a couple or so decades earlier.

It was what had happened to me, what I had experienced in that time, to which I now had to bear witness; justify if you like (as I saw it) my own existence to these, my own latter-day contemporaries.

Like all of this group, of which I now became a focal point, I too was a working film-maker. These six weeks in Poona were to be just a brief break from the ups and down of earning a living with a movie camera: trying to capture with it, to some purpose, something of the pulse and passion of our times. I was well aware that I would be just as much a student myself, learning just as much (if not more) from these who were now my students as they might perhaps learn from me, in this testing time now under way between us, at the Film and now Television Institute of India, here in Poona.

In Poona we talked not of polo and of conduct possibly unbecoming in the mess, but of films. Of *Lonely Boy* Paul Anka and *The Reality of Karel Apell*. *The War Game* was for us no manoeuvre mounted on India's North West Frontier, but Peter Watkins' impassioned film of nuclear annihilation.

For Poona is, and always has been, a great deal more than just a comic-sounding backwater for the Colonel Blimps of a

Author in class - Parbhat Studios - now The Film Institute of India

Author as guru

now obsolete British military establishment (and is now, I discovered, spelt by the Indians *Pune*). Two hundred years ago it was the capital of the mighty empire of the Marathas, fierce Hindu horsemen never conquered or subdued by the Moguls, finally routed by the future Duke of Wellington twelve years before Waterloo. A hundred miles to the south east of Bombay, it is now a centre of light industry, producing textiles, paper, chemicals. It is the seat of one of India's leading universities; and, since 1961, it has been the home of this largest film school in Asia – in the entire world then second only in size, enrolment and scale to Moscow.

Surprising? Not really, and not at all if you realise that India long ago outranked the United States in sheer volume of film making, producing nowadays some nine hundred features and over three thousand short films in just a single year.

No one had told me before I arrived in Poona that the Film and Television Institute of India was in fact a fully-operational medium-sized, and self-contained film studio in its own right.

These former *Prabhat Studios* had been built by a pioneer Indian film-maker, the first to aim a movie camera at India's enormous social problems instead of her phantasmagoric world of religious ritual and make-believe, Rajaram Vanakudre Shantaram. In these studios of his own construction, he made, in 1936, *Amar Jyoti* (Eternal Light), the first Indian film to win a Venice Festival Award, eighteen years before Satyajit Ray's *Pather Panchali* was to hit the headlines at Cannes. Shantaram's *Shakuntala*, based on a 5th Century Sanskrit adaption of an episode in the Mahabharata, was the first Indian film to achieve commercial showing in the United States, opening in New York on Christmas Day 1947 – the same year of Indian Independence and my own arrival in the subcontinent – as a camera-wielding film reporter of the first two turbulent years of freedom from British Imperial rule.

And now, in these same former studios of this Indian pioneer, I screened (and dissected) films that I had then gone on to make in India myself; worked with my own group of students on scripts which ranged in subject from student unrest to the use of insecticide in agriculture; and – as the catalytic agent of a collective – went forth and shot a group film in the villages of the nearby countryside where, thirty-two years before, Shantaram had made *The Unexpected* (*Duniya na Mane*). This had been the story of a young girl married to an old man by family arrangement. Aware of the harm done to this girl Mirmala, and with divorce then impossible, the elderly husband commits suicide. Thereby Shantaram had thrown up another problem into the face of his audience, the stigma of widowhood in Hindu society.

Take nothing for granted is to me one of life's golden rules. But master the rules before you throw them out the window.

I was in Poona, teaching, because I had lived through more and therefore (it could be presumed) acquired more experience than most. Some might say that too much experience is a liability. 'We're not interested in experience – it's flair we're after', a suppliant film-maker friend of mine was once informed by the BBC.

Is experience – a sense of history – a handicap? Here at Poona I was surrounded by history, and not just that of the Marathas. Movie history vaults full of it. Bricks and mortar too. For these *Prabhat Studios* were themselves part and parcel of the history of motion pictures.

Now a hundred year history – which had begun for India with a demonstration at a hotel in Bombay, July 7, 1896. The location for the first British encounter with these moving pictures had been no transient hotel, but had taken place four months before, at the Polytechnic in London's Regent Street, on the 21st February, 1896.

There I too sat in the stalls of its theatre, a hand-cranked projector set up in the aisle alongside, projecting on to a screen short snippets of workers leaving the equipment manufacturers' factory; a baby playing havoc with a family seated on a lawn, a baby being fed outdoors by its parents, Monsieur Trewey doing funny things with a hat – and a train arriving at the out of town station of La Ciotat in France. An anniversary recreation of the original Lumière programme, with the same films, projected in the same way, on the same spot, forty years on, 21st February,

19

1936. There I now was, a sixteen year old schoolboy – mad keen on the movies, and about to stumble on to a film set for the first time, clutching a clapper board, seven months later. So I guess I do have a story to tell, and perhaps an assessment to make.

'His life belongs to the history of cinema and the cinema of history' once wrote of me Dilys Powell, that eminent film critic of the *Sunday Times*. So if you would like to know how it was to film Marlene Dietrich in a bath tub and the Emperor of Japan at the seaside; set up a camera on the stage of Black African protest and the original and ancient Babylonia of D.W. Griffith's *Intolerance* – then by all means read on.

For what I could do at Poona was draw upon and tell my fellow students, and now you, the reader of this book, something of my own history. And it started in a film studio too, a film studio built at just the same time as Shantaram was putting the roof on this one in India.

The country outside may have been as English as the cricket match on the nearby village green. But inside, Korda's Denham was then as Hollywood as Culver City. And so let us first of all flash back to the Thirties, to the heyday of the film as mass entertainment and escape. When the giant screens of those super Palaces, Odeons, Regals, Gaumonts, and Roxys seldom reflected (as is still the case in India) any change of condition more radical than the next bi-weekly programme.

Or did they?

2. FILM AND FICTION

'Korda was a great producer because he was an ex-director.'

Harry Watt

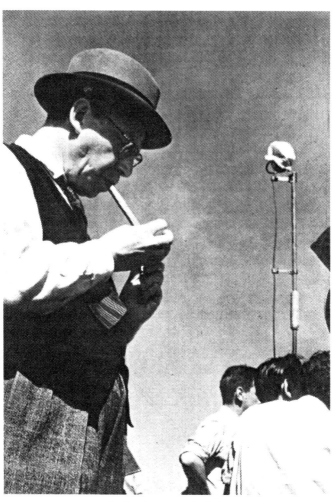

At Denham Korda lights up

'Henry VIII had six wives.
Catherine of Aragon was the first,
but her story is of no particular interest –
she was a respectable woman.
So Henry divorced her.
He then married Anne Boleyn.
This marriage also was a failure,
but not for the same reason.'

The opening title of a film now more than seventy years old. A hundred minutes later Charles Laughton, acting by then the ancient King, summed up his story to camera: 'Six wives, and the best of them's the worst' – and the audience at the premiere in London's Leicester Square Theatre were on their feet, cheering. Twelve days earlier, *The Private Life of Henry VIII* had opened at New York's Radio City Music Hall where, in that same week of 1933, it had already taken only four hundred dollars less than the world record figure for any film at any single theatre up to that time. A British film had conquered America, and its producer was now ready to take on Hollywood.

The irony is, of course, that this now legendary British film was in fact made by a Hungarian, born Sandor Laszlo Kellner. It is a coincidence worth pondering that this middle European who first made British films something to reckon with in the world was born within months of the first commercial showing of films in the United States, which had taken place in an amusement arcade in New York, 14 April 1894. The movies and Alexander Korda were clearly made for each other.

It is generally reckoned that Alexander Korda's career took off with *Henry VIII*. In fact this was no less than the fiftieth film to be directed by the then forty-year-old impresario. As the eldest of three brothers of an impoverished rural family, at the age of fifteen he had set out to seek their fortune in the glittering Budapest of pre-World War One. At first journalism offered a living (of a sort) and this led the way to film criticism and publicity in a succession of periodicals, some of which he launched and published himself; as well as an apprenticeship in what was to prove to be his vocation, augmented by translating into Hungarian the titles of the imported silent films of the time. By 1914 he was directing a film himself. Spared military service because of poor eyesight, he had gone on to direct more than another twenty before the collapse of the central powers and the fascist regime of Miklos Horthy drove him out of Hungary – never to return – and off to Vienna in 1918.

Four films followed, based on Austria, and he was in Berlin. Here he directed six films in less than three years, and was off to Hollywood. Ten in the next three, covering the transition to sound, and he was summarily fired from Fox in a studio revolution. Back in Europe, Korda then took stock of himself and the movie business. He was now thirty-seven years old, with already no less than forty feature films to his credit.

Paramount had a lot of money tied up in France. What more sensible than that this European director with American experience should use some of this for multilingual production? A brainwave which led to a sensitive and successful 1931 filming of the *Marius* of Marcel Pagnol's Marseilles trilogy – and the coming together of all the basic talents of the production team of the great films to come. The fellow Hungarian novelist and playwright Lajos Biro to mastermind the scripts; brother Vincent to design the sets; the French cameraman Georges Perinal to light them and direct the photography.

Paramount had money banked in Britain too, and the British had an Act of Parliament which required the predominantly American renters to make available for distribution a set quota of British-produced films. Korda and his group crossed the Channel and quickly made no less than nine such 'quickies' for Paramount release. With now nearly fifty films and five countries behind him, contacts throughout Europe and the United States, and established at last where this truly genuine internationalist finally felt at home, Alexander Korda decided to make a film to please himself, for the world market as he saw it, his own way. He had at first no distribution, money ran out half way through production, but the rest is history. *The Private Life of Henry VIII* brought as suppliants to his feet the film world of the thirties, his to command. He had huge plans, vast visions; a sense, no less, of mission.

An insurance company, the Prudential, had as always money lying idle, money to invest. Money to invest not as nowadays in property, but then – thanks to the plausible pleading of an Australian who had first of all come along to Korda with a project of his own – films. As a result, about to become Korda's General manager, 'Monty' Marks talked the Prudential into backing Korda. More, he helped to persuade Korda into building his own studios; and, moreover, found the site. Marks bought 193 acres of the English countryside, some twelve miles out of London near the little Buckinghamshire village of Denham, for a mere £15,000.

A schoolboy still in 1935, I stood entranced at the side of the Denham-Harefield Road, and marvelled as the shells of seven enormous sound stages rose high into the incongruous air of this otherwise peaceful English countryside. Then under construction, here was the largest movie studio in Europe, the British Hollywood to be.

At right angles to the main road, the three largest of the huge hangar-like buildings (one of which sub-divided into two) had on each of their respective facades one of the words making up the name of the company which Korda now proudly proclaimed to the world: LONDON FILM PRODUCTIONS. Three smaller, but still outsize sound stages, stood off at right angles to the side of this triplicate of their elder brothers. The main gate opened into the intersection. To the immediate left were the main projection and music recording theatres, L.F.P's own offices above them, the sound department alongside. This was at the head of a long line of separate production offices, stretching the length of the combined studio front and running the width of the four main stages. Not far short of half a mile, the entrance from the particular office to the production with which it was involved on the floor of an adjacent stage was across, or along, a corridor which ran this entire, and seemingly interminable, length.

The one thing everyone who worked at Denham will never forget is this 'corridor'. The longest enclosed dead straight thoroughfare any of us will ever know. The studio's jugular vein. Up its length, down its length, in and out of its cross-sections of entrances and exits, flowed the whole pulse of the place. Producers hurried to conferences, directors to rushes, stars to make-up, and clapper-boys like me with film to loading rooms.

At the far end were dressing rooms, make-up and hairdressing, restaurant, canteen. At the main studio entrance end, and beyond the three smaller sound stages, were to be found plasterers, painters, construction and machine shops, a foundry, metal, blacksmith's, turnsmith's and plumbing shops, modellers studio, electrical and other workshops, property store, and a miniature hospital. To the rear of the three main stages there functioned the biggest electrical generating power station yet to have been built for any private concern in Britain.

Soon to be of particular concern to me, at the other end of Stage Seven (the top half of the subdivided LONDON), and below the stills section, was the Camera Department. Vincent Korda's Art Department had similar space at the rear of the other two main stages. Further on, the car park, and a large outdoor tank bigger than any Olympic swimming pool. Here Korda was to float the Spanish Armada, amongst other naval engagements. On the far side of the tank were the laboratories in which to process the film, exposed mostly in French-built Debrie cameras.

The epicentre of it all was reached by way of a large circular staircase, leading to a balcony running around the rotunda-like interior of the main entrance to the administration area fronting the studios. Off this balcony opened doors – to Korda, by way of a couple of guardians, his secretary, Elisabeth Wright and his production manager David Cunynghame, who had joined him in Paris and who was to remain faithful to the end. So he was only a flight of stairs away from the projection theatres, where he could view the 'rushes' of the daily filming taking place on any one of the seven stages – each of which he could walk to under cover all the way.

To visit units on the 'lot' did require a hat and coat, if not indeed his limousine. The 'lot' was all the acreage of the property not built on by the studios. Still a lot of land. And on these wide

25

open spaces there had already been built and filmed sets too enormous for the studios Korda had meantime been renting for his non-stop flow of productions since *Henry VIII*. Here, although by now somewhat weather-beaten, there still stood the City Hall of the bombed and blitzed Everytown of the H.G. Wells film of *Things To Come*, and a king-sized Scots castle which had been transported to America complete with its ghost in the already released Korda – Rene Clair production of *The Ghost Goes West*.

The appearance and disappearance of the Ghost had been managed for Korda by that wizard of 'Special Effects', Ned Mann. He it was who had already made the world of the future work in *Things To Come* and then gone on to stop the world itself for Korda's filming of another H.G. Wells fantasy *The Man Who Could Work Miracles*. The man responsible for the design and layout of Alexander Korda's movie empire out at Denham back in 1935 was now another American, Jack Okey. This former Art Director of such as the Paul Muni classic *I Am a Fugitive from a Chain Gang* and the Edward G. Robinson *Five Star Final* had also designed studios for both Warner Bros., First National and Paramount. The basic difference to Hollywood here in England was, as he defined it, the need at Denham for covered passageways and corridors to connect every department and corner of the complex. In California, where the sun always shone, this was unnecessary. In Britain, where it rained more often than not, this was essential. Hence that seemingly endless 'Corridor'.

Although outside Denham itself was demonstrably as old and as English as the Domesday Book, once inside the studio gates it could well have been Hollywood. There had been little in that corner of California before the arrival of the movie-makers, other than orange groves and old age pensioners. There had been a village and community centred around estate, church, and pub at Denham for centuries. And this was the peculiar charm and dichotomy of the place. An ancient, then still almost yeoman's England, cheek by jowl with and suddenly confronted by a crowd of cosmopolitan film-makers arriving and departing daily in its midst. Roman legionaries, Dutch burgomaster, Russian revolutionaries, all to jostle each other as they came down together on the 6.20 train from London in the morning, and debouched from Denham's little rural railway station. Overhead balloons went up, magic carpets flew, searchlights crisscrossed the sky as Korda's cameras recreated the Arabian Nights and anticipated the war to come. Snug and secure in their beds at night, the good people of Denham, villager and publican, dreamed happily of all the extra trade and business this meant to their tiny and hitherto little-known village.

The previous owner of the estate now transformed into this studio complex of London Film Productions had been one Lord Forres. There is no record of how many horses his lordship had kept but, suitably refurbished, the stables had now become eighteen cutting rooms. Through the grounds of what had previously been known as 'The Fishery', there flowed the River Colne. On its banks, down the slope from Stage Seven, still stood his lordship's former residence, to be known from now on as 'The Old House'. On the first floor, and by way of a grand staircase, a large bay-windowed room looked out over the river. Here, apart for a while from the studio floor and the cares of administration, Korda was to maintain his real place of work. The prospect was serene. He had, at least so it seemed, achieved every filmmaker's dream – creative independence and control of the factory as well. To the press, at this time, he issued a statement:

'I want to collect here, down at Denham, the people who really matter to the screen, and encourage them in their various ambitions. Here they shall receive all the scope they require, all the credit they deserve, and they shall not be forced to shelve all their best ideas to satisfy the whims of a commercially-minded board of directors.'

In her biography of Korda published some forty years later, Karol Kulik tells us that: 'when film people reminisce about the days of Korda's reign at Denham Studios we get the feeling that it symbolised for many of them a modern-day Camelot. An idealistic and optimistic climate had prevailed over the studio; those who worked there believed that they were part of a film making elite, producing outstanding pictures which would prove to everyone that Hollywood wasn't the only film capital in the world'. Just so.

Korda himself could hardly wait for the paint to dry before directing in these his own Denham Studios the film of his heart's desire, *Rembrandt*. But this was no literal, animated waxworks life of the painter. Korda seized on the Dutchman's life as not only an excuse to demonstrate the grace, range, style and facilities of which his studios were now capable, but to make his own deeply felt and personal statement as himself as an artist, a filmmaker, who had had to make in the past upwards of fifty films for other interests and people before finally reaching this pinnacle of independent and lonely eminence. Into this production went not only his heart and soul but, as his nephew, Vincent's son Michael, has written, 'something of his own pain'.

In the scorn Charles Laughton as the screen *Rembrandt* pours on the Officers of the Night Watch, after they have rejected the masterpiece which they have commissioned of themselves, there is all the rage, frustration and pain of the film-maker trying to interest mercenary-minded little men and sponsors in his vision, in a dream. Already the minions of the Prudential were yapping at Korda's heels, protesting the mounting deficits of London Film Productions.

Of this original creation of Denham I was to hear in further first hand detail from Monty Marks himself many years later. Also of how Douglas Fairbanks, who arranged Korda's film distribution through the original United Artists Corporation which he then controlled with Mary Pickford and Chaplin, had died in a beach house all alone but for the howling of his dog – the very same morning as the press show of *Gone with the Wind*, 12 December 1939. And of how, during the Second World War, Korda had played an important role in British Intelligence, London Film Productions offices and activities in such neutral countries as Portugal and at first the United States, providing a convenient cover. British citizenship had come to Korda on the set of *Rembrandt* and it is now generally recognized that he did a great deal more for his adopted country than his contemporary detractors

28

were aware of at the time and since. His good friend, collaborator and compatriot the actor Leslie Howard – *Gone With the Wind*'s Ashley Wilkes born Laszlo Stainer – with other passengers was shot down and killed when flying back from a visit to Lisbon in 1942. At the height of the war Korda himself made many hazardous flights across the Atlantic.

I myself have known no more satisfying experience than setting up a 16 millimetre projector in the London home of Monty Marks thirty years later, and showing the old man and his artist wife Stella a print of *Rembrandt*. Of the Korda brothers, only Vincent was by then still alive, but unwell and unable to be present. On a makeshift but quite adequate screen, his exquisite sets once again glowed into life, the chiaroscuro of their blacks, greys and whites caught by Périnal's camera in a luminous clarity seldom surpassed. Alone, after the death of Saskia, Rembrandt goes to a tavern. He drinks. The boisterous uproar all around him gives way to silence as, as if to himself, he speaks:

'A creature, half-child, half-woman, half-angel, half-lover brushed against him, and of a sudden he knew that when one woman gives herself to you, you possess all women – women of every age and race and kind and, more than that, the moon, the stars, all miracles and legends are yours: the brown-skinned girls who inflame your senses with their play; the cool yellow-haired women who entice and escape you; the gentle ones who serve you; the slender ones who torment you; the mothers who bore and suckled you – all women whom God created out of the teeming fullness of the earth are yours in the love of one woman. Throw a purple mantle lightly over her shoulders and she becomes a Queen of Sheba; lay your tousled head blindly upon her breast and she is a Delilah waiting to enthral you; take her garments from her, strip the last veil from her body, and she is a chaste Susanna covering her nakedness with fluttering hands. Gaze upon her as you would gaze upon a thousand strange women, but never call her yours – for her secrets are inexhaustible; you will never know them all. Call her by one name only: I call her SASKIA.'

There was no Saskia yet in my young life when, a nervous seventeen-year-old, I first entered Denham Studios. To the head of the Camera Department I brought a letter of introduction from the manager of the then temporarily closed down Ealing Studios, where I had been working for nine months as a clapper boy. It just so happened that they were short of one at Denham, on a film being shot by a cameraman with whom I had worked at Ealing. I got the job.

Like many of the top technicians at Denham in those days, he was American, Phil Tannura. For Korda had not unnaturally filled his studios with colleagues and craftsmen he had known and worked with in Vienna, Berlin, Paris and Hollywood. Five flag-poles stood in line down the front of these Denham Studios of London Film Productions. From the top of each fluttered a Union flag. 'One for every Englishman employed here', a current and cynical wisecrack had it.

Phil Tannura had previously photographed for London Films *Moscow Nights* which featured a young Laurence Olivier in a costume melodrama of pre-Revolutionary Russia. This must have cost him many a wry smile, for as a US Army Cameraman in 1918 he had been assigned to the American Expeditionary Force for Siberia, and actually penetrated as well as filmed the quarters in Ekaterinburg where the Czar and his family had been done to death in the real Russian Revolution.

Operating the heavy American camera for him now at Denham in 1937 was Wilkie Cooper who, in 1950, would himself photograph *Stage Fright* for Alfred Hitchcock at Elstree. For the camera operators on the Denham crews of those days were all to become, in this way, the top lighting cameramen of the next generation of British film-makers. Meantime they went along from picture to picture with the imported foreign talent for whom they lined up and operated their cameras. Robert Krasker worked always with Georges Perinal. Jack Hildyard was Harry Stradling's operator. Jack Cardiff had coped with Harold Rosson on the shooting of *The Scarlet Pimpernel* and *The Ghost Goes West*. On my first Denham film, the operator was Wilkie Cooper. On all three of his previous Denham pictures he had operated the camera for the Chinese-American ace James Wong Howe.

When just a contract director in Hollywood seven years before, Korda had got to know and admire William Cameron Menzies and William K. Howard, fellow film-maker on the Fox payroll. He brought Menzies over to direct and indeed, with brother Vincent, design *Things to Come*. Howard he summoned to Denham to direct *Fire Over England*, an ambitious costume drama of intrigue at the court of the first Queen Elizabeth and the destruction of the Spanish Armada sent to topple her from the throne. Retaining ultimate authority, Korda had turned over the actual production of this one to Erich Pommer, the former head of the great Berlin UFA Company, now a refugee from Hitler's Germany.

Three years before while still at Fox and from a script written by Preston Sturges, William K Howard had directed a truly remarkable film in Hollywood which anticipated *Citizen Kane* in a most uncanny way. From a similar mosaic of various viewpoints this film, *The Power and the Glory*, reconstructs the life story this time of a railroad tycoon, played by Spencer Tracy, who is revered by a faithful few but detested by many.

The cameraman had been Jimmy Wong Howe, who was now to join forces with Howard once again on *Fire Over England*. In the meantime he had been kept busy at Metro-Goldwyn-Mayer. *Viva Villa* and *The Thin Man* are just two of his outstanding films of that period. Later to his credit have been *The Rose Tattoo*, *The Sweet Smell of Success*, *Seconds*, *Hud*, and *The Molly Maguires*. Nominated for sixteen Academy Awards, winning twice, and active well into his seventies, this wizard of light, shade and lens had started as far back as 1922 when he shot his first film as Director of Photography. This was *Drums of Fate* starring Mary Miles Minter. Many years later, on American television, Jimmy Wong Howe told how he got this first job:

'I had photographed a portrait of Miss Minter with my little (still) camera, and she liked it. I enlarged it and gave it to her. She said, "Oh, I look lovely in this picture; could you make me look like this in the movies?" I said, "Why yes". So two or three months later, I'm called in, and they congratulate me, to go down and get my camera – I'm now Mary Miles Minter's cameraman. And she was one of the *big* stars. They said, "She wants to talk to you, Jimmy". I went down, knocked on the door of her dressing-room, and she had the picture lying on her dressing table. She said, "You know why I like these (still) pictures, Jimmy? Because you made my eyes go dark". She had pale blue eyes, and in those days the film was insensitive to blue, and they washed out. And I didn't realise how I'd made her eyes go dark! I walked, and stood where I took the pictures, and there was a huge piece of black velvet. Something told me, "Well, it must be a reflection. The eye is like a mirror. If something is dark, it will reflect darker". So I had a frame made, cut a hole in it and put my lens through, and made all her close-ups that way. It helped her, because it blocked out all the accessories and the people watching her, and she liked it because it made her eyes go dark. That's how I became a cameraman'.

More than half a century later he was still teaching them the tricks of the trade. Setting up his first close-up of the star of 1975's *Funny Lady* he heard a voice say, 'What no diffusion?' 'No, Miss Streisand,' he replied. 'I'm not using any diffusion because this is a beautiful lens. It must have cost five or six thousand dollars and it has wonderful resolution. I'm not going to ruin it by putting a $2.50 piece of glass in front of it. I'd rather get the effect with lights'.

When confronted with *Fire Over England* back at Denham in 1936, Jimmy Wong Howe made a further point about the reflected light which makes our vision, and all motion pictures possible.

'Cameramen don't photograph the object, but light reflected from the object. In California the light is so strong and dry that chemically it is often out of focus. Over here you have what we call the "third plane". Over there, there is foreground and background, but nothing in between. …Here there is a natural mist in the air that Hollywood would give its heart for, because it acts as a soft filter and gives a diffused light …excellent for colour.'

32

And ideal for colour it certainly was, as another Denham film of that era almost immediately proved. For Korda not only brought recognition and stature to the British film – he also brought to it, quite literally, colour.

As a contract director in Hollywood, his agent had been Myron Selznick. Brother David had recently broken away from father-in-law Louis B. Mayer's mighty MGM and, like Korda, similarly set himself up as an independent producer, also releasing through United Artists. A corollary of his financing was that he had to shoot most of his Selznick International Pictures in the Technicolor process, with then only a handful of productions to its credit. *The Garden of Allah*, *A Star is Born*, *Nothing Sacred*, *The Adventures of Tom Sawyer* (Jimmy Wong Howe) thereupon followed in a splendid spectrum. (Screen rights to a just published novel called *Gone with the Wind* were yet to be negotiated – for what now seems the modest sum of $50,000.). Korda too got the message. London Film Productions invested in a British branch of Technicolor. Technicians arrived at Denham and, as if handling nothing less than the Holy Grail, unpacked equipment enveloped in just as much awe and mystery.

But Korda was a canny man. The Paris head of Paramount who had financed his French filming five years before was now chief of his own company, releasing through Fox, and just about to start up production in England. Korda sold Robert T. Kane the idea of shooting the first of his three films at Denham, in Technicolor. It was a subject ideally suited to a run-in of colour in the diffused light of the British Isles, which Jimmy Wong Howe claimed would be so effective chromatically.

Wings of the Morning was the name of a racehorse which won the Derby, and also the title of this film of how it came to do so, the first modern colour feature film to be made in Britain. Production was, nevertheless, entirely American. Cameraman was Ray Rennahan, who had worked with Rouben Mamoulian on *Becky Sharp*, the first American feature to be shot in the new process the previous year. Director was Harold Schuster, a Hollywood editor for whom this was to be his first feature. Star was Henry Fonda, and, playing opposite, Annabella (born Suzanne

Carpentier). She it had been who, at the tender age of sixteen and acting the part of an innkeeper's daughter, had suffered the pangs of unrequited love for Abel Gance's majestic *Napoleon*. Stardom had swiftly followed in such seminal French successes of the period as *La Bandera*, *Le Million*, and *Quatorze Juillet*. Annabella was now on her way to Hollywood and to eventual marriage to Tyrone Power, but at this time her English was all but non-existent. Coached patiently by Schuster and her co-star, she spoke her lines phonetically, with little understanding of their meaning. Nevertheless she gave a perfectly charming performance, and the film was a great success.

The story of *Wings of the Morning* was splendid hokum and romance indeed. Back in 1889 the Earl of Clontarf (Leslie Banks) meets, falls in love with, and marries the daughter of a Spanish Gypsy King. Before their child is born, he is killed when thrown from his horse. A curse is then said to fall on his gypsy wife's descendants. Time marches on, and we are in the then present day of 1936. His widow comes to his native Ireland with a horse with which she hopes to win the Derby. They are joined by her great-granddaughter Maria (Annabella), who has escaped from Spain disguised as a boy. Annabella dressed as a young man in beret and slacks, was a sight to turn indeed the eyes and head of young Henry Fonda, playing the part of 'Kerry', a Canadian racehorse trainer. In the end all the inevitable misunderstandings are cleared up. 'Wings' wins the race, and the curse is removed.

It sounds fun, but working on those early Technicolor films with the three-strip camera at Denham was anything but fun for a junior camera assistant such as I was now myself. Those original Technicolor cameras were designed and built around two 45 degree prisms cemented together in a square block, mounted behind the lens. One of the 45 degree intermediate faces was coated with a partially reflecting surface, which, while enabling the image to pass through to the back, also reflected its identical likeness off at right angles. There were two picture apertures and two synchronised film movements, one to the rear and the other to this side of the prism block, each therefore receiving an identical picture. Above was the magazine, containing side by side three separate rolls of film, a thousand feet each. Two of these negative strips, one behind the other as a bipack, were fed down to the right-angled gate. The face of the prism block through which the picture reached them was dyed magenta. This therefore exposed their image through a combination blue/red filter. The first of these two bipack negatives was an orthochromatic emulsion, insensitive to red, so it only recorded the blue. Its emulsion was on a red-dyed base, so the same image continued on its way through its back to the second bipack negative running behind, which was panchromatic, filtered in this way through red. This second negative therefore recorded the same image, but only its red aspect. In the second aperture gate – in the normal position straight behind the lens – ran the third negative, also panchromatic. But the back of the intermediate prism block filtering the same basic image through and on to it was dyed green, so this negative received exactly the same picture as the other two, but as a green record. So each film strip received a green, a blue, and a red filtered primary colour record of the one identical image but on three different black-and-white negatives. From these, gelatine based relief positives were made, called matrices. Dyed with their complementary colours, these then provided the base for Technicolor's own patented and for a long while closely guarded process of producing – on a single combined film base – release prints in a full range of the entire colour spectrum.

At eight o'clock in the morning, six days a week, the 'Technician' (a title of some importance) would arrive on the set with the optical and mechanical marvel that was this Technicolor camera. First of all, and without fail every day, a colour exposure and registration test had to be shot. I would already have had to ensure that two 'Du-Arc Broads' were correctly set and wired up to flood evenly with white light an exposure chart, on which the camera was focused, with an electronic incident light exposure meter making certain that just exactly the prescribed number of foot candles were registering.

This shot, and duly noted and marked up on my camera report sheets, into the sound 'blimp' the camera would go. In order to silence its running, and to accommodate the size and width of its three thousand feet film capacity, this was nothing less than a large, rectangular padded box, the better part of four feet in height and almost two feet in width. Mounted on an electrically lifting boom on its four-wheeled 'dolly', the operator could tilt, pan and follow the action by handles geared to the 'head' on which it was secured by four heavy screws. Ordinary black-and-white cameras were themselves just a dull black in colour. Technicolor cameras and blimps were painted blue, and this was the only light thing about them. Through a glass plate in the front, the camera exposed all three of its films, firstly through a separately mounted but normal optical lens (there was a choice of four varying focal lengths) and then through the prism block which was the heart of the matter. To change the focus of the lens itself as it followed the movements of the action to and fro, a tiny electric motor was held in the first assistant cameraman's hand, connected by cable to selsenised gearing on the lens mount within. All this we had to have set up and ready for the main unit call at 8.30.

Sounds clumsy and archaic doesn't it? Indeed it was, but those original three strip cameras shot some of the finest colour films ever made (from Miriam Hopkins' 1935 *Becky Sharp* to Jane Russell's 1955 *Foxfire*). See, when you can, Haller's *Gone with the Wind*, Perinal's *Thief of Bagdad*, Polito's *Dodge City*, Cardiff's *Black Narcissus*, to name but four of a great many of that era in which Technicolor all but monopolised the rainbow. But look only at an original, or carefully restored, 35 millimetre print. Because, like old soldiers and the chemically-induced hues of today, contemporary colour print stock starts to deteriorate after little more than five years. Shot as they were in the first place on black-and-white negatives used only occasionally to make the matrices for their subsequent colour printing by dye transfer – original Technicolor motion pictures endure.

And *Star Wars*. In order to achieve the totally imperceptible match between the moving-camera foregrounds and their background action that he had to create in hundreds of composite shots, Special Effects Supervisor John Dykstra resurrected this long obsolete three-colour separation process pioneered by Technicolor. Because, utilising as it did – and for the galactic struggle between Luke Skywalker and Darth Vader once again does – black-and-white film to record each primary colour, it affords a much finer grain than even the latest colour negative materials. And what was the reason Martin Scorsese has given for shooting his 1980 *Raging Bull* in black-and-white? Because 'I have witnessed the deterioration and sometimes destruction of most films I have seen. With the introduction of (single negative) Eastman Color film in 1950, any hope of colour stability vanished'. And Steven Spielberg? To approximate somehow to the awful authenticity of the Holocaust, he deliberately shot *Schindler's List* in black-and-white.

Back then in those old three-strip days at Denham, as well as nipping in and out with my number board in front of the Technicolor camera at the start of each shot, I then had to go in at its end with what was known as the 'Aix'. This was a printed colour spectrum card set alongside and parallel to its black-and-white equivalent, with a contraption of three white cards above, the first aimed straight at the camera, the other two set at angles of 45 degrees to either side. When developed, and printed in colour, these hand tests could tell the laboratory how to print correctly for all the colours in the scene as a whole – as the colours and white cards of the 'lily' were known to be constant. For very distant and wide shots, there was a very big 'lily', with cards a foot high. For close-ups, a very small one, only an inch in height. With one of these after a lighting test of Merle Oberon for a never-made film of *Manon Lescaut*, I all but took the future Lady Korda's nose away as well as I whisked it out of shot. And all the time the star, or set, was being lit, one had to stand at the cameraman's side, light meter in hand, giving him the foot candle readings while he had the electricians adjust the lights. At the back of the report sheets, on which for black-and-white one just noted footages of camera run and takes to be printed, we also now had to write a description of the colours in the particular

37

scene shot. Early on I was reprimanded for describing white as 'white'. It was always 'off-white'. (For a pure white was then the most difficult thing to achieve). For Technicolor all this had to be carried out by that poor dogsbody, the clapper boy, in addition to all the regular work that he had to do on a normal black-and-white picture: numbering the shots, loading and reloading the magazines with film, keeping account of the footages the camera ran, making marks on the floor for the actors to stay on or move to, getting the tea for the camera crew. I marvelled at the results on the screen, but I loathed working with Technicolor back there at Denham on *The Thief of Bagdad*, and previously *The Four Feathers*, two of Korda's own outstanding films in the process.

The Four Feathers was directed by the other one of the three Korda brothers, Zoltan – thanks to the support and encouragement of Alex, by now a well-established film-maker in his own right. After co-directing the then equally unknown Merle Oberon and Robert Donat in *Men of Tomorrow* – a London Films 1932 Paramount quota look at young blood at Oxford University – 'Zoli' had become addicted to tackling subjects in far away places like Africa where, in the Sudan, he was soon to re-stage the Battle of Omdurman. Cameraman for the Denham interiors was, it's almost needless to say, Georges Perinal who, very early on, when filming Zoli's other imperial pageant, *The Drum*, had dispensed with the services and advice of the expert from Hollywood who was wished on every unit then working in the Technicolor process. The theory was that you flooded the scene with light (and at first it had to be entirely arc-light) and that the colours themselves then took care of and created the contrast. This neither appealed or made sense to Perinal. After a few days the expert departed, and 'Perry' lit the way he saw it. The result, and reward, was now not long in coming – an Academy Award for his next film, *The Thief of Bagdad*.

But at least with Technicolor one did not have the final chore at the end of the day, when everyone else was on their way home, of unloading the film from the magazines. This could only be done by Technicolor, at Technicolor's own laboratories. So back they went, carefully guarded by the faithful 'Technician' (as he was called by his Technicolor employers), who, when on location, had quite literally to sleep with the camera and its all-important prism block. The 'Technician' who first initiated me into the disciplines and rigours of Technicolor so far as they applied to a junior camera assistant/clapper boy such as myself was Geoffrey Unsworth. In the years to come he was to be himself responsible for the spellbinding colour photography of *2001: A Space Odyssey*, *Cabaret* and *Superman* – to name but three of his illustrious future credits.

Originally the Technicolor Laboratories were planned to be built at Denham, as part of the overall studio complex. But the local authorities objected to the idea of all those funny coloured dyes running away into the sewage system, and refused permission. A few miles away councillors must have been more enthusiastic film fans, for no one objected to construction alongside what was to be the future site of London Airport.

The three separately filtered but pictorially identical colour record negatives emerging from the Technicolor camera, being black-and-white, could be developed in an ordinary laboratory. And were. At first, the Paramount-owned Olympic. This meant that an immediate – although obviously itself only black-and-white – 'rush' print could be made from one of them for the unit to view the following day, and the editor start to cut. The making of the matrices from all three negatives for Technicolor's own system of inhibition printing into a single combined colour print took a little longer. In the case of *Wings of the Morning* a great deal longer. For the lab in Britain was not ready in time, and colour printing could still only then be carried out at the plant in Hollywood. So at first it was four weeks in those earliest days at Denham before any of them on the picture ever saw anything on the screen in colour at all.

The question of laboratory servicing – particularly in black-and-white – was one that continued to worry the American cameramen working at Denham. Jimmy Wong Howe was quite blunt about it, pointing out that in Hollywood the laboratory department was respected much more than he found to be the case in

Britain and Europe. He instanced a very popular and most successful French black-and-white movie of the time, *La Kermesse Heroique*. (As *Carnival in Flanders*, this was one of the rare foreign films to have scored a hit in the United States.) In his opinion, the cameraman had got beautifully soft highlights and tones, but these were distorted in the processing and their value had been lost. 'Too much bromide – not enough sulphide' was his verdict.

Cameraman of *La Kermesse Heroique* had been an American, Harry Stradling; Director the Belgian-born Jacques Feyder; and the sets had been designed by a Russian, Lazare Meerson. Korda signed up all three and re-united them at Denham. Here they were now to stage no Carnival in Flanders but Revolution in Russia – starring Marlene Dietrich.

In a blaze of box office indifference, that startling partnership of Dietrich and her director-mentor Josef von Sternberg had recently dissolved. *The Blue Angel* had broken records everywhere, but takings had continued to diminish with the sequence of pictures which followed: *Morocco, Dishonoured, Shanghai Express, Blonde Venus, The Scarlet Empress, The Devil is a Woman*. Only once in Hollywood had Dietrich ever made a film with any director other than von Sternberg. Now both had made a couple of films apart from each other. Separation seemed final. Still at Paramount, but this time for Lubitsch, Dietrich had recently made *Desire*; while for Harry Cohn and Columbia, as well as a musical called *The King Steps Out* with Grace Moore, von Sternberg had undertaken *Crime and Punishment*. Of the latter, a contemporary British critic wrote unkindly and most unjustly that this first film since he gave up photographing Marlene Dietrich against bizarre backgrounds was appropriately entitled. 'What von Sternberg did to Dietrich was a crime. This (film) is the punishment'.

Dietrich arrived at Denham by way of Selznick's Technicolored *Garden of Allah* in August 1936. Great excitement surrounded her first make-up and hairdressing test. For the first time British technicians were to be made aware of the cool professionalism of Harry Stradling.

Although with a style of lighting generally smoother and less dramatic than Jimmy Wong Howe's, Stradling came from just as legendary a motion picture background. His uncle, Walter Stradling, had been for many years Mary Pickford's cameraman. Now nephew prepared to light another one of the most famous faces in films.

Great fuss, much temperament, must surely accompany this first filming of – apart from Garbo – the most glamorous of all Hollywood stars in a British studio. Not a bit of it. Marlene had not worked with von Sternberg on all those films as little more than a beautiful but passive object in his series of tonal tapestries of increasingly self-indulgent chiaroscuro. With Teutonic efficiency she had willingly and enthusiastically learnt all there was to know from this visual master of the motion picture. She knew just where lights should go, and why. She could light herself, or the set in which she moved, as well as any, and better than most cameramen. She and Stradling hit it off immediately. They recognised in each other the true professional who never had to make a song and dance, but just gets on with it. A key light here, just around to the front; tip that 5K down for a bit of backlight; move that 'basher' in for just a bit of filler; tighten up the key a whisker – OK, let's go. And that was all there was to it. They at least were ready to shoot the film; and Stradling in later years went on to *Funny Girl* and *Hello Dolly*, by way of Oscars for *The Picture of Dorian Gray* and *My Fair Lady*.

The picture for which Korda had assembled all this talent was a very fine farrago indeed. Dietrich played the part of a Countess caught up and arrested in the Russian Revolution. She is put in the charge of an agent of British Intelligence, masquerading as an assistant commissar of a small town somewhere along the Trans-Siberian railway. Like *Doctor Zhivago* many years later, much of the action takes place on the railroad, and more than a mile of track was laid down on the lot at Denham, complete with station and real train, adapted from locomotive and rolling stock purchased from the London and North Eastern Railway Company. Dietrich and her protector, with whom she had inevitably fallen in love, make their way across revolutionary Russia in Denham, on foot, by train, and down the Volga (for which the ever-present and obliging Colne stood in quite adequately) and after a series of hair-raising escapes from the firing squads of both sides, Red and White, finally make good their escape on another train of the American Red Cross.

This was *Knight Without Armour*, scripted by Lajos Biro and Frances Marion from a novel by James Hilton (whose *Lost Horizon* had first been filmed not long before by Frank Capra, and whose *Mr. Chips* was soon to use the same, but revamped train to wave goodbye to Greer Garson). Although today visually still stunning in the dark sombre tones of its grey design, *Knight Without Armour* was a success with neither public nor critics. One of the latter reported acidly (and they could be very acid in those days) that Miss Dietrich had been photographed with 'elaborate and obtrusive care, but seemed incapable of emotion when taking a hot bath in a moment of respite from being chased'.

Nowadays no film seems complete without its ration of nudity, but at Denham they talked about that sequence in awe for years afterwards. The set, once lit, was cleared of all but those considered absolutely necessary to operate the camera. The first assistant, who had to keep her in focus, was a friend of Korda's son Peter, then only just out of Westminster School, and little more than my own age of sweet and presumably innocent seventeen. He clearly did not count. The camera rolled, the dresser very carefully slipped the robe from Marlene as she slid into the tub filled with exactly calculated and comfortably heated water. All went well and according to plan, Feyder called 'cut', the dresser came forward once again with the robe, behind its cover and protection Marlene stood up – and promptly skidded flat on her back on the soapsuds on the studio floor. A moment of instant, incredulous, and frozen immobility. 'Well,' exclaimed this now fully revealed and total professional, 'thank God there's no continuity to that shot'.

But even so, the Hays Office cut the entire sequence before American release in those seemingly distant days – and Marlene gave every single member of the unit a personally inscribed and engraved wrist watch when all of *Knight Without Armour* was finally shot.

This film cost a very great deal, and took many years to barely recover its negative costs. More than just the clouds of the usually awful English weather now began to build up over Denham, and Korda's head. In the three years their Denham studios had been in production, London Film Productions made seventeen films. Other companies, like Robert T. Kane's New World Pictures, rented space for many more. But with rare exception, unlike *Henry VIII*, the Korda-inspired films failed even to dent the American market and bring back much money; or, if and when they ever did, it took too long for the investment they represented to show a profit.

Alexander Korda never lost either his faith or his vision. He had bought from Winston Churchill the screen rights of *Marlborough* (some say with never any intention of making it). Down at Chartwell, desultory and inconclusive script conferences were held. While Denham was still on the drawing-board, Korda had set out to acquire the rights to T.E. Lawrence's *Revolt in the Desert*, the earlier and abridged version of *The Seven Pillars of Wisdom* in which Lawrence was to create legend out of his exploits against the Turks in the First World War. Their meeting had also proved to be somewhat inconclusive, and of this encounter Lawrence wrote to Robert Graves:

'I saw Alexander Korda last month. (January 1935). I had not taken seriously the rumours that he meant to make a film of me, but they were persistent, so at last I asked for a meeting and explained that I was inflexibly opposed to the whole notion. He was most decent and understanding – it surprised me in a film director – and has agreed to put it off till I die or welcome it. Is it age coming on or what? But I loathe the notion of being celluloided. My rare visits to cinemas always deepen in me a sense of their superficial falsity ... vulgarity, I would have said, only I like the vulgarity that means common man, and the badness of films seems to me like an edited and below-the-belt speciousness. Yet the news-theatres, as they call them (little cinemas here and there that present fact, photographed and current fact only) delight me.

The camera seems wholly in place as journalism: but when it tries to re-create it boobs and sets my teeth on edge. So there won't be a film of me. Korda is like an oil company which has drilled often and found two or three gushers, and has prudently invested some of its proceeds in buying options over more sites. Some he may develop and others not. Oil is a transient business.'

Lawrence's objections to any film in his own lifetime came to a sudden and abrupt end with his unexpected death only four months later, and permission was obtained to film in Transjordan and Palestine, as the area was known and British-administered in those pre-Israeli days. Walter Hudd, who bore an uncanny resemblance to Lawrence, was screen-tested for the part, and 'Zoli' prepared to direct from a script to be undertaken by John Monk Saunders. Within a year this combination had been switched to Brian Desmond Hurst and Miles Malleson, only to be overtaken in turn by an announcement by Leslie Howard – who had previously performed for Korda as *The Scarlet Pimpernel* – that agreement had been reached for him to play the title role and, with William K. Howard directing and Jimmy Wong Howe on camera, to co-produce a Korda production of *Lawrence of Arabia*. The co-producer was quite explicit as to how he saw his planned version of the epic:

'It must be made imaginatively, by a serious-minded and expert craftsman. Above all, it must have no shrieking Arabs riding across the desert in the manner of cowboys.'

Howard visualised the use of soliloquies to make clear and manifest the inner thoughts and torments of the hero or, as we could, and do call him now, anti-hero. But like far too many of Korda's projects this too eventually came to nought; even though, with a unit by then in the Sudan, he later played with the idea of shooting it off the back of 'Zoli's' *Four Feathers*. However at Denham, at that time, there was already working the cameraman who was in fact finally to shoot the film *Lawrence of Arabia* with David Lean a quarter of a century later. Freddie Young was even then shooting in colour, Technicolor, of course, *Sixty Glorious Years* (Herbert Wilcox / Anna Neagle), the life and reign of Queen Victoria.

By the time the debt to the Prudential mounted to well over a million pounds – and pounds were pounds in those days – the Korda group had made more than twenty films at Denham, from the great and enduring, to the grandiose and disastrous. The catastrophe of attempting to film Robert Graves' *I Claudius* had not helped matters very much either.

Hard on her heels, Svengali-like, Josef von Sternberg had arrived in England soon after Dietrich. Out of work, he nonetheless announced grandly that they were going to make three films together. They never did, or any other, anywhere else, ever again. Korda however soon set up a colossal project for a filmmaker he greatly admired. Biro worked on the script. In Hollywood just before the coming of sound he had written one of von Sternberg's better films, *The Last Command*, the story of the disintegration of a Czarist general forced to perform in a studiostaged Russian Revolution, even more remote than *Knight Without Armour*'s. This time it was to be ancient Rome.

Scripted by the same *Rembrandt* trilogy of Biro, Wimperis, and Zuckmayer, both Korda and Laughton were determined to embark on this even more ambitious (and non-commercial) lifestudy. Now to be directed by von Sternberg, this was to be the story of the Roman Emperor Claudius who, despite his own physical handicaps and the plots and conspiracies of the venal Rome of his day, survived to be, eventually, proclaimed a god.

The sequences of this film which were shot and survive are heartbreaking proof that here indeed could have been a masterpiece; its abandonment when incomplete a great tragedy not only for Korda at the time, but for all of us who care for and love the motion picture.

A generation later this could be seen to be true. For all those cans of unfinished *I, Claudius* film found their way to the BBC, and became the substance of a television programme. With surviving participants reminiscing in entertaining but facile comment on the project and its failure, time had dealt less kindly.

'I, Claudius – will tell you how to frame
your laws. Profiteering and bribery will

stop. The Senate will function only in
the name of Roman justice.'

Laughton himself never gave a greater performance; and all
the others in the cast excelled themselves too. Emlyn Williams,
an odious and schizophrenic Caligula, Flora Robson a sinister
Livia, Merle Oberon a lasciviously lovely Messalina. Vincent
Korda's sets were superlative, and the combination of von Sternberg and Perinal on camera stunning. But this time Korda had
really put too much temperament with the talent in the mix.
Laughton went through agonies finding his way into the part,
with little help from a director notoriously unsympathetic towards the hangups of actors. The schedule began to overrun
alarmingly. The great sets tied up stage after stage when they
might have been earning money on other productions. A month
into the production, and after their experience with *Rembrandt*
now on release and playing to empty cinemas, United Artists and
the Prudential shook their dwindling money bags and then their
heads. A car crash involving Merle Oberon, in which she suffered little more than shake-up and bruising, gave them however
the opportunity to recover most of the money from insurance
cover. Production was halted. The film closed down. Certainly
one of the greatest of all that select company of films which
might have been.

A happier collaboration put together by Korda at Denham in
those days was the partnership between director Michael Powell
and scriptwriter Emeric Pressburger. A coming together of an
impassioned Man of Kent and sophisticated Central European
Jew which was to develop into the most original creative partnership in the history of British cinema. But although he had by
then already directed well over twenty films, Powell was, at least
to me, a far from sympathetic character. The moment I walked in
front of Valerie Hobson and Conrad Veidt with my clapper
board marked *The Spy in Black* Scene One Take One, from
Powell, crouched down beside the camera, there had come an
exclamation: 'Well, that's the most cynical looking clapper boy
I've ever seen!'

Cynical I might have seemed. Curious I certainly was. Whenever there was a lull on the set of the picture I happened to be working on, I seldom lost the opportunity to sneak on to the floor of Denham's six other active stages and watch other units at work

One day I took a short cut through the temporarily empty Stage Four. Planned for erection therein no longer the Roman Forum but the quadrangle of an Oxford College. Ignoring the ordinary entrance and exit leading out into the main interconnecting long corridor – and clearly used to taking shortcuts – were two figures attempting to squeeze their way out through the incompletely closed main sliding doors, normally used for the construction of sets. The one tall, thin, and grey. The other short, podgy, and pink. Alexander Korda and Louis B. Mayer. I leant my own modest weight to the proceedings, and the two tycoons were able to emerge into the open air and continue their tour of the premises. Landlord and tenant-to-be. For mighty Metro-Goldwyn-Mayer had announced their intention to produce pictures in Britain, and Denham was their choice of studio.

In those days no less than MGM (who knew a thing or two) clearly held Korda and his studios in the highest regard, but it is intellectual fashion nowadays to sneer at Korda, at the sort of films he made (and sometimes abandoned). Alive at the time of those Depression-ridden thirties, and commanding the resources this central European Jewish film-maker was able to charm out of the British Establishment, *we* of a latter-day Anglo-Saxon social enlightenment would have made altogether different films – wouldn't we! This prejudice is at its most glib in 'The Story of Cinema' published by one David Shipman in 1982, in which readers are told that as an example of what is described as the inefficiency of Korda's Denham operations, 'filming seldom began before midday'. Mr Shipman would have been welcome at the time to help Geoff Unsworth and me line up the Technicolor Three-Strip camera ready for the first shot by 8.30 every morning of a six day week for *The Four Feathers* (and, Mr.Shipman, the *Battle of Omdurman* – and the location for this film was in the Sudan, not Egypt). In the Spring 1986 edition of the British

Film Institute's quarterly periodical *Sight & Sound* there appeared an article on Denham Studios by one Sarah Street, entitled 'The Golden Jubilee of Korda's Folly'. Ms Street, we were informed, 'works at the Bodleian'.

Standing beneath camera author regards Conrad Veidt's and Valerie Hobson's response to Michael Powell's direction of *The Spy in Black*

Prudential Assurance was one of Britain's largest investing institutions, handling more money in a year than many of the world's Prime Ministers or Presidents. Back in 1933, and after the international success of *Henry VIII*, the Prudential certainly did lend Korda all that money, and much of Ms Street's case against him and his wicked ways is based on quotes from their files, bewailing the lack of return on this investment; which, after first of all helping to finance the production of seven more equally prestigious London Film Productions in other rented studios, made possible the building of Denham.

Failure is not folly. It can indeed even be heroic, and the failure we are talking about – and which has bedeviled the British Film Industry ever since – is the failure (with only rare exceptions from *Henry VIII* to *Chariots of Fire*) to make any impact on the American market. After *Henry*'s box office hit, the gentlemen at the Prudential thought that they were on to a good thing, and that the man who had made *Henry* would go on repeating the trick. What they failed to appreciate is that the production cost – let alone profit – from a film's distribution does not necessarily all come at once, or arrive overnight. It takes time. The men from the Pru were impatient. They foreclosed on Korda in less than a couple of years from his first film at Denham.

Where Korda failed to crack the American market, no one else has since or for that matter ever succeeded. At the same time as Prudential money was going into such pre-Denham London Film productions as *The Ghost Goes West*, *Things to Come* and *The Man Who Could Work Miracles*, at Shepherds Bush, Michael Balcon was similarly aiming at the United States. To give Gaumont-British production a transatlantic appeal, he imported amongst other fading American stars and featured players of the period Edward Everett Horton, Fay Wray, Wallace Ford, Richard Dix, Madge Evans, Helen Vinson, Constance Bennett, Noah Beery and George Arliss, the latter British-born but fresh from starring in historical pageantry for Darryl Zanuck. Arliss played the British Prime Minister opposite Walter Huston's American President in *The Tunnel*, a costly epic of the construction of a tunnel under the Atlantic thus linking both nations in lasting physical union. All to no good. Just as the Prudential pulled the rug out from under Korda's feet at Denham, so only a short time previously a reorganised Gaumon-British Board had fired Balcon, and then gone on to close down his studios in Shepherds Bush.

Who came next? J. Arthur Rank of course, who in 1939 acquired Denham and during the next decade from this 'folly' of

Korda's there flowed a steady stream of the most outstanding British films of that time – and some might say of all time. To name but a few, Carol Reed's *The Way Ahead* and *Odd Man Out*, David Lean's *Great Expectations*, Olivier's *Henry V* and that uniquely imaginative and still spell-binding trilogy from Michael Powell and Emeric Pressburger, *The Life and Death of Colonel Blimp*, *I Know Where I'm Going*, and *A Matter of Life and Death*; the construction of the immense moving stairway to and from the heavens on one of Denham's largest stages for the last of these a technical triumph in itself for this much maligned studio.

But despite all this (and not helped by a Denham-made disaster like Pascal's filming of Shaw's *Caesar and Cleopatra* with Vivien Leigh and Claude Rains) Rank too failed to crack the American market, and the shutters fell on Denham. Since then we have seen further attempts to create a viable British Film Industry on an international scale. In the 1970's Bryan Forbes, backed by EMI, mounted an ambitious programme in a refurbished Elstree, only in turn to be ousted when the money failed to roll in. These studios then became the rental base for purely-American-made spectaculars like *Star Wars*. Quite a bit further down market then along came Lew Grade. Where is he now? Immortalised by his rueful remark that it would have proved less disastrously expensive to have lowered the Atlantic than to have set out to *Raise the Titanic*. 'The British are coming!' cried *Chariots of Fire* Oscar-winning writer Colin Welland in 1981. But following on this short-lived euphoria came *Revolution*, the same production group's 1985 epic of what the British prefer to call the American War of Independence. Just as *The Tunnel* of fifty years before, it sunk without trace, dragging the production company down into virtual bankruptcy with it.

Denham was doomed from the beginning by this often heroic, but inevitably disastrous policy of trying to compete on equal terms with Hollywood on British soil. To share the same language but not the same historical experience creates neither an identity of interest or the same emotional response. A product of the polyglot mix that are the English-speaking movies of

America strike a chord, meet with a response, in some way, everywhere. With very rare exception, English-speaking British movies lack this universality of interest and appeal.

If that 'absolutely superb man' as Orson Welles has called Korda, had faults, they were, as Welles has also defined him, those of a 'dreamer'. He dreamed dreams, and Welles understood more than most from his own bitter experience that as these took the form of films he needed lots of money with which to realise them. Should our hearts then be made to bleed for the poor old Prudential, so sorely treated we are told by Korda sixty years ago? I doubt if any widows had to forego their pensions as a result; and many years later Monty Marks told me that in time they got all their money back and then some. The *Night Watch* may well have believed that they had been short-changed by *Rembrandt* but he none the less immortalised them. So whose side, Ms Street, are we on anyway, accountants or film-makers?

For examples of extravagant incompetence at Korda's Denham, her article in the British Film institute's *Sight & Sound* called forth quotes from some of my co-workers there at the time, as interviewed in a BBC programme of 1983. (Why, I sometimes wonder, do so many English veterans when questioned feel that they have to joke about their past experience? Is it a lack of confidence in the presence of the much younger interviewer? Do they feel that they must try to bridge the age gap by deliberately seeming to re-appraise their past endeavours as all somehow slightly comic?). On *Knight Without Armour*, a forest set was left standing, we were told, so long idle on one of the sound stages that the imported trees actually took root. Ha Ha! Simple explanation. The star, Robert Donat, suffered so badly from asthma that production had to be held up until he recovered. When he had, and work resumed with his co-star on this set, 'Welcome back', quipped Dietrich, 'our Knight without Asthma'. Korda is blamed too for shooting much of *Elephant Boy* at Denham instead of entirely in India, whence he had despatched Robert Flaherty to make this film from one of Kipling's short stories. But none of Flaherty's dialogue sequences were usable. He sent back only silent footage, and then only after interminable delays and procrastination. Was this Korda's fault? Should he not surely deserve more praise for being the only British producer after Balcon willing to fund this documentary maverick? And when Flaherty failed to deliver, was he supposed just to write it all off? That would have been extravagant. Instead, to preserve at least the investment, he had brother Zoltan attempt to salvage the picture with dialogue sequences shot at Denham, Another of those interviewed on the 1983 BBC programme and quoted approvingly by *Sight & Sound* told of the overlong and irregular hours we all worked at Denham in those days. Perfectly true – but this was the norm throughout the film industry in Britain at that time. Six day week, eight in the morning to always eight in the evening. Sometimes later. Every Saturday. Sometimes Sundays too. And then off the payroll at the end of the picture. But this was the industrial scene of the 1930s. There was, for example, no such thing as 'holidays with pay' for anyone until 1938. And then only for a single week off work.

I was a clapper boy, known grandiloquently and more accurately at Denham as a second camera assistant. Turning to my 1939 diary, I note that working with second unit director Michael Powell shooting the exterior sequences for Korda's *Thief of Bagdad*, the week ending July 7 – the river banks of the Colne now conveniently transformed into the rustling quaysides of the Sultan's seaport base of Basra – I received four pounds basic salary plus six shillings and eight pence overtime. And that was really good pay, for that job, in those days.

With the outbreak of the Second World War eight weeks later, the finishing touches to this most magical of all fantasy films were made by Korda in the United States. But despite winning an Oscar for cameraman Georges Perinal, it failed at first to fill the coffers. However, a couple of years before production had begun on this saga of the flying carpet, out of all the British studios Metro-Goldwyn-Mayer, the mightiest of all American companies, had already chosen Korda's 'folly' as most suited for their own British production.

From the very beginning the capacity and facilities of Denham had been available to producers other than Korda and companies other than London Film Productions seeking studio space, on a rental basis. This had always been the intention. The very first film actually to go into production in the brand new studios had been the almost instantly forgotten *Southern Roses*, a musical with the popular comic George Robey in a character role. (At Denham eight years later he was to play the dying Falstaff in Olivier's *Henry V*). The independent producer of this first of Denham's many movie milestones was a character called Max Schach – a Nazi refugee, one time head of Universal's European operations, and co-producer of *Moscow Nights*, whose finances were very soon to collapse like a house of cards. But before this imminent debacle he had then very quickly gone on to set up two more companies for two more films: *Land Without Music* with the unlikely double billing of tenor Richard Tauber and Jimmy 'Schnozzle' Durante, and Agatha Christie's *Love from a Stranger* starring Ann Harding and Basil Rathbone. Another company cast Edward G. Robinson in *Thunder in the City*, Pall Mall put Paderewski (no less) in *Moonlight Sonata* with Marie Tempest, and Elisabeth Bergner in *Dreaming Lips*. Previous to *Sixty Glorious Years*, Korda had extended credit to Herbert Wilcox for his initial foray into Victoriana, *Victoria the Great* and from *Wings of the Morning*, Robert T Kane's New World Pictures had gone on to *Under the Red Robe*, a swashbuckler directed by Victor Sjostrom (Annabella, Conrad Veidt, Raymond Massey), *Four Dark Hours*, with John Mills and Robert Newton directed by William Cameron Menzies from an original story by Graham Greene, and *Dinner at the Ritz*, which I had joined at midpoint as clapper boy, and wherein David Niven aided Annabella (once again) to expose a gang of swindling killers of her father; after glamorous pursuit by way of a yacht on the French Riviera (Stage 4) and a luxury houseboat on the Thames (with Windsor Castle painted in, the Colne serving well enough back of Stage 7). And there were others. With his company called not as one might assume 'Regina' but Imperator, Wilcox cast his Prince Albert, Anton Walbrook, in a remake of Ivor Novello's old silent success *The Rat*.

Production of nearly all of these films had been made possible by an obligation on the part of American distributors to make available a proportion of British-made films to British cinemas which, in turn, were obliged by law to screen a proportion of British-produced product. (Produced in Britain that is, by companies registered in the country. With the sole exception of Herbert Wilcox, none of the actual producers of the films listed above were in fact native-born, but the five Union flags still fluttered bravely in the breeze outside Denham.) Without such legislation, there might well have been no British feature film industry worth anyone's attention at all.

At the start of the First World War, a thriving British film industry had been producing more than a quarter of all the films shown in the country's cinemas. While Britain joined with the rest of Europe in that attempt at continental suicide, the American motion picture industry took over. By 1923 the proportion of British-made films shown in home cinemas was down to less than ten percent. Four years later, only one in fifty films shown in Britain had been made there – the rest were all imported, and most were American. Government action was urgently needed to preserve even a semblance of a British Film Industry. The outcome was the Quota Act of 1927. Renters then had to release, and cinemas show, a set proportion of British-made films. It had been a contract to make a series of such quota films for Paramount that enabled Korda to gain a foothold in Britain in the first place. Now, ten year later in 1937, a new and second Quota Act had raised the obligatory screen-time for British films to more than twelve per cent. To make this feasible, for every hundred of the hitherto primarily American films that renters distributed, they now had to include fifteen new British productions. This new Act of Parliament also specified that production of the latter could not be permitted to fall below a minimum cost in order to qualify. Doing away with the so-called 'Quota Quickie' shot for peanuts, in days rather than weeks, and screened, it has since been alleged, to cleaners in otherwise empty cinemas merely to comply with the law. 20th Century Fox for example, after hitherto satisfying their requirement under the old act with the supply of quickies from a little studio in Wembley, were now fulfilling their obligation under the new act by distributing (and part-financing) Robert T. Kane's prestigious Denham-produced New World Pictures.

With a guaranteed home market now therefore seemingly assured, British producers thought they could now afford to look westwards to where the real money was, to the greatest market of all, the United States.

'When', wrote the British magazine *Film Weekly* in May 1936, 'the history of British films comes to be written, the phase through which they are at present passing will be covered by a chapter headed "Getting into America". The end of this chapter is at last in sight ... the progress of the past few years has been almost too rapid. Millions have been poured into the industry. New companies have sprung up everywhere'.

Film Weekly spoke too soon. By the summer of the following year nearly all of those new companies were bust, and Korda himself, before the Prudential closed in, was still struggling hard to get an adequate return from the United States for his London Film Productions. But if British films had not yet succeeded in really getting into America, the biggest studio in Hollywood had made up its mind to get into Britain, in a really big way. Hard on the heels of Louis B. Mayer there now arrived at Denham Clark Gable's director, Jean Harlow's cameraman, *Trader Horn*'s editor.

Hollywood had always made 'British' films – films of British stories and settings, shot in a 'Britain' created just as easily, synthetically, and successfully in its studios as China, or any other non-Californian location. Metro-Goldwyn-Mayer's *David Copperfield* had been as authentically Dickensian – and English – as steak and kidney pudding. In the scenario departments there were always British books and novels, purchased for production, in the process of adaptation. Above all, the Americans and the British spoke, more or less, the same language. Abroad, Britain was the biggest and most lucrative market for American films. Now, with a British studio such as Denham demonstrating a technical facility equal to Hollywood, what more logical than that the American majors should move in and shoot all their 'British' stories and subjects in British studios – as renters of films, as well as producers, ensuring themselves at the same time of a flow of top-flight genuinely British made films now needed under the act.

And so, in 1937, Metro-Goldwyn-Mayer came to Denham.

Only three years later, in those same overhead skies, there was to be fought out the Battle of Britain. It had never occurred to any British company to consider a film about the Royal Air Force. This American giant had not only done so but, as its first full-scale production at what it now chose to call its British Studios, planned an epic on the RAF, to star, no less, Clark Gable.

Gable, with Garbo at that time, was Metro's biggest star, and had just scored a great success in *Test Pilot*; but this meant nothing (or too much) to someone in the Air Ministry. Elmer Dyer, a cameraman of *Hell's Angels* and *The Dawn Patrol*, had already started to shoot background material but, when it was learnt that an American was to star in this saga of the Royal Air Force, all official facilities were abruptly withdrawn. But no one was ever allowed to remain idle at MGM for long. Gable was immediately recast as a daredevil newsreel cameraman in the home-based *Too Hot to Handle*. Fortunately for that gentleman in the Air Ministry, and a great many more of his fellow countrymen, when it really counted just a few years later, Gable flew many missions for real in the United States 8th Air Force, based in Britain and bombing Germany.

Shadow of the Wing was the title of this film of the Royal Air Force never made by MGM before the war in Britain. It had been an idea of John Monk Saunders, co-author with Howard Hawks of *The Dawn Patrol*. Nothing daunted, he came up with another. They may object to the idea of a Yank in the RAF, but they can't object to a Yank at Oxford, for, after all, Americans had studied at that centre of learning for a great many years. So the first Metro-Goldwyn-Mayer British production was indeed *A Yank at Oxford*, a much more ambitious and star-studded

Hitchcock directs Madeleine Carroll and
John Gielgud in *Secret Agent*

incursion into that ancient university than Korda's *Men of Tomorrow* of five years before. Who to produce? For even if (as
they did) Metro planned to bring over key technicians themselves, they could hardly claim the film to be British-produced if
in fact its producer was not himself British. The only equal in
achievement and stature to Korda in Britain was Michael Balcon; and he, born in Birmingham forty years before, could indeed claim to be genuinely native-born.

Balcon had produced his first of more than a hundred films
back in 1922. In charge of production for both Gainsborough and
Gaumont-British, ten years later, he dominated the scene until
the advent of Korda. With refurbished sound stages at his Shepherds Bush Studios, in 1936 he too had planned an assault
against Hollywood. January of that year he announced the signing of his medley of American stars, which now included as well
as Constance Bennett, Victor McLaglen, and Maureen
O'Sullivan (the mother of the Mia Farrow to be). At a press conference he had been asked that, having imported all these American stars 'with the object of conquering the American market,

you will, presumably, make your films in an American style and tempo – not in the British style?'

To which Michael Balcon had then replied:

'There is no British style. Or if there is, it is a bad one.'

For someone who had given Alfred Hitchcock his first film to direct twelve years before and who, at Ealing Studios in the years to come, was to create the most truly English series and style of feature-film-making this was, for the time an astonishing, percipient and penetrating remark (and a sideswipe at Korda too).

The Balcon Gaumont-British films which had succeeded most in making any sort of impression in the United States market were those directed by Alfred Hitchcock. From *The 39 Steps* on, American critics at least sat up and took notice. American stars joined his casts. Sylvia Sidney was brought across to join Oscar Homolka in *Sabotage* while Peter Lorre had previously menaced magnificently in *The Man Who Knew Too Much* and augmented Robert Young in support of Madeleine Carroll and John Gielgud in *Secret Agent*. Now Hitchcock was going his own way, Hollywood beckoned, Gaumont-British was foundering, and Balcon too needed to look elsewhere.

A Yank at Oxford was, however, to be a very unhappy experience for Michael Balcon. Early on he quarrelled with Louis B. Mayer, and found himself ostracised by the top American talent imported to make the film, not his, but Metro's way.

First, the story. The 'Yank', whose scholastic capacities were but marginal but whose athletic prowess phenomenal, is sent on a scholarship from a minor American College to Oxford University. There, some acidly observed young British patronise and rag him, British manners and quaintness are affectionately observed and sent up, our hero is almost sent down, but in a final burst of glory strokes Oxford to victory over Cambridge in the annual inter-varsity Boat Race. Director was Jack Conway. He had been with Metro for years, one of the inner circle which had roistered and revolved around that studio's legendary head of production, Irving Thalberg – dead at thirty-seven only the year

Jack Conway directs Robert Taylor to win the Boat Race
(author back to camera behind Conway)

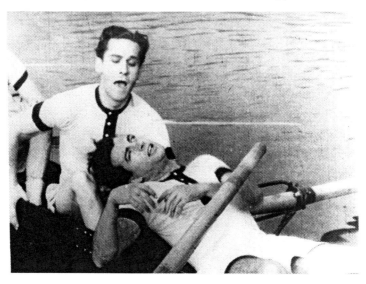

Robert Taylor strokes the Oxford boat to victory – and
collapses at the finishing post

before. Louis B. Mayer (the final M of MGM) had already cast his son-in-law David O. Selznick for the role of what he hoped would be a more subservient semi-replacement. For Selznick Conway had recently directed a sequel to *David Copperfield* – Dickens again – *A Tale of Two Cities*.

But he, like all contracted directors of that time, had to be, and was, totally adaptable. No one could have been better suited to the fast, wisecracking, iconoclastic pace of *A Yank at Oxford*.

'You can bet your life', Conway had said early on, 'the Dons won't like this picture. Well, who cares? I'm not making it for the Dons, anyway. To me it's just another subject like *Libelled Lady* (which had starred William Powell and Jean Harlow), a good excuse for a slickly-made comedy drama'.

Cameraman was Harold Rosson, not long ago married to and quite recently divorced from Jean Harlow, whose films he had frequently photographed. It was said that the studio had forced this marriage – any marriage – on Harlow in order to give their free-living star a more 'respectable' image in what was then a very hypocritical Hollywood. Rosson had in fact long been in love with her and, like Barkis, was willing. But such an alliance of what was basically only Metro convenience had soon blown apart. Now, nursing his wounds and grumbling at his assistants, 'Hal' Rosson was safely out of the way here for a while, back in Britain, where he had previously shot three of the pre-Denham films for Korda, *The Scarlet Pimpernel*, *The Ghost Goes West*, and *The Man Who Could Work Miracles*. A rather nasty little man, was the unanimous opinion of the former Gaumont-British camera crews Balcon put together to serve him, but none of us was then aware of his problem.

Not long before, Rosson had photographed Selznick's first Technicolor production, *The Garden of Allah*, starring Marlene Dietrich. Eight years later, still working for Metro, and after, amongst others, *The Wizard of Oz*, he found himself assigned to photographing tests of her once again for *Kismet*. After viewing the results, Marlene is alleged to have turned to him and said, 'Hal, I don't think you're giving me close-ups as good as you did on *Garden of Allah*'.

'Miss Dietrich', was Rosson's reply, 'I'm sorry, but I'm not getting any younger'. If this old chestnut is true in his case, then it is the only recorded witticism of an otherwise unforgiving taskmaster; and it would explain why *Kismet*, when released, credited Charles Rosher as Director of Photography. Once upon a time Mary Pickford's cameraman, he too had also shot a film for Korda at Denham: *Men Are Not Gods*, directed by Walter Reisch, with Miriam Hopkins and Rex Harrison.

Similarly brought across from the home studios was Thalberg's supervising editor, Margaret Booth. Seemingly as humourless and, in appearance, certainly as uptight as Rosson, this formidable female picture-saver was to breathe down poor Charles Frend's neck throughout his editing of Metro-Goldwyn-Mayer's first British baby. For Thalberg, she had recently cut – and nobody could say other than brilliantly – *Mutiny on the Bounty*. Of her professional capacities there could be no doubt.

And the star? After Gable, the next in line in Louis B. Mayer's stud farm out at Culver City was Robert Taylor. Born Spangler Arlington Brugh, and first seen in *Buried Loot*, a short film in the series *Crime Does Not Pay*, this morbidly modest but quite strikingly handsome young man had just confounded sceptics and astonished critics by holding his own against Garbo, as Armand, in *Camille*. To one feminine columnist of the day, he reminded her of 'a magnificent, perfectly mannered horse, going courteously and charmingly through its paces'.

On the set, this was no more than the truth. Always and unfailingly word-perfect, Taylor would perform and play his part as almost a well-oiled and programmed automaton. Never any fuss, never late, never (so far as he was concerned) need for a retake. Between takes he would sit quietly, and quite politely, not talking. Gossip had it that his heart was back in Hollywood, with Barbara Stanwyck. So far as Taylor was concerned, the 'Yank' was quite clearly just another part, to be done as well as possible, and as quickly as possible.

And authorship? Hard to define. Crediting J. Monk Saunders with the original idea, the finally finished *Yank at Oxford* listed no less than five other scribes: Malcolm Stuart Boylan, Walter

Perris, George Oppenheimer, Michael Hogan; and, very ill at ease amongst this line-up, Sidney Gilliat (yet to co-script *The Lady Vanishes*), whose major contribution was to be the introduction of a lusty young local woman designed to create havoc amongst undergraduate heartbeats.

Now legend has it that Scott Fitzgerald also worked on this film, during his own sad and final sojourn in Hollywood. As a Princeton man, they must have thought him wise to the ways of academe, even 'Cardinal', the fictitious Oxford foundation to which they consigned the 'Yank'. But we officially received final confirmation of this much later. In Matthew Bruccoli's 1982 biography of the doomed Jazz Age chronicler, we learn that he was assigned to the picture, for little more than a week, and that he himself was only able to claim the writing of just one single sequence as his own.

Wouldn't it be good to know just what sort of dialogue the author of *The Great Gatsby* wrote for *A Yank at Oxford*? Well, we can. By looking at the copy of the script to which, as a mere clapper boy, I had absolutely no right but which I grabbed just as soon as I found someone's lying around the set. (And on which incidentally, there is no writing credit whatsoever).

The only person who is at first at all kind to Lee Sheridan – the 'Yank' – is Molly, the 'nice girl', played by Maureen O'Sullivan. As a choir sings from the top of Magdalen Tower, and this choral music drifts across the water, early one May morning he takes her out on the river. The setting is serene, the mood almost elegiac. The dialogue is Scott Fitzgerald.

SCRIPT

SCENE 242: EXTERIOR: RIVER BANK

(The setting is idyllically beautiful. Lee is trying to hold the punt against the bank with the pole. Molly tries to step in. The river swirls the boat under the laburnum trees. Molly must leap for it. Lee catches her almost like a dancer in the air. The punt tips perilously as he holds her for a moment.)

LEE (naval etiquette)

Good morning. Glad to see you aboard!

MOLLY

Such a good morning, and it's a perfect miracle that I am aboard.

(They are standing together a little off balance. Lee is holding the pole and the girl as the boat swings out.)

LEE (indicating a seat)

Won't you sit down ... before it's too late?

MOLLY (to Lee)

Thank you.

(Just then the boat lurches, and she sits down abruptly and heavily; frowning at the stream)

Old Man River.

LEE (looking at her with deep appreciation)

I suppose you know you're beautiful.

(He is so intent on looking at her that the boat swings sharply around into the stream)

MOLLY

Why, I've hardly got the sleep out of my eyes.

(She begins rubbing her eyes with both hands)

LEE (tenderly)

If that's sleep, don't rub it out ... it's beautiful sleep ... it's the loveliest sleep I ever saw.

MOLLY

You're an idiot ... and I hope you never regain your sanity.

(He makes a vigorous stab of the pole and the boat shoots ahead. The pole, however, does not come out of the mud easily. Lee hangs on to it until the last possible moment, and then lets go. He sits down in the punt, and takes a paddle from the bottom which he uses more expertly.)

LEE

Well, we got rid of that bally thing anyway.
(he seems surprised at his own use of the word)

Was that me? I say! I'm getting more British every minute. If my father heard that, he'd snap an ear drum.

MOLLY

I'm sure he's wonderful (mischievously) even if he is an American.

LEE

He's great, and he thinks you are wonderful too.

MOLLY

He doesn't even know me.

LEE

Oh, yes he does. Old Man Griffin, the postman, stuffs you
under the door twice a week.

(Molly laughs)

Then my father picks you up, turns you over, and slits your
wrapper.

MOLLY

Mercy!

LEE

Gee, I'd like to have you in my town ... wouldn't you like to
see it?

MOLLY

I'd love to

When the film was released, Scott Fitzgerald wrote about it
to his mother:
'Very few lines of mine are left in *A Yank at Oxford* ... but the
sequence in which Taylor and Maureen O'Sullivan go out in the
punt ... is mine, and one line very typically so – where Taylor
says, "Don't rub the sleep out of your eyes. It's beautiful sleep." I
thought that line had my trade mark on it.'
Catching the May morning magic of that 'beautiful sleep'
proved to be more easily writ than done. The sequence had to be
shot no less than three times, in three different locations. Firstly
out on the ever obliging river Colne, a few miles down the road
from the studios near Uxbridge. Not so good. Try again. This
time, and still out in the real open air, afloat on the exterior tank,

back of the studio car park. No one entirely happy with the way the scene played. Finally one major inadequacy of Denham Studios just had to be faced: not one of the seven stages had under its removable floor boards a 'tank' which, when filled up, made possible the design, construction, and completely controllable interior settings for such watery scenes, whatever the weather might be up to outside. The older Ealing Studios, where I had got my first foothold the year before, did have one, as well as scenery doors to the sound stages which lifted automatically at the push of a button. For aqueous interior sets at Denham, 'tanks' made up of water-tight canvas suspended from off-camera wooden uprights had to make do. Such as, for example, the Mediterranean lapping the sides of the villain's yacht Annabella had to swim out to in *Dinner at the Ritz*, held in focus as she did so by a temporarily promoted clapper boy suspended above the 'waves' on a camera boom. So for the third attempt at the Yank's aquatic courtship of the 'nice girl' we all trooped to the other big studio which was properly equipped for this purpose, and which has just been built not far away in the grounds of another country mansion, from which it had taken its name: Pinewood. There, with Rosson's lighting sparkling in the water from the spot-rail overhead, and free from any extraneous interruptions from passing traffic, Taylor and O'Sullivan finally did do justice to Fitzgerald's invention; the mood of which might well have been a scene between Jay Gatsby and Daisy Buchanan in his most famous and twice filmed novel. For was not *The Great Gatsby* always claiming to have been an 'Oxford man' himself?

But the sequence which really stays in my mind came earlier in the story. For this was not only the very first to be filmed, but we had also already shot it at least half a dozen times previously to try out candidates for its key supporting role of the 'scout' – the college servant who looked after the 'Yank' while at Oxford.

'Testing' in those days meant more than just the reading of a scene or two from the script, followed by a 'Thank you very much, don't call us we'll call you' routine. It involved a complete production crew's filming of the aspirant under consideration, in costume if required, and in the actual performance of a key scene the character being cast would be called upon to play. Producer and Director would then assess the outcome on the screen the following day, and make their decision. No one was more into this preliminary visualisation than David O. Selznick For the year's most coveted part – that of the starring role in *Gone With The Wind* – no less than thirty were put through their paces in this way before he finally found his Scarlett O'Hara. On one such occasion, David Niven was even borrowed from Sam Goldwyn to feed lines to one of these glamorous hopefuls.

At the same time Selznick was also setting up *Rebecca*, and one evening at the former Fox Studios at Wembley I ran a focus measuring tape out to just between the sparkling blue eyes of Dorothy Hyson, then under consideration for the lead. Despite being lit by Harry Stradling, who was soon to join Selznick himself, this very English rose lost out as we all now know to another damsel already on the doorstep, Joan Fontaine.

But then how else could producers in Hollywood effectively assess artistes recommended by their British representatives all those thousands of miles away?

To England at this time came William Wyler, as much to take a look at real Bronte country as to find himself a Heathcliff. He was sure he had succeeded with the then little known Robert Newton, brought to his notice by the sullen power Bobbie had already displayed in a succession of character parts in previous productions for the Korda group. Up at Denham went a set of *Wuthering Heights*, and with his ever meticulous attention to perfectionist detail, Wyler directed Newton in several scenes from the already scripted film. Viewing the result shipped over to Hollywood, and despite Wyler's pleas, Goldwyn would have none of it. Together with his own *Henry V*, this is surely the screen role for which Laurence Olivier will always be best remembered.

Testing artistes for key roles on such a lavish scale was so very much Metro's way. All in all, for *A Yank at Oxford*, there were no less than four weeks of such altogether full time preliminary filming – which must have cost as much as an average 'Quota Quickie' of old. Time and again Robert Taylor was called upon to turn up on an improvised set just to feed the lines to a whole succession of candidates hoping to play the part of his Oxford College 'Scout'. Every one of us on the unit knew it all, word for word, before it finally went to Edward Rigby. Lee Sheridan, the 'Yank' played by Taylor, has just been unmercifully ragged and made to look a fool by the British students on his arrival at 'Cardinal', the fictitious college invented by MGM.

SCRIPT

SCENE 93: INTERIOR : LEE'S STUDY

(It is rather bleak and bare, but with the towers and spires of Oxford visible through the window. As he enters, the various bells begin chiming in harmonious disagreement. Note: these bells reflect the passing moods of the boy and continue throughout this scene. Lee looks about, then goes through a door into his bedroom.)

SCENE 94: INTERIOR : LEE'S BEDROOM

(As he enters. During the following pantomime his manner suggests the small boy who is going to do something defiant but knows, secretly, that he is being silly. His suitcase is in a corner. He grabs it up angrily and almost dislocates his arm because it is empty. The lid drops open and he looks at it, astonished. He crosses to the wardrobe to discover that his clothes have been hung up. He bangs open a drawer to find it filled with his smaller articles. He snatches a handful of handkerchiefs and socks, and begins repacking when there is a knock at the door.)

LEE

Come in.

(From Lee's angle toward the door for a...)

68

SCENE 95: CLOSE SHOT: SCATTERS

(A sturdy little old man with side-whiskers and a gentle smile, He stands bowing and smiling in the doorway.)

SCATTERS

Good evening, sir.

SCENE 96: LEE AND SCATTERS

LEE (frowning, inquiringly)

Yeah?

SCATTERS

I'm Scattergood – your scout, sir.

LEE (suspiciously)

What is this – another gag?

SCATTERS (not understanding)

Beg pardon, sir?

LEE

Well, then – what are you scouting for – Indians?

SCATTERS

No, sir... At the moment there are no gentlemen from India at Cardinal.

LEE

Skip it ... What can I do for you?

SCATTERS (protesting)

Oh no, sir – it's my job to do for you.

LEE

I've *been* done for – thanks, Mr. Scattergood.

(He viciously throws some of his clothes in a messy pile into his valise and turns to get more. Scatters starts removing them and folding them neatly.)

SCATTERS

Just call me Scatters – it's customary.

(Lee turns, sees Scatters removing his clothes, and thinks he's trying to unpack.)

LEE

Here – what are you doing?

SCATTERS (with a gentle smile)

Packing for you, sir ... How much will you be wanting to take with you?

LEE

Everything.

SCATTERS

Very good, sir.

(He proceeds to pack slowly and deliberately.)

SCATTERS (suddenly notices a large hole in one of the socks he has been packing)

I'm afraid sir, you've a hole in one of your socks. (He puts it aside.)

SCATTERS (continues)

I'll have it as good as new for you when you get back.

LEE

Don't bother.

SCATTERS

Oh, no bother at all sir. (There is a pause, while Lee looks out of the window disconsolately.)

I don't suppose you've seen much of Oxford as yet, sir.

LEE

I've seen everything I want to see.

SCATTERS (with a little laugh)

Oh, that's not possible, sir – not in one day ... It takes years, really – and each time you see it there's something new – something you hadn't noticed before ... It sort of grows on one.

LEE

It'll have to grow mighty fast – as far as I'm concerned.

SCATTERS

I'm afraid it doesn't happen that way, sir ... Oxford's too old to do anything fast ... Now, take the Cathedral, for example, part of it has been standing for a thousand years. (with a little pride) That's a long time sir.

LEE (beginning to show light interest, pointing out the window)

Is that it over there?

CUT TO

SCENE 97: LONG SHOT OVER LEE'S SHOULDER

(With towers and spires silhouetted against an evening sky. Scatters looks up from his packing toward the view out of the window, as Lee points)

SCATTERS

Oh no, sir ... That's Magdalen Tower – and rare beautiful too, isn't it sir?

LEE (begrudgingly)

Not bad.

SCATTERS (with a little twinkle)

No, sir. I'd say it was my favourite spot of all – there's hardly a night that I don't pass there and stop for a moment. (He laughs apologetically) It's almost like visiting an old friend.

(Lee's face softens – it is obvious that he is moved.)

SCATTERS (continuing)

You'll be finding friends like that, too, sir – before long.

LEE (bitterly)

I could do with a few of them right now.

(Suddenly the bells begin to increase in volume. Lee's face lights a bit – he leans out of the window.)

SCATTERS

Do you hear those bells, sir? ... Centuries old, some of them – and still as clear as the day they were cast. (He stops his packing) You know sir – sometimes I can almost see Sir Walter Raleigh and many of the other great gentlemen who came here standing in this very room, right where you're standing at that same window, and hearing those bells just as we're hearing them now.

LEE

Gosh – that's kind of spooky – isn't it?

SCATTERS (smiling)

Some of my gentlemen who come back, claim they hear them all through their lives ... I'd venture to say, sir, that you, too, will carry the sound of those bells with you wherever you go.

(They stand there in silence for a moment. Then suddenly Scatters breaks the silence.)

SCATTERS

I am sorry, sir ... Here I've been chatting away – forgetting all about your packing. (He moves over to the bag.)

LEE (hesitates for a moment, then decisively, with embarrassment)

I – ah – you needn't bother packing any more, Scatters ... I'm going to – I mean ...

SCATTERS

I quite understand, sir.

(With a happy little smile he starts unpacking the bag.)

FADE OUT

With a credited collective of half a dozen other writers, authorship in this case is anyone's guess; and with such a streamlined script, there was little if any need for revision during actual filming.

As production proceeded, Denham's *Yank at Oxford* had visitors. To the set one day came William Powell. On a European vacation gloomily; like our cameraman but in his own way and for his own reasons, also trying to get over the sudden and mysterious death of Jean Harlow. Fresh from Hollywood too, and the part of Louis XVI to Norma Shearer's *Marie Antoinette*, arrived a young but already substantial Robert Morley.

And Sidney Gilliat's 'bad girl' in the story, instrumental in nearly bringing about the downfall of our Yank at Oxford – who was to play her?

Discovered in the London theatre four years before, Korda had signed, and then starred in three of London Film's Denham productions, Vivien Leigh. She was to be just perfect as the local coquette who set all the undergraduates in Metro's story panting at her heels. Legend has it that she was unknown when intro-duced by her agent Myron Selznick to his brother David, busy at that time burning down Atlanta on his own back lot at the com-mencement of *Gone With The Wind*. Not so. She had already been seen on American screens nationwide in *A Yank at Oxford*. In this minor but key role named, believe it or not, Elsa Craddock, there was already more than a hint of Scarlett O'Hara.

In the Korda group's *Fire Over England* Vivien Leigh had been cast opposite Laurence Olivier – and there had occurred almost nuclear reaction. Now the future Lord Olivier sat, satur-nine and gloomy, a visitor to the set every time she was called, following her every move and line before camera. Finished for the day, he would, just as silently, disappear with her – at the start of an odyssey which was soon to take them both to Holly-wood. She to Scarlett and he to Heathcliff.

Most of what little real fun there was in the making of this on-screen very funny film was had by the second unit, shooting the many athletic events in which Taylor always triumphed. The Oxford and Cambridge boat race was shot both on the ever-reliable and handy Colne, and the actual Putney to Mortlake course of the Thames. It had been many years since Oxford had in fact beaten Cambridge. The film was first shown at the Em-pire, in London's Leicester Square, the following spring the ac-tual week of that great and annual sporting event. Lo and behold, just that year of 1938 the real Oxford did indeed vanquish Cam-bridge, and the first run of *A Yank at Oxford* had in its pro-gramme a newsreel of that ancient university's genuine win over her traditional rival. A certain young cynic, who might have been a clapper boy, was heard to wonder if Metro might not have bribed Cambridge.

The film was a huge success, and broke every record at the Empire since the original *Broadway Melody* of 1929. In the *Sun-day Express*, Stephen Watts wrote that Metro-Goldwyn-Mayer had 'made a swift, exciting, amusing picture, with all their Hol-lywood polish and punch, which will, I am sure, rank with the best films of the year – not just with the best *British* films of the year'. Of its re-presentation on British television in the summer of 1990, the TV Times had to say of *A Yank at Oxford* that it was 'remarkably entertaining'. Why not – with all that talent?

The most cautious, as well as the most prestigious, of all the Hollywood giants, Metro-Goldwyn-Mayer marked time as far as further British productions were concerned until this successful outcome of their first was confirmed and assured. Meantime, and like many then and now, I was out of work. Despite the new Quota Act, the high hopes of a flourishing British Film Industry had blown away with the reality of mounting bank overdrafts. Gaumont-British had already collapsed as a direct result of 'the failure to get into the American market'. January 4th, 1938, I went over to Denham, to find out what I could. Most of the seven sound stages were empty, the others becoming idle. After this New Year visit, I recorded that 'they think London Film Productions are bust'. At a union meeting of unemployed technicians in March, I learnt that Korda would have nothing on the floor of a studio until maybe May. Three weeks later, at last, just two days' work at Denham materialised: second camera on a musical number in 20th Century Fox's first directly produced major British picture, *We're Going to be Rich*, In this optimistically entitled attempt to launch Gracie Fields into the American market, the lassie from Lancashire battled Victor McLaglen for the custody of a kid and the.loot of a 19th Century gold rush. But the worst of this slump in the fortunes of the pre-World War Two British film industry was soon to be all but over. The camera operator of *A Yank at Oxford* took me on for a four week minor film at Shepperton Studios; and, most exciting development of all, forty-eight hours later there landed in Britain from Hollywood King Vidor. The director of *The Big Parade*, *The Crowd*, *Hallelujah*, *Billy the Kid*, *Street Scene*, *The Texas Rangers* and many another great American movie was here, to make for MGM their second major British production, *The Citadel*.

The Citadel had been a runaway best-selling novel on both sides of the Atlantic ever since its publication the previous summer. It is the story of an idealistic young doctor who starts his work and career amongst the poverty-stricken coal miners of South Wales; who falls foul of local prejudice as he seeks a cure

King Vidor with Welsh miners setting up *The Citadel*

for the silicosis for which, in those pre-National Health days, they received no pay when laid off; who moves on to London at first to a slum practice which in those days had to be bought; where a stroke of fortune has him called to a dress shop to treat an hysterical 'society' woman. She falls for his rugged good looks. Before long, social doors are opened for him, he has set up shop in Harley Street, acquired an expensive car, alienated his wife, and all but forgotten the days the two of them set out in the Welsh valleys to conquer pain and disease. The death of a friend, at the hands of an incompetent but fashionable fellow practitioner, brings him face to face with his loss of integrity. *The Citadel* ends with his joining a small group to practise medicine, co-operatively, on a semi-socialised basis.

It is said that, on the basis of a synopsis, Sam Goldwyn had his story editor make an immediate offer for the film rights to *The Citadel*. But, by the following day, still smarting from the overnight preview failure of his latest but quite unrelated picture, he had changed his mind. 'All doctor stories', he then announced, 'lose money'. MGM thought otherwise (after all, their Dr. Kildare was to prove quite a moneymaker) but the rights had mean-

77

time been acquired by the independent British producer Victor Saville – and with whom, in order that they could make the picture, Metro had now joined forces.

Victor Saville had been Michael Balcon's original founding partner, and he had directed many films for him in the years which followed. Recently a Producer-Director with Korda, he had made four films at Denham, *Action for Slander*, *South Riding*, *Dark Journey*, and James Bridie's *Storm in a Teacup* (the last two starring Vivien Leigh). As now their new British Producer, MGM were to give him a much freer hand than Louis B. Mayer had been disinclined to extend to Balcon, and from now on the plan was to bring over from Hollywood only the director, and maybe a star, for their British productions.

As soon as he had originally acquired the film rights to *The Citadel*, Saville had set scenario writer Ian Dalrymple to work on a script. As soon as they acquired it, MGM assigned playwright John Van Druten to work on it further in Hollywood. As soon as he was signed up to direct it, with his wife Elizabeth Hill, King Vidor worked over it all again to his own satisfaction. Finally, and most sensibly, Saville brought in Emlyn Williams to provide genuinely Welsh-sounding 'additional dialogue' (he was also to give one of the film's best performances as a progressive miners' leader).

South Riding had been shot for Saville by *Knight Without Armour* and *Kermesse Heroique*'s Harry Stradling. Now he was to be cameraman on *The Citadel*, but he didn't want some kid called Peter Hopkinson as his clapper boy. Furiously I argued. Fearlessly I pleaded with mighty Metro-Goldwyn-Mayer.

Successfully I made it, and finished up on the picture as Denham's highest paid second assistant cameraman to date – £4 a week.

Immediately I set about designing a new and what I considered to be a correctly screen-proportioned number board (Denham's had hitherto been upright and vertical) and prepared to learn all I could not only from a great cameraman, but also from a legendary film-maker, King Vidor.

Oscar-winning Jack Cardiff and camera crew filming *Black Narcissus*

Lining up Technicolor camera for special effect shot in *Black Narcissus*.
Crouched below, director Michael Powell

The story of King Vidor is the story of Hollywood, of the American film.

The grandson of a Hungarian immigrant, named by his mother 'King' after her favourite brother, as a film-mad teenager Vidor had got himself a job in 1910 at three-and-a-half dollars a week as a ticket taker in his local cinema. With a school friend, and a home-made camera, he shot a hundred feet of a hurricane in the nearby Gulf of Mexico. They sold copies to the cinemas in his native state of Texas. Three years later, at the age of eighteen, with a hand-cranked camera on loan in return for a share in any sales, he became a newsreel freelance. He went on to make a couple of locally successful two-reel shorts, and on the proceeds of a film for a sugar-refining company married his girl, bought a Model T Ford, and set off for Hollywood. They paid their way from Texas to California by the sale of snippets of travelogue shot en route. With his seventeen-year-old bride bringing in ten dollars a week as a sort of understudy to fellow Texan beauty Corinne Griffith, Vidor sat down to write. He wrote fifty-two scenarios before he sold one for thirty dollars. He continued the rounds of the studios; watched D.W. Griffith shoot *Intolerance*; got a job at Universal as an accounting clerk; under another name bombarded its scenario department with scripts. Got a break directing a series of shorts on the rehabilitation of juvenile delinquents. Stuck three of these together into a feature, and failed to sell it. Now or never. Put heart and soul into an original story of how its hero faced up to life, and sought an answer, after the death of his young wife in childbirth: *The Turn of the Road*. It was indeed. Production backing was forthcoming from a syndicate of nine doctors. The film was a hit. Capital was now available. As a virtually independent film-maker, eleven features now followed before, in 1923, *Peg O' My Heart*, his first for the Metro Company. Six years and fourteen films later, in a speech to students at the University of Southern California, Irving Thalberg – by then the legendary head of production at Metro-Goldwyn-Mayer paid Vidor this tribute:

'King Vidor is as much a realist as Griffith is an idealist, and his pictures have been an attempt to mirror life of today as it really is. I have discussed scenes with him so many times, and have asked him to do this or that to heighten the dramatic effect, and his worst fear has always been to make any character do anything that wasn't natural for him to do.'

Another generation of students at that same University of Southern California has since sat at his feet, for when in his own seventies, and retired from active production, Vidor himself became a greatly respected teacher of film; in between flying from one international film festival to another as the official and greatly respected American representative. By then a grand old man of movies, his penultimate film had been the 1956 version of Tolstoy's *War and Peace*, starring Audrey Hepburn and Henry Fonda.

Now, at Denham in 1938, King Vidor was at the height of his powers, and about to shoot his forty-first film. He had none of the somewhat crude aggressiveness of Jack Conway, none of the frequently flamboyant and often temperamental tantrums of not a few of Korda's continental imports. He was quiet, patient, unassuming, but total master of every aspect of making motion pictures. On the set relaxed, at all times articulate; and not only about what he wanted from technicians and actors but about his work and film making in general. He was the first director to even notice my existence as a fanatical film buff as well as a clapper boy. He talked to me, with me. Told me of his early days in Hollywood, of his struggle to get started. That, as he saw it, European cameramen tended to concentrate on lighting the set, while American cameramen lit the star. He told me that while stars in Hollywood often got the cameraman they wanted (the outstanding examples being Garbo and William Daniels), directors were seldom so fortunate. And telling me all this was the man who had directed Laurette Taylor, Sylvia Sidney, Dolores Del Rio, Barbara Stanwyck, Anna Sten, Lillian Gish and Marion Davies. Marion Davies, the great and good friend of newspaper magnate William Randolph Hearst. Vidor was one of the few directors *Citizen Kane*'s prototype had approved of, at least so far as the handling of his protégée in front of the cameras was concerned.

Likened by a British reporter to a 'JB Priestley on the water wagon', on arrival at Denham to film *The Citadel*, King Vidor very early on made his attitudes clear. (Clearer, indeed, than in the autobiography he wrote fourteen years later, but by then Hollywood was under 'investigation' and it had begun to look very much as if 'it had already happened there'.)

'In America movie makers like myself are up against such things as censorship and diplomatic relations which spoil one's plans all the time, To name only two very famous recent novels both overwhelming successes in America – Sinclair Lewis's *It Can't Happen Here*, a picture of how a particularly brutal Fascist demagogue could gain power in America, and Franz Werfel's epic of Armenian heroism under the Turks, *The Forty Days of Musa Dagh*. Both these stories were bought by Metro, and both are stories I'd love making into films. It still isn't certain that we won't be able to do one or even both, but at present, no.' (In reality neither Vidor nor anyone else for that matter has ever made either.)

Forty Days was abandoned, so the studio claimed, in order not to offend the Turks. A similar concern on the part of the British Foreign Office inhibited Korda's attempts to set up his version of *Lawrence of Arabia*. What, one wonders, was so special about Turkish susceptibilities in those days?

'I do feel good', Vidor continued, 'about *The Citadel*. Here you have a profession that every normal person is inevitably interested in – we've all been to the doctor at least once in our lives. And the author has taken an ordinary, well-meaning, simple man – neither patriot nor pacifist, as it were – and thrown him into his complex calling.

'He shows us what happens – the choices he has to make, the people he meets, the parts of the country he has to go to. It's not just a debunk job – not merely an exposure of Harley Street. That would be much too narrow – people would think we'd got chips on our shoulders. No, it's the panorama of a life, an ordinary man journeying through an exceptionally important profession. Moral and ethical questions are involved, and all these aspects, properly done, can make a great film to appeal to every one'.

By 1983 millions more of a later generation had become aware of *The Citadel* by way of a BBC TV serialisation.

In the 1930's the average running time of a cinema film was little more than ninety minutes, and in 1938 MGM and Vidor had barely a couple of hours in which to dramatise Cronin's story. By the very nature of their spread across consecutive weeks (or evenings) TV book-based mini-series are nowadays able to include most if not all of the author's original narrative. Moving on from Cronin, Vidor was forced in 1956 to cope with *War and Peace* in the by then road show luxury of three and a half hours; but the BBC, in later association with *Time-Life*, were able to spread Tolstoy's canvas across eighteen hours of twenty serialised segments. Back in 1923 that wild man of the American silent cinema Erich von Stroheim shot a film based on a novel by Frank Norris, which in his first cut it is said ran nine hours. The horrified studio cut *Greed* to a quarter this length.

What screen adaptations had to aim for in those pre-television days was more the *essence* of a novel rather than its literal narrative line. After all, the New York Jewish writer Ben Hecht's script for Goldwyn of *Wuthering Heights* ran for only an hour and forty minutes. But in the hands of William Wyler it caught a kind of passionate exuberance wholly absent from later, longer, and more ponderous TV versions of Emily Bronte's English gothic masterpiece.

Nowadays ten hours or more are nothing in the overall running time of the average television drama. In 1985 *Heimat*, Edgar Reitz's sixteen hour chronicle of the people of a mythical German village over sixty three years of their turbulent ups and downs, was screened by the BBC in eleven separate episodes (and in cinemas complete over a single weekend). The HBC's serialisation of *The Citadel* ran to a more modest nine hours in ten fifty five minute episodes – but for Vidor forty-five years earlier it had all had to be done in a matter of a hundred and thirteen minutes. Playing the young doctor hero in the BBC's 1983 version was Ben Cross, fresh at that time from his triumph in

Chariots of Fire. For King Vidor and MGM in 1938 it was to be Robert Donat. In fact MGM had secured rights to the book just so that he – and only he – could do so.

Born in Lancashire of a Yorkshire mother and a Polish father, and then a youthful thirty-three years old, Robert Donat was at that time the most popular and highly paid British film star. Once again it had been Korda who discovered him for the screen, an up-and-coming stage actor with an already considerable achievement in the theatre.

Apart from striking and sensitive good looks, Donat possessed an extraordinarily beautiful speaking voice; a quality of diction and a combination of attributes seldom seen before, or since, in someone still undeniably masculine. Korda had first of all cast him in three of the films he made in Britain for Paramount quota, and then as Thomas Culpeper, the courtier who cuckolded his king. As with all concerned in *The Private Life of Henry VIII*, this small but effective part made an immediate impact on American audiences. Korda thereupon lent his handsome property (at a fair profit to London Film Productions) to Edward Small in Hollywood, as the latter's *Count of Monte Cristo*. Donat loathed Hollywood, and never went back. Instead, Hollywood was now coming to Donat. Korda had then gone on to lend him out once again, this time to Michael Balcon and Alfred Hitchcock for *The Thirty Nine Steps*; finally at last finding him a suitable film of his own, the title part of *The Ghost Goes West*. It was a foregone conclusion that Robert Donat was the only British star of sufficient calibre to share top billing with Marlene Dietrich, and it had therefore accordingly fallen to him to pilot her through the perils of the Russian Revolution as that *Knight Without Armour*. Who else but Robert Donat, all alone with the beautiful and vulnerable Marlene, waiting in an abandoned railroad station for the unlikely arrival of a train which might save both their lives, could have got away with just quoting Browning: 'Fear death? – to feel the fog in my throat, the mist in my face, When the snows begin, and the blasts denote I am nearing the place, The Power of the night, the press of the storm, the post of the foe...'

Knight Without Armour. Dietrich flees the Bolsheviks - and takes a tub

Almost neurasthenic in his sensitivity, Donat worried and anguished long over which of many offers to accept next. His name above a title now did more to guarantee the success of a British film in the United States than anything else. For this simple reason MGM wanted him, and what Metro-Goldwyn-Mayer wanted, they got. It was reported that Metro were so keen for Donat that they offered him a contract for seven years, without any option clauses at all, accepting his stipulation that all his pictures had to be made in Britain, at £60,000 a year; and that was a lot of money all those years ago. The only other star to have been offered anything approaching this was Clark Gable.

So here, at Denham, May 1938, was *The Citadel*'s and Metro's Dr. Andrew Manson. Let his original creator, A.J. Cronin, now describe the opening of his story:

'Late one afternoon in the year 1924, a shabby young man gazed with fixed intensity through the window of a third class compartment in the almost empty train labouring up the Penowell Valley from Swansea. All that day Manson had travelled from the North, changing at Carlisle and Shrewsbury, yet the final stage of his tedious journey to South Wales found him strung to a still greater excitement by the prospects of his post, the first of his medical career, in this strange, disfigured country. Outside, a heavy rainstorm came blinding down between the mountains which rose on either side of the single railway track. The mountain tops were hidden in a grey waste of sky, but their sides, scarred by ore workings, fell black and desolate, blemished by great heaps of slag on which a few dirty sheep wandered in vain hope of pasture. No bush, no blade of vegetation was visible. The trees, seen in the fading light, were gaunt and stunted spectres. At a bend in the line the red glare of a foundry flashed into sight, illuminating a score of workmen stripped to the waist, their torsos straining, arms upraised to strike. Though the scene was swiftly lost behind the huddled top gear of a mine, a sense of power persisted, tense and vivid. Manson drew a long breath. He felt an answering surge of effort, a sudden overwhelming exhilaration springing from the hope and promise of the future.'

And now, as our Study Course at Poona was all about Script Writing, let us see how this introductory sequence of *The Citadel* was in fact scripted:

SCRIPT

INT. CORNER OF THIRD-CLASS COMPARTMENT OF TRAIN CLOSE SHOT ANDREW MANSON. DAY.

(A rugged young man in shapeless, shabby but serviceable tweeds. He looks impatiently at his watch, a big silver 'Turnip' on a chain, on which hangs (if this is correct – insert?) his 'Hunter Medal', then gazes out of the window eagerly.)

MOVING SHOT AS SEEN BY MANSON (RAIN) OF A DREARY LANDSCAPE.

(The small industrial town of Blaenelly begins to come into view – foundry, a steel mill, a quarry at one side; dismal rows of cheap workers' cottages; poor muddy streets, etc.)

INT. OF COMPARTMENT

(The train begins to slow down. Andrew watches the scene in quiet, eager, excitement; he is a man curiously looking for the first time at the locale of a new phase of his life.)

GLARE OF A FOUNDRY

(Illuminating a score of workmen, stripped to the waist, their torsos straining, arms upraised to strike etc.)

BLAENELLY – RAIN

(Train slowing down preparatory to stopping. A street or road in the rain.)

INT. RAILWAY COMPARTMENT

(Andrew, sensing his destination, prepared to get off. He grabs his belongings eagerly, overwhelmed with a sudden exhilaration, springing from the hope and promise of the future.)

But as constructed and shot in the studio by Vidor, this sequence became on screen twice as many shots and cuts:

LONG SHOT and distant view of the train approaching in Welsh Valley. (Actual location).

MEDIUM CLOSE SHOT, Manson seated alone in compartment of train, he looks out of the window. (The Welsh scenes in background were back projection plates, shot at the same time as the cutaways which follow).

MEDIUM LONG SHOT, his eyeline, camera moving past pithead and Coal Mine.

MEDIUM SHOT, closer on Manson reacting, background through window of train now miner's back-to-back tenements, running up the line of a hill.

LONG SHOT, his eyeline, camera moving past miners' homes.

MEDIUM SHOT, cut back to Manson. He draws out of his pocket, and looks at, his watch.

MEDIUM CLOSE SHOT, camera (as if in train) passing men hammering at forge.

MEDIUM SHOT, cut back to Manson, his head turning as he passes this scene.

MEDIUM CLOSE SHOT on miners' back-to-back tenement homes passing by.

MEDIUM SHOT, cut back to Manson. He gets to his feet.

MEDIUM CLOSE SHOT, Railway Station sign BLAENELLY.
Back to camera, pouring rain, a macintoshed man is waiting.

LONG SHOT, camera further back, the train pulls into the station.

Apart from the opening shot itself, the train in the last two shots was the old *Knight Without Armour* railway and rolling stock, its restored locomotive puffing more proudly now that it was called upon to act out a role in a story a little nearer home. Elsewhere on the lot, most of Cronin's Blaenelly was built. The drab lines of miners' cottages, the pithead itself, the smoking chimneys of a South Wales coalfield; designed by the same Lazare Meerson who had previously created on the same site the Nevsky Prospect and the wastelands of Siberia for that earlier super-production of Dietrich's at Denham.

All *The Citadel*'s interiors were built, and shot, inside one or other of the studios sound stages: including the coal face, and the primitive surgery in which Manson is confronted with his first decision. He has been called, almost immediately on arrival, to a case. An obviously very sick woman. It is clear to us that he hasn't a clue as to either the cause, or the nature of her illness. Back in the surgery, he ponders his predicament, and wonders what to do. Back to the script:

33 INT SURGERY – NIGHT – RAIN ANDREW (Deep in thought. He searches on shelves for bottles; setting out two (spirits of nitre, salicylate of sodium) beside an empty one. He writes name and address of patient on label of latter and prepares to concoct a prescription. He thinks a moment, takes medical book from shelf, opens it, then crosses to window and lowers shade to

keep from being seen. Now back to his compounding, he is yet perplexed over his diagnosis.)

34 ANDREW (Looking quizzically from the bottles to the book. The surgery door opens with the ping of a bell. He quickly closes book and looks round guiltily.)

35 THE DOOR OF THE SURGERY (A man, rather older than Andrew, thickset and powerful, enters, wearing an old velveteen suit, pit stockings, and hobnail boots, with a sodden oilskin cape over his shoulders. He is accompanied by a very muddy mongrel wire-haired terrier. He walks slowly into the room, staring curiously at Andrew, who comes into scene as CAMERA DRAWS BACK. The newcomer pauses, nods carelessly at Andrew, then speaks in a voice politely ironic and annoyingly well-bred.)

DENNY

Thought I'd like to welcome you. I'm Denny. What you are to the revered Doctor Page, I am to the esteemed Doctor Nicholls, L.S.A. That, in case you haven't met it, is the Licentiate of the Society of Apothecaries, the highest qualification known to God and man.

ANDREW (holding out his hand)

How do you do?

DENNY (takes and releases his hand casually – then to dog)

Sit down Hawkins.

(Denny looks toward the sink and insolently strolls forward, Andrew looking after him curiously.)

90

36 THE SINK (Denny comes to the sink – takes up bottle – smells it.)

DENNY

Splendid! You've begun the good work already. One table-spoonful every three hours. It's reassuring to meet the dear old mumbojummery. But, Doctor, why not three times a day? Don't you realise, Doctor, in strict orthodoxy the tablespoonfuls should pass the oesophagus thrice daily?

(he pauses, becoming more blandly offensive than ever)

Sweet spirit of nitre! Wonderful! Won't hurt 'em, won't help 'em, makes 'em feel they're being treated, and they can swill it by the tubful, while Nature makes 'em well.

(Silence, except for the rain on tin roof. Denny laughs, a mocking appreciation of the blank expression on Andrew's face.)

DENNY (derisively)

Science apart, Doctor, you might satisfy my curiosity. Why have you come here?

ANDREW (retorts grimly)

My idea was to turn Blaenelly into a health resort – a sort of spa, you know.

DENNY (his laugh an insult)

Witty, witty, my dear Doctor. Unfortunately, I can't recommend the water here as being ideally suited for a spa. As to the medical gentlemen – in this valley they're the rag-tag and bobtail of a glorious, a truly noble profession.

91

ANDREW

Including yourself

DENNY (nods)

Precisely! (His tone though bitter becomes serious) Look here, Manson, I realise you're just passing through on your way to London, but in the meantime there are one or two things you ought to know. There's no hospital, no ambulance, no X-rays, no anything. If you want to operate you use the kitchen table. Page, your boss, was a good old Doctor – three years ago, but he'll never do a hand's turn again. Nicholls, my owner, is a tight little money-chasing midwife. As for myself – I'd better anticipate the gay tidings – I drink like a fish. Now, I think that's about all – (snaps fingers) Come on, Hawkins.

(Andrew, troubled, watches as Denny starts out.)

37   CLOSE UP OF THE DOG

(Asleep – Completely uninterested, Hawkins rises from a deep slumber and follows his master to the door.)

DENNY (at door – looks at label on bottle)

By the way, you know, some of these cases in Glydar Place aren't exactly typical. If I were you I'd look out for – typhoid. (tosses bottle to Andrew. He goes out.)

ANDREW (alone, thunderstruck, doubting, disbelieving, thinking. Suddenly realisation comes)

ANDREW (banging his forehead and half-articulating) Typhoid!

(He turns to the sink, eagerly opens the book and furiously searches through it)

FADE OUT

This was the first sequence to be shot. For the first time, all the temperaments and talents involved came together in the cramped confines of a set. Vidor decided to shoot it all in one long unbroken take. Nowadays not so surprising, when flexibility of filming and improvisation of dialogue is more often the rule than the exception. But rare in those days of tightly-scripted speech and rigidly controlled camera work and lighting. Rarely indeed did a European director demand of his actors such a sustained scene, or of his cameraman and crew the complex and laborious shifts of camera and focus required, as they manoeuvred in harmony with a complex of carefully rehearsed movements within an at all times exactly calculated frame. The Americans seemed to take this for granted. Jack Conway had started *A Yank at Oxford* in exactly the same way, by shooting first of all the long scene with 'Scattergood, your scout Sir', in just one such long uncut take. It now took us all day on *The Citadel* to rehearse and finally achieve coordinated balance between actors' speech, their movements within set as they delivered their lines, and the more than half dozen movements of camera, tracking and panning with them as they did so, in this first scene.

Seldom free of nervous tension, Donat was high-strung enough on this first day's shooting. Playing against him as Denny, (in a part for which Metro had originally and briefly considered Spencer Tracy) Ralph Richardson had considerable difficulty remembering his lines. We even had an animal to contend with as well. 'Hawkins' the dog, would as often as not fail to sit down on cue, and wander off set to sniff the legs of one or another of us crouched behind camera range. But by late afternoon the first, full unfluffed take was in the can, and by the end of the day Vidor had several more to his satisfaction. Large sighs of relief all round – turning to groans of anguish when we reassembled the following morning. Overnight the film had as usual been developed and printed The result on the screen was far from satisfactory. Although the scene itself played well, its pictorial appearance was bleak, harsh, and uneven. Had Harry

Stradling overdone his dose of Welsh realism? No, it was another case of what Jimmy Wong Howe had described as 'too much bromide, not enough sulphide'. Up the road, the laboratory had contrived to all but ruin that first day's work. There was nothing to be done but just simply do it all over again.

By now nerves were even further on edge, and it took even longer to get the first all round satisfactory take. Retake after retake, something went wrong. Richardson fluffed a line, Donat made a false move, one or other missed a mark. More and more film flowed through the camera, as I loaded one magazine after another. The scene running as it did over 300 feet uncut, as soon as we had shot over 650 feet of our standard 1000 feet rolls of 35 millimetre film, the camera had to be once again reloaded. At last, at last, a perfect take. Footage counter on camera, 975. Got it with 25 feet to spare. Open camera. No film in gate. Even second assistant cameramen can make appalling mistakes. Instead of a full 1000 feet, I had mistakenly loaded only 950. Richardson's last line, and Donat's reaction had been spoken to an empty camera.

'Please dear God', I prayed, 'make him do it again' as, 'Camera Reloading', one pretended all was routine. 'That's just fine', said Vidor. 'Now we've really got it, let's just try one more.' And they did. And it was even better. And he never even asked to have printed the take on which I ran out of film.

After this initial agony, all went well on the happiest and most relaxed feature film on which I ever worked. Soon we were all getting along so well together that Donat was the first to enjoy a rather elaborate joke at his own expense.

Few film actors have ever 'lived' his parts the way Donat did. So long as *The Citadel* was in production, Robert Donat was Andrew Manson. The clothes he had carefully chosen to wear as the young doctor he lived in and wore off the set as well. In his own words, 'I let things sink into me'. He had already spent long weekends wandering about the Rhondda Valley and the Welsh coalfields, on his own, in these clothes. Six months later, in his next film for Metro, I watched this then thirty-three year old man at the end of a long hard day's work as the seventy-eight year old

The Citadel. Donat delivers the baby

Mr Chips, in a tearing hurry to get home, rush down that long corridor at Denham Studios – but only as fast as, and at the pace of, the septuagenarian schoolmaster he would not be called upon to play until the following morning. Donat hated fresh faces, and visitors were barred from his sets. Even those of us technical crew he had to endure, positioned around camera and lights, he liked to be as inconspicuous as possible. To accommodate and assist him in this, large ten feet high folding black screens were made, and stood around the empty fourth wall of the set, concealing from him as much as possible of the remainder of the studio, with all its irrelevant paraphernalia of painters, carpenters, electricians, clapper boys and what have you – any of whom, catching his eye, was liable to throw him off balance and fluff his lines. (Just in the same way as Jimmy Wong Howe's huge piece of velvet around the camera and its attendants had similarly relaxed Mary Miles Minter.)

This idiosyncrasy amused Vidor no end. Our second week we came to the scene where Donat has to tell his bedridden and incapable employer of the outbreak of typhoid. A small, bedroom set. Built right up against the studio wall, door at back. Start of scene, Donat waiting for cue, all alone in the cramped space between back of set and studio wall. On cue, opens door, comes into set, up to man in bed, plays scene, takes leave, out back through door, closes it behind him, waits in confined and lonely isolation for director to call 'cut'.

Final good take. Vidor happy. 'Just one more please, Bob.' Donat obediently stations himself once again behind closed door at back of set, out of sight of any of us. Quickly the screens are put up in one unbroken line, from one side of the set to the other, completely enclosing and sealing it off from the outside world. All of us, including camera, now behind this blank and black wall. All in the joke, except Donat. All go through the motions of turning the camera. 'Eighty-seven Take Five', calls out sound. 'Whack', make I with the clappers. 'OK, Bob', calls Vidor. Peering through the chinks in the screens, we all watch Donat go through another faultless performance. 'Cut', calls out Vidor, 'That's just fine, Bob'. Only then does Donat look round at this voice of approval – not a soul in sight, just the long blank black wall of his own unbroken screens. From behind, Vidor is the first to join him in laughter all round.

More than most, *The Citadel* is a film of set-piece sequences. And none more striking than that when the young doctor brings life to a miner's stillborn child.

First, A.J. Cronin, and his book:

'It was a long harsh struggle. Then, as the first streaks of dawn strayed past the broken edges of the blind, the child was born, lifeless. As he gazed at the still form a shiver of horror passed over Andrew. After all that he had promised! His face, heated with his own exertions, chilled suddenly. He hesitated, torn between his desire to attempt to resuscitate the child, and his obligation towards the mother who was herself in a desperate state. The dilemma was so urgent he did not solve it consciously. Blindly, instinctively, he gave the child to the nurse and turned his attention to Susan Morgan who now lay collapsed, almost pulseless, and not yet out of the ether, upon her side. His haste was desperate, a frantic race against her ebbing strength. It took him only an instant to smash a glass ampoule and inject pituitrin. Then he flung down the hypodermic syringe and worked unsparingly to restore the flaccid woman. After a few minutes of feverish effort, her heart strengthened, he saw that he might safely leave her. He swung round, in his shirt sleeves, his hair sticking to his damp brow. 'Where's the child?'

And now, to script.

56 CLOSE UP OF ANDREW
(Slapping the baby, he waits for the breath of life but it doesn't come – he tries again, now more frantically. Still there is no cry.)

57 CLOSE UP NURSE (The tragedy shows on her face.)

58 CLOSE UP GRANDMOTHER
(When she sees that the baby doesn't breathe she covers her face with her old hands – in horror.)

59 MED. LONG SHOT
(Andrew now passes the still form of the baby to the nurse, who quickly covers it with a blanket, and brings it forward. [The CAMERA PULLING BACK as she does so.] She places the baby in an old chair or on a table. In the background Andrew gives his attention to the mother.)

60 MED. CLOSE UP
(Andrew feels the mother's pulse. It is weak. Still holding the woman's wrist, he reaches for his medicine kit. Searching frantically through the bag he finds the pituitrin. He smashes the glass ampoule and with the assistance of the nurse, who has slid into the scene, he administers an injection. He works even now with determination, with positive definite movements. No green medical student here. He flings down the hypodermic syringe and works unsparingly to restore the flaccid woman. After a few minutes of feverish effort, her heart strengthens. She opens her eyes.)

MRS MORGAN (murmurs)
Boy or girl?

ANDREW
A boy. Now you must go to sleep.
(A little smile passes over Mrs Morgan's features. She lets her eyes close. The old woman, who has come up beside Andrew, looks down at the sleeping smiling face.)

OLD WOMAN (grimly)
She wanted a boy.

(Andrew turns away from the bed, holds the old woman's glance a moment, and then turns to the nurse.)

ANDREW
Where's the child?

(The nurse makes a frightened gesture.)

61 CLOSE SHOT ANDREW (He crosses to the child. As he picks it up –)

ANDREW (to nurse)
Get me hot water and cold water! And basins! Quick! Quick!

NURSE (she falters, her eyes on the pallid body of the child)
But, Doctor …

ANDREW (shouting)
Quick!

(The nurse goes. The old woman follows. Snatching a blanket, Andrew lays the child upon it and begins artificial respiration. The two women return with basins, ewer, and a big iron kettle. Frantically, he splashes cold water into one basin; hot water into the other. Then, like some crazy juggler, he hurries the child between the two, now plunging it into the icy, now the steaming bath.)

62 CLOSE SHOT OLD WOMAN AND NURSE
(The old woman still gazes heartbrokenly and accusingly at Andrew.)
(The nurse reacts nervously.)

OLD WOMAN
The child's dead – it's God's will. Let it alone!

63 CLOSE SHOT ANDREW

(Still working on the baby. He pays no attention to the woman. Sweat runs into his eyes, blinding him. One of his sleeves hangs down, dripping. His breath comes pantingly. The floor is a draggled mess. Stumbling over a sopping towel, Andrew almost drops the child, which is now wet and slippery in his hands, like a strange white fish, as he puts it on the blanket again. He rubs the child with a rough towel, crushes and releases the little chest with both hands, trying to get breath into that limp body. And then, as by a miracle, the pigmy chest gives a short convulsive heave. Another ... and another ... A smile, almost hysterical, comes over his face. He redoubles his efforts. The child is gasping now, deeper and deeper.)

OLD WOMAN (sobbing hysterically)
It's come alive – merciful heaven, it's come alive!

(She begins to weep motionless, tears fall down her cheeks as one might who has seen a miracle performed. Andrew hands over the child. He has given life to a morsel of flesh. Elation, pride, ecstasy play over his face. He slowly straightens and turns towards the women.)

As shot, and finally edited, on screen this sequence was broken down into thirty-five cuts.

LONG SHOT (The Group around the bed. Manson straightens up with the baby.)

CLOSE UP   Grandmother.

CLOSE UP   Manson. (He slaps the baby. Twice, No sign of life.)

CLOSE UP   Nurse.

CLOSE UP   Manson. (Slaps baby a third time.)

CLOSE UP   Grandmother

CLOSE UP   Manson. Puts stillborn child down (below frame)

LONG SHOT   The Group. Manson is centre, hunched over stillborn child, which he hands to the Nurse (in silhouette).

CLOSE UP   Grandmother. (Puts shawl over her head in the presence of death.)

MEDIUM LONG SHOT Group. (The Nurse goes out with stillborn child, Grandmother moves over to the head of the bed. Manson turns to the mother lying on it.)

MEDIUM CLOSE SHOT (Manson takes Mother's pulse)

CLOSE UP (Manson taking pulse.)

MEDIUM CLOSE SHOT (Group round Mother on bed)
Mother: 'Boy – is it a boy?'
Manson: 'Yes, a boy. Just go to sleep'. (He bathes the Mother's forehead, and straightens up.)

LONG SHOT   The group. (Manson moves to foreground and sits dejectedly)
 Grandmother (moves over to him): 'She wanted a boy'.
(Manson turns, stands up. To nurse): 'Where is the child?' (The Nurse points to the floor. Camera PANS as Manson picks it up, by fireplace) 'Get me basins quick – get me two basins – quick.' (He unwraps the stillborn child)

CLOSE UP   (He starts artificial respiration)

MEDIUM SHOT Nurse (enters frame with basin, placed down in foreground)
Manson: 'Hot water and cold water – quick'.

CLOSE UP   Manson, rubbing the baby's chest.

CLOSE UP   Grandmother (Sound of other basin put down)

101

CLOSE UP   Manson. Holding child (below frame – sound of splashing water)

CLOSE UP   Nurse

VERY BIG CLOSE UP   Manson. Camera panning and holding him left to right as he moves the child from one basin to the other (below frameline)

MEDIUM CLOSE UP   Grandmother: 'The child is dead – it is God's will'.

VERY BIG CLOSE UP Manson.
Voice of Grandmother. 'Leave it alone.'

CLOSE UP Nurse.

CLOSE UP Manson, water splashing all over his face, then rubbing the child's chest (below frame)

MEDIUM CLOSE SHOT Grandmother.

CLOSE UP   Manson, breathing on to the child's lips.

MEDIUM CLOSE UP Grandmother.

CLOSE UP   Manson, breathing on to child. IT CRIES OUT. Its little hand, just visible, jerks.

MEDIUM CLOSE UP Manson. The child's crying heard over.

MEDIUM CLOSE SHOT Grandmother. She lifts her hands in supplication.

MEDIUM SHOT   Manson hands the now living baby to the Nurse. Seen for the first time, the two basins on the floor in foreground. He slowly stands up.

It is Admiral Bligh who, in Metro-Goldwyn-Mayer's *Mutiny on the Bounty*, maintains that a midshipman is the lowest form of animal life in the British Navy. A clapper boy, it has been said, is the lowest form of animal life in a movie studio. Be that as it may, I soon found myself very much an accepted element in MGM's British operation.

I greatly preferred the company and attitudes of the Americans to those of my own compatriots in the studios. All that mattered to them, all they cared about, was motion pictures. This went, and has continued ever since to go for me as well. Punctually at nine-thirty every morning, on to the set would walk Ben Goetz, in executive charge of production. 'Hi, Bob', he would call out to his star. 'Hi, King', to his director. And then without fail as part of this ritual, 'Hi, Peter', to my relatively insignificant self.

At the end of every day, the 'rush' prints of the previous day's filming would be screened for director and editor, cameraman and crew. The latter would then go off home. Not so the director. King Vidor would sit on, and as often as not there would then be run for him the latest picture over from the home studios. In this way Robert Taylor appeared once again, starring now in Metro's just completed version of Erich Maria Remarque' *Three Comrades* – with a credit this time for co-scriptwriter Scott Fitzgerald.

I stayed on. No one objected. And, more than this, an ever greater privilege and experience, I sat in on the editing of *The Citadel*. A chronological story in the first place, taking its hero step by step, place to place, from his first job in Wales to final self-discovery and enlightenment in London, Vidor shot the film in sequence. As a result, by the end of each week, Charles Frend, the editor, was able to put up for him on the screen a cut reel of film after an evening's rushes. Together they would analyse and discuss it. Vidor would suggest changes. Frend would bring it

Building Denham - 1935

Destroying Denham - 1980

104

back again a night or two later. I sat still, alone in my seat in the corner. No one objected. I watched. I listened. As a result, I discovered that what the textbooks said was true. By day, on the studio floor, the film was certainly shot. Now, in this editing process at night, it was made.

The climax of the story comes when a society doctor, with whom and his ilk Manson has come to make common cause, carries out a very simple and straightforward operation in which Manson assists. As a result of incompetence, this seemingly superior surgeon makes a botch of it. The patient dies on the table. Shattered, Manson walks out on the fashionable profits-conscious and phoney medical world as Cronin saw Harley Street. Face to face with his loss of integrity – and consequent share of responsibility in his friend's death – he decides to start all over again, as one of a small collective group, practising medicine not for profit but for humanity.

To tighten up the script at this point, and give the film added impact, Vidor had decided that it should be good old drunken Denny who dies in this way. Piling on the agony, Cronin also kills off Manson's wife Christine, very soon after. But who could have done such a thing to Rosalind Russell, brought over from Hollywood to play the part of the schoolteacher wife Manson marries in Wales? (Originally Elizabeth Allan had been lined up for this part, but box office consideration demanded an American name to co-star with Donat.)

In the book, Manson's reaction to the climactic trauma of bungled surgery is described as follows:

'How long Andrew remained in the office, his forehead pressed against the cold marble of the mantelpiece, he did not know, but at last he rose, realising that he had work which he must do. The dreadful shock of the calamity had caught him with the destructive violence of an explosive shell. It was as though he, also, were eviscerate and empty. Yet he still moved automatically, advancing as might a horribly wounded soldier, compelled by machine-like habit to perform the duties expected of him'.

105

Cronin himself had said that if the most was to be made of this sequence on the screen, it would have to be handled with 'something like the subtle, psychological penetration achieved by Sternberg and Jannings in the opening scenes of *The Blue Angel*'. The script was not very helpful. The operation is over. Denny is dead. Leaving Christine, his wife, behind, Manson walks blindly out of the Harley Street Nursing Home.

SCRIPT

222 CHRISTINE

(She gazes after Andrew, compassion and understanding in her face, then suddenly follows him.)

223 EXT. STREET

(Andrew walks blindly along the sidewalk, bumping into people, narrowly missing others. Some thirty feet behind, Christine, steadily watching him, follows. He leaves the curb and heads out into traffic. The policeman waves his arm. Buses and cars stop for Andrew, others swing to avoid him, as the policeman urges him toward safety.)

224 CHRISTINE AT CURB

(As she starts across the street after Andrew, the policeman waves the traffic on. Christine returns to the curb and stands there, not far from tears, her eyes seeking Andrew through the maze of cars and traffic.)

225 – 229 SHOTS OF ANDREW WANDERING
THROUGH STREETS OF LONDON

(These shots to be composed with Mr Vidor and Mr Meerson, finally ending with a shot on the Embankment, where Andrew throws a stone into the water as he leans over the balustrade.)

It was these Numbers 225-229 which could make or break the film of *The Citadel* – the 'Shots of Andrew wandering through streets of London'. Here was a sequence that could be constructed only in terms of cinema, and one which would have to encapsulate both the entire theme of its story as well as the psychological dilemma of its 'ordinary man' protagonist.

Two years previously the London Film Society had shown to its members an Austrian film on the subject of lost identity, *Die Ewige Maske*, directed by Werner Hochbaum, a young German whose chequered and now forgotten career offers interesting pointers for our times. The maker of highly acclaimed anti-Nazi working class films in the days of the Weimar Republic – and at that time busily engaged at Berlin's UFA Studios – this was one of his equivocal in-between films made in Vienna. (He was soon to fall foul of the Nazis once again, and then in turn with the Anglo-American occupying powers of his country after the war.)

Die Ewige Maske is the story of a young doctor who loses a patient during an epidemic, and who becomes obsessed with the idea that the man's death was due to a new serum injected by him against his superior's orders. The doctor loses his reason and attempts suicide. The highlight of the film was an expressionistic attempt to depict and delineate the young doctor's state of mind when he is, for a while, insane. This reel was brought down to Denham and run for Vidor at one of the evening screening sessions. I thought it was marvellous. In very much a Caligari-like style, the hero wandered in a strange subterranean-like labyrinth, to the accompaniment of weird music, and impressionistic monsters and shapes of his own fantasy. But although this might have been all right for the Film Society, it would not quite do for MGM. As finally worked out by that romantic King Vidor, here is a shot-list for *The Citadel* climactic sequence:

SCRIPT

MEDIUM LONG SHOT PAN   Manson among crowd, Harley Street.

LONG SHOT   PAN   Christine following.

LONG SHOT   PAN   Manson as he crosses main street.

LONG SHOT   Cut back to Christine starting to run after him.

LONG SHOT   Manson reaches the other side of the busy street.

LONG SHOT   Christine reaches the crossing. Traffic fills the street. She cannot see him. She has lost him.)

LONG SHOT   Her eyeline – crowds hurrying along. No sign of Andrew.)

FADE OUT   FADE IN

MEDIUM CLOSE UP   Tracking ahead of Manson as he walks along city street at night.

DISSOLVE

MEDIUM CLOSE UP   Profile tracking shot of Manson walking. He looks at…

MEDIUM LONG SHOT   … old man and barefoot child helping themselves to scraps of food in garbage bin.

MEDIUM CLOSE SHOT   Manson looking at this scene as he walks on.

DISSOLVE

MEDIUM CLOSE SHOT   Manson, from other side as he walks. He looks up at…

LONG SHOT   … with clanging bell, an ambulance drives through the night traffic.

MEDIUM CLOSE SHOT   Back to Manson once again, still walking.

BIG CLOSE UP   Manson walking, walking, his expression still both lost and agonised.

MEDIUM SHOT   Camera tracking past a blind beggar

CLOSE UP   Manson reacting to this sight.

MEDIUM CLOSE SHOT   Manson still walking, and wrenching open his shirt collar.

MEDIUM SHOT   Moving past a Pub, outside a baby in a pram, with it a little girl but barely eight years old, opening the door and peering in.

MEDIUM CLOSE SHOT   Manson, looking back at this.

MEDIUM LONG SHOT   Small boy on kerb, runs out right in front of a bus, and is almost knocked down.

CLOSE UP   Manson reacting to this as he still walks on.

DISSOLVE

MEDIUM LONG SHOT   Manson walks into shot of the Thames Embankment. Back to camera, he leans on the parapet.

MEDIUM SHOT   Reverse, on to Manson leaning over the parapet above the river. In his hand he has coins, which he flips as if unconsciously into the water.

CLOSE UP   Coins falling into the water.

MEDIUM SHOT   Manson leaning over parapet above river.

And now the most radical departure from the book, and the script. Worked out by Vidor and his wife Elizabeth Hill, who was with him on set throughout production, we now hear the voice of the dead Denny, the same who walked into that tumble-down Welsh surgery at the beginning of the film and, in his embittered way, welcomed him to their profession at the start of the story.

DENNY   (voiceover)   Doctor Manson – Doctor Manson. This isn't your individual sorrow. You can't take this responsibility alone. You're not one man fighting a battle alone, you're one of a great profession, a profession continually fighting for the benefit of health, for life, for humanity.

CLOSE UP   (Manson, with voiceover of the dead Denny continuing)

DENNY

You can't stop now, you understand that, don't you? You'll see many deaths, many heartbreaks, many tears, before you're finished. But you must carry on. You must keep on, hoping and trying. That's a doctor's job. That's your job, Doctor Manson.

MEDIUM SHOT   (Manson still leaning on parapet.)

MEDIUM LONG SHOT   (Reverse. He turns, straightens up, and camera tracks very fast into Close Up.)

110

Soon, all too soon for me, it was over. Ten weeks after that first false start in Lazare Meerson's set of a Blaenelly surgery, with a concealed camera we shot Robert Donat and Rosalind Russell losing sight of each other in the real Harley Street. Keeping up with the flow of sequential film and nightly editing sessions, Charles Frend had a cut picture only ten days later – and out it went to a sneak preview, unannounced, on an unsuspecting audience. For this was Metro's way, long pioneered and practised by Thalberg, of whom it was said that he did not so much make pictures as remake pictures. In this case, there was no need. It was simply judged necessary to shoot a few more close-ups of Donat, to cut into strategic points of the story. *The Citadel* was a complete motion picture.

Premiered that Christmas week of 1938, C.A. Lejeune, film critic of the London *Observer* was moved to write that it was 'a rare film that could rouse so many people to such a fine rage'. In the United States, the National Board of Review voted *The Citadel* just simply:

THE FILM OF THE YEAR

In that same year of 1938 there was an average of more than three new feature films released from British Studios every week. But for the film industry in Britain this was, alas, no more than the backlog of its most spectacular but short-lived boom. For Hollywood, it was still the Golden Age, its huge studio-complexes dream factories for the world, crowding into two to three thousand seater cinemas for a twice weekly rendezvous with the illusion and magic of the movies.

Now an era already of legends and myth, a vast storehouse of cheap entertainment, often impeccably made by great craftsmen, surviving today as the cheap raw material and mileage of television's miniaturised movie slots. But it was not always a cinema of evasion, a screen of escape. Such men as Vidor, such films as *The Citadel*, attempted to use it as a screen of change. Sometimes they succeeded, but the nature of a profits-orientated mass entertainment bankers' industry more often than not stopped in their tracks a *Musa Dagh* and an *It Can't Happen Here*. The tight all-inclusive mini-worlds of the Metro-Goldwyn-Mayer's were all the provinces of politics. Studio politics, Wall Street politics, international politics.

No one even dreamed of suggesting that the solution of the social ills exposed in *The Citadel* might be a National Health Service – socialised medicine. For that would be politics.

And so what about politics – on the screen?

3. FILM AND POLITICS

'All realism is a readjustment'

Andre Malraux

Louis de Rochemont overlooking Elia
Kazan's direction of *Boomerang*

113

Back in 1936 someone had in fact succeeded in putting *It Can't Happen Here* on the screen – or at least a snippet. In this filming the setting is a typical American middle-class home of the period. A knocking on the front door. The householder goes to aswer. Enter a couple of uniformed bully boys.

'What's the trouble?' asks Mr America.

'We're having a book burning on the green tomorrow night.'

'A what?'

'We're going to burn up all this subversive literature. A lot of smutty stuff that's corrupting public morals – have you any objections?'

'Well, you won't find any subversive books here.'

(Over by the bookcase) 'Huh – now how about this one. Now this fellow Charles Dickens – wasn't he a Communist?'

This filming has been established as taking place on stage, in a theatre, while voice over informed us that 'In twenty-one cities simultaneously, WPA actors appear in a dramatisation of *It Can't Happen Here*, novelist Sinclair Lewis's enactment of a Nazified US at the mercy of sedition-hunting fascist storm troopers'. WPA stood for the Works Progress Administration by way of which, in those Depression-dogged days, Roosevelt's New Deal attempted to create jobs for the millions of American unemployed, in this case actors, playwrights and directors like Joseph Losey.

Titled 'An Uncle Sam Production', this extract from *It Can't Happen Here* was just one item in a radically new but by then already established film series which, claiming to be 'A New Form of Pictorial Journalism', had already lit up American cinema screens with such as the controversy surrounding the newly created public power system of the Tennessee Valley Authority; the dictatorial ambitions of the then Governor of Louisiana, Huey Long; and the fascist-style broadcast preachings of the Irish-American prelate Father Charles E. Coughlin. From overseas had come what we would now call in-depth (and sympathetic) looks at Soviet Russia; Ethiopia facing up unaided to Italian fascist threats; China embroiled in Japanese aggression. Nothing like this had ever been seen before on American commercial cinema screens, prompting David Selznick to declare that it 'will prove to have been the most significant motion picture development since the inception of sound', and the Academy of Motion Picture Arts and Sciences to award its producers that same year of 1936 a special 'Oscar' for its significance to motion pictures and for having 'revolutionised one of the most important branches of the industry – the newsreel'. By the time of its Academy Award, this short black-and-white two-reeler, running barely eighteen minutes, was a regular feature, every four weeks, in 5000 cinemas in the United States and more than 700 in Britain, with an estimated audience of 15,000,000. It was called the *March of Time.*

With its invention, the motion picture camera had entered immediately into journalism. The newsreel is as old as the cinema itself. The first films ever made were direct recordings of happenings. A catalogue of 1895-1900 lists *New York in a Blizzard*, *Easter Parade*, *The Henley Regatta*, and *Czar Nicholas in his Summer Palace.* Movie screens in 1910 reflected *The Funeral of King Edward VII*, as well as the fisticuffs of the *Jeffries – Johnson Match.* For the next quarter of a century, while such as Griffith, Eisenstein, Gance, Mizoguchi were maturing the motion picture into a great new mass art, the newsreel, although a popular and indispensable part of the programme, hardly changed at all. Even with the coming of sound, it still remained a superficial catalogue of fires, floods, and earthquakes, the ingoing and outgoing of politicians, the ups and downs of new flying machines, the parades of fleeting fashions, the drilling of armies, launching of ships, and the comings and goings of royalty.

For one newsreel cameraman, this was not enough. To have scooped the world (and bluffed a British censor) with film of rioting following an arrest of Gandhi was not sufficient. To have then become, in time, director of short subjects for Fox Movietone News was inadequate fulfilment. Louis de Rochemont aimed to revolutionise the newsreel. What he wanted to get on to motion picture screens was a great deal more than just a mere assemblage of snapshots of sporting events and catastrophes. Just as newspapers dig into the detail and background behind their headlines, so he wanted to project, in the same way on film,

115

the story behind the news. Like all revolutionaries, he had to find support from somewhere outside the establishment. The men who controlled the newsreels were neither journalists nor film-makers. Their interest lay in the profit to be made from feature films. The newsreels were merely put together as part of a package, as a sideline to the block booking of the endlessly profitable assembly line of Hollywood product. De Rochemont's idea would cost money, and who was going to provide this, when newsreels could never be a source of profit in themselves?

Broadcasting. Yes, in that pre-television era of the early 1930's, the answer lay in the technique, and the sponsorship, of a radio show. Two bright young men of the Yale Class of 1920 had already accomplished in the printed word what de Rochemont now aimed to achieve for the motion picture. With their brash new news magazine *Time* (and *Life* its pictorial counterpart to come) Briton Hadden and Henry Luce had revolution-ised the reporting, and the interpretation of news. *Time Incorporated*, as their corporate progeny soon came to be called, looked for new fields to conquer. For a generation raised on TV with radio miniaturised into a source of transistorised pop, the broad-casting scene of the mid-1930's is remote indeed. But it was lively, and already (before the phrase became current) mass media. It had its stars. Bing Crosby, and the husband and wife cross- talk team of Burns and Allen. Hollywood took note. The *Big Broadcast of 1936* featured all three, plus many other favourites previously known only by the sound of their voices, or their music. In the United States radio was, from the beginning, commercial. And this meant money.

Time Inc. decided to get into radio. Not to broadcast weekly readings from its news magazines, but to dramatise actual happenings, and those that made them happen, in the news. They called their programme the *March of Time*.

Again remember that this is not only pretelevision, but also quite a long time before the tape recorder and video camcorders of today, which make possible the interviewing of those in the news with such effortless facility (if not always matchless integrity.) What recording systems did exist back then in the early

116

thirties were far too cumbersome and rigid to move around in a pack slung from a shoulder. What went out on the air had to originate in a studio. It had to be reenacted. Actors read dialogue parts from tightly-written scripts based on *Time* and *Life*'s own voluminous files of intensively researched investigative journalism.

The *March of Time* radio programme was also a welcome source of additional employment for New York actors. Parts were played by members of Orson Welles's Mercury Theatre. (The master himself was to base his own *War of the Worlds* invasion from Mars – which took him to Hollywood and into the movies – on its technique of convincing and literal immediacy.) It was his job to impersonate the voices of Abyssinian Emperor Haile Selassie, German President Hindenburg, armaments king Basil Zaharoff, and Japan's Imperial Ruler Hirohito. Agnes Moorehead, the mother-to-be of the *Citizen Kane* yet to be made, was the voice of the President's Lady, Eleanor Roosevelt. The vibrant and sonorous Voice of Time itself, linking the reenacted sections with narrative, was provided by the amiable but omnipotent sounding Westbrook Van Voorhis.

The mind of Luce and, in particular, his circulation manager Roy Larsen, had not overlooked the movies. After all, if they could put something up on cinema screens which regularly proclaimed that 'The Editors of *Time and Life* present a new form of Pictorial Journalism' this would help to sell the magazines too – and justify an investment. And this is what they did. For Louis de Rochemont called on Larsen with his idea to transcribe and transform the *March of Time* method of radio investigation and re-enactment into film. Larsen had already been thinking along much the same lines, and Luce agreed to the making of some experimental reels. That was good enough. De Rochemont quit Movietone, retaining only a call on its film library. For he proposed that current freshly-shot footage be worked in with archive material, and that reenacted dialogue scenes be incorporated whenever necessary in order to give each film report of hard-hitting news analysis a unique and persuasive perspective of integrated, *personalised*, and dramatic impact.

117

The first issue of the *March of Time* in the movies had opened at the Capitol Theatre on Broadway February 1, 1935. For the next seventeen years it was to be as much a part of the cinema scene as Mickey Mouse.

It has become fashionable to poke fun at the *March of Time*, at its portentous voice of doom – 'TIME MARCHES ON!' But a non-stop narration rattled out by an authoritative and anonymous voice was the convention of the time; and, in any case, from its earliest issues the *March of Time* used sound-on-film newsreel cameras for direct statements, snatches of dialogue, and interviews with those involved in its reports. Commonplace now in television, such snippets of conversational realism – and quite often reconstruction – were used to break up, intercut, and highlight its otherwise Time Magazine-style commentary (which had its origins in radio) so easily parodied. Parodied most memorably at the beginning of *Citizen Kane* when, immediately after the death in his castle-like fortress, in little more than nine minutes, the life and times of Charles Foster Kane flash on the screen in 'News On The March'.

In her New Yorker essay on *Kane*, Pauline Kael tells of how 'The *March of Time* was already a joke to many people' when she was a student at Berkeley in the late thirties. So let us list some of the subjects covered during the year we were making *The Citadel*, the year of 1937-38. 'Child Labour', 'Scotland's Highland Problems', 'Poland and War', 'US Dust Bowl', 'War in China', 'Ships, Strikes, and Seamen', 'Ulster v. Eire'.

Yes, at least one of these is still with us, well over sixty years later, and still not very funny.

According to Miss Kael, 'there was always laughter in the theatres when the *March of Time* came on'. One can only conclude that she and her fellow students were a great deal more sophisticated and less socially committed than that far from frivolous Scottish 'Father of the Documentary Film', John Grierson, who had his own young directors out enthusiastically shooting subjects for the *March of Time* at just that same time. Harry Watt, for example. In 1936, for the series' Second Year Issue Number 4, he did a report on the Tithe War. This now forgotten

1. Dateline title - Hindus sitting (10')

2. ls Government building (6')   From a capital city of Asia in January 1949 came a warning

3. closer shot same (6')   of deep significance to a world dominated for centuries by the

4. mls congress in session (6')   powerful nations of the West. It was the voice of Jawaharlal Nehru,

5. ms Nehru and Patel (6')   Prime Minister of the new state of India, speaking out to and

6. sign "Broadcasting House" (4')   for the three hundred and twenty million newly,

7. ms technician at board (6')   liberated Indians, and for all Asia as well.

8. ms male commentator - super- (11')   REGULAR SOUND TRACK #1 - INDIAN VOICES
imposed title - "The role Asia
has been playing has not been pro-
portionate to her size, population
or real importance "

9. cu woman commentator - super- (10')   "
imposed title - "The Western
World has been thinking of Asia
as a fringe of Europe."

10. ms male commentator - super- (10')   "
imposed title - "A resurgent New
Asia no longer intends to take
a secondary role in world affairs."

11. map - Asia (13')   VOT: Underlining the dramatic sign-
LAP DISSOLVE   ificance of India's new leadership were developments in China, where the once largest republic in Asia was breaking up.

12. ls Chinese troops retreating (5')   With the disintegration of the
thru hills   Nationalist army which

13. mcu poorly clad Chinese soldiers' (8')   had long fought against Communism, China
feet   could no longer be counted among the democratic nations.

14. mls Chiang Kai-Shek getting out of(4')
car at airport

15. mcu Chiang getting into plane (7')   Generalissimo Chiang Kai-Shek relin-
quished his leadership after twenty-two years as China's dominant

16. cu Chinese refugees (8')   political figure.
The way was left clear for Communism to swallow up the

17. ls Chinese refugees past ruins (6')   largest nation in Asia.

March of Time script/commentary - *Asia's New Voice*

confrontation was between English farmers and the Church of England. From time immemorial the farmers had had to pay a tithe, a tenth, of their crops to the land-owning church. Pure feudalism, well into the twentieth century. The farmers of that day refused. The church forced sales of their goods. For the *March of Time* the future director of *Target for Tonight* and *Where No Vultures Fly* reconstructed a raid on a farm by church militants, the sounding of the alarm, and the rush of farmers back from the fields to defend themselves. In Harry Watt's own words, 'I suppose it was the first time dramatic reconstruction of a contemporary event had been done in British documentary...'.

A more substantial charge against the *March of Time* nowadays is that it was 'right-wing', if not indeed itself fascist. Readers of W.A. Swanberg's life of *Time Incorporated*'s owner and tycoon Henry Luce are certainly given this impression; and in his 1979 investigation into the American communications industry, David Halberstam writes of Luce that 'in a sense he was by 1940 already the (Chinese) ambassador to America. It was not just his magazines, but his *March of Time* newsreels, showing the brave Chinese standing up to the barbarism of the Japanese, which became perhaps the most successful and influential propaganda of its time in making Americans care and think about China and identify with Chiang Kai-shek'.

Well, including 'Formosa – Island of Promise', a look at Chiang's final eclipse on Taiwan, (the series last release in 1951) out of 290 *March of Time* reports during the sixteen years of its existence, only six were devoted to Chiang Kai-shek and Nationalist China.

'The creative treatment of actuality' is Grierson's definition of documentary, and another charge levelled at the *March of Time* finds it guilty of the currently heinous crime of 'faction'; frequently setting up scenes, staging events, *without informing its audience of this device*. What says the record? In the original announcement of the launch of the series, 12 February 1935, the world at large was informed that 'from hundreds of stories and thousands of feet of film from all over the world, the best of these are taken and woven together in radio *March of Time*'s curt, concise manner, *reenacting* complete, *dramatic episodes* of the world happenings you've read and wondered about'.

Why do I go on about it like this? Does it really nowadays matter? Well, it does to me – for I worked for the *March of Time* as Cameraman/Reporter of its international subjects for six seminal post-Second World War years. A period which bent the series into the visual rhetoric of the United States' Cold War with the Soviet Union, rendering a young left-leaning Brit like me increasingly ill at ease at its change of direction. What was it then that led me to take up its offer of employment in the first place?

Well, for a start, the innovative and far from ignoble record that I have just described; and, having spent most the war years as an army cameraman which gave me the opportunity to set up and shoot, on my own, semi-documentary film reports on such as a Yugoslav guerrilla outpost in the Adriatic and the establishment of a free press in a liberated Rome – I had no desire then meekly to return to pulling focus on cameras in make-believe film studios. Moreover this wartime experience had led directly to my appointment as Cameraman/Reporter for the United Nations Agency brought into being to help Europe to get back on to its peacetime feet; and this, pre-Cold War, included the Soviet Union's two westerly republics of Byelorussia and the Ukraine. Whatever I shot there, at that time, was going to be unique, if not sensational, and it was. So much so, that the *March of Time* picked it up as a special release – and me along with it. For what as a consequence my filming was able to show, on American screens, were people who had suffered appallingly in the recent war, appearing at that time in no way either able or anxious to start another one. With the title the *March of Time* gave to its edition of my work, I could find no fault: *The Russians Nobody Knows.*

Everything up to then seemed to have led me to this point. Reflected in their films, it had been American attitudes and ways of doing things that had been so much of rny own obsessive film-going childhood; and major American films, and film-

Ruins of the Byelorussian city of Minsk - *The Russians Nobody Knows*

The Russians Nobody Knows - Young Russian's best foot forward

122

Author films in the
ruins of Minsk

makers, with whom I had felt so at home as an otherwise insignificant clapper boy at Denham. To this day I cannot believe that any British organisation would have put someone on that sort of payroll sight unseen – and unheard – judged and not found wanting solely on the strength of their work, my Russian material, viewed on a screen in New York. Back of it all was a disenchantment with Britain – a belief that its time had passed.

At the end of John le Carré's *Tinker, Tailor, Soldier, Spy* the traitor, Haydon, attempts to justify himself to Smiley:

'At Oxford, he said, he was genuinely of the right, and in the war, it scarcely mattered where one stood as long as one was fighting the Germans. For a while, after forty-five, he said, he had remained content with Britain's part in the world, till gradually it dawned on him just how trivial this was. How and when

123

was a mystery. In the historical mayhem of his own lifetime he could point to no one occasion: simply he knew that if England were out of the game, the price of fish would not be altered by a farthing. He had often wondered which side he would be on if the test ever came; after prolonged reflection he had finally to admit that if either monolith had to win the day, he would prefer it to be the East'.

For me, the reasoning was the same – but to me, for all these primarily filmic reasons, it was to be the West. Had not Henry Luce himself, in a special article in his *Life* magazine, not long before declared that 'We are the inheritors of the great principles of Western civilisation – above all Justice, the love of Truth, the ideal of Charity. It is in this spirit that all of us are called to create the first American Century'. There seemed little reason to doubt this, in 1947.

Fifty years after its original launch, Mr Luce's very own *March of Time* burst into life all over again. Under the creative guidance of *Flashback* Producer Vicki Wegg-Prosser, between 1985 and 1990 Channel 4 Television mounted no less than sixty retrospective screenings of this pioneering current affairs pacesetter. Veteran participants in its original production were interviewed. Lothar Wolff, Associate Producer; Edgar Anstey, Director; Mary (sister of Joseph) Losey, Writer-Researcher; Maurice Lancaster, European Manager; Peter Hopkinson, Director-Cameraman. All of us speaking of our own contributions and confident that what a new generation would now be seeing on their TV screens would confound Jay Leyda's 1964 ('Films Beget Films') strictures on the 'invariably conservative point of view (and) reactionary slant' of the original *March of Time*. With maybe less of an axe to grind, *Flashback*'s Presenters Fred Halliday, Jacqueline Fear and Murray Sayle got the perspective of the years between just about right.

Viewers were now to see reports by the *March of Time* in which its editors' sympathies were clearly with the unemployed seen seizing the New Jersey State Assembly House and protesting the ending of their dole payments in the United States elections of 1936; with John L. Lewis's organisation of the American coalminers and their British counterparts calling in 1937 for the nationalisation of the pits; with whites from the north beaten up by southern racists in Arkansas attempting to smash a union formed by sharecroppers demanding a dollar and a half for a ten-hour day; with Fiorello La Guardia's success in breaking up corruption as Mayor of New York city in 1938.

International subjects screened in *Flashback*'s Channel Four retrospective evidenced the *March of Time*'s support of Czechoslovakia's defiance of Hitler; its concern for the refugees already pouring out of central Europe and Spain in an issue directed by Edgar Anstey in 1939; its hostility to Mussolini's plan for a Mediterranean empire; and, above all, with *Inside Nazi Germany*, its stand against Hitler when no other film, on any screen in either Britain or the United States, had yet to attack – let alone criticise – his genocidal ambitions.

Unlike the bland and anodyne newsreels, as a creative short film series in its own right, before release in those days every issue of the *March of Time* had to be viewed first of all by the British Board of Film Censors. Of *Inside Nazi Germany* its Vice-President, a certain Colonel J.C. Hanna, had this to say: 'In my opinion the public exhibition of this picture in England would give grave offence to a nation with whom we are on terms of friendship and which it would be impolite to offend'.

A previous 1938 issue, *Arms And The League*, had indicated the betrayal of the League of Nations and the principle of collective security, highlighting the recent resignation of Anthony Eden in the face of the Chamberlain government's appeasement of German, Italian, and Japanese aggression. The voice over laid it on the line:

'In England', reported this *March of Time*, 'crowds are dismayed as Chamberlain, in order to be free to bargain with the Fascist nations who smashed the League's powers, drops his Foreign Secretary Anthony Eden, champion of the League'.

The British Board of Film Censors banned this issue outright. Director Edgar Anstey now told Channel Four viewers how he had thereupon arranged a private screening for Winston Churchill.

'Mr Anstey', Churchill had said, 'I can tell you that this film should be seen by every man, woman, and child in this country. But I am powerless to help you. As you know, I am out of office, and I have no standing or status in this country at the moment'.

Right from the beginning, and enthusiastically supported by no less than John Grierson himself, the *March of Time* made a point of its policy to include British reports in its regular scheme of things. To the American film industry Britain was always the most lucrative and therefore the most important overseas market. British attempts to gatecrash Hollywood could not therefore be ignored. In *Challenge to Hollywood*, J. Arthur Rank was shown in conference with Hollywood tycoons, and stating that all he asked for was a fair share of the American market for English-speaking British-made films. In this same 1945 release, American audiences were also shown excerpts from British films in production at that time, including *A Matter of Life and Death*, and Gabriel Pascal incoherently directing *Caesar and Cleopatra*. By then the British documentary movement which Grierson had launched with *Drifters* in 1929 had gained international recognition – not least as a result of classic wartime productions like *Listen to Britain* and *Target for Tonight*. Directing this *Challenge to Hollywood*, the American George Black included a sequence of the then Ministry of Information's Film Chief, Jack Beddington, in conference with his documentary dominies. Glimpsed amongst them could be seen *The Citadel* scriptwriter Ian Dalrymple and my future companion at Poona, Basil Wright, very uncharacteristically puffing away at a pipe. And this 1945 *Challenge to Hollywood* had not been the first time that attention had been paid to the British film industry by Time-Incorporated's 'new kind of pictorial journalism'. In only its second year of 1936 the de Rochemont-Larsen series had screened for British audiences shots of Denham Studios under construction, Alexander Korda studying scripts, and clips of the airborne technocrats about to descend on Everytown from his production of *Things to Come*.

'Voice to the future of British cinema', the portentous tones of Westbook Van Voorhis had informed us, 'is given by a British author of world renown, who has given up writing books entirely in favour of the cinema, Mr H.G. Wells, just back from inspecting America's Hollywood as the guest of Charlie Chaplin'. On screen we saw Korda standing sphinx-like behind his desk while, in foreground with his squeaky little high-pitched voice, the author of *Things to Come* pitched in:

'At the present time there are great interests which oppress man's minds, excite and interest. There's the onset of war. There's the increase of power, the change of scale and the change of conditions in the world. And, in one or two of our films here, we've been trying, without any propaganda, or pretension, or preachment of any sort, we've been trying to work out some of those immense possibilities that appeal we think to every man. We are attempting here the thing of imaginative possibility. That at any rate is one of the challenges that we're going to make to our friends and rivals at Hollywood'.

The onset of war. The war Wells and Korda had already anticipated so dramatically in *Things to Come*. In Europe, it had in fact already started. Spain. The Spanish Civil War was, in its day, just as much an ideological culture clash as Vietnam was to prove to be in the years to come. Progressive film-makers then flocked to Spain, to help the Republican cause get its story on the screen. Ernest Hemingway joined forces with Joris Ivens and John Ferno for a film they called *The Spanish Earth*, shot in Madrid under siege and a village twenty-five miles away along the road to Valencia. On this straight-forward and moving report of a people at war – human guinea pigs in this dress rehearsal for the greater war soon to come – the *Motion Picture Herald* was pleased to write that: 'its partisanship and propagandist non-objectivity tend to vitiate whatever message it may carry'. Its message was clear enough to the German Ambassador in London. Von Ribbentrop was present at its 1937 screening to the British Board of Film Censors. A total ban was only relaxed after all references to German and Italian intervention had been deleted.

Technicolor camera blimped for sound

Geoff Unsworth   Chris Challis

Michael Powell   Emeric Pressburgger

A Matter of Life and Death

Who wants a screen of change? Some then did, in the United States, at 369 Lexington Avenue, New York, where the *March of Time* was put together every four weeks, under another roof and altogether different management from its *Time* and *Life* parenthood. For where, blocked by censorship, Hemingway and Ivens

128

failed to reach an audience in Britain with *The Spanish Earth*, the *March of Time* got through. With *Rehearsal for War* the series revealed how the Spanish Civil War was being used by both Hitler and Mussolini as a testing out of the social democratic countries will to fight.

The *March of Time* was as much a child of the thirties as *The Left Book Club* and *The New Deal*. Roosevelt's election and his 'New Deal' had re-energised the American ethic, given new hope to an ideal then almost smothered in the post-World War One boom years of Harding, Coolidge, and Hoover. The *March of Time* was as much the forerunner of what it had chosen to call a 'new kind of pictorial journalism' (which we now take for granted in television) as it was the pacesetter in a fresh drive to put the real and the genuine of America on screen. It was believed to be a time to attempt amends for the ruthless human and physical exploitation which had been the background to the jazz age. Roosevelt's own administration made movies too, and chose a noted film critic to produce them. Pare Lorentz.

Pare Lorentz made his first film for the Resettlement Administration (the predecessor to the Farming Security Administration). It covered ground to be worked over later by John Steinbeck in *The Grapes of Wrath* and already screened by *March of Time* – the worked-out prairies of the mid west, and the dustbowls which a ruthless greed for profits and no care for the future had turned them into. This Lorentz entitled *The Plow that Broke the Plains*; but his lasting achievement, and most famous film was his next, *The River*. With an eloquence altogether alien to Timespeak, Lorentz spelt it out:

'From as far West as Idaho, Down from the glacier peaks of the Rockies – Down as far East as New York, Down from the turnkey ridges of the Alleghenies – Down from Minnesota, twenty-five hundred miles, The Mississippi River runs to the Gulf...'

But *The River* is no picturesque travelogue of the Mississippi. It is a fast-flowing chronicle of the havoc wrought over the years by private enterprise along its banks and the land through which, with its tributaries, it flows. Paced to his editing of

Willard Van Dyke's and Floyd Crosby's visuals, and counter-pointed with Virgil Thomson's score, Lorentz created a commentary of protest which combined all the elements into a poetic and tragic elegy on an environment in danger of destruction by man, machine, and short term profit.

'We fought a war and kept the West bank of the river free of slavery forever. But we left the old South impoverished and stricken. Doubly stricken, because, beside the tragedy of war, already the frenzied cotton cultivation of a quarter of a century had taken toll of the land. We mined the soil for cotton until it would yield no more, and then moved west. We fought a war, but there was a double tragedy – the tragedy of land twice impoverished...'

Sponsors of *The River* included several agencies of the New Deal's Department of Agriculture: the Agricultural Adjustment Administration, the Farm Security Administration, the Bureau of Agricultural Economics, and the Soil Conservation Service.

'We built a hundred cities and a thousand towns but at what a cost. We cut the top off the Alleghenies and sent it down the river. We cut the top off Minnesota and sent it down the river. We cut the top off Wisconsin and sent it down the river...'

The answer, the film summed up, was Federal Aid and intervention on a massive scale. Socialised power. The dams of the Tennessee Valley Authority, generating power for the land as well as controlling its flooding, provide both solution and climax to this classic motion picture study of land and human conservation.

Pare Lorentz was a close friend of King Vidor. With the completion of *The River*, Lorentz needed a break and a change of scene. Vidor suggested that he come with him to England, and that they worked together on *The Citadel*. The two film-makers sailed from New York on the *Manhattan* April 20, 1938. But MGM had other ideas, and the quota of American employment on the picture was already fixed. Lorentz stayed on for a while in London, saw *The River* premiered on BBC Television – yes, BBC Television, back in 1938 – and was made much of by John Grierson, Robert Flaherty, and other documentary dominies. For

Vidor, it was Denham, Lazare Meerson sets, and studio-rooted situations and dialogue.

On arriving at Denham from Hollywood two years before, Jimmy Wong Howe had wondered how it was 'That your producers shut themselves up in studios? A wall in a British studio is just the same as a wall in Hollywood'. This had occurred to me as well. But that was the time when everything originated in a studio, everything was built in a studio, everything was made to happen in a studio. The only shots of the real Oxford in *A Yank at Oxford* are behind the titles. The only shots of the real Wales in *The Citadel* are cuts from the studio train in the opening sequence.

This was not the Grierson way. This was not the Lorentz way. This is not the way of the screen of change. Back in the United States, by coincidence, Pare Lorentz also made next a feature length film of the trials and tribulations of a young doctor. *The Fight for Life*, based on the first section of a book by Paul de Kruif, was for the most part shot on location in the Chicago slums.

'Of course', said Lorentz, 'I wanted to show the housing conditions of the industrial middle west as a background to the medical story. In fact, I wouldn't have made the movie had I not been allowed to broaden it to give some indication of the unemployment and living conditions as prevailed then, not only in Chicago, but in all the industrial United States'.

Shot in and around a Maternity Centre in the heart of that city's slums, *The Fight for Life* was banned by the Chicago Police Department. It was to be twenty-one years before this film first appeared on Chicago screens – and by then they were television screens.

Those who object to 'politics' on screen are always telling us that we should be instead 'objective'. That reporting of this Orwellian era in which 'Peace is War and War is Peace' should somehow be above the battle. And in case anyone thinks that the newsreels of the 1930's were without exception as puerile and pallid as they may seem to be when in portion revived in television programmes like *All Our Yesterdays*, let's flash back to the bombing of Shanghai in 1937. In a Paramount newsreel, for the first time on cinema screens, audiences saw the maimed and bleeding victims of aerial aggression. Uproar. It is the job of the film to entertain, not to shock or get involved in politics, was an outraged and immediate reaction. Said Jeffrey Bernerd, Editor of Gaumont-British (one of Paramount's four rival newsreels of that time):

'It is the duty of the newsreels to present news, but not to put on the screen material for a political purpose...'

Paramount's crusading Editor G. T. Cummings swiftly countered this argument: 'It is our duty', he said, 'to give the news. These things are happening, and we have decided to show them. The only way to stop war is to give people a proper idea of what it means'.

Paramount's was a lone voice in those dismal days, and we had to wait forty years before we were able to see some of the anti-Nazi and anti-appeasement material and interviews they shot – but had censored – at the time. *Before Hindsight* was the name of this evaluation which, written by Elizabeth Taylor-Mead, edited by Jonathan Lewis and narrated by James Cameron (Presenter BBC *One Pair of Eyes*, not *Titanic*), in 1977 incorporated this archive material in a self evident projection of the inadequacy of the newsreels of forty years before.

Their inadequacy lay in their failure to report the reality of what then happening in Hitler's Germany, and the threat that this presented to the survival of any sort of civilised existence anywhere.

One of those interviewed in *Before Hindsight* was Edgar Anstey, correctly captioned as 'Director of Production, *March of Time*, London 1936-1937, 1938-1939. Foreign Editor, *March of Time* New York 1937-1938'. He did not have much trouble in pleading the cause of the *March of Time*, *Before Hindsight* concludes with clips from the series' report of how it was to be, at that time, *Inside Nazi Germany* – screened in its entirety in Channel Four Television's more recent rerun of the series in December 1985.

132

The racism of the regime is made manifest. Jews are seen victimised and on their way to what was all too soon to become the 'Holocaust'. The screen fills with Hitler's marching legions and parades of aggressive weaponry. And then, in what is perhaps the most effective end sequence in *March of Time* history, we come upon an elderly lady, doing needlework in what must be her German home. (That this had to be set up and shot in New York is surely absolutely irrelevant.) The commentary has meanwhile been telling us that now – that is, to audiences in 1938 – 'Germany is fashioning the greatest war machine history has ever seen. And throughout history machines of war have led only to one thing. War'.

By now we are on to the old lady in her modest German home. On the wall behind her we have glimpsed two photographs, hung side by side. Close-up shows them to be of two young Germans in the uniform of the First World War. Around the pictures – black crepe and medals. Clearly – without the need for any words to say so – these are the sons of this widow, killed (like her absent husband) in that previous war. And as their lifeless faces fill the screen, out booms the pay off – 'TIME MARCHES ON!'

This desperate and doomed search for impartiality that we are told must now follow, for objectivity between victim and aggressor, progress and reaction, capital versus labour, good (if you like) and evil, exemplified in a fascinating programme devised by the old London Film Society that same year of the Cummings-Bernerd confrontation over reporting the Japanese invasion of China. This time the subject was another war, also under way at the same time: fascist Italy's invasion of Haile Selassie's African Kingdom of Abyssinia. The programme was made up of alternate reels of two different films, shot on either side of the firing line. Firstly, the Italian Luce Films' ambitious, spectacular and pretentious *The Path of the Heroes*. This consisted of elaborate arrangements of smoothly flowing, carefully selected and staged groups of scenes, each designed to illustrate some single aspect of the conquest, proclaimed by a preceding title in French and German accompanied by its Italian dialogue equivalent. The other film was entitled just simply *Abyssinia*, shot by a couple of Russian newsreel cameramen of Soyuzkino-chronika. This was a straightforward narrative, with no funny treatment. By 'intercutting', as it were, alternate reels of each, the audience was able to see the smirking smiles of fascist airmen as they admired the precise and formal patterns their bombs made, exploding on the ground far beneath them, with the effect of these bombs on the ground itself – a Red Cross hospital in ruins, and the blinded and bleeding faces of their flesh and blood targets.

But even with all due respect and homage to cameramen in Vietnam, no war in history has been such a heady mixture of passion and politics as the Spanish Civil War. The newsreels of the time reflected a great deal less than objectivity. Under the aggressive editorship of Cummings, British Paramount News was unashamedly on the side of the legally elected government of Spain, fighting for its life against a rebellion aided by Fascist Italy and Nazi Germany. British Movietone, on the other hand allied to the Rothermere interests and the *Daily Mail*, reported and publicised Franco as a gallant Christian gentleman and saviour of civilisation against the onward march of Bolshevism. As kids, we would fill a row of seats in newsreel theatres, cheering the one and booing the other.

Few remained uncommitted to the Spanish cause. If Franco was allowed to win, then a total European war was a foregone conclusion. Fresh from involvement in the Chinese Revolution, André Malraux arrived in Spain and raised an international fighter squadron in support of the Republic. And more, he made a film about it. *L'Espoir* is the story of an international group of aviators, flying the Republic's obsolete bombers against Franco's up-to-date German and Italian-flown fighters. The last reel of this film, which Malraux wrote and directed himself, is little short of epic. After a raid on a fascist fighter base, a bomber is shot down. Its crew were Belgian, French, Arab, Spanish, and anti-fascist German. The pilot is dead. His body is recovered by peasants. Strapped to the back of a mule, it is brought down from the mountains. At every village along the route, more and more join this funeral cortege. Until, at the end, all Spain seems to be in pilgrimage across the face of the land, behind this corpse of a foreigner, dead for Spain, in the fight against fascism. A sequence which is a striking parallel to *Battleship Potemkin*'s concourse of people filing on to the mole at Odessa, passing in homage before the body of the sailor Vakulinchuk, dead 'on account of a spoonful of bortsch'.

Civil War in Spain, back in those still seminal thirties. Civil war in Britain in our own time. What the BBC chose to attempt in Ulster was to report both sides of an armed conflict impartially. But with the intervention of a self-styled 'army' based on the other side of an international border, it became more and more difficult to maintain – let alone justify – this laudable intention. With a confrontation soon clearly seen to be as more than just a clash between two communities confined to six counties of Britain, the *British* Broadcasting Corporation's attempt to balance Ulster loyalist with gunmen of the *Irish* Republican Army came in for mounting criticism. As a result, both the ethic and the principle of the BBC's being above the arena were called into question.

Is it ever possible to film, report, a war impartially? How can you, unless you film both sides, giving each adversary equal time as it were, remain totally uninvolved and aloof from the political and military commitment of either? I was able to do this, just once; but wound up almost facing a firing squad as the price of my protested objectivity.

As with Ulster, the issue was religious. That same old intolerance still marching on down through the ages. But this clash was not between Catholic and Protestant Christian but between Hindu and Muslim Indian; and the setting, the roof of the world in the far off Himalayas. Both, however, had their origins in British colonial rule. Forced to give freedom to Ireland, partition was the price in 1922, with civil war its legacy then and in 1972. With the coming of freedom to India in 1947 agreement to the separate Muslim State of Pakistan was the price the Hindu had to pay. Each side claimed the previously independent state of Kashmir. They went to war over it.

135

By then myself a Cameraman/Reporter for the *March of Time*, India had been my first assignment. In front of my camera there was passing the greatest migration in human history. All the Hindus in the Pakistan side of what was now the divided province of the Punjab in the north west were fleeing eastwards into India. All the Muslims, suddenly finding themselves in what had now become for them the wrong side of the border, trekked west. All in all, twelve million people moved in this bloody exchange of populations.

Like my latter-day successors in neighbouring Afghanistan, my problem then was to get in there, find, and film a war; at that time the first (undeclared) war between India and Pakistan over the state bordering the Punjab to the north, Kashmir. The only overland route in was by then from Pakistan. I was in India. But I had a good friend in Delhi's Ministry of Defence, and he got me on to a plane flying reinforcements up to Srinagar, the capital of Kashmir. By this same route India had flown a regiment of Sikhs to that airstrip just in time to throw Pakistan-supported tribesmen back the month before. Now they were perched high up in the lower Himalayan peaks fifty miles to the West. Indian artillery lobbing shells up at them, and ammunition convoys winding their way through this awesome scenery, were the most dramatic scenes I was able to shoot before the first fall of winter snow closed the airport and I took off and away on the last flight out that season.

My task and objective was then to get to the other side, the receiving end of those shells. It took me three weeks to reach the Headquarters of the Pakistan Army in Rawalpindi, where everyone denied and disclaimed all knowledge and any involvement in this war going on up the road.

I ate a lonely and depressed dinner in a faded Kiplingesque hotel called Flashman's (yes, that's true!). Across the room, similarly solitary with the baked jam roll which generations of cooking for the British had persuaded Flashman's to be the height of *haute cuisine*, was a Pakistan Army Colonel I had met on the plane the previous day. We drank coffee together. 'I'll get you into Kashmir', he said. 'Be ready at the hotel after lunch tomorrow.'

Standing with camera and equipment at the portals of Flashman's the following day, as if awaiting a taxi, I was prepared for anything. A truck drove up. Its driver motioned me aboard. We drove off. Nobody spoke. I was volunteered no information. My questions remained unanswered. By evening we were on the border of Kashmir, a great gorge through which thundered one of the great Himalayan rivers on its way down to irrigate the fields of the divided Punjab, now behind us in Pakistan.

We passed the night in a deserted frontier post. Then across the river gorge on a crazy suspension bridge on foot. Mules awaited on the other side. By some mysterious means, word of my mission was preceding us. Equipment strapped to the sides of these docile beasts, we walked on. Walked and walked, climbed and climbed. For two days. Up and down mountain tracks, just below the snowline, all the time passing and repassing 'volunteers' coming in from Pakistan, laden with weapons and ammunition, the insignia of the Pakistan Army only just removed from their battle dress. We reached the headquarters of Pakistan's first campaign to wrest Kashmir from India: a village, where I was at once taken before the 'Leader'. I was made welcome and invited to film a meeting he planned to address that same evening. I pleaded lack of light by then, and my own near exhaustion, as an excuse to decline. I lay down on a makeshift bed in a mud hut. Bang! Crash! Whoosh! Whoomph! All hell suddenly broke loose outside. I dashed out. Indian Spitfires were rocketing and machine-gunning the village. They accounted for twenty-seven Kashmiri peasants, dead and wounded.

Regretting that in those days there was no practical and portable sound recording equipment available to cameramen alone and on the hoof like me, that night I talked long with this 'Leader' of 'Azad' (Free) Kashmir, Sardar Ibrahim. From him I heard at first hand the origins of a still festering conflict which by 1990 had threatened to become nuclear.

Guerilla fighters in Kashmir

Adjacent to the north west area of the Indian subcontinent which had become Pakistan, Kashmir also has a primarily Muslim population. But its Ruler was a Hindu Maharajah. Over which of the two new nations between which his fiefdom was sandwiched he should join, he dithered. Whereupon a revolt took place in his territory, demanding accession to Muslim Pakistan. Panic-stricken, the Ruler immediately signed up with India: Pakistan meantime unofficially making the way clear for the fellow Muslim tribesmen of its own northwest Frontier Province to sweep down to the support of their co-religionists in Kashmir. Thereupon India claimed this to be aggression against what had then become, in strictly legal terms, a newly joined State of the new Indian Union; and to this day has refused a referendum as to what the wretched Kashmiris themselves would really like to do.

Up there in the foothills of the Himalayas, I at least felt fine, and very pleased with myself. Even without an on-the-spot original sound recording of the Pakistani-Kashmir case, I had a scoop, and spent the following day filming Ibrahim, his rugged headquarters and ragged followers, in action. No other cameraman had then penetrated this side of the Kashmir story, at all.

With the same guide who had led me up from Pakistan in the first place, I then set off on the return journey. At the river frontier border crossing we halted. No further, I was told. Why, I asked? No answer. At least not vocally, but abruptly physically. I found myself seized, separated from camera and film, and flung into a cowshed with its door bolted behind me. A surprising and unexpected twist in my fortunes indeed – and for why? I gave up wondering, and went to sleep. Outside picturesque, but, so far as I was concerned in this predicament, plainly hostile guards patrolled all night. Was it because I had failed to film that evening meeting called by the 'Leader', possibly because I knew in advance of the planned Indian air attack, and in some way had been able to communicate with a camera which might, in another of the cases of its equipment, have been really a radio? No doubt it was known that I had already filmed the other side, and was a cameraman accredited to the enemy in Delhi as well. A plague on both your houses was certainly now my attitude, and the force of G.K. Chesterton's dictum that 'the man who sees both sides of a question should be hit on both sides of the head' seemed about to become a reality as far as I was concerned.

However, the next morning I was let out, camera and film were returned undamaged. Without a word of explanation, I was led, all in one piece, back to Flashman's. I lost no time in getting the exposed film away; and, despite this somewhat brusque treatment and experience at the hands of Kashmir's freedom fighters, continued to plead the Pakistan case with my editors in New York. They, like most of the world then and for many years to come, tended to see only the Indian side of things.

In Kashmir, although I could not but see the justice of Pakistan's case, I operated a strictly and deliberately neutral camera. In combat, I defy anyone to shoot with a genuinely uncommitted camera. In fact I deliberately threw mine aside on one occasion, to assist actively, as a combatant, my own side in mutual survival.

This was in Greece, in 1944, towards the end of the Second World War. The Germans were pulling out. I was then a uniformed British Army Film Unit cameraman. I had talked my way into being allowed to join a small force of commandos, landed as a reconnaissance force at an abandoned airfield two hundred and fifty miles to the west of Athens. In just four jeeps, and less than a week, with one captured enemy gun, we had chased the retreating enemy to within less than thirty miles of the Greek capital.

But before they finally evacuated Athens, the Germans decided to turn around and test our strength. We were encamped on an abandoned airfield at Megara. Advancing down on our little handful was the rearguard of nothing less than the entire German Army Group in the Balkans.

Now the uniform I wore, and not the viewfinder of my camera, dictated my actions. I was ordered down to the beach at our back, to see if there were any signs of an enemy landing to our rear as well. All clear. And then, the most miraculous sight of a lifetime. Overhead, the sky suddenly filled with huge four-engined troop transports. Ours. They carried the leading elements of the airborne brigade of the main British force scheduled to liberate Athens.

A ground wind was blowing at more than thirty miles an hour. More than enough to call off any drop. But seldom, if ever, could reinforcements have been more urgently needed. Our own commando fired off a green smoke signal – announcing to those in the sky above that the ground was still in our hands. This was in fact the signal for chaos. The Germans started to shell us while, at only five hundred feet over our heads, the paratroops poured out of their aircraft. I was almost too excited to hold my camera steady – and soon I didn't even hold it at all. For as soon as those paratroops hit the deck they were dragged by the wind in their still opened chutes over the ground at more than thirty miles an hour. Within minutes many were out in the sea, bleeding and broken, their ammunition and weapon containers likewise strewn all over the place. If any of us hoped to survive the now developing German counterattack, the task was to get as many and as much of these men and their equipment into action as soon as possible. Two of our four jeeps had gone back for supplies. That meant that my own vehicle was half the entire mobile and available transport. Frantically we dashed about in it, picking up survivors and weaponry. The paratroops' radio set was fished out of the sea; enemy shells bursting all the time in our midst.

Should I have just stood my ground, and shot all this with my camera? By not doing so, I missed what could have been possibly the most dramatic and exciting coverage of World War Two. Never before, or since, has a cameraman been already on the ground *before* an airborne invasion of his own side dropped on his head, in broad daylight. But what one was able to do with the invaluable jeep and one's own bare hands (of which there was only another one of the first and barely another thirty of the second) saved that airborne descent – and that particular liberation of Greece – from disaster.

It was such excitements, and what seemed at the time such fulfilments with a hand-held camera in World War Two that decided me against any return to a film studio. Cameras, I now believed, should be out and on the streets. An obvious move on my part would have been into the then booming and confident world of the British Documentary film. But for what I now wanted to do, what I now wanted to say, I needed a motion picture format more abrasive, less English middle-class if you like. Journalistic rather than aesthetic. Less Film Society – more Fleet Street.

Based very much on the layout of *Life*, in Britain the weekly news magazine *Picture Post* had also pioneered the pictorial report of news in depth. I had subscribed from its first issue October 1, 1938. Many of its reporters and cameramen were to be the nucleus of television's new breed of communicators when, in the fifties, it succumbed (as too for a while would the UK itself) to the new electronic medium. In its issue of January 21, 1939, *Picture Post* ran a story on the plight of Britain's 2,000,000 unemployed. It was reported of Bob Davies, a thirty-nine-year-old Welsh coalminer, that he had been out of work for seven years on end. Once a strong young boxer, he was finished as a man, coughing his lungs out with silicosis, for which he had received

An airdrop brings the British back to Greece - Megara 1944

Wounded paratroops at Megara

no compensation. Had any British feature film dared to put this human and national disaster on the screen? At that time, no. But we at pre-war MGM had done so, and it was called *The Citadel*.

The classic British documentary of this subject, at that time, is *Coal Face*. But Cavalcanti's film is more poetical than political. Music was by Benjamin Britten, and words by W.H. Auden – including direct quotations of the statistics of death in mining disasters. But the manner of this presentation, combined with the inadequacy of the sound recording system then available to the Grierson group, lessened the impact of its appeal for mass action.

In the tenth issue of its second year of 1937, the *March of Time* came up with *Black Areas*, directed by Edgar Anstey. Here was the direct reality. Unemployed Welsh miners begging in the streets of London; two thirds of Britain's miners unemployed for thirteen years; boycott of a company union; a lockout; demands for the complete nationalisation of Britain's coal mines and industry.

Only three months before I had at last succeeded in gate-crashing a studio and entering the make-believe world of the pre-war British feature film, the *March of Time* had come up with its first report of the 'British Hollywood' and 'the giant strides in the growth of the British film industry'. Always it had seemed to be where the real action was, reporting in a direct and muscular manner the true facts of a flesh and blood world. It was to be the *March of Time* for me.

Towards the end of the war against Germany I had shot film for the United Nations Relief and Rehabilitation Administration. UNRRA coped with the colossal economic problems of a wrecked continent, while simultaneously attempting the return home of the millions who had been uprooted by Hitler's war. The *March of Time* acquired some of this film and, on the strength of it, offered me that job, based in their London office. In 1947 I had not hesitated.

But by then time had indeed marched on from those halcyon and hopeful days of the *New Deal* and the *March of Time*'s own aggressive youth. Soon there was another war on, the 'Cold War'

143

between the United States and the Soviet Union. As this intensi-
fied, more and more the *March of Time* did indeed come to reflect the narrow and blinkered anti-communism of its parent
publishing house *Time-Incorporated*. The era of Roosevelt was
no more. The junior senator from Wisconsin, Joseph R.
McCarthy, was beginning to make his bigoted way in the land. I
had to admit to myself that I might have made a mistake. The
arteries of the *March of Time* were hardening. Louis de
Rochemont had moved on by way of Hollywood into factual feature production. His original MOT series was now becoming increasingly non-objective in the doctrinaire nature of its reporting
that 'We of the West' were the 'goodies', 'They' of the Communist
East the 'baddies'. Previously filming for UNRRA in Eastern
Europe and the Soviet Union immediately after the Second
World War, I knew that there was more to it than this sterile
over-simplification. But objectivity in this developing situation
was beyond the scope or powers of my new masters. However,
before its final end, the *March of Time* was to attempt one bold
issue of genuine impartiality.

By 1950 the world was truly once again at war, in Korea.
China, now under Mao, appeared to many to be bent on aggression. In Europe, an American general once again headed up a
coalition of ten other nations, poised to counter the presumed
Russian threat from the East. It was a time to take stock. The
calendar reminded the editors of the *March of Time* that the human race had reached the midpoint of the twentieth century.
Where were we heading? And so, in *Mid Century – Half Way To
Where?*, the *March of Time* reviewed man's progress to date, and
assembled an intercut series of interviews with the presumably
farseeing, and certainly prestigious in their various fields of human endeavour.

'Though outwardly at peace, the world at mid-century is split
into two conflicting concentrations of power', an introductory
title proclaimed. The capitals of these conflicting concentrations
of power were of course Washington and Moscow. Easy enough
for the *March of Time* to film and record statements from the
mighty in the first, but how to balance with the point of view of

144

their Marxist adversaries in the Kremlin? No American Communists were available or, at that time, able to speak. The twelve members of the Board of the American Communist Party had been indicted by a Grand Jury on charges of teaching and advocating the overthrow of the Government of the United States by force and violence. The call came to us in London. Same language, but safer if the message came from our side of the Atlantic. Off to King Street we went, to the headquarters of the British Communist Party, and to its General Secretary Harry Pollitt.

Mid-Century – Half Way to Where? World Communism, says
British Party chief Harry Pollitt for the *March of Time*

It seemed he had received approval from his masters – or was his welcome an indication of left-wing deviationism on his own personal part? Whatever the case, Pollitt quite clearly relished this opportunity to bear witness by way of the apparatus and lackeys of the imperialist enemy. I filmed him in his office: a Spartan interior – desk, plus a few chairs; on the mantelpiece, a bust of Karl Marx; on the wall, portraits – Lenin, of course, and Stalin – and one other. I peered hard. Pollitt noticed, and re-

145

minded me. It was Ralph Fox, the British writer, killed with the International Brigade in Spain.

Camera set up, sound channel checked. Pollitt needed no prompting: 'The working people of all capitalist countries will become the masters of the wealth they produce, as in the Soviet Union, China, and the People's Democracies'. In close-up: 'poverty, unemployment, war, will be abolished. Mankind will rise to heights of social, economic and cultural progress undreamed of in the past. All roads will lead to Communism, and British and American imperialism can do nothing to stop this inevitable development'.

One dedicated and committed Marxist's view in 1950 of where we would be in the year 2001. What did others forecast for the *March of Time* and mankind in *Mid century – Half Way To Where?* A leader of labour on the other side of the fence, by then so-called 'iron curtain', the CIO's President, Walter Reuther: 'Democracy's most challenging problem is to find a way to translate technical progress into human progress, and prove that men can enjoy economic security without sacrificing their political freedom. The Communist masters in the Kremlin offer the promise of economic security at the price of political and spiritual enslavement. While rejecting Communism, American labour is equally determined to resist the abuse of economic power in the hands of the great monopolies. While labour maintains that the rights and dignity of the individual are supreme to the state, we also insist that people are more important than profits, and that human rights come before property rights'.

A voice from the past, and a ration of rhetoric – from Winston Churchill, addressing a mid century convocation at Massachusetts Institute of Technology: 'Do not suppose that half a century from now you will not see seventy or eighty millions of Britons, spread about the world, and united in defence of our traditions, our way of life, and the world causes which you and we espouse. Let us move forward together in discharge of our mission, and our duty, fearing God and nothing else'.

The Chairman of the Board of RCA, David Sarnoff, speaking up for technology: 'In the next half century, people will see as well as hear around the world. Pocket-sized radio instruments will enable individuals to communicate with anyone, anywhere. Newspapers, magazines, mail and messages will be sent through the air at lightning speed, and reproduced in the home'.

For the arts, Herbert Read, also filmed by us in London: 'During the past fifty years all the arts have had to accept the triumph of the machine. Traditional forms of painting and sculpture have no function in our streamlined existence. If they are to find a place in the civilisation of the next half century, the visual arts must effect a compromise with the machine. This must be done only within the terms of what we call abstract art'.

Spokesman for the military machine, so much the catalyst and customer of the mid century industrial complex and infrastructure, the then Chairman of the Joint Chiefs of Staff, General Omar Bradley: 'How a future war will be fought depends on when it is started. Begun tomorrow, it would be much like World War Two. Ten years from now, war can only be more destructive than the last. Science and technology, with the development of the guided missiles, target-seeking projectiles and other weapons has multiplied tremendously the destruction possible on the battlefield, at sea, and in the air. But this very scientific progress of weapons may be the ultimate deterrent to any future war. The more I work on the plans for defence, the more I am convinced that war is not inevitable'.

And finally, from Princeton, the voice and image of a servant of science; and the father, so-called, of the Atomic Bomb, to be hounded from public office in the years of inquisition which lay just ahead, J. Robert Oppenheimer: 'Science has profoundly altered the conditions of man's life both materially and in ways of the spirit as well. It has extended the range of questions in which man has a choice. It has extended man's freedom to make significant decisions. No one can predict what vast new continents of knowledge the future of science will discover. But we know that as long as men are free to say what they think, free to think what they must, science will never regress, and freedom itself will never be wholly lost'.

147

And now that we have indeed reached that then distant Millennium would anyone care to give screentime to where we might all be in 2050?

4. FILM AND PERSONALITY

'If you want to engage people you must do so on a personal level.'

Jacob Bronowski

Author films Japanese Emperor and his Empress

Seeing it again after all those years, what does date the *March of Time* is the deadpan and so easily parodied pomposity of its voiceover narration (its quite frequent use of irony even then quite too often taken at face value) and some of its undeclared re-enactments. Not all were as successful as the First World War widow who winds up *Inside Nazi Germany*. Particularly embarrassing are some of the little inserted sequences of phoney dialogue. When he reviewed Channel Four's *Flashback* rerun of the series, nothing amused Max Hastings more than a staged scene of a bogus peer of the realm trying out his robes (*Coronation Crisis 1937*). 'What about the sword?' he asks the servitor. 'Perhaps you'd like to take it home and practise with it?' Whatever may now be perceived to be its latter-day shortcomings, the *March of Time* did however succeed in opening up the screen to controversy, paving the way for all the *Panoramas*, *60 Minutes* and *Worlds in Action* of the television age to follow. Moreover, believing that the essence of a story lay in an awareness and understanding of the people involved, its dramatisations and reporting always set out to focus on a particular personality concerned – and thereby the complex and. impersonal was rendered understandable, if not indeed entertaining, in human terms. The individual caught up in, influencing, or being influenced by the situation or circumstances under scrutiny and analysis.

The story of trade unionism in the United States in the thirties was the story of the mineworkers' leader John L. Lewis. The story of social change in the Middle East was the story of Mustapha Kemal, *Father of All the Turks*. The story of the new breed of politicians, swept into office with the New Deal, focused on New York's colourful Mayor, Fiorello La Guardia. A report of what and where was Albania, next on Mussolini's hit list in 1936, was centred on the tragicomic figure of that little Balkan country's diminutive King Zog. The entire immense American war effort – Roosevelt's 'Arsenal of Democracy' – was focused on just one modest little factory in Ohio making items of equipment for military aircraft. *Bill Jack vs Adolf Hitler* they called this one, Bill Jack the manager of the cooperatively run plant.

150

If personality is indeed the essence of television, and a great deal of its documentary and current affairs reporting, then film and personality are quite clearly more mixed up together than ever before.

Throughout its history, the feature film always concerned itself with personality. But as often as not it has tended to reflect more the personality of the film-maker than the individual portrayed on the screen. No one ever pretended that Korda's *Private Life of Henry VIII* was a picture of the public life of the English Reformation. And nobody was around with camera and tape recorder at the time providing raw material for later reinterpretative hindsights. The Warner Bros' biographies of the 1930's like *The Story of Louis Pasteur*, *The Life of Emile Zola* and *Juarez* were as much vehicles for actor Paul Muni as platforms for their progressive writers whereon to draw contemporary parallels. The David Lean – Robert Bolt *Lawrence of Arabia* is less historically clinical than Terence Rattigan's screenplay of *Ross*. And Lawrence's retreat into that later anonymity is more the clue to his character. Francis Ford Coppola and Franklin Schaffner would not have written and directed *Patton* the way they did in 1970 if Vietnam had not by then called into question, if not contempt, the mystique of military glory personified by their 'hero'. By bringing its miniature magnifying glass to bear on the nature of personality, television has enormously enlarged and enriched the range of screen biography. Until Ken Russell made his television film of Elgar for the BBC, a vast majority who had never bothered to listen to any of his music other than *Land of Hope and Glory* had dismissed this English Mahler as little more than a musical Kipling.

Elgar had been dead for thirty years by the time Russell made his film portrait. Time enough for perspective and reassessment by another generation. But what of the still living, those at the height of their powers and influence, who are so often the subject matter of television profiles? The easy way out is to shoot interviews with a selection of those who have known and worked with the person concerned, intercut with sections of a longer such interview with him or her, backed up with archive

151

material along the road to success. But the result is usually only too bland and predictable, particularly if a politician is concerned. For one veteran and committed journalist this was not good enough. A pioneer photo-essayist for *Picture Post*, James Cameron 'suggested that what television needed was a visual approximation of a signed personal column, from which if necessary the organisation could dissociate itself, but which could have intrinsic value not necessarily sterilised by the BBC imprimatur'.

After some hesitation the Corporation agreed, and Cameron found himself making the first three in the series of *One Pair of Eyes*. The personality so indulged was permitted, to a very great degree, his or her own choice and direction of programme. By letting him or her tell and show how it is, or was, to them, we sometimes caught an aspect and understanding of their personality which they might not even be aware of themselves. Certainly it dispensed with the need and artifice of an interrogator to interpose his own personality between us, the audience, and the person we would like to know better.

With *One Pair of Eyes*, personality was all. An outstanding example of success in this authored series – whether you liked and approved of the man or not – was its programme back in August 1972 devoted to, and taken over by, the Liverpudlian Marxist Mystic Sculptor Arthur Dooley. The very opening shots of sparks flying from the metal he worked set your teeth on edge right away. They were meant to. This programme let you know where it stood from the word go. No attempt at 'balance' or 'impartiality' here. It was Us and Them. Arthur Dooley let the audience know without hesitation where he stood. He identified himself with the artisan, not the artist, the shipyard workers with whom he had learnt his craft. And if you too were not from the Liverpool working class, living from pay packet to pay packet, and worshipping your gods on a Saturday at the football ground, then you were one of Them. Dooley took us, through the film camera, on a tour of his beloved Liverpool. We looked at, he showed us, the Cathedral, the University, the high-rise flats and the run-down warehouses. As we looked, he talked, speaking with scorn of the politicians, the planners, the sociologists, the architects, and all of You who were ravaging his city. It was possible to find Dooley inconsistent in his denunciation of education while yet seeing hope in it. You might have thought him parochial when he appeared to think that Liverpool had broken new ground in letting its working class artists sell their paintings in the open air. But that's just the point. For aren't we all irrational and inconsistent in our opinions and attitudes? It's only the plastic and the phoney who come up on that little screen with everything worked out as neatly and as tidily as a public relations consultant and an autocue can devise. Whatever you thought of Arthur Dooley, even if he annoyed and irritated you, you were compelled to watch and listen to his world, through his *One Pair of Eyes*. For we had, of course, the Mersey Sound too, the latest songs of protest. 'Now you can walk on the Mersey, for the river is sludge to the sea.' Dooley railed at pollution as well; but, as a television film programme, it was all constructed to lead up to a testament of this one man's faith and work, and this one small corner of the decaying western world. In this final third of the twentieth century, Arthur Dooley found Christ in the Liverpool streets: his working class could build the New Jerusalem. We were shown, and he explained, the artefacts in which he expressed his vision. His Dachau Crucifixion, his Stations of the Cross and his Splitting of the Atom.

Personally authored and hardly impartial, television series like the pioneering *One Pair of Eyes* and the BBC's much later *Byline* give us a much greater understanding of individual personality than *cinéma-vérité*, of which so much was claimed in the Sixties. To film the Mayor of New York back in 1938, Director Jack Glenn, his cameraman, and their assistants had to hump around a 35 millimetre sound-on-film camera (no tape in those days) and the spontaneity of this La Guardia profile is a tribute not only to their ingenuity but also their stamina. By the 1960's a film-maker could do the whole thing virtually on his own.

The development of lightweight tripodless 16-millimetre hand-held sound cameras, the zoom lens which made (for this type of filming) the cut from setup to setup unnecessary, portable tape recorders with directional microphones and, above all, high speed film which made any lighting equipment additional to that existing superfluous – all this now enabled the individual film-maker to become to all intents and purposes a one-man film production unit. As such, he or she could be accepted within a group, as part of that group, by the individuals within it whom he or she was setting out to portray on film. It was claimed that now, at last, the filmmaking person was no more conspicuous than just another fly on the wall. Everything that took place in front or his or her camera was therefore real, never contrived. Studies of people under stress lent themselves to this technique of filming them from morning to night, from teeth cleaning to tippling, and generally throughout a period of crisis.

Institutions too. Hand-held cameras penetrated and intrigued us with the conflicts of enclosed worlds in microcosm. Strip Clubs, British 'Public' Schools, Military Establishments, Lunatic Asylums... Out of the mountain of film which resulted, there was edited what was claimed to be a 'truer' image of that person, that establishment, than would otherwise have been the case. We witnessed the sentencing and last hours of a man condemned to death in the electric chair. We shared the agonies of an actress awaiting the morning reviews of a Broadway opening.

We accompanied a pop star on tour. We became the surrogate father of quintuplets. With *The Family*, in Britain between elections in 1974, we followed the fortunes of the Wilkinses of Reading. Unlike the intellectually-anguished Louds of California in the American Public Broadcasting System's similar familial saga, these working class Britons were refreshingly earthy, frank, and seemingly stable (although in due course, and some time after the programme was aired, divorce was to follow).

But can you be sure that awareness of a camera and tape recorder following and recording your every move and every word does not in itself influence what you do, what you say; consciously or unconsciously make you a performer? And it is so passive. We, the audience, are merely shown what is claimed to be a mirror image. By its very nature, *cinéma-vérité* did *not* investigate or explain. It could never attempt to show us *why*, or *how* it might be different, or how it came about in the first place. This is how it is, it said, for better or for worse. Take it or leave it. In fact, such technique – or lack of technique – verges on voyeurism. We are spectators, never participants. We are back in the days before the *March of Time* when events, happenings, were chronicled, uncommented, by anonymous and uncommitted cameras: really all in a super newsreel, if not even a king-size home movie, confusing identification with involvement. It absolves the audience from any feeling of shared responsibility. Finally, by the nature of its deliberate non-involvement in personal drama and difficulty, *cinéma-vérité* rejected – if not mocked – Grierson's original definition of documentary as the *creative treatment* of actuality.

Is truth, like objectivity, subjective and not absolute? Is a personality, like Citizen Kane's, only what it appears, to different people, at different times, in different ways? Were you really here, at Marienbad, last year, or was it someone else, and maybe it wasn't me either? Can the motion picture camera capture more than a chemically or electronically recorded image of the person's reflected physical surface? Can, should, the film-maker subjugate his own personality, with all its own quite natural and inbuilt prejudices, to give us a portrait of another personality as he or she really is, or was, or seems to be? Light years separate the mask of Tutankhamen from the boy Pharaoh.

The twentieth century has seen no greater personality than that which dominated the Indian scene for so long, and whose cunning example wrested freedom from the British. The centenary of Mahatma Gandhi's birth coincided with the opening of our study course at the Film and Television Institute of India. A five-and-a-half hour long (no less) compilation film on his life was the official motion picture centenary tribute. It was screened to us the first Sunday after my arrival in Poona. Every foot of film, from every possible source, must have been included. There was Louis de Rochemont's original newsreel footage of the riots following Gandhi's arrest after his famous salt march to the sea. There were many very human and revealing scenes, unknown to archivists outside of India. Gandhi on an old Peninsular and Oriental Steamship on his way to an abortive conference on Indian freedom in London in 1931, refusing a cabin and eating and sleeping out on the deck; attended by a very stiff and formal and clearly most embarrassed ship's captain, as well as being shaved in sight of the Rock of Gibraltar with a cutthroat razor. There were at least six synchronous sound sequences with his voice clearly recorded. The little, dhoti-clad man cheered by the poor of London's East End, and unemployed Lancashire mill workers. The British working class feeling an affinity for the impoverished of Asia in those depressed days. Visiting Italy on his way back to India, Gandhi is asked his opinion of a run-past of young fascist warriors (the invaders of Abyssinia four years later). His reply, with an ironic twinkle in his eye, 'very good exercise for them'.

The only film material of Gandhi missing from this monumental life study was the sequence I had shot with him in Delhi a month before his assassination. This, like all the million and a half feet of *March of Time* film, was still jealously hung on to by *Time Incorporated*, pending the day it might all possibly be a source of revenue and sales promotion once again on television.

With Gandhi I had exchanged not a word, for my filming had been arranged for one of his self-denial Days of Silence. That in those days I did not have with me a sound recording camera therefore did not really matter – but what a pity. With Gandhi's disciple and heir, free India's first Prime Minister, Jawaharlal Nehru, I spoke plenty. The principal and most challenging assignment I ever received from the *March of Time* was to shoot a series of its film reports on the reality and promise of independent India and newly-created Pakistan. I was in the subcontinent, completely committed to and absorbed by this task for sixteen months, 1947-1949.

As a later generation has now entered pictorial journalism, primarily in television where the action now is – questioning not only the ethics of the medium but also their own response to its disciplines – there has been a revival of interest in the *March of Time*, stimulated even further nowadays by *Flashback's* revival

156

NEHRU

The public private person

157

of the series for Channel Four. How did they go about it in those days, and was their prescribed, reenacted method of dramatisation an interference with reality – in short, a cheat?

Writing of the influence of the *March of Time* in the fifth volume of her definitive 'History of the British Film', Rachael Low tells us that: 'The real change in the British documentary movement brought about by the *March of Time* was the abandonment of the vestiges of the early visual editing (based on silent Russian film techniques) for an entirely literary style, the editing of shots accompanied neither by their recorded sound nor by sound counterpoint but made to fit a commentary bearing the burden of the message'.

In his complete account of the entire MOT series published just a year before the above – that is in 1978 – Raymond Fielding includes an interview with associate producer Lothar Wolff: 'Stylistically what (made) the *March of Time* different from everything else is in many instances the script dominated the picture, rather than the other way around ... Louis de Rochemont was the first man, in my opinion, who gave words and image the same value, There is a documentary maxim that the picture should tell the story. I never subscribed to it. I think it's an oversimplification, just like *cinéma-vérité*'.

And Fielding added a postscript from editor Morrie Roizman: 'If the script didn't fit the picture, we'd make the pictures fit the script, and we'd work until we had a happy marriage'.

Now I believe this may give rise to a misconception in the mind of anyone who did not experience the methodology of the MOT – and that must include virtually every reader of this book.

Scripts were hardly, if ever, written for *March of Time* productions. Shooting Scripts: that is, with on one side of the page a detailed descriptive list of visual images to be filmed, with an indication of how they were to be filmed; and in parallel on the other side of the page the words which would accompany them. What Lothar Wolff refers to are not 'scripts', but commentaries. *March of Time* releases originated on paper more in the form of what might be described as 'Treatments' – story outlines. When I set off for India on the basis of a cable which simply said 'India approved for schedule with Hopkinson covering by himself', all the documentation I had to go on was a typewritten page from the associate producer listing what he thought should be filmed, and this was little more than a listing of political notables. For my later assignment to *Formosa, Island of Promise* (deliberate irony on our part) I was better served. Researcher Nancy Pessac had prepared for me and associate producer Sam Byrant a thirty-page background paper on the entire history and current significance of the place.

For, although always an editorial law unto itself, the *March of Time* could, however, call on the informational facilities of its parent organisation, the Henry Luce publishing empire of *Time*, *Life*, *Fortune*, and their extensive reportorial data, both present and past. At the same time, MOT maintained its own staff of diligent researchers, whose responsibility could range from the correct pronunciation of a Chinese General's name to the current cost of a British cup of tea. The intention of both Bryant and myself was that once I got to Formosa (now better known as Taiwan) I would follow up and personalise the story of the Formosans themselves, those willy-nilly hosts to Chiang Kai-shek and his cohorts expelled by the Communists from the mainland. In India, on the other hand, events happened so fast that any pre-planned programme just went by the board. I had barely arrived and begun to check off my shot list when communal massacres broke out on a hideous scale in the north west, war exploded in Kashmir, and Gandhi was assassinated in Delhi.

So one shot very much off the cuff, guided in the first place by a New York story line, and in the second by one's own experience and appraisal of the story on the spot. Not, according to his autobiography, as did, in the early days, Harry Watt: 'Having found you'd been given a subject, you wrote a commentary only in your version of Timese ... You then went out and shot to illustrate the commentary, word for word ... You shot dozens of snippets around every scene ... because all they were wanted for was to carry words ...' He then goes on to express surprise that not a word of his 'commentary' ever finished up in the final film. Surely he must have realised that a commentary cannot be written – let alone recorded – until you have a final cut of the picture.

This was certainly not my experience – or indeed method. And few, if any, shot more footage, away from head office, on their own, as I did. Back in New York with, for example, all the film I brought back from Formosa, while editor Leo Zochling made an assembly of the material, Sam Bryant and I drafted a commentary – bearing in mind all the time what we needed to say and show in the space of eighteen minutes' screen time. Writing of commentary and editing of film proceeding in parallel – with commentary more often than not setting the pace. Commentary written in the well-known punchy MOT style, so much a hallmark of the series.

The more orthodox way of going about things is, of course, for director and editor first of all to put their material together in the cutting room, and only when they and all concerned are happy with the result does someone say, right – now let's get so-and-so to do a commentary. It was this immediate shotgun wedding of word and picture that gave the *March of Time*, for better or for worse, its own particular style and impact. And, to match sentences which never wasted words and always conveyed another level of information related to but not literal to the action on the screen, shots were kept short. Never any camera movement, for this would delay the rat-a-tat rhythm in ears and on screen. The average length of a shot in a typical MOT was seven feet of 35mm film – that is, less than five seconds.

But every now and then the *March of Time* broke out of the limitations of its stylistic straightjacket and short film series format. Some time before Pearl Harbor brought the United States into the Second World War, Louis de Rochemont had used the other element in its technique – that is on-the-spot dialogue location filming – as the basis of *The Ramparts We Watch*. A feature-length reconstruction of how an American small town reacted to the events leading up to the First World War: a deliberate anti-isolationist parallel. India presented a similar opportunity. For with the fall of China to Mao Tse-tung, it now appeared to the American public at large that the one hope for western

160

style democracy in Asia – at least as understood by their own founding fathers – lay in that vast subcontinent only recently free from British colonial rule. An experience with which Americans had considerable historical sympathy themselves, and at this time therefore no little interest. As well then as the scheduled releases, *Asia's New Voice* and *The Promise of Pakistan*, I received instructions to set up and shoot a feature-length study of the life and times of Prime Minister Jawaharlal Nehru, and the hundreds of millions of people over whose destiny he then presided.

Out-takes from the coverage I had already made for the regular releases would obviously be incorporated. I had already filmed Nehru at work in his office, at a meeting of his cabinet, reviewing troops in Kashmir, and addressing a giant gathering of the Congress Party. I had been introduced to and had a long talk over tea with his daughter Indira, who was in time to follow in his footsteps as a most controversial Prime Minister of India herself. I had met and filmed Nehru's sister, Mrs Vijaya Laksmi Pandit, in turn India's Ambassador to the Soviet Union, the United States, and Great Britain.

The last thing I had in mind was a Lowell Thomas-like travelogue. Could Nehru, about to visit the United States himself for the very first time, be, I wondered, the peg and personality as it were on which to hang the story of his contradictory, turbulent and wonderful land? But the true nature and essence of this extraordinary person, a fusion of high-class Brahmin with British public school, a patrician scholar with political activist, completely escaped the camera. Before which, like every politician and doubtless every one of us if the truth be known there was, always, a performer. If he spoke, it was for posterity. When he acted, it was for effect. A little *cinéma-vérité* might indeed have helped a bit here.

I brooded, I pondered, and I read. I read book after book on Nehru, about India. I read Jawaharlal's own autobiography. At our second meeting I asked him to autograph my copy. Willingly he did so, telling me, however, that he thought more highly of *The Discovery of India* which he had written for his daughter when imprisoned by the British. And then I realised that to get the personality of Nehru on the screen I had to capture nothing less than something as intangible as the Indian Personality. And this, I think to a small degree, I finally did – by building my film around six personalities, representative of the spectrum of Indian life. An Untouchable, outcast to the Hindu hierarchy – and a highborn Brahmin Priest, highest of the high. A poor peasant, on the eve of his wedding to a fourteen-year-old he had never met; and a Maharajah who had just spent over a million rupees on the marriage of his daughter. A half-caste (as the West calls those of European origin with coloured blood) schoolteacher, teaching his beleaguered community the English language their sires and forefathers had brought as another element in the Indian tapestry – and a young highborn but progressive intellectual working as a subeditor on a Calcutta newspaper. This final character and personality exemplified the new and outward-looking India Nehru strove to create – and once himself was.

In this young man, Satyabrata Chatterjee, this wheel of multiple personality – every individual a facet of Nehru's own – came full circle. *The Discovery of India* was the discovery of Nehru. The *Discovery of Nehru* was the discovery of India.

Still in pursuit of the personalities, and the personality of the time, late September 1949, I had then flown from India to Japan. There, in Tokyo, I had a date with *The Mikado* – in fact with two Mikados, the one in every way the mirror image of the other.

The dichotomy of Japan's defeat in World War Two, dramatised through the personalities of victor and vanquished, conqueror and conquered, was the subject of my next assignment for the *March of Time*. Two men dominated this story, preeminent in their respective persons and myth – the Emperor of Japan and General of the Army Douglas MacArthur. Cultural personality, and the clash of cultures expressed through personality, was the keynote of the approach to this one. MacArthur appeared in a picture book newly issued to Japanese children for the furtherance of democracy, a political concept which the American Occupation was serenely certain of having taught the Japanese in the short span of four years. One first saw this Supreme Commander Allied Powers – SCAP – at prayer, his head not only bowed, but uncovered. Four officers stood at attention behind this picture of MacArthur. They were, so it was captioned, praying with him for the peace of the world, and it was in keeping with this spirit that the General wore none of his military awards. Other illustrations showed Japanese children bringing him flowers, and doves hovered over his head. In one, he was offering to share his office elevator with a humble Japanese. This was entitled 'Kindness'.

I thought I could do as well as the compiler of this picture book, but, as it turned out, that somewhat imaginative artist had an advantage over me. Although the General viewed the *March of Time* with the greatest possible favour and approval, I was never able to film him actually at work in his office, high in a requisitioned insurance company's building known as the Dai Ichi (Number One) in Tokyo, or at the American Embassy where he lived. No pictures had ever been permitted of SCAP at his desk, or at his home, and none ever were. In time I fathomed the reason: MacArthur never attended any social function, and was never photographed other than outside his office when, as a serving officer, he of course wore his military cap. To be seen without it, to be photographed without it perched on his head, above that jaw-jutting profile would have revealed to all the world that his fast thinning hair was indeed that of a balding man approaching seventy.

But that Japanese children's book and the *March of Time* did have one picture in common. By arrangement with MacArthur's liaison officers, I mounted camera and lights on the corridor outside his office. They had previously explained to me that, for all his rank and eminence, the General was really no more than a simple soldier; and, as evidence of this sense of identity with those under his command, he would, if confronted by an enlisted man waiting to take the elevator to the ground floor at the time of his departure from the Dai Ichi, invite the soldier to ride down with him. Would not this example of the General's own modest magnanimity make a good sequence for the film?

Indeed it would I had replied. And now, somewhat nervously, a sergeant from MacArthur's own office waited within camera range. Right on cue MacArthur strode into view.

'Waiting to ride in the elevator, Sergeant?'

'Yes, sir.'

'Well, come on in then.'

The dialogue was spontaneous, which was more than can be said for the action.

Many years later I learned that I had been exposed to an even more elaborate charade than it even appeared to be at the time. Reading William Manchester's monumental 1979 biography of MacArthur, *American Caesar*, I realised that this elevator routine was part of the standard SCAP repertoire: 'On one occasion which became famous throughout Japan, the General was entering the Dai Ichi elevator when a small Japanese, already in it, began to bow himself out, MacArthur signalled him to remain. Later he received a letter which, translated, read 'I am the humble Japanese carpenter who last week you not only permitted but insisted ride with you in the same elevator. I have reflected on this act of courtesy for a whole week, and I realise that no Japanese General would have done as you did'. Newspapers ran the story, a one act play was written about it, and a Tokyo artist painted a heroic canvas of the elevator confrontation which was reproduced and hung in Japanese homes. And, with the set redressed, and another performer to back up the star, I realised that I had followed on to put this priceless performance on film.

To resurface, forty years later, in the first instalment of *Nippon*, the BBC's monumental 1990 series of Japan since the war: still and always the only image of the great man actually inside the fastness of the Dai Ichi.

Across the road from the Dai Ichi, beyond a moat, and inside a great walled enclosure, there dwelt that other personality, an older but more diminutive divinity: and my approach to this Imperial Household was altogether more successful.

SCAP had let it be known through the right and proper channels that the inclusion of the Emperor in this film would be considered a good thing, and I was introduced to the Marquis

Hirohito

Awaits instructions

Yasymasa Matsudaira, the Head of the Bureau of Ceremonies, in order that we could discuss something for which there was no precedent. Like every one of his eighty million subjects, Hirohito was anxious to please, and to do what was considered right in the eyes of those who had so suddenly propelled him with his people into this unaccustomed democracy; but there was some hesitation all the same at being revealed to all the world as something less, or more, than a little man on horseback endlessly reviewing bowing troops sworn to serve him unto death.

Many a monarch of the modern democratic world had appeared in *March of Time* was my argument. To prove my point and argue my case I had a copy of the recently completed *Sweden Looks Ahead* flown out from New York and delivered to the Imperial Household. In due course it was returned, with the word that we too could go ahead. Apparently the spectacle of the octogenarian King Gustav wielding a nimble tennis racquet in the intimacy of his palace grounds at Stockholm had done the trick.

Two hours' drive from Tokyo, past Yokohama and villages crowded in amongst abrupt and miniature hills, winding now and then along the coast, by way of the great Buddha at Kamakura, I drove with Matsudaira to the small seaside town of Hayama on the shores of Sagami Bay. Through a guarded gate let into a high wall veiled with shrubbery, the chauffeur steered us up a short, white-pebbled and carefully raked drive to the front entrance of the low, black-tiled building which was the Emperor's summer retreat. And now there approached a straw-hatted and knicker-bockered little man who, until three years before, had been worshipped as the living descendant of Amaterasu, the Sun Goddess and the creator of both heaven and earth.

Giggling with shyness at this wholly unaccustomed experience, Hirohito chatted with his consort, the plump and matronly Empress Nagako; and, with these scenes of an obviously happy and simple middle-aged couple enjoying a stroll in their garden successfully recorded, we adjourned to the beach – where precedent and custom were wholly abandoned.

In the past, no one – but no one – had ever been permitted a greater literal eminence than the Emperor. At his passage through the streets of towns and villages the upper stories of buildings had been rigorously cleared and shuttered. No one could ever be permitted to look down upon this passing incarnation of their divine destiny. But now, with sleeves rolled up, Hirohito grubbed about amongst the flotsam and jetsam of the rock pools left behind by the receding waters of the Pacific; while, looking over him, I directed his exploration of the aqueous world in which he found solace and escape from his people's predicament. An acknowledged expert in marine biology and author of the 'Opisthobranchia of the Sagami Bay Region', Hirohito carefully filled his test tubes with the hydrozoa and amoebae whose company and study he obviously preferred to the duties and responsibilities which an accident of birth had forced upon him.

The next day Matsudaira drove me further down the coast to Numazu, where the Crown Prince – and future Emperor – was enjoying his summer holiday with his younger brother Masahito. Then a poised and confident sixteen-year-old, Akihito splashed about and swam around for the benefit of my camera.

Ever a practical people, the Japanese had decided that because the Americans had beaten them, the American way of doing things might well be better than their own. In order to prepare this future emperor for a Japan very differently situated and oriented from the land of his own upbringing, Hirohito had engaged an American tutor for his elder son. A Philadelphian Quaker, Elizabeth Gray Vining was accordingly 'opening windows' on this wider mid-twentieth century world for her illustrious protegé. Amongst other books they read together was Kipling's *Kim*.

Forty-four years before this study session, the Japanese had defeated the Russians and smashed the Czarist fleet at Tsushima – an event that had led not only to mutiny aboard the battleship *Potemkin*. but also the appointment by Theodore Roosevelt of MacArthur's father as American military attaché in Tokyo and chief observer with the Japanese Army in Manchuria. So impressed had been the President with General Arthur MacArthur's reports that he had then assigned him to a complete study of all the colonial lands of the Far East, and the then twenty-five-year-old lieutenant had accompanied his father in what was to be one of the most formative experiences of his life. The grand tour had sailed from Yokohama direct for India and the North West Frontier, the land of Kipling's fame and fable; and SCAP legend had it that MacArthur was so carried away at the time by the adventures of Kipling's *Kim* that he too had walked on foot, down the Grand Trunk Road, in search of enlightenment.

Now another Arthur MacArthur held pride of place in the General's heart, the twelve-year-old son of his second marriage; but, having met and filmed the attractive and gracious Mrs Jean MacArthur deputising as usual for her husband at a diplomatic reception, I turned down the suggestion of a sequence of the General's wife and son shopping in the occupation forces' exclusive Post Exchange stores – 'just like everyone else' – as a substitute for further scenes of the great man himself. For I had no taste for any more charades and was sick of the whole mystique of *MacArthur's Japan* – which to me was a depressing compound of the fake and the fallacious.

From the moment of my landing at Tokyo's Haneda airport I had loathed its atmosphere. Unmet, ungreeted, I had been driven in a GI bus for mile after mile of semidarkness through depressing and seemingly endless slums. At last, the Press Club finally discovered, I found myself master of a cell in which there was just sufficient space to stand between wall and bed. I descended into a bar that boasted every known brand of whisky, four fruit machines forever spinning, and the most mediocre company conceivably assembled.

The cream of correspondents covering Japan had all made their homes in private houses and seldom visited this depressing dormitory. Seldom did it see such veterans of the Japanese scene as Frank Hawley of the London *Times*, an erudite scholar whose despatches, based on twenty years' involvement in Japan, were to incur MacArthur's Olympian wrath; and Carl Mydans, chief of *Time* and *Life*'s Tokyo bureau.

Hawley had been a Japanese prisoner and had spent eight months in solitary confinement. Both Carl Mydans and his wife

Shelley had been captured in Manila, to be finally repatriated by way of Shanghai and neutral Goa where, with fifteen hundred other American and Canadian citizens, they had been exchanged for a similar number of Japanese interned in the United States via the steamships *Teia Maru* and the *Gripsholm*.

But in the dispiriting misery of the Press Club one personality stood out like a beacon, *Time* magazine's Frank Gibney. A former naval interpreter of my own age, Gibney was the possessor of a sceptical sense of humour which, allied to his deep love and understanding of the real Japan, was to lead to his writing, in *Five Gentlemen of Japan*, the definitive book of the period. Together we cut loose from the depressing apron strings of SCAPery and, with his fluent mastery of the Japanese language aiding our freedom as correspondents to visit the premises and people of a land 'Off Limits' to its occupying force, the ten weeks of my stay became tolerable after all.

In Japan, around the personalities and backgrounds of its two dominant figures of that time, I tried to bring into focus the confusion of an experiment as new as the inculcation of democracy. Women, for the first time, were now to 'exercise their influence on a political and social course of Japan's destiny'. At Tokyo University, I filmed something which was still an innovation – a co-educational class; and, in a newly formed women's club whose premises overlooked the great naval base at the mouth of Tokyo Bay, photographed some rather perplexed participation by this presumably gentler sex in the civil affairs of their own community.

Novelty rubbed shoulders with survivals from an age-old past. Japan now had her own advocates of Western ways in the form of *Nisei*, Japanese-Americans formerly resident in California. During the War these American citizens of Japanese origin had been regarded as potential Fifth Columnists, and interned. Back in Japan, with the war over, and now in American uniform, they toured the country extolling the democratic way of life. And less than twenty-four hours after I had filmed them at work in Kyoto, my camera recorded the passing of the *Yamahoko Junku* of the Gion Matsuri Shinto festival – in appearance very much a miniature variation of the Juggernaut – the idol of Krishna – that I had previously filmed in southern India.

My companion, interpreter, and Man Friday, with whom I at last drove out, by jeep, from the SCAPist suburbia of the Occupation into the Japanese countryside, was the office boy from the Tokyo bureau of the *Time* and *Life* magazines. His name was Honabusa, but Frank Gibney had christened him 'Dagwood', after one of the real immortals in the mythology of the comic strip, the much put-upon husband of 'Blondie' (whose trials and tribulations were now being syndicated to a Japanese newspaper). Dagwood's youth and cynicism had saved him from any participation in his country's recent past, and he had a healthy disrespect of all authority. He combined this with an eagerness to serve, a highly developed sense of self-mockery, and a very fair command of English.

With Dagwood as interpreter and contact man, I established myself for a time in a country inn a few miles from Maizuru, on the shores of the inland sea. All was peace in my little apartment of eight tatami mats – the units of the floor about an inch and a half thick and approximately six feet by three, by the number of which the size of a Japanese room is calculated. The walls were of plain plaster, divided into segments resembling the floor by narrow strips of wood. The doors were sliding panels covered in thin paper, and the whole of one side was a window with sliding glass doors in wooden frames leading straight out into a garden by way of a verandah. On one wall hung a painted ideogram. But there was no other furniture, decoration or colour. Lying at night in the bedding made up on the floor of this austere room I felt relaxed and at ease for the first time since landing at Haneda Airport six weeks before.

Half of Japan's cultivated land had been owned by less than one tenth of her farmers, of whom the great majority, in the past, had been forced to pay as much as three quarters of their crop as rent for the privilege of working land they did not own. In its most enlightened reform SCAP had swept away this agrarian feudalism, and all absentee landlords had been forced to sell their land to the government. A bearded and ancient farmer radiated approval at a village meeting that we filmed in the rice fields near Maizuru.

But what had really brought me to this corner of Japan was another injection into the Japanese psyche and personality – little short of schizophrenic this time.

Faithful to his promise to join the Allied struggle against Japan after victory had been achieved in Europe, Stalin had attacked Japan's continental flank from Siberia forty-eight hours after the first atomic bomb had burst over Hiroshima. In the course of rendering this now superfluous assistance to Japanese defeat, the Soviet Far Eastern forces had gathered up most of the machinery from Manchuria's highly developed industry and scooped up as prisoners a million Japanese.

For years nothing had been heard of Japan's lost Manchurian army. It had vanished into the Siberian silence. But, four years after their capture, on a windy and overcast July afternoon, I focused my camera across the waters of the Bay of Maizuru towards the lighters that were bringing the first of these missing men home.

'Are these men or beasts the Soviets are sending back to Japan from their prison camps? It is no wonder that an anguished mother welcoming her long-absent son should cry out: "What have they done to my son?" This was the anguished tone of the *Nippon Times* two weeks later, for these prisoners of war were being sent home as thoroughly 'brainwashed' as any to be taken in the Korean War yet to be fought, which would destroy MacArthur and render the technique so familiar. Glaring at my lens, striking aside the hands eagerly proffered to help them ashore, ignoring the little nurses pathetically bowing their rejected welcomes, these sullen-faced men formed up and marched off into the land of their birth – where it was hoped they would now assist in the task of making it over into the image of their captors.

'Where is their individuality?' the *Nippon Times* went on to ask. 'Where is their feeling for family and home? Where is their sentiment for their native land? Where is their respect for law and order? Perhaps the repatriates themselves should not be

171

Japanese prisoners returned from Manchuria

172

judged too severely for they are the products of Communist training. They are the ones so well indoctrinated that the Soviets allowed their return. They are Communists.'

Waiting to greet them with open arms, however, was the Communist Party of Japan; and, thanks to Frank Gibney's contacts, its Central Committee welcomed me and my camera to a dingy headquarters in a back street of Toyko's Yoyogi district with far less formality than we ever experienced in penetrating MacArthur's sanctum in the Dai Ichi. Around a table sat a triumvirate of revolution: Sanzo Nozaka, who had learnt his Marxism the hard way, with Mao Tse-tung in the formative years of Yenan; Yoshio Shiga, the intense young editor of *Akahata* (Red Flag); and Kyuichi Tokuda, the party's theoretician.

That my *March of Time* report penetrated in any way the Japanese personality I cannot claim. We had to wait twenty-five years for that, for the Yorkshire Television – Antony Thomas trilogy of films called *The Japanese Experience*. But as a record of the country at that time, pegged on the two leading protagonists of its contradictory situation, *MacArthur's Japan* will serve. By its very deadpan and 'objective' observation of the two cultures side by side but in collision, it did at least make the point that no contact existed between them whatsoever, except the purely and immediately expedient.

Today Japan is once again a power in the world.

In Europe that screen of change is more and more often than not a Japanese colour television set. Our roads choke up with cars, and more and more of them are Japanese. We are now even employed by them, in our own homelands, in the factories they are building and the real estate they are acquiring, from the Welsh valleys to Rockefeller Center. And already, back then in 1949 – and despite SCAP control and prior censorship of all scripts planned for production – the whole world was about to be made aware of the particular genius and original achievement of Japanese cinema. If any single film could be said to exemplify this breakthrough, this was Akira Kurosawa's *Rashomon*: within a couple of years to sweep all before it at the Venice Film Festi-

Shiga

Tokuda

Nozaka

Central Committee of the Japanese Communist Party

val. Japanese films then went on to win this same Golden Lion premier award for the next four years running, all to be directed by Kenji Mizoguchi – who had made his first motion picture back in 1922, and who had already more than sixty to his credit prior to the American occupation of his homeland.

What an astonishing success story – but always in its heart a contradiction. Shame at losing the war – but no guilt in precipitating it in the first place and then waging it so ruthlessly. By the 1970's the giant pre-war capitalist combines were once again paternally in place – and Communist representation in their government although still marginal had more than doubled. The Japanese themselves seem to be just as puzzled and perplexed by the contradiction in their own nature and character as do we of the rest of the world. In his film *The Ceremony* (which he shot in 1971 under the tile of *Japan and the Japanese*) Nagisa Oshima used as his central narrator a character returned home after the traumatic experience of surrender to, and capture by the Russians in Manchuria. Masuo, his 'Man of Manchuria', left a formalised and traditional Japan to fight and maybe achieve the mystique of death for his Emperor. Shipped back a failure, in defeat, he finds himself both disoriented and rejected by the new Japan of his generation of frantic economic development. In the climactic ceremony of a marriage which is simultaneously a mutual suicide – to which, like all else which has happened in and to his country since his return he bears witness – the Man of Manchuria sees a final confirmation of the loss of everything he once believed in, and which formed his personality as a Japanese.

MacArthur's Japan, as the *March of Time* called the film I shot there in 1949, was very much Hamlet without the Prince. The great man himself only appeared three times. In original newsreel clips of him accepting the Japanese surrender four years before, for once capless at an open air diplomatic reception soon afterwards – and in my own filming of him offering to share the elevator in the Dai Ichi building with a sergeant from his office.

The title was in fact ironic. Although the audience was able to share briefly in the home and working life of an automobile worker at the Toyota plant, there was nothing personalised in the format of *MacArthur's Japan*, still produced like all other such factual documentaries and newsfilm for large cinema scale screens. The voice which accompanied the pictures and told you all about it was not only authoritative, but anonymous. Television was to change this altogether. Now a personality comes into your home, on that little screen in the living room, and you go along with him, or her, to wherever the story leads you both together, electronically hand in hand along the yellow brick road of discovery and enlightenment.

Within less than a year of saying 'Sayonara' to Honabusa and the others in *Time*'s Tokyo office, I was already into the new format on the biggest and most far reaching story of post-war Europe.

Before landing in Japan, the *March of Time* had sidetracked me to China, assigned to film the activities of the United States Economic Cooperation Administration. ECA. How's that again? This was the official designation of the organisation put together to administer the Marshall Plan, the major American post-war effort to help in the rebuilding and recovery of primarily Western Europe. All told, United States taxpayers contributed multiple billions of dollars to this salvage operation. Apart from claiming this as necessary to combat the threat of Communist takeover, the question was how, in a short programme, to render this palatable to the mass taxpaying TV viewing American public across the land. To use the definition soon to become basic to the TV vocabulary, who could *present* this enormously complex political economic story in an understandable and personal way? Still held in great affection by Americans, the answer was a woman. Eleanor Roosevelt. Endlessly energetic wife of the four times President of the United States, Franklin Delano Roosevelt. Widowed since his death in the closing year of the war, in no way retired gracefully from the public scene. In fact some were to say that it was only now that she was really coming into her own.

176

MACARTHUR

The private public person

In the Spring of 1950, Mrs Roosevelt was invited by the Government of Norway to unveil a statue of her late husband in Oslo. She accepted. As soon as this was known, to be showered by follow-up invitations throughout Western Europe – where of course the Marshall Plan was by then well underway and showing results. Hearing of this itinerary in Washington, the ECA's Administrator Paul Hoffman – a former head of General Motors – and his advisors saw the opportunity. Hoffman persuaded Mrs Roosevelt to cooperate in the making of a film for television of her trip abroad, in which she could be seen to witness and heard to describe the success of Western European recovery. Who then to make this film?

Headed up by a former *March of Time* producer, Lothar Wolff, ECA's own film division located in Paris had already proved to be a great shot in the arm for documentary film-makerthroughout Western Europe, commissioning many producers to salute and dramatise its achievements on screen, together with its implied aim of European Economic Unity. Most ambitious, and already in the works, was a five part *Changing Face of Europe*, in which the renowned British documentary director Humphrey Jennings was to meet his untimely and accidental death in Greece.

The *March of Time* had itself already made one of its own regular releases on the Marshall Plan, following Hoffman around the countries and problems involved. In the Cold War rhetoric of the time, this they called *Answer to Stalin*. No surprise then when the *March of Time* got the contract to make the film with Mrs Roosevelt. And who to shoot the film? Who else but our globe-trotting cameraman-director now based in London.

Unfortunately when Mrs Roosevelt agreed to do this film of a similar such tour, she had failed to realise that this meant a cameraman going along with her all the way. And not just she alone having to put up with this. Accompanying her would be her third son Elliott, together with his teenaged son and daughter, her grandchildren; the former First Lady planning it all as very much part family vacation. Elliott was to be enraged at this, and all along the way was to do his best to get me dumped off the aircraft at one or another stopover. It was to become a duel of wits between the two of us. He had expected the film to be assembled from material shot by different and local cameramen, in the various locations, left behind in each case on departure – not by an outsider, and a non-American at that – imposed on them all the way on what he regarded as a private family affair.

Apart from the filming, I therefore did my best to keep my distance. The entire length of the aircraft flying us from place to place for a start. The four Roosevelts were always up front. Right at the rear, and on the port side of the plane, *March of Time* cameraman. Alongside, and across the aisle, unless summoned forward, Mrs Roosevelt's devoted longtime secretary Malvina Thompson. No one else. Just we six passengers. However in Ms Thompson I found an ally. She understood the situation and appreciated the commitment. Making certain that whatever false and later departure times Elliott sent my way, I was always there for the take-off. Her own main commitment was to transcribe and transmit Mrs Roosevelt's unfailing dictation of 'My Day'. Her daily column syndicated and published as it then was in up to three hundred newspapers stateside. This I also included in my filming.

So there I was, near Midsummer Day 1950, in Oslo, negotiating a good camera setup from which to film the unveiling of the statue of President Roosevelt, which the people of Norway had subscribed to as a symbol of their respect and gratitude to FDR and the American People.

From the unveiling ceremony itself, we had then been whisked to a reception by the Foreign Minister, to be airborne after two further days of hectic sightseeing for Sweden. From a breakneck tour of the factories and social institutions of that model welfare state, the former president's wife had flown along the rim of the Soviet world to Helsinki. At Rovaniemi, on the Arctic Circle, I filmed their excitement at the spectacle of the midnight sun which refused to sink beneath the horizon; whence, as we watched, it began a stubborn climb back into a sky from which it was never absent in summer and sadly missed in winter.

But the cold air of northern neutrality was as nothing to the frigidity between Elliott and myself. In their off-duty hours I could at least relax with the captain and crew of the United States Air Force plane which was flying us around. In Finland our hosts invited us to the intimately convivial atmosphere of a sauna, which Elliott refused; and in which, at that time, I would willingly have boiled him alive.

Being part of the Roosevelt family group, and not therefore entirely dependent on the formal ECA itinerary, really did however pay off. Adding to the film an altogether personal and human dimension.

Back we had flown once more to the lands of the Marshall Plan and the model cooperatives of the Danish countryside, and a meeting with Mrs Eugenie Anderson: until the appointment of Henry Luce's consort to Rome, the United States' only woman Ambassador. There we had transferred ourselves into automobiles, and driven to Holland – and to a moving welcome in the little town from which one Claes Martenszen had sailed to New Amsterdam in 1636. Once settled in the New World this Dutchman had decided to be known by the name of this, the village from which he had emigrated – Rosenvelt – and here I filmed the three latest generations of this illustrious American family against their original European background.

The late President's maternal ancestors, the Delanos, had come from Luxembourg, and so that little duchy had been next on our list. There his grandchildren, pursued as ever by my camera, visited the old castle of the Delanois, now a hotel. On we had driven, to Bastogne, and the site of the encircled General McAuliffe's classic refusal to surrender during the 'Battle of the Bulge'; and on to the nearby grave of George Patton, resting place of this most dashing commander of a victory which had made his country the new master of Western Europe; to Paris, for a call on President Vincent Auriol, and a tour of Versailles. Here at last the parting of the ways for Elliott and myself. Much to our mutual relief.

The next item on his mother's programme was to be an address to the Headquarters Staff of the United States 3rd Air

Force just outside London. I flew ahead of her, and routed out the *March of Time*'s British crew and their sound recording equipment. Knowing that Mrs Roosevelt would invite questions from her audience, I had then prevailed upon an American airman, carefully placed within camera range, to rise immediately to his feet and ask her what impressions she had formed of European recovery.

Mrs Roosevelt rose to the bait exactly as I had hoped, and launched into an enthusiastic reply. This provided the film with the perfect climax and summing up that it needed. Later that same day, at a press conference in London, further interrogation had been forthcoming from British journalists. What, she was asked, did she think of the attitude of the American airmen serving overseas whom she had visited that morning? Whereupon this dear sweet lady had replied that she had been most impressed by the intelligent nature of their questions.

My Trip Abroad turned out to be the most successful of all the films of European recovery televised coast to coast by the American Broadcasting Company.

It was however not long before I was back once again with the British-based United States 3rd Air Force, and this time for real. For this was SAC, Strategic Air Command. The other side of Marshall Plan coinage, and the nuclear answer to Stalin. The *March of Time* had come up with a release to be focused entirely on this constantly alert, constantly airborne, nuclear strike force. Its targets already pre-planned and programmed, deep inside the Soviet Union. For what the editors chose to call *Flight Plan For Freedom*, along with my camera I flew on one such rehearsal for Armageddon. Deep in the belly of a B52. Only a few feet above the bomb hold. But it was not as yet – or so I hoped – either aboard, let alone primed.

5. FILM AND WAR

'Go there, see it, tell it, bring it back.'

Kate Adie

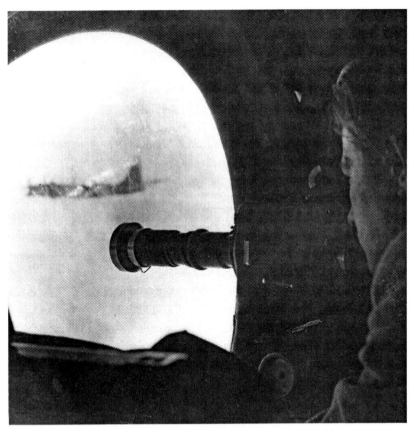

Author flying and filming on a nuclear bomb run with the American Air
Force - The Cold War, 1951

MacArthur was one of *The Commanders*, a BBC series of prominent military leaders of World War Two, presented on American television in 1975, thirty years to the day after he accepted Japan's unconditional surrender. A series, claimed the BBC, which 'examines the way that a few unusual men of different nations rose to the challenge of high command'. Other eminent warriors in further episodes, which mixed reminiscent interview with archive material, were Britain's Sir Arthur 'Bomber' Harris who 'took out' Dresden and Sir William Slim who reconquered Burma, the Soviet Union's Georgi K. Zhukov, Germany's Erwin Rommel, Japan's Isoroku Yamamoto, and the United States' Dwight D. Eisenhower.

The format was simple. Interviews with aged but still surviving colleagues – from now, of course, both sides of the battle – were intercut with film of their various campaigns and conflicts shot at the time.

On the screen, war in general, and World War Two in particular, exercises endless fascination. Programme after programme, series after series, high camp or deadly serious, continues to stream forth on television. One of the reasons for this is of course the cheap availability of all that mileage of movie material shot on film by hundreds of combat cameramen, on each and every side of the firing lines. Now producers can really put together programmes of a World at War showing it how it was on both sides of a battle at the same time, and take a more 'objective' view of who was really to blame and did we really have to bomb Dresden.

With old wars and new wars still taking up so much time on our screens, and some of us still actively involved in actually filming it – at Poona one of the students was soon to don a uniform and shoot the battle for Bangladesh – so why don't we take a look at how war has been portrayed on film, how film has gone to war, and what it feels like to film it?

A war correspondent claimed to have set up a 'cinematograph' camera during an early Greek and Turkish scrap back in 1897. This same Frederic Villiers has described his attempt at film coverage of the Battle of Omdurman – forty years before

Zoltan Korda restaged it in Technicolor for *The Four Feathers*. But it was over on the shores of the New World that the motion picture camera first deliberately chose to go to war, and one of the cameramen concerned has left us with a racy account of their experience.

Carrying their camera up the gangplank of a troop transport loading in Tampa, Florida, Albert E. Smith and J. Stuart Blackton were hailed and halted by Teddy Roosevelt, then embarking his 'Rough Riders'.

'What are you young men up to?' he asked.

'We are the Vitagraph Company', was the reply, 'and we are going over to Cuba to take moving pictures of the war'.

The year was 1898. Only nine years after Edison had first produced and projected a motion picture in the peepshow form of the *Kinetoscope*, Manifest Destiny – and the Monroe Doctrine – had brought the United States into conflict with Spain. With a loss of more than two hundred American sailors, the Battleship *Maine* had blown up in Havana Harbour. 'The Spanish in colonial occupation of Cuba must have been responsible for this outrage', cried newspaper publisher William Randolph Hearst, seizing on this excuse for the war he eagerly sought and energetically propagandised. 'You provide the pictures and I'll furnish the war', Hearst is alleged to have cabled the artist he had despatched to seemingly nonexistent battlefields. 'You provide the prose poems, I'll provide the war', cables in turn Orson Welles' Citizen Kane, at that point in the movie's parallel of the tycoon's life and times.

Billy Bitzer, later to photograph *The Birth of a Nation* and *Intolerance* for Griffith, attempted to snatch shots of this earlier Cuban – American conflict with a *Biograph* camera so cumbersome that it had to be horse drawn. For the opposition *Vitagraph*, Al Smith and Stuart Blackton also did their best to give Hearst, and the American public, moving pictures of this turn of the century war in the Caribbean.

But the equally unwieldy inadequacies of their own primitive equipment, and the hit-and-run nature of the fighting, utterly defeated their attempts at genuine combat coverage. The original

184

Edison camera was so heavy that it required at least two men to move and handle it. An inventive pioneer in his own right, Smith had designed and built a much lighter model himself, incorporating the basic mechanical method of the former but encasing his adapted mechanism in a more compact and less weighty wooden box. He also cut the weight down by the use of separate, external and detachable wooden boxes to house and take up the unexposed and exposed film. Magazines as we now call them. To improve still further on Edison, he had set his heart on a lens of a longer focal length than the wide-angles then standard for the full and static one-take long-shot general views that were all that the 'films' of Edison's Kinetoscopes ever amounted to. A friend whose father made magic lantern slides found a three inch lens in a box in the family shop. So off to war went Smith, with his own self-designed camera, equipped with a lens which would get him an image closer to the action than any item of motion picture apparatus hitherto available in those primitive days of the cinema's infancy. Even so, it still weighed the better part of fifty pounds, and had to be mounted on a tall non-collapsible tripod before it could be worked by the crank handle jutting out from its side.

When Teddy Roosevelt's 'Rough Riders' set up their own more lethal equipment with which to shoot that Spanish-American war in Cuba, they lay flat on their faces, only getting to their feet as they scrambled up the hill behind Santiago in an attempt to seize that key port from the land to its rear. Hauling camera, tripod, and film along with them, Smith and Blackton had a tough time trying to keep up, and after two Spanish bullets had smashed their way through the solid mahogany of their camera's casing, they judged it time to retreat.

For *Vitagraph* they had material of the original landing, troops in camp and on the move, artillery manoeuvred and fired. Exclusive excitement enough and indeed for the folks back home and very saleable at so much a foot. On a troopship returning to Tampa, they heard gunfire over the horizon. This was the battle at sea which decided the campaign, the United States Navy destroying the Spanish fleet as the latter tried to make a run for it.

Our two cameramen disembarked to this news, and the realisation that they had not a foot of this victory, a naval action which cleared the Caribbean of seemingly hostile shipping until Khrushchev sent his missiles into Cuba sixty years later. What were Smith and Blackton to do? The resources and ingenuity which had built the camera in the first place could surely recreate the Battle of Santiago Bay, and in Vitagraphs' rented office on the top floor of New York's Morse Building this they accordingly did.

Blackton was by way of being something of an artist. One of his larger canvas-covered frames was placed behind an upside-down table, covered with water an inch deep. On this canvas background he painted white clouds on a blue sky. On the water in the foreground floated cutout photographs of ships of the rival fleets, brought from street vendors outside. Little shelves on which they were nailed supported these cutouts, and provided a hidden platform behind them on which pinches of gunpowder were exploded as battle commenced. Thin thread pulled the 'ships' along in the right order. Blackton set off the powder flashes with a wire taper concealed to the rear of all this contraption. Smith cranked the camera. Mrs Blackton puffed cigarette smoke under its lens, and an enthusiastic office boy added to the atmosphere with the single most expensive item of equipment, a ten cent cigar. And so on to American screens, and into the history books of the cinema, pass *The Battle of Santiago Bay* and *Fighting With Our Boys in Cuba*.

One year later an expanding and ambitious Vitagraph despatched Smith to another war, in another continent.

'Great quarrels,' Winston Churchill once wrote of the Boer War, 'often arise from small occasions but never from small causes'. The Dutch had been settling in South Africa since the seventeenth century, but by the end of the nineteenth they were outnumbered in their landlocked republics by the British, driving in from the coast. Gold it was that beckoned, the largest and richest reef of this metal ever to be discovered, right under the surface of the sanctuary to which these Boer descendants of Dutch settlers had trekked in search of a homeland of their own.

They just wanted the world to leave them alone. But it was not to be. Came this clash between Boer fundamentalist, happy to raise his family, farm his fields, obey his Bible, and energetic British ambition, gobbling up territory and raw materials at this height of industrial and imperial expansion.

Boer Commandos hold position against the British – Boer War, 1900

Leaving Blackton behind not only to set up but also produce and direct the growing number of truly fictional single reels Vitagraph were now turning out, with his faithful camera Smith landed in Durban early in December 1899. The main British base was sixty miles to the north. He joined forces with Hearst's correspondent Richard Harding Davis. They hired a horse-drawn cart, put two Africans on their payroll, one to cook and the other to look after the animals, and set forth. They were in time to join up with the force setting out to break through to the British besieged in Ladysmith. General Buller's relieving column had to ford the Tugela near Colenso. Marching as on parade, they were picked off like flies by the superior Boer marksmen on the other side of the river. Back at base, Smith sat down to figure what, if anything, he had got of this defeat. Virtually nothing on film of the actual fighting, as a non-combatant forced with his cumbersome camera and tripod to remain at too far a distance. But if he could stage the Battle of Santiago, so too he would refight the Colenso. He talked some British soldiers into putting on Boer clothes, and going through some mock skirmishes within range of his camera. Firing from behind boulders, they charged his camera, and Vitagraph once more had film from the front.

This time American cameramen were not alone in the field. The Boer was, after all, a British war, and its coverage greatly stimulated the early newsreel. Half a dozen operators sent back scenes such as 'The Scouts in Pursuit of the Boers', 'Bringing the Maxims into Action', 'A Charge and General Fusillade'. Cameraman Joe Rosenthal went along with General French's army to the relief of Kimberley, and Kitchener was filmed on a white charger as he rode in to receive the surrender of Kroonstad. Credited with Edison as the inventor of the first practical movie camera, the British William Kennedy Laurie Dickson was out there filming for a subsidiary of the American Mutoscope and Biograph Company. He had his problems. 'One military officer high in authority has done everything to block my path, and to prevent the world from seeing these views. I have yet to discover his motive.' Sounds all too familiar.

The pioneering British producer Cecil Hepworth brought proceedings to a close with a hundred-and-fifty allegorical feet entitled *Peace with Honour*. A portrait of the victorious Kitchener was seen to be unveiled by an Edwardian beauty dressed and made up as Britannia. A khaki-clad 'soldier' gave three rousing cheers, and then offered the hand of friendship to a 'Boer', led into camera range by our Britannia who beamed approval as the two reenacted adversaries enjoyed a smoke together. The Hepworth Company's publicity release summed up its synopsis with the pious hope that 'may so end all Great Britain's wars'.

Not so the next, and so-called Great War.

The French had cameramen in the field from the beginning, but the War to end wars was already a year old before a War Office Topical Film Committee was formed, and 'Official War Office Kinematographers' sent off to the British front lines..

Representative of this small band of resourceful men was Geoffrey Malins, and he has left us a chronicle of his adventures in a book published some years later, which he somewhat egotistically and exclusively entitled *How I Filmed the War*. He describes how he attempted to overcome the problem of heavyweight equipment with, believe it or not, a camera driven by compressed air. He tells us that another and essential part of his equipment was a foot pump with which to recharge its cylinders; and that while filming gunners in action in a sea of Flanders mud, he ran out of air and his camera ground to a halt.

There was nowhere solid under foot in which to place his machine and the foot pump with which to recharge his cylinders with air. He found some pieces of brick, and with them made a little foundation. Started to pump. After every few thumps on the pump he had to put more bricks under it to prevent it sinking out of sight in the mud . He claims it took him three-quarters of an hour to recharge his 'battery' cylinders in this way, on this occasion, surrounded by gunfire.

Next time back home at base in London, he exchanged this *Aeroscope* camera for a more orthodox but larger hand-cranked machine, and the inevitable tripod on which it had to be mounted. But filming the battle of Neuve Chapelle he must have regretted this. Running for cover from enemy bombardment, he tells how he dropped and lost the crank handle. Nothing daunted, he quickly made a substitute out of a piece of splintered wood and an old nail he found behind a blown up tree trunk.

Because of the lack in those days of any adequate long focus lens, he overcame this even greater disadvantage of not being able to get action close-ups by planting his camera on the parapet in the front line trench, and indulging in a little self-protective camouflage. Told that at dawn the following day the Germans in a blockhouse only a hundred and fifty yards away and dead opposite would be bombarded he arranged, so his story goes, a wooden cylinder through the sandbags that made up the top of

A Canadian Cameraman prepares to ascend in a balloon

French Cinematographer films a wounded Scot

World War One camera unit advances under fire

Cameraman in the ruins of Lens

the British trench, through which to shoot his film more or less protected.

Under cover of darkness that night, two other sandbags were placed in front of its aperture opened out into 'No Man's Land'; so by daylight the line of the sandbags above the British trench would appear unbroken to the enemy, a mere stone's throw opposite. As soon as dawn heralded the start of the bombardment, Malins tells how he pushed the covering bags down from behind with a stick, in order to give his camera, focused as it was down the cylinder, a clear field of view, He overdid it. All the bags fell down. A movement which brought German bullets battering all around his loophole. But he stayed put, and got his film of the blowing up of the German blockhouse.

According to his own account, he commenced his filming of the Battle of the Somme by cranking away with his camera aimed at a point in the enemy trenches underneath which he had been told twenty-two tons of high explosive had been buried to be blown up at H Hour, 17.20, July 1st, 1916.

World War One German camera team setting up on the Balkan front

192

Official German film section on the march

Up it went, certainly producing one of the most awe-inspiring shots of that war. Malins then says he swung his camera round on its tripod and filmed British troops swarming over the parapets of their own trenches, to take what remained of the enemy position by hand. German shellfire sent both him and camera flying, blasting half his tripod away. We are told how he tied it up with pieces of wood, telephone wire, and string, picked up in the surrounding shambles, getting his equipment back into action in time to film the first wounded, now beginning to stream back from the failed 'Big Push' which was supposed to end the War. 'Was I in the picture, sir?' he says they called out as they were carried past.

More recently both Malins' film and the book he wrote have been exhaustively studied by Kevin Brownlow; and in the latter's masterly account of how silent film and silent film cameraman faced up to war, *The War, The West, and The Wilderness*, he quite reasonably maintains that *How I Filmed the War* is so filled with 'preposterous exaggeration that (Malins') real achievements

193

suffer by comparison with his imaginative exploits'. Certainly, and as its title implies, Malins' chronicle could almost be retitled 'How I Won the War', but, having followed in his footsteps (mud included) the next time round, let's not be too hard on him.

The descriptions in a subsequently reminiscent book of graphic filming – not evidenced when viewed in actual projection on a screen – can lie in a combination of two factors, one subjective and the other objective. Filming vast emotional action, like men going bravely to their death, can create an impression of participation which the camera, unless it becomes itself a participant, is failing to communicate in the static long-shot views of an unimaginative photographer. The cameraman, as a human being, is caught in close-up in the action. The camera, as a machine operated by non-creative film-makers like Malins, is not. It is therefore perfectly possible, unless you are yourself a creative film-maker, directing to a degree action as well as camera, to believe that because it is happening all around you and you are cranking away at that handle, that it must all be going on film as well. Malins quite likely did believe that what he described he had also filmed. And so he had. But only in the general views of the manner of his time. The newsreel cameramen of the Second World War worked much the same way. It is nearly always in long shot. Even though they would emerge themselves shaken from involvement in the action at which they had aimed their cameras.

Viewing not long ago the newsreel footage shot of the 1950-53 Korean War, I found that there are still no close-ups – except those of Chinese prisoners. The enemy – strange, inscrutable, Oriental which, working still in the mould of the Second World War, cameramen clearly found more fascinating than their own men. And, as prisoners, they could not object if you thrust a camera right into their faces.

And moreover, it is perfectly possible that in retrospect Malins did come to realise the fundamental inadequacy of his filming – and decided to justify himself in print. After all, what am I doing right now!

194

In the lengthening years since we filmed World War Two I continue to ponder the approach of myself and other British Army cameramen to the coverage of that conflict. It seems to me that we suffered a psychological blockage. We were, to start with, first and foremost soldiers. We had all of us had some year or so of military training, in the ranks, before ever being accepted as combat cameramen, to be issued a camera alongside a revolver and ammunition. Although often very bloody-minded, we still regarded ourselves as soldiers, were numbered and issued orders as soldiers. If we came across a blown up face, a shattered body, friend or foe, we merely muttered 'poor sod' and moved on. It just did not occur to us to take a picture; unless he was still alive and gave us – like Malin's survivors of the Somme – a cheery grin and a 'thumbs-up' sign. Then it was another 'one of our brave lads'. Were we failing in our duty? Our duty as cameramen, if not as soldiers? It did appear, and still appears, that this was a 'just' war. As military moviemakers, our task – with which we willingly identified – was to record the onward march of our own victorious side, hailed as it was by tears of joy by the peoples of Europe, as it triumphantly fought its way through the remnants of Mussolini's Empire and the ruins of Hitler's Third Reich.

But despite the liberation of hellholes like Dachau and Belsen that this brought about, in essence there is nothing noble about war. There is no greater obscenity. And it only remained for Stanley Kubrick to dramatise its final nuclear lunacy with *Dr. Strangelove*.

War is indeed the ultimate ego trip. And this holds true as much for the commander in chief as the combat cameraman. Both are exercising power. The one over the lives of men in the belief that he is saving his country, serving its cause. The other, through his viewfinder, in the belief that in some God-given way he is able to serve as a channel through which others may share in the excitement and 'glamour' of war. It has been left to a later generation of cameramen to identify totally with the rank and file, and attempt to act as self-appointed exorcists of its horrors.

Arnhem

Arnhem cameramen

Dutch nun nurses wounded at Arnhem

San Pietro

197

Let us not forget Bob Capa and Larry Burrows, both dead in Vietnam.

The other factor distancing the picture on the screen from the report on the page in either one of the two world wars was the absence of any worthwhile telephoto lens. No British Army cameraman in 1914-18, or 1939-45 for that matter, had adequate long focus lenses. There just were not any available for the 35 millimetre clockwork hand cameras which were all we had. (Although newsreelers, like *Movietone*'s Paul Wyand in Italy, might have had one – but essentially static and tripod-bound.) So although it was happening all around us, with very rare exception, the most we could ever really hope to get were at best wide angle general views. Nothing had really changed since the Boer War. Writing of Rosenthal's coverage then, the pioneer producer Charles Urban commented back in 1904 that: 'Modern battles are at long distance; the bullets go 'zip, zip', but you can't see the men who fired them: they are too far off. In the olden days it would have been different, when everything was at close quarters. But there were no Bioscopes then'.

So, if an audience was ever to be made to feel participatory in the action of the first two world wars, it became necessary to reconstruct – set up – some action showpieces. With his usual exemplary diligence, Kevin Brownlow has discovered that the famous 'going over the top' sequence in *The Battle of the Somme*, hitherto presumed to be Malins-like actuality, was in fact arranged for the camera at a trench mortar school well behind the lines. Until there developed hand held cameras with real long focus lenses, together with a new breed of combat cameramen who were not militarily committed to the war they had to film, there really was no other way. Compare, for example, the blood and thunder, total close-up 'you are there' on the spectacular re-enactment of *A Bridge Too Far* with the total lack of impact of the sparse material shot by the army cameramen actually dropped with the airborne troops at Arnhem at the time.

The 1920s saw a spectacular number of re-enactments of the great engagements which were already passing into the legend of the previous war. Harry Bruce Woolfe, for the hopefully named

British Instructional Films, produced a series of compilation films made up of original shooting from Malins and others, mixed in with sequences set up and directed later at home. *The Battle of Jutland* employed model ships and tactical maps to trace on the screen the course of that indecisive naval confrontation. At greater length, and with additional reconstructions, *Zeebrugge* demonstrated how the Royal Navy attempted to cut off the North Sea to German submarines by blockading the entrance to the Belgian port which served as one of their main bases.

The most exciting, successful and glamorous British victory at sea in World War One took place, and was fought out, not in home waters at all, but in the far and distant Pacific and Southern Atlantic. At the outbreak of hostilities, two enemy cruisers, an earlier *Scharnhorst* and *Gneisenau*, were reported somewhere off the coast of China, and roaming ominously at will in the path of the convoys bringing Australian and New Zealand troops to France. In the end, no less than two battle cruisers, one battleship, half a dozen heavy and two light cruisers of the Royal Navy – together with the then allied Japanese Fleet providing a distant cover flank – were needed to send these two Germans to the bottom of the sea off the shores of Chile and Argentina in this forgotten battle of World War One. But there was no film of this now legendary British naval engagement in the First World War, let alone a reconstruction, and unlike the army and the air force the navy had no film unit of its own to call on in the Second. This led to a couple of us army cameramen being borrowed to film at sea what all concerned believed would prove to be a real spectacular. In short, a German 'Dunkirk'.

The warfront in North Africa had now narrowed to a tiny area in Tunisia. Bottled up by the victorious American and British forces in a peninsula jutting out into and surrounded by the Mediterranean, the defeated Germans and Italians had but two options – to surrender or attempt to get away by sea. Naturally it was assumed they would do their best to go for the latter, and the Royal Navy concentrated a large force around this Cape Bon to intercept and blow them out of the water.

But no cameramen on the ships to film what would be a truly spectacular climax to the war in Africa.

So, flown out from Egypt to this new battlefront, and by way of Algiers, one day in May 1943 I boarded a Royal Navy destroyer, and for ten days we two army cameramen to and froed, up and down, offshore Cape Bon. Not even a rowing boat ever put out to sea. While every night we listened to the drone of aircraft overhead. The Germans flying out key personnel in the darkness all around us. But not a foot of film had we shot when word reached us that the entire enemy army group, surrounded still intact on land, had surrendered. The war in Africa was accordingly over.

Winched aboard a landing craft which came up alongside to take us back to dry land at Bizerta, we waved goodbye to *HMS Laforet* – to be sunk with all hands on an Arctic Convoy to Russia a few months later.

Bruce Woolfe, and British Instructional Films (on the Board of which there served for a while that imperial romancer John Buchan) received lavish official assistance in their plans to recreate this one decisive British naval victory of World War One. Their film of *The Battles of the Coronel and Falkland Islands* was backed by the Federation of British Industries. The Admiralty lent ships, including some of the actual participants, still in service. Photographed by Jack Parker and Stanley Rodwell, and released in 1927, the result was a great contemporary success, popular with public and critics alike.

More than half a century later, audiences at home were to cheer or swear at their TV screens as a British Task Force once again went into action off these bleak islands in the South Atlantic. The images were this time brought to them by video cameras – delayed by distance and, at times (like Dickson in the Boer War) official and deliberate intention. The 1982 'Battle of the Falklands' brought a new dimension to the screen of war. For the first time, on their nightly TV news, a British audience saw pictures from the other side as well. By way of satellite transmission, their adversaries in the Argentine often got their coverage onto the screen ahead of the British cameramen, plodding along bravely with their ENG equipment towards Port Stanley – by way of San Carlos, Goose Green, and Bluff Cove.

Another British producer saw the destruction of the First World War in more human, if not indeed sentimental terms. In his story of a widow who lost all of her three sons in the last few weeks of the fighting, George Pearson ended this film, *Reveille*, in 1922, four years after the Armistice. By then the symbolic significance of the two minutes' silence on the anniversary of the signing of peace, eleven o'clock on the morning of November 11th, 1918, had become a sacred institution, in which everyone the length and breadth of Britain stopped whatever they were doing and stood with bowed head for a full two minutes; a ritual which was to last unbroken until the next round with Germany broke out the morning of September 3,1939. The climax of *Reveille* is this two minutes' silence. The mother is frozen in the grief of her memory. A problem for the maker of the silent films – how to convey the impact of silence?

This was not such a difficulty for Pearson as it might seem to later film-makers who think that 'silent' films were silent. As viewers of the Thames Television's series *Hollywood* have now been made well aware, they were never shown in silence. From the beginning there was always a sound accompaniment. Either an upright piano, or an orchestra ranging from a few instruments to a full symphonic ensemble. For *L'Assassinat du Duc de Guise* a score was composed as far back as 1908 by no less than Saint-Saëns. Films like *Reveille* were shown with full orchestral score, to which literal sound effects were added by mechanical means. All Pearson had to do, when one of the musicians struck a bass drum to accompany above him on the screen the firing of a gun in close-up signalling the commencement of the silence, was to instruct the conductor to stop playing for two actual minutes – the total silence in the theatre to be only broken two minutes later by a bugler playing an actual Reveille. How many film-makers today would dare to kill their soundtrack dead like that, for as long as that, one wonders?

Four years earlier, Griffith had brought his own silent film epic of World War One to a climax with *sound* alone. On the edge of a battlefield, his heroic French people huddle together for shelter in a ruined farmhouse. Terrified. Then a sound. What was that? Tramp, tramp, tramp. Yes – marching feet. Louder and louder. Nearer and nearer. (Feet of course, of stagehands, tramp, tramp, tramp behind the screen.) Our anguished innocents, staring out of the window of their shattered farmhouse. The whole scene still only played on their faces. And now, at first faintly, but increasingly in volume all the time, a band. A military band, in rhythm with the tramp, tramp, tramp of marching feet. Louder and louder (all the brass in the theatre orchestra now going full blast below the screen). But on the screen, still only the faces of our innocents – now joyful, tears of joy. For only now, in yet another of his famous last minute rescues, do we cut to what they see – the American Army. The New World coming to the rescue of the Old. Line after line, column after column, of American soldiers, marching into battle. Led by the band visually at last on the screen, but actually in the theatre, blaring out the rousing tune of 'Over There'. Cameraman Billy Bitzer's assistant Karl Brown was at that 1918 premiere of *Hearts of the World*. One of a stunned audience who found their feet instinctively beating time, in triumphant and deafening unison, with those *silent* marching men.

The non-talking film reached perhaps its apotheosis with the vast and complex visual metaphor that is Abel Gance's *Napoleon*. The battle for Toulon takes place in pouring rain, at dead of night. The attacking French fall back, despairing and dispirited. Our hero – whose great chance this is – calls for a beating of the drums to rally his troops. But all the drummers are dead, swallowed up in the mud and mire of battle. Supernatural intervention. The rain turns to hail, which beats on the abandoned drums in a furious tattoo. But to what effect? This was a *silent* film. Don't you believe it. At this point the tympanist in the orchestra below the screen (the Paris Opera for the premiere) beat out a rapid and synchronous tattoo on his own drums – and swept us all along to triumph.

With. a few notable exceptions such as King Vidor's *The Big Parade*, most of the films of the First World War originating in

American and British studios were little more than adventure stories. As Paul Rotha summed up the era: 'The barbaric thrill provided by modern methods of war is too exciting to be dampened by a pacifist message. Box office appeal demands only that romance should play its part'.

The arrival of synchronously recorded sound – initially to provide cinemas with an already packaged full orchestral accompaniment (plus crashes and bangs) without the need to pay for live musicians – brought not only the added excitement of real gunfire, but Russian born Lewis Milestone's production of the German Erich Maria Remarque's *All Quiet on the Western Front*. Nobody wins in this one. Death at the instant of reaching for the unattainable and incongruous beauty of a butterfly perched on the edge of a shellhole is its climax, and final comment.

At the time, Paul Rotha believed that this was even eclipsed by a British film. As a climax to their series of reconstructed First World War land battles, of which *Ypres* and *Mons* had also caught the public fancy, Bruce Woolfe and British Instructional Films produced a sound film on the Gallipoli campaign, which had been Churchill's plan to knock the Turks out of the war in 1915 by landing on their coastline in the Eastern Mediterranean. Nowadays only the play *Journey's End* captures the Rupert Brooke-like dialogue on the part of its young heroes – before the reality of war hits them. And only the Russians in their original epic reconstructions of their own revolution had hitherto bettered Geoffrey Barkas's re-enactment, and Anthony Asquith's editing of the Dublin Fusiliers storming ashore from the converted freighter River Clyde which served as their assault craft. *Tell England* was the title of this film. Tell England indeed! 'Tell it what?' Rotha wrote in later hindsight, forty years later. But at the time Grierson too shared his earlier enthusiasm. 'The biggest job,' he wrote, 'so far performed in the history of English cinema … It is in a higher category altogether than other English films ... (but) a film of Gallipoli to be genuine must either be a rollicking farce like (Chaplin's) *Shoulder Arms* or a drab tragedy which finishes in honour but in futility'. As ever, Grierson proved to be a prophet. In 1981 the Australian Peter Weir directed *Gallipoli*, a film in which all honour is given to his countrymen who bore the brunt and futility of fighting in that stricken peninsula.

'I have striven to be, and I have tried all the time to realise that I was the eyes of the millions of my fellow-countrymen at home. In my pictures I have endeavoured to catch something of the glamour, as well as the awful horror of it all. I have caught a picture here, a picture there; a scene in this place, a scene in that; and all the time at the back of my mind has always been the thought: that will give them some idea of things as they are out here'. The *cri de coeur* surely of all combat cameramen, summed up by Geoffrey Malins after his years of filming the trench warfare of World War One – and expressing something of what I myself felt as I set out to follow in his footsteps twenty-three years and another World War later.

As I embarked on a troopship in early December 1941, quite unbeknownst either to myself or my companions of the first muster of a newly formed 'Army Film and Photographic Unit' was a letter which had preceded us, sent from on high only a few weeks before. On the 27th of October, from the War Office where we had just paraded in full battle order, the Secretary of State for War had written to the Commander in Chief Middle East, whence we were now bound. 'My dear General (he was thus addressed and informed) there has been strong criticism in certain quarters of our failure to compete with the Germans in the production of battle films and photographs for propaganda purposes. The demand for battle photographs here and (in the then still neutral) USA is almost insatiable'.

Well, we had accordingly been whisked out of the hodge-podge of different units where we had been languishing since first called to the colours, and were off now to see what we could now do about it. Unfortunately we film men had as yet no cameras with which to do so – although we were assured they would be there and waiting for us when we arrived in Egypt. Obviously they had to be, and eventually were, hand cameras. The American Bell and Howell Eyemos, holding a hundred feet of 35mm in daylight loading spools, with three lenses of varying focal length mounted on a revolvable turret, with a hand grip screwed into the base were, at that time, the most suited. They had become the badge and hallmark of the intrepid newsreel cameraman as played by Clark Gable in *Too Hot to Handle*, and as operated for real by such as Arthur Menken of Paramount News, covering the aerial bombardment of Shanghai and Nanking. But while we of the fledgling British Army Film and Photographic Unit were making our lengthy and laborious six-week voyage in a troopship to the Middle East the Japanese had gone on to bomb Pearl Harbor. One immediate outcome of this was the requisitioning of all Eyemos for the United States Army Signal Corps, as a direct result now also expanding and preparing to film their second World War as well. The only British portable camera was the still too heavy single-lens mounting hand-built magazine-loading Newman Sinclair, and there were only a few of these very solid jobs available anyhow. We were still twenty years away from the development, and complete acceptance of sophisticated l6mm equipment and film really needed for the get up and go, smash-and-grab nature of news and combat reporting.

For we British, now to become increasingly the poor relations of our richer and more powerful ally, it was to be De Vry cameras, very much the poor man's Eyemo. These were little better than sardine cans, hinging in half to be charged with only a hundred feet of 35 millimetre film in daylight loading spools, mounting only one of their three separate lenses at a time on a single socket in front, on the same principle as clipping in an electric light bulb (and only a little more secure); their clockwork motors wound up by a separate crank one was always in danger of losing. None the less, these mechanical lightweights were soon to shoot most of the material for the film which James Agee put highest of all of World War Two. *Desert Victory*, awarded the Oscar for Feature Length Documentary that year of 1943.

Apart from one eighteen inch lens mounted on a very carefully rationed and rarely operated Newman Sinclair camera, the longest focal length lens we had on our De Vrys was a six inch.

Desert battle

Desert victory

Forty years on from the Spanish-American war, we had still only halved our distance from the action – and Rommel fought from far further off than Teddy Roosevelt. So we were still little, if at all, better off than our forebears in Cuba. And it is this, apart from the nature of the fighting, which distinguishes the material shot in Vietnam a quarter of a century later from that older coverage of World War Two. We could never get close enough to the action, in any case dispersed all over the place in that Egyptian Desert in which was fought out such as the Battle of Alamein. With what are nowadays regarded as virtually wide angle lenses, if we ever got close enough for a genuine close-up, then we were dead. As indeed not a few of the more gallant of our little gang were to go on to prove to be the case.

The Second World War produced many a misconception of the popular image of war. Filming the British 2nd Army's assault crossing of the Albert Canal into Belgium, cameraman Jock Gordon was pinned down by crossfire in what little protection he could find underneath a railroad truck. From this restricted position he was at least able to point his camera in the general direction of infantry plunging forth in assault boats from the canal bank below. For his pains he was rewarded with a report from the armchair viewing committee back in England that 'you really must try and get more action and a greater variety of angles – looks like a Sunday afternoon on the river'.

Gordon's armchair critics had viewed his material from the isolated comfort of a projection theatre at Pinewood, now doing its duty as Britain's foremost propaganda film factory. Both Denham and Pinewood Studios had been acquired by the Rank Organisation. Of the two, they decided early in the war to concentrate all feature film production at Denham ('Korda's folly') leasing Pinewood as a base for both the Army and RAF Film Units. Here too was established the Crown Film Unit, now able to make full use of all the artifice available at this major film studio with which to embellish the realism of its documentary tradition. For a tribute to the Merchant Navy called *Western Approaches*, director Pat Jackson, who had previously seldom been able to work with more than a clockwork camera and a few rolls of black-and-white, was now able to construct interior sets of the inside of an enemy submarine, flood, and film its sinking in Technicolor no less. To Pinewood had also been evacuated for safety from the bombed City of London the headquarters of the Royal Mint. (And no one has so far accused Korda of trying to get his hands on that.)

In the North African desert, and the mountains and river valleys of Italy, the Second World War never even remotely resembled the spectacular blood and thunder of the Hollywood reconstructions that cinemagoers had been brought up to believe in as the real thing. 'Viewed as a drama, the war is disappointing' D.W. Griffith is reported as saying when visiting France in 1918. Eisenstein's epic reconstruction of the mass storming of St. Petersburg's Winter Palace in his film *October*, ten years after the event, has now, thanks to its use again and again as a clip in television compilation programmes on the Russian Revolution, become accepted as a visual reality, how it was. In point of fact, the premises were actually occupied by a handful of sailors, few stone-cold sober.

War, like the death it brings and celebrates, is so huge and total an experience in all its entirety, that its genuine and grisly essence can rarely, if ever, be encompassed in a single shot; and only and rarely caught, fleetingly, in a passionate overall view of the pity of it all.

For a twenty-two-year-old combat cameraman in the Second World War, determined to be a film-maker, this was another kind of torment. The cranking up of my De Vry, and its aiming at – so far as its angle of view was concerned – distant bangs and crashes as we were bombed and shelled by day, was in no sense a capturing of the image of war. The real hand-to-hand, gut-to-gut fighting almost always happened at night, so it was unfilmable. All the camera could see by daylight were separated holes in the ground, into which victors and vanquished had scratched themselves hurriedly before dawn; blobs, humps, and smudges in a calcined arena of otherwise emptiness. Tank battles were fought out in much the same way, with much the same tactics, and over as relatively as wide an horizon as the naval encounters of the previous world war. Not alone, I despaired.

Others were more realistic. Before our arrival in the Middle East Pathé Newsreel's cameraman had already started to stage his own actions. A team of our own Army Film and Photographic Unit was permitted to follow this example. At the height of the Battle of Alamein they shot the most famous still picture of that desert campaign, the storming of an enemy position through smoke. Its location – back of the cookhouse at Rear Headquarters 9th Australian Division, five miles behind the actual front line. The most dramatic sequence of the film *Desert Victory* is the tremendous barrage of gunfire which precedes the British attack, and then the Scots Highland Division assault through the German minefield defences, bagpipes playing – seen as well as heard to be played – as they battle their way through. And all, as of course it was, in the darkness of the middle of the night of 23rd October 1942. Did anyone in audiences around the world ask themselves, or anyone else, how those scenes had been shot, in the distant desert, at night? A technical impossibility, of course. The sequence was set up, and shot, back in England, at Pinewood.

But did this matter, does this matter? Does it diminish, or invalidate *Desert Victory*? Those Highlanders did storm those minefields, their piper did play them through. It was not for want of courage on our part that they were not filmed in the desert, in the act of doing so. Optical photographic film cannot, by its nature, capture an image in darkness. Some amongst us even failed to get the gunflashes. I was one myself. The barrage was so colossal that it appeared to one's own eyes as one continual ripple of flashing light. But the movie camera turns at 24 pictures a second, its shutter revolving as the film is pulled down at this speed cutting the individual exposures by a further half, to all but a fiftieth of a second. It only needed the gunflash to take place in the other forty-nine fiftieths of a second for nothing to go on the film at all. This had not occurred to me.

Of the opening of the historic Battle of El Alamein I proudly turned in a hundred feet of perfectly blank film.

By the time we had crossed over the Mediterranean by way of Sicily, and were stuck in the mud of the mountains south of Rome, this inability to supply our masters in the distant War Office with the type of film they envisaged as bursting and blazing from the battlefield had reached a crisis. In Naples we were shown the American Signal Corps films *With the Marines at Tarawa* and *To the Shores of Iwo Jima*, staggering in their impact.

Iwo Jima. The strategic linchpin in the island chain outpost guarding the home islands of Japan itself. On to just three thousand yards of beach, five hundred landing craft had put ten waves of American marines ashore – in broad daylight. They endured seventy-two hours of continuous pounding on the beach before they were able to move forward. With them there were cameramen of the United States Navy, the Marine Corps, and the Coast Guard. Dominating everything was Mount Surabachi. In the words of one of the marines 'they chased us off there five times. We came back six'. It took them twenty-six days to secure the island – in due course to become the airbase for the nuclear strikes against Hiroshima and Nagasaki. How could cameramen in such a setup miss, we asked ourselves? But to Pinewood all wars, anywhere, in whatever terrain, should have appeared just as horrifically spectacular.

Led by one of the few Hollywood stars to see real combat – Louis Hayward, now a Marine Captain and formerly *Son of Monte Cristo* – those American cameramen just could not go wrong. There they had been, flung down on a postage stamp-sized beach, with all hell happening all around them in broad Pacific daylight. In Italy we were now confronted with widely dispersed and now mountain warfare, in which virtually all of what little action there was at that time still took place at night. Was reconstruction – faking if you like – to be the answer, our solution? The enemy had never had any qualms about it.

Right from the beginning, the Germans had artfully and carefully staged and cut scenes and incidents into the mass of genuine combat material which made up *Baptism of Fire* and *Victory in the West*, their films of the invasion of Poland and conquest of France. The Russians' *Defeat of the Germans near Moscow* has

210

previously knocked out German tanks blown up again more thoroughly for the benefit of one of the fifteen cameramen concerned, as well as a restaged mass charge by ski troops to build up real but inevitably sporadic and uncoordinated coverage of the recapture of a village.

At the end of the war with Japan I was in Saigon, and came upon the vast store of film which the Japanese had been distributing throughout South East Asia. I screened this treasure trove, amongst which was *Marei Senki* (Malayan War Record), which featured the sinking of the British battleships *Prince of Wales* and *Repulse*. Sent to the bottom of the South China Sea, this ensured British defeat in Malaya and Singapore. The two ships on the screen were obvious models, settling down slowly in a studio tank. The *Battle of Santiago Bay* all over again.

In Italy, in early 1944, we continued in our attempts to catch the image of war, the hard way, losing lives and limbs in the endeavour. But we were never able to satisfy our armchair critics back in London, ensconced in the comfortable isolation of their viewing theatres. I held long talks about all this with our own chief in the field, Geoffrey Keating, one time Fleet Street photographer, Rifle Brigade Major, Officer Commanding Number Two Army Film and Photographic Section. In the relative sanctuary of a drain on the road to Rome, which I was sharing with an American rifle company, on the 2nd March 1944, I wrote to him my views on the subject:

'During any feature of the existing campaign, or as an entirety in future operations (a Production Unit) would shoot a coherent and complete document of operations, for Pinewood use only, which would serve as a framework to any film of that operation. Thus, and only thus, would the previous charge of the Pinewood Editors that the material of the Section lacks continuity and imaginative treatment be overcome ... Instead of attempts at making feature documentaries of campaigns from existing, miscellaneous material, each item of which shot as an end in itself, a complete framework to such a work would be in existence, designed by one mind, viewing and interpreting cinematographically the operation as a whole, in the creative terms

211

of the cinema. It is thus that films are made, and only thus can documentaries of the army in action in the field be satisfactorily produced. The miscellaneous material from the other cine operators in the unit, with whom close liaison would be maintained, would be cut into this existing framework, and a balanced documentary of the entire operation result. The need for such an approach is admirably summed up by a quotation from the Nazi brochure on the German propaganda film *Victory in the West*: 'You get no documentary by joining together documentary stills. You get no history by joining together historical events. It is ORDER, the showing up of relations which turns chronology into history. And thus it is the WILL, the IDEA behind the film which turns dead celluloid into a living documentary'.

What I was trying to do of course was usurp the prerogatives of the producers back at Pinewood Studios. David Macdonald and Roy Boulting *Desert Victory*; Frank Capra and Hugh Stewart *Tunisian Victory*; the following year Garson Kanin and Carol Reed *The True Glory*, as was to be believed and entitled the liberation of France and the downfall of Germany; and finally David Macdonald once again repeating success with *Burma Victory*, the defeat of Japan at the gateway to India. What a hope! I was, after all, at that time of writing, just a twenty-three-year-old wartime sergeant who had been issued with a camera instead of a gun. It was only with my joining and filming the resistance movements across the Adriatic in Albania, Greece, and Yugoslavia later that same year that I finally came to terms with myself as a cameraman in World War Two.

What I was not to know when I wrote that memorandum to the man in charge of British Army cameramen in Italy is that only a few miles away, and a few months before, an American had approached the filming of the war in just that way. Considering that not so long ago in Hollywood he had directed with conspicuous skill *The Maltese Falcon*. This was not so very surprising.

Captain John Huston had arrived in Italy with a Signal Corps camera team led by his friend Jules Buck, commissioned a lieutenant. As the Mediterranean area was an Anglo-American theatre of military operation, with them to make up the balance was the British author-screenwriter Eric ('Mask of Dimitrios') Ambler who, with Peter Ustinov, had recently scripted Carol Reed's *The Way Ahead*. In just the same way as the *March of Time* had personalised the immense American home front war effort on just one small factory in Ohio, so they decided to concentrate their efforts on a single battle, and just one infantry regiment, the 143rd of the 36th Texas Division. North of Naples, the way to Rome lay up the Liri Valley. Commanding its approaches was a little township, typical of the tens of thousands which cling to the hills and mountainsides of the Italian peninsular, and which were seemingly identical and never-ending bloody stepping stones the American and British armies had to take and fight over to get to Rome. This one was called San Pietro.

The night of 15th December, 1943, the Texans were ordered to take it. Dug into the mountain slopes all around, the Germans fought back like fiends. Concentrated on the narrow regimental front, with ten or more inch long-focus lenses on their Eyemos, up there with the infantry, mortared in what should have been the serene surroundings of olive groves, hanging on while counter-attacked by intensive and heavy shellfire, Huston's cameramen got the closest and most vivid combat coverage of the Italian campaign. Huston wrote, and spoke, his own commentary. 'The price paid for the ground gained was at the rate of a man a yard'. Out of sixteen tanks sent forward to take out the enemy strong-points, only three got through into the village, and none of these even survived. The 143rd, like the other regiments in the Division, was decimated; reduced to the strength of less than a rifle company before they finally succeeded in pushing the Germans just five miles further back along the road to Rome. 'The lives lost were precious lives. Precious to their loved ones. Precious to themselves'. Huston's film ends with the burial of the American dead. One after another the bodies are lowered into hastily-dug graves. And as these dead men finish their war, and lives, in holes in the ground, so we are shown living people emerging from other holes in the ground. Out from cellars and shelters beneath their battered buildings emerge the inhabitants,

Author 'cleaned up' outside Cassino

the Italian peasants for whom was presumably fought *The Battle of San Pietro*.

When they had at first succeeded in getting into the ruins of San Pietro with the surviving forward elements of the 143rd, Huston and his companions had been shelled out before they had been able to shoot even a foot of film. Ambler later had this to say:

'Captious critics of war documentaries, too, should have rules: for every gallant fighting man peering over the top of a slit trench as the barrage flickers, we ought to remember a camera operator with his buttocks in the air and his back to the enemy. Unless, of course, the critic prefers straight newsreel coverage'.

Only finally shown fifteen months later, the United States Army Pictorial Service tacked a final title on this film which comes close to conveying what Hemingway called the ultimate loneliness of what is known as combat. 'All scenes in this picture were photographed within range of enemy small arms or artillery

214

fire. For purposes of continuity a few of these scenes were shot before and after the actual battle of San Pietro'.

Even that cookhouse back at the division's rear headquarters at the Battle of Alamein could, at a stretch, have been defined as being within range of enemy artillery fire. But all reconstruction, of whatever nature, however close to the firing line, was soon to be totally prohibited to the British Army Film and Photographic Unit; and by the time they went ashore in Normandy the following year, they at last had cameras, with lenses, made for the job. The Germans all along had had their Arriflexes, originally designed in the first place as combat cameras for this war.

Only the Americans had colour on any practical scale. That ancient mariner manqué, John Ford, covered in this way *The Battle of Midway*. Under the direction of Edward Steichen, United States Navy cameramen shot a mint of sixteen millimetre Kodachrome on an Essex class aircraft carrier in action in the Pacific. Louis de Rochemont produced and edited. Robert Taylor spoke the commentary. All concerned deserved the Oscar they earned for *The Fighting Lady*.

Directed by Harry Watt and Humphrey Jennings, *London Can Take It* had demonstrated this to be only too true during the Blitz of 1940, but fifty years on there are now very mixed feelings about that war as waged from the air. *The Battle of Britain*, refought on the screen in 1969, was more tactfully retitled for German audiences *Achtung Spitfeuer*, but it has to be remembered that for years the only way the British could hit back at the enemy heartland was from the air. Soon after Pearl Harbor had brought the United States into the war, and forsaking such as Donald Duck and Goofy for the cause, the Walt Disney studios combined live action with animation to argue the case for *Victory through Air Power*.

In Britain Bomber Command, and its controversial Chief Air Marshall Arthur Harris, were pledged to this concept, and its execution. Climaxed in February 1945 with the aerial assault on Dresden which killed at least 35,000 people and destroyed most of the city. The argument rumbles on. In 1991 the RAF's 'Bomber Command Association' set out to erect in the heart of

London, which had known very well its own Blitz, a memorial statue to their former Commander in Chief, 'Bomber' Harris. The mayor of Pforzheim, a German city which suffered 20,000 dead in this way, pleaded please don't.

Two by now legendary documentary films of World War Two featured, and in one case actually flew with bombing aircraft and their crews at that time. The one British and the other American.

Having restaged a tithe war for the *March of Time*, Harry Watt, and now with the Crown Film Unit, came up with *Target for Tonight*. Although genuine Royal Air Force pilots and personnel performed their actual combat roles, all the scenes inside the aircraft fighting off flak and unloading its bombs on to an oil storage depot down river from Hamburg had to be mocked up on a sound stage at Denham. This is not to belittle the director, or his crew. There just was no room to spare for any passenger with a movie camera inside that cramped Wellington bomber codenamed in the film 'F for Freddie'. For the director of *Wuthering Heights* and *Mrs Miniver* there was no such inhibition or necessary subterfuge. William Wyler and his cameraman William Clothier did it the hard way. What made this possible was the more than twice as large and daylight-flown B17, the aptly named 'Flying Fortress'.

In 1938, and soon after official objection to Clark Gable starring in MGM's proposed British feature *Shadow of the Wing*, the future Rhett Butler had safely landed in *Test Pilot* the prototype of a new Boeing long range intercontinental bomber, the B17. For the same studio, six years later, and with the United States by then three years into the war, King Vidor climaxed his own *American Romance* of an immigrant turned tycoon with his hero's mass production of these same Flying Fortresses. And as Wyler's actual wartime combat film of a single crew's final mission in one of these aerial behemoths came to be reinvented and restaged by David ('Chariots of Fire') Puttnam as recently as 1990, let's take a look at how they made and flew the original *Memphis Belle*.

It was to be some time before the RAF came up with any-thing comparable to the B17, the *Lancaster*, and in any case they had believed in bombing by night. The United States Air Force preferred to do it by day, confident at first in what they believed to be the protection of the all round arcs of fire possible from B17's flying together in mass formations. So if you could squeeze aboard a B17 with a hand-held sixteen millimetre cam-era, you too could shoot more or less whatever happened. During five different combat missions over Germany, this is just what Wyler and cameraman William Clothier set out to do, and indeed did. In his own description of himself as a twenty-four-year-old kid, Clothier had been one of upwards of twenty youngsters like himself armed with hand-held cameras filming 'anything and everything' that flew for William Wellman's silent epic of World War One, *Wings*. Years later he was to photograph in Cinema-scope, for the same director, *The High and the Mighty*, together with no less than eight pictures for John Wayne, including *The Alamo*.

But as he was airborne from a base in East Anglia in the au-tumn of 1942, all this lay in the future – if they got back. On this first flight, over the enemy target of Vegesack, for Lieutenant Colonel Wyler, Major Clothier shot the first aerial motion pic-ture of an actual bombing attack in the Second World War. At an altitude of 28,000 feet, the temperature was sixty-five degrees below zero. All the guns in the aircraft froze – and so did his camera. Finally, and with the help of the bomb aimer, Clothier was able to get it to turn, and shot through the open bomb doors. The meagre footage he was able to bring back was the beginning of the 16,000 feet that he and Wyler were then able to bring back in mission after mission over the next few months. And make no mistake about it – this *was* in colour. Sixteen millimetre Ko-dachrome. Just as Louis de Rochemont's *Fighting Lady*, to be enlarged after Wyler's final edit into 35 millimetre Technicolor, for theatrical release, in this case by Paramount.

The Memphis Belle was the name one crew had given to their Fortress, and Wyler saw that this whole story of the American air assault on Germany from Britain could be focused on the crew of just such an aircraft. And this of course he did. His material edited into and around their final mission, their twenty-fifth, before relocation back home to the United States. The drama and the tension transferred in this way into audience identification as well as participation. Would they survive this final raid over the U-boat pens at Wilhelmshaven, to live on in movie history, these twelve young men of the original *Memphis Belle*?

'Pilot Captain Robert Morgan, industrial engineer from Ashville, North Carolina... Second Pilot Captain Jim Varinis, business administration student at the University of Connecticut... Radio Operator and Gunner Sergeant Bob Hanson, construction worker from Spokane, Washington... Navigator Captain Chuck Layton, chemistry student at Ohio University... Engineer and Top Turret Gunner Sergeant Harold Locke, from Green Bay, Wisconsin, used to be a stevedore... Tail Gunner Sergeant John Quinlan, of Yonkers, New York, clerk for a carpet company... Ball Turret Gunner Sergeant Cecil Scott, pressman for a rubber company in New Jersey... Bombardier Captain Vincent Evans, operated a fleet of trucks in Fort Worth, Texas... Waist Gunners Sergeant Bill Winchell chemist for a paint company in Chicago and Sergeant Tony Nostale, nineteen years old and used to repair washing machines in Detroit...' The original combat crew of *The Memphis Belle*.

And of course Lieutenant Colonel William Wyler and Major William Clothier. Originally there was to have been a third member of this Hollywood contingent, Sound Recordist Lieutenant Harold Tannenbaum, like Clothier also from RKO Studios. But sent across to follow them from the United States by sea, all their equipment had been sunk. Wyler was able to scrounge camera equipment from Lieutenant Commander John Ford of the United States Navy – but no sound. Forty-seven-year-old Tannenbaum volunteered to fly none the less, and Clothier showed him how to use a camera. On an earlier raid and over enemy coastline, this veteran of Astaire-Rogers musicals had been reported missing, his Fortress shot down over St Nazaire. Not so lucky as the twelve men crew of the original *Memphis Belle*.

How did these films of World War Two look to a later generation whose battle scars were spelt Vietnam? To mark the thirtieth anniversary of what the then victorious still call VE Day, in the United States WNET TV Channel 13 mounted a massive retrospective. Reviewing the programme in the *New York Times* of May 8th, 1975, John O'Connor wrote of *San Pietro* that, apart from its closing sequence still 'dazzling', it 'is less a masterpiece than a historical – and thoroughly absorbing – curiosity'. Of Frank Capra's *Prelude to War* (the first of seven in the *Why We Fight* series) he was less than kind. 'The distortions are glaring. The emotional accuracy and justification are startling'. The entire programme, which also included Wyler's *Memphis Belle* and outstanding episodes from the NBC compilation series *Victory at Sea*, was summed up as a 'first-rate source of image manipulation and bemused nostalgia ... The films are innocent, naive and righteous, and they have every reason to be an accurate reflections of the nation at that particular moment in history. The lines between right and wrong, between good and evil were clearly drawn – and 'we' were on the right, the angelic side. The rare unanimity of opinion may never be recaptured'.

All very true. Naive we certainly were. Filming the opposed landing on the beaches at Salerno back in September 1943, when the Anglo-American 5th Corps invaded Mussolini's Italy, was British Army Film Unit and formerly Paul Rotha's cameraman Harry Rignold. He was killed, and of him someone [Alan Moorehead] wrote this elegy:

'He saw for those at home who could not see,
And banished distance for a million eyes,
Through him they gazed beneath strange foreign skies
Where exiled father, husband, son might be.
He helped those lonely hearts to understand,
Comfort he brought, then war's realities
Which stirred a thousand factories
Till lathes worked faster for his steady hand.
Steady amidst the thundering crash of war,
Steady to hold the world's eye of his lens –

His only weapon. Here was work well done,
To face the ultimate that he might pour
Fresh inspiration out to everyone.
For those who mourn, there is no recompense'.

It is not only our attitudes which have changed. Like the equipment with which it is now filmed, war too has changed its ways and its means. Lightweight 16 millimetre and electronic video cameras with super telephoto lenses and soft on the feet guerilla raids by 'freedom fighters' is the contemporary combination of tactics. But for quite a while after the Second World War those bulky old 35 millimetre film cameras, still often on tripods, were humped into action.

Author as World War Two combat cameraman using camera with which
he filmed Yugoslav, Albanian and Greek resistance fighters

The defeat of the ruling colonial powers, followed by the 1945 surrender of Japan and the attempted crawl back of these same colonial powers, now no longer seen or respected as supermen, led as a matter of course to localised but nonetheless bloody wars of national liberation, to which we are still witness.

A couple of weeks after the Japanese surrender in 1945, I stood on the causeway linking Singapore to the mainland in Malaya. There approached a figure familiar from my time with Tito and other Balkan guerilla fighters of the previous year. Submachine gun, cartridge belt over shoulder, five-pointed red star in cap – but this one was Chinese.

The Malayan Communist Party had come into being in 1930, to be almost immediately outlawed. Its capacity for the clandestine, and its long record of anti-Fascism, had enabled it to form a British sponsored guerilla force during the Japanese occupation. Arms, ammunition, uniforms, and instructors were parachuted in from India. By the time of the Japanese surrender its strength was upwards of ten thousand, but only a little more than half of these surrendered their weapons to the returning British. The remainder went back, with them, to the jungle. In Chin Peng they had a brilliant leader, and able disciple of Mao Tse-tung. He waited just three years before launching the terrorist campaign designed to lead by way of three further stages of insurgency to the total victory of his People's Anti-British Army. It took the British twelve years to beat him.

By the time what was then regarded as a text-book counter-insurgency campaign was in its fifth year, I was back in New York with the *March of Time* attempting to come to terms with television. In preparation was a list of subjects for me to shoot around the world in 1953. I suggested Malaya. There was little response or even interest. But then, that same week, *Time* magazine itself came out with a cover story on the colourful and newly appointed British General Templer, and the significance of his struggle for 'the hearts and minds of the Malayan people'. Resistance to my proposal immediately crumbled. As finally shot by cameraman John Peters, this *March of Time* film on Malaya, never shown in Britain but televised coast to coast in the

United States, was an early attempt to put on the screen the new type of warfare. Soon to be followed up by my friend and former Desert Army Film Unit chief David Macdonald, who took a unit out there and came up with *Operation Malaya* the following year.

Before he had gone off to Hollywood a young man in his twenties, David Macdonald had been a rubber planter in Malaya. He knew the country well. From the viewpoint of the occupying power, his new film concentrated on the military struggle against what had come to be called Communist terrorists: their methods of attack and intimidation, the countermeasures of patient and persistent patrolling, the destruction of their jungle camps, the resettlement of village people. A highlight was the trial, and sentence to death, of a captured guerilla, the verdict received by the Chinese with awe-inspiring indifference.

If this Asian war, euphemistically described by the British only as an 'emergency', at first failed to interest my editors in New York the next to blaze out on the other side of the Pacific met with an instant editorial response. For the first time, sitting at home, Americans not only saw but heard from their men at war – in Korea.

Film cameras have been able to record spoken interviews since the coming to the motion picture of synchronised sound. In fact the showing of the first synchronised sound film at the Manhattan Opera House, August 26th, 1926, was prefaced with a filmed and spoken introduction by Will Hays, President of the Motion Picture Producers' and Distributors' Association. The newsreels had made much of this added dimension to their reporting, but in battle their heavy 35mm sound-on-film cameras and recording equipment had been hitherto almost exclusively trained on and tuned in to little more than the crump of bombs and the platitudes of generals. John Huston however had filmed interviews with some of the men of the 143rd before they went into action at San Pietro. They spoke sincerely and eloquently of what they believed the future would hold for them, and their country. Later Huston set up a camera as their bodies were laid out for burial. In his first uncut version of the film be had their living voices speaking of their hopes in this way over close-ups of their dead faces. But then he felt that this would be just too much for audiences of the time. 'The present generation,' he wrote of this later, 'might be up to it, it's become inured to anything'. But now, nine years and another war later, another American would bring voices, as well as pictures, back from the latest battlefront. Edward R. Murrow.

Murrow had followed and reported war before. Tuned into the Columbia Broadcasting System in 1938, American listeners had heard his voice from Vienna, as he awaited the arrival of Hitler in the Austrian capital. 'They lift the right arm a little higher here than in Berlin, and the Heil Hitler is said a little more loudly'. It was not long before they were to hear him broadcasting from London that 'the noise you hear at this moment is the sound of the air raid siren. A searchlight just burst into action, off in the distance, an immense single beam sweeping the sky above me now. People are walking along very quietly. We're just at the entrance of an air-raid shelter here, and I must move the cable over just a bit, so people can walk in'.

Is television basically a miniature motion picture with sound – or is it animated radio? To Murrow, the true function of words in TV reporting was to enhance in parallel the picture by giving it a further dimension, by qualifying and even complementing. Which, after all, has always been the art of truly effective commentary writing. 'Never call your shots', Louis de Rochemont used to tell his writers on the *March of Time*. Words should be a counterpoint to picture.

But by now the *March of Time* was no more. After a few unimaginative attempts at series of its own (which had included my Malayan story) it had failed to make the transition to television.

The torch, if we can put it like that, was picked up by Ed Murrow, a reporter with a microphone – with now a camera too – and at first unequivocal support from his network, CBS.

'This is Korea, where a war is going on. That's a marine, digging a hole in the ground. They dig an awful lot of holes in the

Murrow in Korea

ground in Korea. This is the front. Just there, no man's land begins, and on the ridges over there the enemy positions can be clearly seen. In the course of the next hour we shall try and show you round Korea a bit'.

The introduction to *Christmas in Korea*, televised by CBS December 29th, 1953. And Murrow, and the others of co-producer Fred Friendly's team, did just that. Through television they took their audience to war, with sound on film. This milestone programme in the series *See It Now* dropped in on French, Ethiopian and British amongst the many making up the United Nations forces out there on that stricken peninsula fifty years ago. The filmed programme comes to an end on a series of close-ups of the men in a rifle company, as their sergeant assigns them their roles in the reconnaissance patrol on which they are then seen to set out.

'Chambers, you will be number one scout. Ball will be number two, second man in the file. I'll be third scout. Wallace, you carry the AR, the basic load of ammunition. Van Fleet, you're the assistant AR. Waley, you be first rifleman. Archebeck, you follow Waley. Smith, you come after Archebeck and Kim, follow Smith. Smothers, behind Kim, and Leo carries the radio. Sisson, you pack the wire, and Sergeant Lammar, you are second in command. You will be in the rear. All right, let's move up on to the ridge line and we'll take a look at this route we are going to follow tonight.'

Back to Murrow, watching them go: 'There is no conclusion to this report from Korea because there is no end to the war...'.

That Korean War of the early 1950's brought us right up to the nuclear threshold of a Third World War. Despite immense volumes of aid, and the unstinting support of Henry Luce, Chiang Kai-shek had been driven off the Chinese mainland and, as the prologue to the *March of Time* I shot in India 1947 - 49 had it, 'underlining the dramatic significance of India's new leadership' were developments in China, where the once largest republic in Asia was breaking up'. In Europe, Stalin seemed able to call all the shots. Italy and France appeared to be tottering into Communism. In Korea, American troops had suffered a major defeat at the hands of the Chinese – then seen to be as one with the Russians. At his HQ in the Dai Ichi in Tokyo, MacArthur called for the use of atomic weapons in counterattack. In his finest hour, President Truman sacked him.

Compared to then, the tensions of the later 1980's were almost tepid. In October 1951, the mass circulation American weekly magazine *Collier's* brought out a special issue devoted to how war against the Soviet Union would be fought and won and, after defeat, how the Russians would be led back to democracy. The cover of the magazine was a picture of American paratroops dropping over Kharkov, and no less than J.B. Priestley was a contributor as to how, after occupation, the arts would be encouraged along more liberal and progressive lines. In the more

225

prestigious pages of the *Atlantic Monthly* five months later, Bertrand Russell of all people argued the case for a pre-emptive

Author in centre distance filming a flypast on an American airbase in
Britain at the height of the Cold War in 1951

strike against the Russians in order to create a single world order of western liberalism.

What then had happened to Luce's proud boast that if the 19th had been the British Century, then the 20th was going to be the American? Unacceptable it had to be that the United States might perhaps have misread the situation. The only explanation therefore was that all this could only be the outcome of conspiracy, and moreover conspiracy within the United States itself – amongst the Foreign Service, the Armed Forces; and, above all, the Media.

As the author of *The Little Foxes*, Sam Goldwyn's sometime scriptwriter Lillian Hellman has described it, it was indeed a 'scoundrel time', and no more vicious scoundrel took greater advantage of this to serve his own ambitions than that member of the United States Senate, Joseph R. McCarthy; and by so doing wreck the original truly liberal spirit of the United States.

Nothing – and certainly no opinion – was safe or secure except an unquestioning acceptance that Uncle Sam had been betrayed, and moreover betrayed by subversives active in the media. Careers were ruined, major film-makers forced to flee the country and seek work abroad – like for a while Jo Losey – under assumed names.

And out of all this nightmare came what many still recall as the new electronic journalism's finest hour (or to be more precise, half hour).

See It Now had already by then gone underground with coal miners in West Virginia, ridden with blacks in school buses following court-ordered desegregation, reported on housing problems in Harlem and a Chinese immigrant barred by neighbours from buying a house in a Californian suburb – and already the clash of black-and-white in South Africa.

On March 4, 1954, came *See It Now*'s 'Report on Senator Joseph R. McCarthy'. Together Murrow and Fred Friendly assembled sufficient footage to damn the demagogue out of the deceit of his own mouth. At the close of this devastating documentary programme, Murrow stepped right out of the role of reporter. Looking up, directly into camera, he addressed his audience, the American public: 'We will not walk in fear, one of another. We will not be driven by fear into an age of unreason...

'The actions of the Junior Senator from Wisconsin have-caused alarm and dismay amongst our allies abroad and given considerable comfort to our enemies.

'And whose fault is that? Not really his. He didn't create this situation of fear, he merely exploited it; and rather successfully.

'Cassius was right. The fault, dear Brutus, is not in our stars, but in ourselves'.

To film *Christmas in Korea*, Murrow had taken no less than five 35 millimetre sound on film cameras and crews to the battlefront. By the time another generation were committed to war in Vietnam, 16mm and tape had replaced such cumbersome equipment. In Saigon, filming the Japanese surrender back in 1945, I had had only an army issue 35 millimetre clockwork hand-held Eyemo camera with which to film the return of French troops, disembarking in the hope of reimposing colonial rule on what on most maps was then marked as 'French Indo-China'. Already bullets were flying around, fired by a hitherto allied resistance force known as the Viet Minh. Soon to be renamed Viet Cong. In this Asian peninsula soon to be renamed Vietnam. Twenty years later it was to be American troops disembarking into this colonial quagmire, and by then most of the veteran war correspondents of World War Two had retired to write their memoirs. Making way for a new generation of newshawks eager to gain a Pulitzer Prize by way of combat fatigues. Outstanding amongst this new generation of audio visual reporters – and also like Murrow working for CBS – was Canadian-born Morley Safer.

CBS assigned Safer to Vietnam, and in August 1965 he joined a group of American marines on their way to a village claimed to be an enemy firebase. Cam Ne the name.

Vietnam - CBS reporter Morley Safer

They reached it. There had been no enemy fire. No enemy sighting. Nonetheless the marines tore the place apart. They torched it.

With grenade and flamethrower they incinerated the terrified unarmed inhabitants. Although horrified, but ever the professional newsman, Safer shot the story.

Back at CBS in New York, there was consternation when first his radio report was heard, and then his picture screened.

CBS reporter and cameraman in Vietnam

229

These were early days for the United States in Vietnam. American troops had never been seen behaving like this before. Anywhere. What to do? Should they broadcast? They did. In network evening prime time news. To receive the next day a blistering telephone call from the President, Lyndon Johnson insisting that American troops would not have acted in this way and that Safer, whom he claimed could only be a Communist, must have bribed the marine officer concerned to set it all up for his camera.

It was a watershed. A turning point. To its lasting credit, CBS supported Safer – and kept him out there. From then on the full filth, futility, and finally failure of Vietnam was to penetrate more and more American homes by way of that little electronic screen in their living rooms. No war in history has been so photographed, debated, filmed and anguished over as Vietnam. CBS News put out a Special Report on Vietnam: *How We Got In - Can We Get Out?*, and all told this one American network was continually to report and debate this agonizing question in upwards of two hundred programmes. Before he became an uneasy and short-lived Director of the United Sates Information Agency, Murrow had risen to the Board of Directors of the Columbia Broadcasting System, so it was not surprising that his own tradition of humane and personalised reporting was the hallmark of CBS programmes from Vietnam. Early on history repeated itself on the TV screen with the 1965 *Christmas in Vietnam*, and with a special report five years later on *The World of Charlie Company*. Outstanding was Isaac Kleinerman's *Hill 943*. This one-hour CBS News Special dealt with the futility of the war as seen through the eyes of a platoon assigned to capture a specific hill, and its withdrawal from that hill forty-eight hours after what was left of them had reached its top.

Murrow once said that 'the decline of British power is one of the sensational chapters of history', and although fought out in an area where the British still had extensive economic interests, Vietnam was a war from which they excused themselves. This, so it seemed to some, gave them a moral superiority from which to pass judgement. Certainly British television came up with plenty of film programmes on how it was to be the unfortunate and innocent local inhabitants of this tortured territory which, in colonial days, had been French Indo-China.

Towards the end, a Granada *World in Action* team on their way to film *The Siege of Kontum* moved on to Laos, and shot a programme on the Meo people for the series *Disappearing World*. The Meo are a hill minority, slowly over the centuries pushed down from North China. Their livelihood and relative prosperity had been gained from growing opium. Producer Brian Moser and his crew lived in the house of a priest-cum-medicine man. They contrasted the peaceful life of his village with another to the south, where ten thousand Meo refugees had fled from the war. Weekly, supplies were dropped to them by American planes. They could no longer grow their own rice.

Most of the reporting and film making of that American war to be fought for questionable aims in an alien land inevitably comprised a collage of talking heads and shots made with very long telephoto lenses. No one under the strain and isolation of real combat can really talk about it clearly and articulately, and what he says may be almost invariably presumed to be so said because of the very camera he says it to. Camera and microphone thrust at you, you've got to say something, haven't you?

'Take a picture of my mate, go on. He's been blown to bits. Go on. Go on. Take his bleeding picture. Bastards. Bastards.' An anguished screamed appeal to me during the breakout from Alamein. However as this shattered tank gunner was helped away to safety, I did not press the button. But this incoherent appeal remains with me always as the epitaph for all that desert bloodshed.

As Hemingway said in the commentary he wrote and spoke to the film he and Joris Ivens made of the Spanish Civil War: 'Men cannot act before the camera in the presence of death'. The strange, dislocated impression the super telephoto lens gives us is an impression, but only an isolated impression, of a momentary and fleeting image, but foreshortened, fragmented, and fractional of the whole. The very dissociation in appearance of this style of filming and reporting may in itself have contributed to alienation from the Vietnam War.

That by continually emphasising its brutalities in American homes television did much to erode support for the Vietnam War – and thus undermine his own Presidency – became an article of faith with Lyndon Johnson. The day following his formal announcement that he would not seek re-election in 1968, he addressed the National Association of Broadcasters. 'Historians', said Johnson, 'must only guess at the effect that television would have had during earlier conflicts on the future of this nation, during the Korean War, for example, at the time our forces were pushed back to Pusan, or World War Two, the Battle of the Bulge...'

And with failure in Vietnam, the image of war finally ceased to be in any way heroic. *Catch 22* took care of World War Two and Korea is now spelt *M.A.S.H.*

For those that believe that truth lies somewhere in the greater sum of all the parts, there can be no substitute for the *creative* treatment of actuality; and war is reality, however terrible a one. *The Deer Hunter*, *Apocalypse Now*, *Full Metal Jacket*, *Platoon*, *Hamburger Hill*, *Born on the Fourth of July* ... all American reconstructions of Vietnam, with a vengeance. A vengeance for what, defeat? Short of organising your own battles – and your own comments on your own battles – on a studio-style back lot in this way, you have to be there, camera ready, when it happens. And luck has a great deal to do with it.

The eastern Mediterranean was the setting for not only the seemingly endless conflict between the Arab world and Israel and the internecine bloodshed of Beirut – where cameramen were apt to be taken hostage – but also in 1974 the Turkish invasion of Cyprus. The best film of this assault came from a British ITN crew. But it was not planned that way.

With other newsmen, reporter Mike Nicholson and cameraman Allen Downs were in Nicosia's Ledra Palace Hotel, waiting for it to happen. Flash – the Turks were landing at Kyrenia, the costal port to the north. Off to the action everyone raced, in their own or in rented cars. Less than halfway there, the ITN car broke

Contemporary irregular warfare - author lines up Kalashnikov riflemen

down. Furious and frustrated, Nicholson and Downs watched everyone else overtake and pass them, leaving them stranded. And then, in exactly the same way as it had happened to me on the mainland of Greece, on the outskirts of Athens, thirty years before, the sky overhead filled with planes, out of which, and down on top of them, poured paratroops. It was the Turkish airborne follow-up. Just like myself at Megara in 1944, they just couldn't miss. Still close to Nicosia, they were then able to get back and their film out. Which is more than their competitors were able to do, by then cut off in Kyrenia, for five days.

'Six in the morning and in the van,
The Reporter, the Photographer, and me, the Sound Man,
Driving off to Suchi 'stead of getting a sun tan,
And there's Captain Lopez with a G-3 in his hand.
All that Chicago producer would say was 'Oh, Goddam!'

233

The Limey Reporter said 'I think it's time to scram!'
I got the Salvador Blues,
Working for the Network News...'

The late at night lament of TV crews in the bar of San Salvador's Camino Real Hotel. The 1980's and the dubious and messy wars of Central America. But the networks (just like our Pinewood warriors of old) continued to demand blood and guts coverage; and, by now, thanks to 'electronic news gathering', what that camera caught could be transmitted almost instantly back to base by satellite. Getting from the fire fight with your ENG tapes of the action had now become just as frantic a business as getting the picture in the first place.

No one has spoken more eloquently of this new hazard than the BBC's Kate Adie. In a 1989 speech to the Royal Television Society she told of the difficulties of getting the tapes of Tiananmen Square out and on the air from Beijing. 'As the clock ticks round, you're first of all trying to get into the place (the local TV studio). Normally, it's run by a military noodle – most television stations are run by military noodles and have men with guns outside who are absolutely impervious to shouts of 'My God! My satellite is up'.

The good Kate was to ride with the British 1st Armoured Division in the really spectacular Persian/Arabian – depends which side you are on of it – Gulf War of January 1991. And now an immensely significant new dimension opened up in war and war reporting. Not just so-called 'smart' bombs which zeroed in down the ventilation shafts of enemy command bunkers, but for reporters and cameramen 'carry your own folding satellite dish and new suitcase-sized transmission units', making possible the despatch of almost instant imagery from the battlefield itself. Time and again the highlights of British television during the bombing build-up to the land offensive came from the first in the field with these new twin accessories: CNN, the American Ted Turner's Cable News Network, its Baghdad-based reporter Peter Arnett taking his own degree of flak from those protesting his Iraqi-monitored pictures of the pitiful human results of bombing not always quite so 'smart'. But once the land offensive opened up and the tanks swept up and into a defeated Iraq in less than a week, Kate Adie was not the first to have discovered that 'It's not like in the movies'.

In his own way, and much later on, Steven Spielberg made up for my disinclination to film all that remained of a blown to pieces tank man at Alamein – which would not have been shown anyway – with large scale feature reconstructions of combat in World War Two. Outstanding in this way were *Saving Private Ryan* and his recruitment of Tom Hanks for their *Band of Brothers*. No holding back in the ration of blood and guts in these two.

Vietnam was the first television war for Americans. For Britain it was to be Ulster; counter-insurgency in the homeland, on the doorstep, where cameras have themselves been accused of creating conflict.

In 1985, the producers of the BBC series *Real Lives* came up with matching profiles of two adversaries in Ulster, Gregory Campbell, the leader of the Protestant Democratic Unionist Party, and Martin McGuinness of the Catholic Provincial Sinn Fein, each advocates of violence against the other's community. On the screen they emerged as amiable family men, articulate in their mutual antipathy; an attempt at balance – 'objectivity' – which brought down the fury of the Government, whose Prime Minister had recently been a target of attempted assassination. Alerted by the Home Secretary, the BBC's Board of Governors called for a ban on the broadcast, in the event only postponed. The Northern Ireland Governor, one Lady Faulkner, was later to write that 'the shots of McGuinness – who says he would be proud to be the chief of staff of the IRA – were like those foxes produced years ago for the anti blood sports campaigners, pretty animals, like collie dogs. What one didn't see were the fowl in the hen-run with their heads pulled off'.

Previously making contact with the Provisional Irish Republican Army, a BBC *Panorama* team received a call that the IRA were mounting a roadblock in a village called Carrickmore, just a few miles from the border with the Republic.

'You provide the pictures and we'll provide the war' - Belfast, 1989

236

Once the camera had filmed this, the IRA and their roadblock simply melted away.

So we're really back where we started, the Spanish-American War of 1898, and Citizen Kane – Hearst:

'You provide the pictures, and we'll provide the war'.

Ulster, Northern Ireland, was in fact a British Civil War, although few were prepared to admit it. Civil is defined in my dictionary as 'polite' and 'obliging'. What a misnomer for the most foul of all armed conflicts. Claiming as victims men, women, and children from either side of the same street. As the vicious twentieth century drew to its close, nowhere more vile than in the territories of what had once been called Yugoslavia. Gulping their disgust, photo journalists having to aim their cameras and create pictorial compositions of bits and pieces of kids and old women, deliberately blown to pieces in the school playground and buying the groceries.

Ten years on from the Gulf War, the focus of conflict centred on Iraq. Computerised and digital technology had rendered sound and film equipment even more transportable and even less conspicuous. Instant transmission back to base was also now feasible. Preparing to leave on assignment, veteran reporters' refrain could now well be 'Pack up your camera, discs, and videophone in your old kit bag…'

But let WH Auden have the final word on capturing the imagery of war.

'The man with the camera, effacing himself in order to spy on others, is a homeless fugitive. He can document experience only if he is excluded from it; the machine he wields enforces his alienation.'

Part Two

6. MIDPOINT AT POONA

'I prefer the idea of digesting the world, observing it and trying to transform one's observation into something personal, but with observation as a starting point.'

Jean Renoir

How it once was

If it's your job to make films at the end of the twentieth century, when most of your life will be lived in the twenty-first, you have to face up to a revolutionary situation: a revolution moreover not only in the methods and mechanics of communication.

If we are coloured, we have to get on at least equal terms with the white man who has hitherto exploited us economically, politically, psychologically. If a race, a people, a nation even, fighting to preserve our own identity, we have to do battle with multinational business conglomerates, of which some are stronger and more powerful than many a national state. And as we breed more and more of ourselves, of whatever colour, and use up more and more of our natural resources, all of us, as a species, are threatened with extinction.

As you get your hands on a movie camera perhaps for the first time, what should you do with it? Surely put it to work in the service of revolution. For this is what all of us are now faced with: a revolution in the way we need to face each other; white and black; have and have-not; rich nation; poor nation. A revolution in how we have hitherto come to regard ourselves and everyone else in a fast-contracting world, seemingly set on a course of even greater polarisation between the one and the other. We and Them.

Constantly criticised, both within and without (but it's all we've got otherwise) are the instruments and the agencies of the United Nations. It is the task of UNESCO (The United Nations Educational, Scientific and Cultural Organisation) to translate such pious acronyms into action. Just simply – across this great widening gulf – help the one to communicate with the other. And it was the job of Basil Wright and me at Poona to try to translate this into some sort of practicality for our students – and all the millions upon millions of impoverished people they represented and, one hoped, would go on to serve.

The Russians provided us with a good example.

In the office of Jagat Murari, Principal of the Film Institute of India, was a framed photograph of Eisenstein. For much of the methodology at Poona was based on the principles and experi-

241

ence of VGIK, the State Cinema Institute of Moscow. Its syllabus owed a great deal to Eisenstein.

Trying to reconcile his concept of intellectual cinema and hitherto experience of the silent film with the arrival of sound and Stalin's demand for now 'Socialist Realism' in all the arts, the director of *Potemkin* and *October* had suffered a real creative block throughout the early 1930's. No film materialised from the master at all during this period. However he had, to a certain extent, worked out his frustration by pouring out his ideas and thoughts on to paper – and teaching a new generation of younger Soviet film-makerat the Moscow Film School.

Eisenstein set out to teach that the ideal film-maker should be first and foremost a master of all the arts: social and political as well as aesthetic. His students were supposed to have at least a working knowledge of architecture and design; of the bases of physical movement, and temporal-spatial orientations. They should be sociologists, aware of the interplay of evolution and history. They should read Balzac and Plato as well as the then obligatory Lenin and Marx. In order to understand the processes of creation, Eisenstein believed that the lives of innovators and inventors like Edison and Ford should be studied just as closely as the films which bore his name as well as those of other masters. In short, this eclectic and renaissance man believed that unless one was aware of and had studied all the forces and phenomena in a given situation, then no worthwhile film would result – certainly no work that could make a forceful and constructive contribution to the screen of change.

Eisenstein was however out of fashion. We were being urged to follow more the example of a contemporary of his, Dziga Vertov. In the immediate aftermath of the Soviet Revolution of 1917, this fellow Russian film-maker issued a stirring manifesto: 'The lens of the camera has the power of the moving eye. It can and does go everywhere and into everything. It climbs the side of a building and goes in through the window; it travels over factories, along steel girders, across the road, in and out of trains, up a chimney stack, through a park – into the houses of the rich and poor; it stands in the street, whilst cars, trams, buses, carts flash by it on all sides ... it follows this person down that alley and meets that one round the corner...'.

Did not this sound very familiar, and indeed almost contemporary? For is the *apologia*, if not *credo*, of the maker of so many of what have been called teledocumentary films. The entire emphasis placed on the camera, what it could see, what it could get. Since Vertov originally enunciated his technique of *Kino-Pravda* (Film Truth), a new school arose making this some sort of argument for *cinéma-vérité*: what you are really doing is letting the camera do all the work for you, even the thinking. 'We don't need a script', had not one of us said already at Poona? Since Vertov's time, now more than sixty years ago, super long-focus telephoto lenses have come along to make it all the easier for the man with the movie camera to get, from an uninvolved and detached distance – and hence the claim for a greater 'objectivity' – sufficient shots of seemingly unaware people in action to build up in edited combination an impression of an overall situation, even a point of view. Vertov actually called what has come to be his most famous film *The Man With the Movie Camera*; and that's what it was, a film of a man with a movie camera moving in and out of the cunningly cut material which he was seeing and supposed to be shooting.

We even now have another name for his sort of *collage* of moving pictures projected on a screen, Pop Art. It was then only natural that many of those working in this style made films of pop music festivals.

'My definition of a documentary film', says Donn Alan Pennebaker, maker of the film *Monterey Pop*, 'is a film that decides you don't know enough about something, whatever it is, psychology or the tip of South America. Some guy goes there and says, "Holy shit, I know about this and nobody else does, so I'm going to make a film about it". Gives him something to do. And he usually persuades somebody to put up the money who thinks this is the thing to do. Then you have the situation where this thing is shouting on the wall about how you don't know something. Well, I think that's a drag. Right away it puts me off. There are a lot of things I don't know about, but I can't stand having someone telling me that … On the other hand it's possible to go to a situation and simply film what happens there, what goes on, and let everybody decide whether it tells them about any of these things. But you don't have to label them, you don't have to have this narration to instruct you so you can be sure and understand that it's good for you to learn. You don't need any of that shit. When you take off the narration, people say, "Well, it's not a documentary any more". That's all right, that's their problem. That's why I say that films that interest me to do, I wouldn't consider documentaries'.

Now listen to another voice from the past, to words written nonetheless sixteen years after Vertov's original proclamation of *Kino-Pravda*:

'I look on cinema as a pulpit, and use it as a propagandist; and this I put unashamedly because, in the still unshaven philosophies of cinema, broad distinctions are necessary. Art is one matter, and the wise, as I suggest, had better seek it where there is elbow room for its creation; entertainment is another matter: education, in so far as it concerns the classroom pedagogue, another; propaganda another; and cinema is to be conceived as a medium, like writing, capable of many forms and many functions. A professional propagandist may well be especially interested in it. It gives generous access to the public. It is capable of direct description, simple analysis, and commanding conclusion, and may, by its tempo'd and imagistic powers, be made easily persuasive. It lends itself to rhetoric, for no form of description can add nobility to a simple observation so readily as a camera set low, or a sequence cut to a time-beat. But principally there is this thought that a single say-so can be repeated a thousand times a night to a million eyes, and, over the years, if it is good enough to live, to billions of eyes. That seven-leagued fact opens a new perspective, a new hope, to public persuasion'.

John Grierson, like Eisenstein, also considered today somewhat old-hat. These two attitudes expressed by Pennebaker and Grierson are not only generations, but worlds apart; and this might seem an academic, even sterile debate, had it not polarised our attitudes at Poona.

In the twenty-four years between my filming of Japanese surrender and my arrival in Poona, much of my work in film had been in developing countries. Filming in Thailand (and with Paul Rotha his co-director in Mexico) Basil Wright had already made for UNESCO *World Without End*. In many ways, this was the preparation for the course 'in documentary, short film script writing' we had been called upon to run at the Film and Television Institute of India.

Although India produces hundreds and hundreds of escapist films a year, these are only seen in the cities. The vast majority of India's then 509,000,000 lived in villages. The only motion pictures they ever saw were those brought to them by mobile 16 millimetre projector units. The average village, we were told, at that time enjoyed this type of film show only once every three years. To help improve in any way their quality of life, what this burgeoning audience of Griersonian billions needed more than anything else was information. Information on simple but improved methods of agricultural self-help, irrigation, family planning...

The motion picture – the screen of change – could do this, if we can ever get our priorities right.

They knew what I meant when I said this at Poona, and so I suggested that the path we should follow as socially committed film-makers was less the self-indulgent way of Pennebaker and Vertov, and more the apparently didactic examples of Eisenstein and Grierson. And this meant building a film up from within, before a foot of film is ever shot in the first place. This is much more difficult, much harder work, than just shooting a talking head reflecting our own prejudices, or merely spraying a happening with a movie camera and then enjoying a subsequent burst of editorial razzmatazz. It means that you have to attempt to become more expert – and more humble at the same time – than the experts themselves in the field and subject area of whatever it is you are committed to make a programme about; as well as being expert in your own field, in the techniques which you will then have to call upon in order to turn it all into a cohesive motion picture on the screen of change.

And this therefore cannot mean *cinéma-vérité*. But it does mean using *vérité* techniques, wherever and whenever they can help get what is wanted on the screen.

To arrange, readjust, to direct an action for the camera – if it is necessary to the overall concept of the film – is not a crime. To attempt to awaken the world to the perils of Fascism, was it wrong of the *March of Time* to set up the old girl with her medals at the end of *Inside Nazi Germany*? Did anyone of the New Left yell 'fake' at Gillo Pontecorvo's film of *The Battle of Algiers*? But that was all set up for the camera in 1965, after the shooting was over and the French had pulled out. And why not? What was the alternative? A newsreel-like collage of hand-held long-focus shots, snatched at the time, smuggled out, if lucky, under the noses of the French? Such creative reconstruction, on its actual sites, with the actual people involved, is the only way to picture the real heart of a drama: yes, and I shall say it, its inherent and universal truth. For a newsreel of bomb blasts in Algiers, intercut with surreptitiously-shot talking heads, would have been no more than just that. As Gillo Pontecorvo conceived and created it, *The Battle of Algiers* is a very great deal more. It is a metaphor, an allegory, of all resistance against what is perceived to be alien rule. Algiers became Saigon, Jerusalem, Belfast...

It is surely high time to move on from this sterile debate as to whether or not 'reconstruction' of an event, dramatisation of a fact is, or is not, 'honest'. As Basil Wright reminds us in *The Long View*, to get his camera back far enough to show Nanook and his Esquimeaux family bedding down for the night, Robert Flaherty had to cut their igloo in half. The sound recording equipment available to Harry Watt and the British Post Office Film Unit in 1936 was neither sensitive nor flexible enough to catch the dialogue of the letter sorters rattling along in their *Night Mail*. So they built a railroad coach in their studio. An exact facsimile, and the sorters were real, doing their own thing, as they knew it.

When Lisa Pontecorvo arranged a screening of old *March of Time*s at Britain's National Film Theatre in 1971, was she aware,

I wonder, that what she was really doing was in fact paying homage to what had led the way to her own cousin's film of *The Battle of Algiers*?

This is not an outrageous or partisan view of my own. In his account of 'Documentary in American Television', William Bluem wrote in the same year that Pontecorvo was making his film that the *March of Time* stretched the limits of journalism by implicitly arguing that the picture as well as the word was, after all, only symbolic of reality. 'What mattered was not whether pictorial journalism displayed the facts but whether, within the conscience of the reporter it faithfully reflected the facts'. For reporter read film-maker, and there we are.

Writing of Flaherty in *The War, The West and The Wilderness*, Kevin Brownlow makes a plea that a comment of his be stamped upon the front of every documentary film script: 'One often has to distort a thing to catch its true value'. And of his *Medium Cool* (the adventures of a man with a movie camera in the America of the Nixon years) the Director-Cameraman Haskell Wexler argues that 'a re-enactment taking on elements more real than the actual statement is an accurate description. It is naïve to think that film-makers cannot create powerful reality images. I feel confident enough to defy anyone, after they have seen *Medium Cool* (his film of the riots outside the Democratic Convention, Chicago 1963) to discriminate between an actual happening and a rehearsed scene'.

That he had reached these limits with the *March of Time* no one knew better than Louis de Rochemont. At the end of World War Two, leaving his brother in charge of the shop, he went to Hollywood. But not to film in its studios. To extend *March of Time* techniques into the full-length feature film. To take the latter out into the streets. To film real stories, reconstructed, and reenacted, in the real locales of their actual happening. To accomplish this he was able to draw at first on Twentieth Century Fox's roster of directors. For *The House on 92nd Street*, an authenticated case of the international espionage (with which we were soon to become so sickeningly familiar) they gave him veteran Henry Hathaway; for *Boomerang*, a real life murder mys-

247

tery in a small Connecticut community, a newcomer from the theatre, Elia Kazan.

These films, and this man's example – which brought a more genuine reality to the American feature film and gave the documentary film report a new dimension in feature film form – still point the path today. And we are more fortunate than the directors and cameramen on de Rochemont's early features. They still had to work with the cumbersome studio equipment of the time. We now have a new generation of lightweight cameras and portable tape recorders.

It is this that made possible *cinéma-vérité*, which all really began in 1961 with *Chronicle of a Summer*, made by Jean Rouch. On a day that the battle of Algiers seemed to be ending, and France therefore about to be free at last from foreign wars, the film-maker stopped people at random in the streets, and asked them if they were happy. This he followed up weekly with such interviews, finally filming everyone involved (including himself) as they were confronted with the results. Of this technique, which has then gone on to flourish one way or another in many parts of the world, Satyajit Ray wrote (just before we all foregathered in Poona) that this 'face to face technique also presents problems. How can we ever be sure that an interviewee is making honest statements and not merely saying what he believes is the right thing to say ... Half the time I'm inclined to disbelieve what they are saying, but all the time I am fascinated by how they say it. The sharpest revelations of truth in the cinema come from details perceived through the eyes of artists. It is the sensitive artist's subjective approach to reality that ultimately matters, and this is true as much of documentaries as of fiction films'. Confronted with this point of view, Rouch stood the argument on its head. In his opinion, the function of the movie camera is 'not to film life as it is, but life as it is provoked'. Such a point of view certainly provoked Grierson: 'One *ciné-vérité* derivation which has always been particularly attractive to the provincial (is) the secret camera's talent as a peeping Tom, and its ingenuity in catching the embarrassed reaction to the embarrassing question. Like all harlots, the *cinéaste* of easy virtue is apt to run into power without responsibility; and it can go to his head'.

Let us then stop confusing form for substance.

Believing as I still do in the first of all hard work approach of homework before even picking up a movie camera – let alone aiming it – and subscribing as I certainly did then more to Eisenstein and Grierson than Vertov and Pennebaker, what then now follows is a set of film case histories. How, and working in this way, I went about the making of a film of the African Personality; a study of a nation at a turning point in its history; and an attempt to restore an environment lost in an earlier age as we are now well on the way to destroying our own. Subjects and themes of ultimate concern to every one of us; and of particular concern to the group of younger film-makers we had now met up with at Poona.

Taking then what now follows in the same way as examples – if assigned to tackle these subjects yourself – you would therefore have been urged to be just as interested in related history, geography, sociology, ecology, as in the sheer fun of filmmaking itself. For like Eisenstein, that Leonardo da Vinci of the cinema, it had long been an article of faith with me that you cannot be a really effective and worthwhile film-maker in a screen of change unless you are.

And even without access to, or interest in a movie camera, from what now follows, kind reader, you may learn more of the origins and reality of Black Power; how it is to lose an empire and your way at one and the same time; what Arabs first set out to do with all that money from their oil. Having to get to grips with all of this before turning a foot of film in a camera on the whys and wherefores, I certainly did.

7. FILM AND THE ENVIRONMENT

'How is the hammer of the whole earth cast asunder and broken! How is Babylon become a desolation among the nations!'

Jeremiah

'... And Babylon shall become heaps - without an inhabitant...'

An evening in early November 1988. The Dominion Theatre in London's Tottenham Court Road. The place packed. Not a spare seat to be had and people turned away at the doors. Apart from the appearances of pop stars and rock musicals which now more frequently kept it in business, the Dominion had seen nothing like this since it first opened its doors for the February 1931 European premier of Chaplin's *City Lights*, with Charlie himself in the audience. But what the customers had now come to see was an even older film, made back in 1916, by that founding father of the American cinema, David Wark Griffith. *Intolerance*. Prior to broadcast, Thames Television's representation of a freshly restored and colour tinted print, the screening accompanied by a newly commissioned music score, performed in synchronised accompaniment by a full sized symphony orchestra, conducted by Carl Davis. As audiences had first experienced seventy years before, a packed house now found itself similarly poleaxed by Griffith's immense bombardment of impassioned imagery. In the accelerating counterpoint of what has been called the only film fugue, Griffith brought to a simultaneous climax the last minute rescue in modern times of a man about to be hanged for a crime of which he was innocent; a Protestant family threatened with massacre in 16th Century Catholic France; the foundation of the Christian era with the preachings and crucifixion of Christ; and, in the most spectacular sequence of all, the downfall of pagan Babylon five hundred years before. The wide angle general view of Belshazzar's court, thronged with literally thousands of extras dwarfed by the life-size elephants surmounting the great columns towering hundreds of feet above them on either side, made from the top of the tower on which Bitzer's camera then advances in the cinema's first great crane shot, has become legendary – the enduring icon of the American 'silent' screen.

But what of the real Babylon?

In those far-off biblical days, Babylon had been indeed a mighty civilisation, the greatest of its time in the world. What's left of it still stands, in a dusty corner of Western Asia. Two and a half millennia after the Persians sacked the city, and forty years on from Griffith, I set up a camera on its ramparts, and panned across its ruins. You can imagine my feelings.

What brought me back across the centuries in this way was the making of a film which would picture an attempt to reverse the *March of Time*. A project which would bring waters back to Babylon, restore life to a land now barren where once it flourished, revolutionise an environment.

Babylon was then little more than a name on a signpost off the main road south from Baghdad to Basra, in the country called Iraq. On all sides was desert. Four thousand years ago Iraq had been the granary of the ancient world, when its rivers Tigris and Euphrates enriched not only Babylon but the Assyrian empire as well. This land was once the most productive in all history; it could support those Babylonian and Assyrian splendours which have since become so fabled that they are now veritable cities of the imagination, enthroned in the memory of mankind. But the time came when no captives could hang up their harps upon the willows of the nearby stream and sit down and weep by the waters of Babylon – for there were no waters: the cities fell, crumbled and disappeared into all but legend. But what happened was the result of no curse by an impatient Jehovah, appearing by magic as writing on a wall, but simply deforestation along the higher reaches of the rivers. Seeking more water for their irrigation crops, and more land to replace their exhausted soils, the plainsmen of those days cut down the hill forests – and were rewarded with uncontrollable floods that overwhelmed their fields and swept away their irrigation works. As a result, the land, and the people, died.

We know all about ecology these days. We certainly pay at least lip service to conservation, threatened as we now are with the destruction of our own environment. Back in the thirties, Pare Lorentz captured our imagination with his film of *The River*, which showed how greed for short-term profit cut down the naturally balanced sources of the Mississipi and turned the heart of America into a dustbowl, like most of Iraq had become. (In its indictment of this outcome of uncontrolled private enterprise, *The River* came to be considered too controversial, to be withdrawn from official circulation.) In my filming in Iraq twenty years later, we went back to demonstrate that the source of all survival is the tree – cut them down at our peril. We hoped to do at least as much good as Lorentz.

And so for me, it was back to Baghdad once again: that drab and far from glamorous city – far from Korda's magical fantasy – from which, an army cameraman, I had set out to make my first film, of wartime aid to Soviet Russia by way of Iran, the country next door to the East. Then I had had to make do with a single lens clockwork camera picked up in a local photographer's shop on Rashid Street. Now I had the very latest Arriflex, with a full battery of lenses, including a new wide angle of 18 millimetre focal length, at that time still something of a novelty and regarded with suspicion by the more orthodox film-maker. This outsize optical combination, originally four full inches in diameter, gave the camera a wider field of view than ever before, and at the same time a greater degree of overall sharpness from very close-up foreground to very distant background. How Eisenstein would have loved it, and what further miracles of construction and design he would have wrought with its tremendous range and depth. Using one myself for the first time the year before, I now swore by it. Now we could really play with perspective, relate face, figure, to a huge and pin-sharp background: the very reverse of the effect produced by the long-focus zoom.

The pictorial possibilities were endless, and I was eager to create with this new aid a fresh look at people in relation to their environment – now here in Iraq about to be radically and simultaneously changed by the impact of a new found wealth from the oil which had been discovered beneath its surface.

'Film-makers are encouraged to make films about subjects which demand and deserve thought. The next critical step is to make the audiences aware of film technique as well. If they were so conscious, we might get some real advance in technique – for technicians are at present devoting more and more time and energy to giving the pictures a highly polished surface which is admirable – admirable and dull. Almost every film today is technically competent – competent and nothing else. Portrayal has become entirely subservient to the thing portrayed: the frightening rattle of the conveyor belt is heard today around the studios and cutting rooms'.

Thus, eight years previously, spoke John Shearman, the producer of the film I was then about to make, in now the Spring of 1956. My concept that it should attempt a visual synthesis between environment and people now in conflict and development should, it seemed to me, satisfy both his creative ambition and guarantee our successful collaboration. But first – absorb the background to the story that we had to tell.

Baghdad itself seemed little changed since I had first trudged its streets, an impatient young army cameraman. Lacking any style or character, the bulk of the city still sprawled along the eastern bank of the Tigris, and the same wide bridge still led me reminiscently back to where I had then been billeted on the other side of this dingy but fast-flowing river. Heavy, red, single-decker British-built buses honked their way through the stream of traffic flowing fast and furious down the narrow main street, which was still a jumble of poky and colonnaded little shops, and on the corner by the bridge the same photographic shop displayed what seemed to be the same still pictures of Armenian family groups and Iraqi royalty. But the little King Feisal who had then been portrayed as a wide-eyed ten-year-old, in the shadow of his uncle the Regent, had now come into his inheritance. He was now twenty-four, and busy fulfilling his duties as monarch of this kingdom itself only thirty-five years old.

Prominent in every such Iraqi portrait gallery was the likeness of the then seemingly perennial Prime Minister, Nun al-Said. Nun had fought the Turks with Lawrence of Arabia, pledged to place Feisal, son of the Sheriff of Mecca, on the throne of an independent Arab state. For a short time Damascus had seen the latter, carried forward on the wave of the Arab Revolt, so ensconced, but the French had claimed Syria. Thereupon the British had unrolled their maps, created a new country called Iraq around the yet to be exploited oilfields of Mesopotamia, and offered this synthetic kingdom to their protégé. Now his grandson maintained the tradition of a monarchy which had, in fact, but two more years of life.

So much for history, and anticipation. But as I mused on these matters, and walked – as usual much to everyone's surprise – around the highways and byways of Baghdad, I realised that a new element had entered into at least café society.

Every street still had its *chaikhana*, its tea house, where Iraqis (always the menfolk – never the women) drank glass after glass of sweet and milkless tea, endlessly discussing for hour after hour the business of the day, the promise of tomorrow. But as the sun set, a huge red orb in the waters of the Tigris, and millions of lights started to twinkle, in every *chaikhana* one light flickered brighter than all the rest. It was a picture, and it talked. Television.

Only recently an industrial and trade fair had been held in Baghdad. A British company had set up and demonstrated a complete closed-circuit television installation. It had been the hit of the show. Other exhibits and pavilions had folded their tents and moved on, but this electronic complex remained. Taken over by the government, and now installed in a large house on the east bank, here was now the first television service in the Middle East. Restricted in range so far only to Baghdad, nonetheless, in the land which had pioneered pictographic writing in the fourth millennium before Christ, here there now flickered the instant communication of the twentieth century. And it was this that I had to thank for my coming to Baghdad.

For my experience in TV journalism and factual film reporting had made possible my assignment to this film. To achieve any appeal, any acceptance, any success, it must talk to the Iraqi audience, for whom it was intended, in their own language. The orthodox and anonymous voice of an unknown commentator, preaching away as pretty pictures passed by on the screen would certainly in this case lack any impact or conviction. The story of the redevelopment of their country must be told to Iraqis not just in their own language by other people but dramatised on the screen by their own selves. They, the people of Iraq, had to be the then protagonists and spokesmen of this, their film.

This concept had happily been accepted; and, as I had demonstrable experience in making both the more traditional as well as the more recently reportorial TV documentary, I had got the job.

My walks back to a hotel named after the Assyrian princess Semiramis, side by side with another named after Sinbad the Sailor – the only touch of magic about either – took place to a sound track which was a medley of music poured forth from radio as well as television sets. I developed an acute pain in my right ear. But however dissonant Arabic music might sound to one at that time more used to Beethoven and Brahms, this was not the cause. On the flight out, in a far from adequately pressurised aircraft, this ear had failed to 'pop' after takeoff. Pressure had become pain; and now I was reduced to lying in bed, restricted to one side, the afflicted ear against a miniature hot-water bottle, lifted off only for the periodic insertion of unguent oils. A ridiculous posture and situation, but one which I redeemed by reading all the literature available on the subject of the film: *The Development of Iraq*.

Sandwiched between Syria and Iran, a portion of its western frontier marching with the similarly synthetic Kingdom of Jordan, Iraq comprised some 172,000 square miles of bleak landscape in which there then lived only 6,000,000 people: the population of greater London in an area a little larger than California. But hardly as prosperous; most lived in mud-built villages, scraping an existence from worn-out soil alongside the animals they herded. Now all this was going to be changed, if all the plans, papers, and reports that I waded through meant anything.

The government had set up a Development Board, to be directly responsible for a programme of capital works for economic development; and allocated to it for this purpose seventy percent of all its revenue from oil.

Now Iraq had lots of oil, lots of money as a result, and very little of anything else – except water, and there was too much of that.

From the day of the original flood, when Noah came to rest in his ark on the summit of Ararat, the melting snows of this and other Turkish mountains to the north had poured, in their tons of millions of tons, down into Iraq; spreading out over the plains, inundating communities, ruining harvests. Only two years before the Tigris had burst its banks, flooded Baghdad itself as well as a large area of central and southern Iraq, washed away crops, animals, homes, and destroyed roads and railways. To control these ruinous waters was priority number one for the Development Board, and a safari and survey along the course of the country's huge and twin rivers accordingly the first piece of fieldwork for myself.

'Will you carry some of the dialogue over sequences of silent shooting?'

'Unless the 18 millimetre lens is set up straight on to the subject, won't all the verticals in the picture be distorted?'

Two of many questions fired at me by my new companions, Mohamed Shukri and Abdul Latif Saleh, young Iraqis in their twenties, director and cameraman from the unit the London-based Film Centre had set up in Baghdad as film consultants to the Iraq Petroleum Company.

The British-American-French owned Iraq Petroleum Company of those days was known to one and all as IPC, and in Iraq it was in fact three separate but associated companies. Down south, what was called the Basra Petroleum Company shipped oil along a pipeline a hundred miles from its Subair field to the combined mouth of the Tigris and Euphrates at the head of the Persian Gulf, where tankers could load and take it away.

We boarded a company boat in Basra, and set off in style down both rivers now flowing together in one great unison known as the Shatt al-Arab. On our left was Iran, on our right Iraq. On our left there soon appeared the towers and columns of the biggest oil refinery in what we then still called the Middle East, Iran's Abadan.

A third of Iraq's oil went out from a tanker terminal which had been built at Fao, the end of our river trip, where I once again sniffed that mixture of salt water, heat, humidity, and petroleum which has become such a prevalent perfume of present-day Arabia. But before I could continue my own survey of present-day and future Iraq, I had to take a journey back into a past so ancient that it would only be accomplished by that modern time machine, the motion picture camera.

Throughout the previous year Film Centre had been making a film of the archaeological, cultural and historical past of Iraq. A story which began over six thousand years ago, in the days of the earliest inhabitants, the Sumerians. Filmed in museums in Baghdad, London and Germany, now on the screen were examples of the metal they had smelted, the pottery they had moulded, the bricks they had baked, the images they had carved, and the language they had originated. Leading on to the Babylonian, Greek and Roman eras, in this way it was possible to show how each age had absorbed the land into its own empire, and how each vanished as its power crumbled. A gallop of horses and a flourish of flags introduced the coming of a new leader, the Prophet Mohammed. Then, with the filming of medieval manuscripts, the *Rivers of Time* went on to illustrate the profound scientific achievements of Islam, and showed how Baghdad and Damascus became centres of the arts and sciences. With a reminder to European audiences of how far the influence of Arab civilisation had then spread – from France and Spain in the West to China in the East – the film came to a contemporary close. But it had no start, no beginning. I was asked to devise, and film one.

Here was a film which portrayed the very origins of man, in the place of his oldest recorded habitation and environment – a country which was itself the scene and location of much of the Old Testament's story of Genesis.

Sequences for the film had already been shot in Babylon, still almost miraculously preserved despite the prophetic writing on its walls which confounded Nebuchadnezzar:

'And Babylon, the glory of kingdom, the beauty of the Chaldees' excellency, shall be as when God overthrew Sodom and Gomorrah. It shall never be inhabited, neither shall it be dwelt in from generation to generation; neither shall the Arabian pitch tent there'.

Here was a prophecy which had come true. I was soon to walk the great procession street of that once mighty metropolis:

empty, deserted, desolate, but vibrant still with the curse that had befallen it all those thousands of years before:

'And the owl shall dwell therein, and it shall be no more inhabited forever'.

In search for an opening for this latter-day film, turn then back to that first of all chapters:

'In the beginning God created the heaven and the earth. And the earth was without form, and void; and the darkness was upon the face of the deep ... and the Lord God planted a garden eastward in Eden, and there he put the man whom he had formed '.

Where could I, for the purpose of this film, find an Eden? An hour's drive from the hotel. For 'a river went out of Eden to water the garden; and from thence it was parted, and became into four heads ... and the fourth river is Euphrates'.

To the northwest of Basra was a huge lake and marshland, the delta of this same Euphrates. Shukri led me to it and an obliging boatman ferried us into its private and remote world of crossed and crisscrossed channels and waterways; all around were reeds and wild fowl, and at dawn an eerie silence. Crouched in the boat, we awaited the coming of day. Mist and vapour breathed over the face of the waters. All was total silence – in the aqueous and future killing fields of the war to come between Iraq and Iran. Now, alone, in this then still pacific wilderness, with camera encompassing its primeval perspective, and with lens set to catch the first shades of light to fall across its surface, we did indeed feel present at the beginning of things.

To the east, a lightening of the firmament. With camera heavily filtered, I shot straight into the huge red globe as it appeared over the horizon, then directly into the waters in which its light and life was soon sparkling. As the sun climbed into the heavens, I composed a series of abstract shots and patterns of its reflected progress; and those patterns of dancing light and shade – in the waters which had 'flowed out of Eden' – together became an impression of creation which, edited into the opening sequence of *Rivers of Time*, sent that future award-winning film off to a flying start.

Back to Basra, and the more immediate and urgent present. North, by road to Qurna, where the waters divided and became the present-day Euphrates, its course now eastward into central Iraq, Syria and, doubling back in the north, to its source in eastern Turkey; and Tigris, along the banks of which we now drove. Stark desert, with now and then an occasional settlement amongst an oasis of date palms. Dust. A place called Kut. The scene of Britain's most ignominious defeat in the First World War. Here, in what was now a town as nondescript as any I was to see in Iraq, the invading British, with their Indian troops driving on Baghdad, had been surrounded by the Turks. After a five-month siege, they had surrendered to a man. A melancholy place, where now new bridges were being built over roads which had known the march of Assyrian legions.

Into the environs of Baghdad, and eastwards back again into desert and the Euphrates at Ramadi. Here a new barrage had just been built across the river. Continuing on our way north, sixty miles upstream from Baghdad on the Tigris, we came to an even more impressive dam. This coordinated control of the two rivers north and east of Baghdad and was the Development Board's pride and joy.

Between Tigris and Euphrates here lay an immense pear-shaped hollow, enclosing 900 square miles of land considerably larger than the area of the Dead Sea, called the Tharthar Depression. The bottom was 230 feet below the surrounding ground, and below sea level. As far back as 1908 a British engineer had declared that, if ever the money were forthcoming, it could solve most of the problems of Iraq. A dam across the Euphrates to divert surplus water at Ramadi into the nearby lake at Habbaniyah, and a dam across the Tigris here at Samarra, with a diversion channel dug from there into this Tharthar Depression, would once and for all end the seemingly inevitable and divinely ordained flooding – which had devastated central Iraq every year since 'the flood was forty days upon the earth; and the waters increased, and bare up the ark'.

Now a new miracle had been wrought, and the waters controlled.

Both my companions, Mohamed Shukri, assistant director, and Abdul Latif Saleh, camera operator, were of course Muslims; although Shukri, who was half Turkish, was more typical of the young agnostic intellectual of his age anywhere. Possibly as a result of his mixed blood, the latter was the more febrile personality. He dabbled in abstract art, and wrote poetry. Latif was more down-to-earth, more ponderous in his movements and reactions. Physically he somewhat resembled Egypt's former king, Farouk; a likeness that seldom ceased to amuse Shukri. But they got on well together, the introvert and the extrovert; and each was as keen as any acolyte, apprenticed to the art of the moving image hitherto without roots in their country.

Works of an older art and faith abounded, and stood high for all to see. In the desert outside Samarra rose an enormous tower – the minaret of the largest mosque in the world. Eleven hundred years old, its height was 175 feet, 99 cubits: for all the world the Tower of Babel as pictured in children's story books. It was in fact modelled on that legendary erection, the foundations of which eager guides would point out to incredulous visitors in the present day ruins of Babylon.

Ninety feet from the base of this tower still stood the north wall of al-Mutawakkil's masterpiece, the Great Mosque of Samarra. All four walls were still intact, more than eight feet thick, enclosing an immense rectangle of more than forty-five thousand square yards. The roof and its supports had long since disappeared, and this colossal edifice now stood, still four-square, but open to the winds of heaven. It was quite deserted, completely abandoned.

What a fabulous setting for a film, I thought. No studio could ever hope to emulate its enormous and extraordinary dimensions. Surrounded by desert, by space, huge and alone it emerged out of the blood-red dawn of our departure from Samarra, a vision of another world, another age.

The Old Testament was still a more profitable guide on this journey than any other literature. What was this smoke and fire, bursting out of the very ground itself, a hundred miles to the North East of Samarra?

261

The zigurrat at Samarra

'Nebuchadnezzar the king made an image of gold, whose height was three score cubits, and the breadth thereon six cubits: he set it up in the plain of Dura, in the province of Babylon. Then an herald cried aloud, "To you it is commanded, O people, nations, and languages, that at what time ye hear the sound of the cornet, flute, harp, sackbut, psaltery, dulcimer, and all kinds of musick, ye fall down and worship the golden image that Nebuchadnezzar the King has set up: and who so falleth not down and worshippeth, shall the same hour be cast into the midst of a burning fiery furnace".'

I walked to the edge of the flames, the brittle surface of the desert flaking and crumbling beneath my feet. From the imprint of my very footsteps, smoke and further flame burst forth. These were in fact the eternal fires, no less, into which Nebuchadnezzar had cast the prophets Shadrach, Meshach, and Abednego.

Whence came this divine fire? What magic had fed these flames since long before the days of Daniel? From the top of a nearby hill the answer stood clear. In the distance great towers and silver columns rose out of the plain, the minarets of contemporary materialism – the oil refinery of Kirkuk, powered by the same field which had nearly succeeded in incinerating those Old Testament prophets. Petroleum.

Here was the heart centre of the oil company's empire, plumb in the centre of some sixty miles of oilfield, feeding more than twenty million pipelines every year.

There were two Kirkuks: an old Arab town, perched on a little hill, a labyrinth of narrow streets, overhanging roofs and walls, and the smell of animals and men. Six miles away was the Kirkuk of the Iraq Petroleum Company: pumps and power-houses, air-conditioned homes, floodlit swimming pool and tennis courts, the smell of paint and petroleum, and the clipped accent of the English abroad.

My host, however, spoke more with the accent of Bordeaux than Bournemouth. At last, in an IPC then one-third French, I had found a Frenchman, Leo Teyssot, the General Manager of the Kirkuk oilfields. Over a dinner which made a welcome change from the uncompromising Anglo-Saxon fare of the company rest house, I heard from him of how an American had first struck oil in Iraq.

A drill had been thrust down into the surface of the desert a mile of so from the Eternal Fires. In charge of operations was an American crew, led by one H.A. Winger. Midnight on October 13, 1927, the drill was down to 1,500 feet, and an Iraqi took over. Winger went to bed. The Iraqi driller decided to pull up the bit of the drill, and clear the borehole of cuttings. He had raised it to twenty feet of the surface, when a roar of escaping gas blew it out in his face. Huge fountains of oil gushed high over the derrick and into the surrounding darkness.

For six days this bonanza was completely out of control. Oil roared out of the well at the rate of more than 12,000 tons a day, streaming away in a river 100 feet wide. The people of Kirkuk, lining the flat rooftops in dumbfounded awe, were implored to light no fires – and the Eternal Fires themselves were hurriedly doused with sand. One spark and the 'Burning Fiery Furnace' of Nebuchadnezzar would have been a refrigerator in comparison.

Twenty wells were sunk in the next three years, and 1,200 miles of parallel pipeline laid across the Syrian desert to tanker terminals on the Mediterranean coast at Banias and Tripoli. Here at least it was thought, was one Middle East oilfield whose output need never be at the mercy of whoever controlled the Suez Canal.

Another pipeline, however, ran north, bringing down into the mainstream the output from IPC's third associated company, the Mosul Petroleum Company. We too now drove on north, through country which at last gave us something to look at for the first time since leaving Baghdad.

In all my wanderings I have never been to a country quite as featureless or bereft of character as Iraq. It is all one great monotony of flat nothingness. And it is not even a nothingness which has that strange appeal and grandeur of the real emptiness of the Arabian desert. There the very absence of anything seems profound. Iraq, to me, seemed by contrast wholly negative. The vast and ruined monoliths of earlier and vanished civilisations, with which its sterility is scattered, only served to depress me further; monumental reminders as they were to the ephemeral and transient nature of human hopes and ambitions.

But now to the left of our road rose mountains, down from which flowed two great tributaries of the Tigris; named, like a couple of prehistoric monsters, the greater and lesser Zab. Here was natural irrigation, and good farmland as a result. Camels no longer meandered along, in search of the occasional oasis; but donkeys and oxen worked water wheels, and corn stood high below terraced hillsides.

We pulled up at a *chaikhana* in the market town of Arbil, drank tea, ate meat on skewers, and turned off to the east. Soon we were driving through a different landscape again, flat, but every now and then pimpled by large mounds, rising sometimes smooth and pregnant-like, as high as hilltops. A century before, the Englishman Austen Henry Layard had thrust a spade into one of these – and dug up a palace. Nineveh, the city of Senacherib, the capital of Assyria, the dominant power of the contemporary world for three hundred years; buried and lost for the next two thousand.

Twenty feet tall, two great carved and winged bulls, with the faces of bearded men, stood side by side where they had been excavated at the portals of this ancient and ruthless residence. Only a mile away, to house their descendants, the Development Board was building a new housing estate, out of the plaster and cement of our now, less flamboyant age. On the outskirts of Mosul, new water tanks and towers were being welded, alongside yet another mound. This time the tomb of the prophet Jonah, on the summit of which a mosque proclaimed the revelation of that other prophet, Mohammed, and the now very much alive and increasingly militant faith of Islam.

'A camel is not an animal, an Arab is not a human being'. Such was the opinion of the people amongst whom we now found ourselves: rugged, independent hill men, of whom the Arab said in return 'There are three plagues in the world, the rat, the locust and the Kurd'.

We were now in an area which has long claimed and fought for its independence from Iraq, and the rest of the world. Kurdistan, the home of the Kurds, a people tougher than the Arab, more hot-tempered, less quick-witted and genial; more thrifty and hard-working; tribal in sentiment, dwelling in strongly fortified stone houses, proudly perched on the hillsides and mountain tops of this meeting place of northeastern Iraq, Turkey, and Iran. Their homeland divided by the borders to these three adjacent countries, whose frontiers mean nothing to them, and out of which they hoped one day somehow to carve out their own state.

The Kurds resembled somewhat the tribesmen of India's northwest frontier, both in temperament and dress. They wore brightly coloured clothes, wide-sleeved shirts, thick felt waistcoats and short jackets. On their heads they wore striped turbans, and on their feet leather slippers with turned-up toes. Long baggy trousers were tied round the waist with a girdle on which hung knives, for use as well as ornament.

Most of the labour in the Am Zala oilfield was Kurdish, but the management of the Mosul Petroleum Company was as English as Cheddar cheese. Once again I had to endure indigestible and formal meals from which, by virtue of their inferior and Iraqi status in the organisation, Shukri and Latif were spared. It was a relief to be on the road again, and headed for an area where the three of us could breathe an air purer than the compound of petroleum and protocol which so characterised our now immediate environment.

Eastwards now, almost to the borders of Iran, deep into the turbulent territory of the Kurdish homelands. Through ravines, over mountain torrents; down into rich and fertile valleys where, at work in the fields, male and female returned our gaze look for look, eye to eye. Here was none of the reticent and withdrawn retreat of a sometimes inhibited Islam. Here were a proud and independent people who regarded southern Iraqis such as my companions with contempt, and talked with my alien European self as more than an equal.

'When the Turks were driven out in 1918, you English promised that we Kurds would have our own state.' My informant was the *Mutassarif*, the Governor, of Sulaimaniya. We had now reached, and established ourselves in, the most northeastern of Iraqi provincial capitals. Shukri had taken me along and introduced me to this first citizen of what was in fact a predominantly Kurdish city.

'Look here', he said, and I read that in May 1919 the British Government had authorised its Acting High Commissioner in Iraq 'to take in hand the construction of five provinces for Iraq proper... You will also proceed with the creation of the Arab province of Mosul fringed by autonomous Kurdish states under Kurdish chiefs, who will be advised by British Political Officers'. This I saw would have meant a Kurdistan run on much the same lines, and enjoying the same nominal degree of independence, as the former native states of British India.

Author on his way to film the marsh Arabs of Southern Iraq

'But you were not sincere', my host went on. 'As soon as our leaders started to make their own decisions, your army marched on us here from Kirkuk, and occupied Sulaimaniya.'

I had done some homework too, and was aware that the new element which had then entered into the situation was the rise to power in Turkey of Mustafa Kemal. Rallying his defeated and stricken nation, Ataturk had once again made her a force to be reckoned with. The British Government feared that truly independent Kurds in Iraq might combine with the Kurds in Turkey, who were then being encouraged to invade and reoccupy the Mosul area from which the southerly winds were beginning to waft the scent of oil. Royal Air Force planes bombed the supply routes into Sulaimaniya, and the newly formed and British controlled Iraqi army marched for the first, and by no means the last time into forward positions, and in its own turn occupied Sulaimaniya.

'What now?' I asked.

'We are part of Iraq, and we expect our own fair share of the country's revenue from oil. It is really our oil you know – much of it comes from these parts.'

But the original, in those days, Iraqi Kurds had little to complain of in the Development Board's plans so far as I could see. Up here in remote Kurdistan were some of the most impressive and ambitious of all the new schemes of development. At Darband-i-Khan on the Diyala, and at Dokhan on the Lesser Zab, great dams were being built across these powerful tributaries to the Tigris. At Dokhan we stayed with the French engineers sweating away at their huge task of diverting the course of a river around a mountain. British consultants had picked the site in a mountain gorge, but the engineers had discovered that the actual mountain sides were too weak to act as safe buttresses of the dam itself. Thousands of tons of concrete were being injected into these two flanks in order that the dam, when cast between them, would not tear them away under the pressure of the millions of tons of water which it was designed to shore up and store.

Stagnant water means mosquitoes. They too were under attack. Teams drove out into the villages, and with DDT sprayed them into extinction. As a result malaria, which had cost so many Kurdish lives in the past, was ceasing to be a threat to their health and livelihood.

Sulamainiya itself was having a facelift. New homes had been constructed, and roads laid in the paths of bulldozers and trucks driving to and from an almost completed cement factory on the outskirts. Incongruously dressed in their baggy pants and turbans, perched high on rooftops, hands encased in black rubber gloves, Kurds wired up cables run from a new power station. Public gardens had been laid out. On a Friday, the Muslim Sabbath, we picnicked on the grass, beside a babbling brook, and in the shade of trees.

Trees. In the desert that was southern and central Iraq, apart from the occasional date palm, there were none. Outside Sulamainiya nurseries had been established, growing the seedlings which in time would come to shade the new highways of more than just this one northern province. The year before, a Forest Law had been passed, and regulations had followed for setting up State forests; the manufacture of charcoal for commercial purposes forbidden for a trial period pending the introduction of controlled cutting, and a forest police force created. A fifty-year programme for afforesting an area of two thousand square miles was now under consideration. Meanwhile, a twenty-year plan of afforestation had been drawn up to cover a hundred square miles, mostly in the areas to be furnished by the new irrigation projects. These measures were designed both for the protection of crops and to serve the commercial needs of the country in the supply of industrial hardwood and wood pulp. Over the same period it was proposed to plant seven hundred and fifty miles of avenue between the main towns. An organisation had been created for research and experiment on the varieties of tree most suited to the country's conditions and requirements, and on the control of the insects and pests which attack them. It was experimenting on poplar and eucalyptus, and the plane, tamarisk and conifers were also under trial.

In what was, to all intents and purposes, a desert country, this quest for home-grown timber seemed to my mind the most encouraging and imaginative ambition; and in this search for a good home-made plank lay the peg on which we were to hang the whole story of the Development of Iraq.

Back in Baghdad it was now time to take stock. From our survey of the length and breadth of Iraq we now had thousands of feet of film of the development projects we had shot along our way. Together with sequences of the land and its people themselves, these could have been put together into a creditable, but orthodox, documentary film. The disembodied voice of an anonymous commentator could then have told the story alongside this assembly of scenes, but it was our intention to involve the Iraqis themselves in this telling of their own contemporary story. All the silent filming that I had therefore amassed was but so much flesh to be grafted on to a skeleton not yet completely devised. This framework-to-be would consist of dialogue scenes and statements, in which their involvement in the whole story would be made manifest to the audience by their own spokesmen, in their own language.

The great question was just who would be our Iraqi archetype? Around what sort of figure, representative of what type of occupation, could we most effectively personalise the country's development? Whoever we chose must be a composite character which would strike an immediately responsive chord with our audience, who should be able to identify themselves with this celluloid counterpart of their own doubts and desires.

In the north the Development Board had been growing trees, timber. What could be a more effective symbol of progress in a primarily desert country? And who worked with wood, who fashioned timber into a hundred-and-one different uses and applications? A carpenter. And so a carpenter it was; a village carpenter, and we called him Usta Rzuqi.

The film, which came to be called *The Great Question*, opened with a close-up of a piece of wood, filling the screen, and close enough for the audience to see that this was not new timber, but merely a piece of an old packing case. Hands were attempting to plane some sort of practical shape out of it. They gave up, and in disgust their owner marched out of his workshop, through his village street, and into the local *chaikhana*. As he walked along he heard a news broadcast, from a car radio, from a transistor set slung on a bicycle, from the loudspeaker in the forecourt of the teahouse.

In glib and impersonal tones, the announcer painted a glowing and optimistic picture of the country's development: so many new dams, so many power stations, so many new projects nearing completion.

'Bunk', said our hero, settling back to enjoy a glass or two of tea with his friends. 'Talk, talk, talk. Why, a man can't even get a good piece of wood with which to hammer out a decent living for himself.'

'What would you do then, Usta?' ask his friends, as more tea was ordered.

'Why, that's easy. I would...' Pause. He's not so sure. He's tired. 'Don't bother me. Any fool knows the answer.' He gets up and leaves, goes home, lies down, and drifts off to sleep. He dreams. A new voice is heard.

'Usta, Usta Rzuqi'. He sits up. 'What's this – who are you?'

'We are the people of Iraq', says this voice on the sound track. 'Answer the question: how would you make everyone rich and happy?'

'Easy', says our self-appointed expert. 'Divide up into equal shares all the money we get from oil.'

The screen fills with bank notes. Town criers give them away. Young and old queue up for their share. Children sleep, cradled in currency.

'There are more than six million of us', the voice of the Iraqi people reminds Usta Rzuqi, 'and last year we got seventy millions from oil – so that if we followed your plan we would all of us have no more than ten pounds a year'.

'Alright', countered Usta, 'Then we can buy all we need from abroad'. Shops bulge with imported consumer goods. Ships are seen to sail up the Shatt al-Arab and discharge their cargoes at Basra. Aeroplanes land and unloaded freight at Baghdad.

271

Oilfield in Iraq

Barrage on the Tigris

'But what if we ran out of oil', Usta is now asked. 'What if the world no longer wanted our oil?'

A donkey wanders amidst a derelict and abandoned airfield, the only sign of life on the screen as the desert creeps back. The flames of the Eternal Fires flicker finis to this transient attempt to draw off their fuel.

'Therefore we are building dams...'

'Dams', roars Usta. 'Don't make me laugh'. But nonetheless he does, in great guffaws. 'What good are dams to me?'

The barrage across the Euphrates at Habbaniya and the Tigris at Samarra are followed on screen by a map of an intensive and countrywide irrigation network. Into picture steps an engineer. Against this background he talks directly to the camera, to the audience – now one and the same with Usta Rzuqi.

'This is the answer to your problem. Power. The power we shall get from the force of all this water which we have previously allowed to run to waste'.

The Dokhan dam is seen a-building, but the voice of the engineer is suddenly interrupted. In his place appears an irrigation engineer: 'That is not enough. We must get this water on to the land. We must feed it through a completely new irrigation system, and then we shall no longer have to live in a desert'.

Water pours through channels cut in the desert soil near Babylon and Samarra. At Sulamainiya little seedlings are carefully nursed. Corn is tossed in the air as Kurds separate wheat from chaff. Cattle roam through a new green landscape. Water flows everywhere, and tall conifer-like trees grow high against the sky. But another expert butts in: 'You cannot just let that water run into the fields without a proper drainage system – or they will all salt up'.

Dried-up mud flats, salinated soil, old bones, and the ruins of Zubair now replace what was an energetic abundance. Drainage engineers are seen at the headworks of great pumping stations near Hilla.

Yet another interruption. This time a doctor. 'But all your water can bring disease and death...'

Splashing through a ford, a medical team drives into a Kurd-

Babylon

ish village, and sprays with insecticide the homes of the malaria-carrying mosquito, breeding in stagnant water. A mobile unit X-rays the inhabitants of another, southern village. Leaning against his filing cabinet, the doctor comes back on screen. 'That's the answer. Health. Everyone fit, disease vanquished. Then we can build a strong nation'.

But even he, in his turn, is interrupted – by a teacher, standing by his blackboard: 'But we need schools – otherwise there won't be any engineers, irrigation and drainage experts, doctors. Without education we shall always be poor. We have to teach and equip the children of a whole new generation – our real future'.

Building and yet more building now takes over on the screen. New houses, new hospitals, new schools, new colleges. Inside are seen lecture classes, laboratory work, electronic tuition. Power cables are hoisted and power stations switched on. In the freshly irrigated fields agronomists are shown at work, veterinary experts with new breeds of cattle, chicken, sheep. Combine harvesters move through a sea of soft green alfalfa; crops are sprayed from the air; cotton is spun in a mill. A cement factory is built, and its product creates new roads and bridges. A little girl turns on a tap, and out flows water. Another licks an ice cream. The desert has disappeared – and in a factory timber is mass-produced into furniture.

'It's all very simple really', says Usta Rzuqi, who now reappears on the screen, talking now in his own turn to the audience. 'Everything relates to everything else. We can't have one thing without the other. *There are no short cuts.* We need engineers, irrigation experts, doctors, and teachers. We must dam the rivers, irrigate and drain the land. We must train our children – we must grow trees. Trees. That's the answer. It will take time, but I know – because I'm a carpenter!'

The original script had been written by John Rowdon, a one-time writer with All India Radio; an apprenticeship which had given him a good ear for the dialogue of peoples not necessarily his own. As well as Sinclair Road, our Executive Producer from London's Film Centre, we were now joined in Baghdad by a man

The Chaikhana at Ctesiphon

'Usta Rzuqi' - our Iraqi 'man in the street'

Debating the Great Question

276

named Jabra Ibrahim Jabra.

Jabra was an Arab, engaged in the writing of the commentaries of the other, more orthodox documentaries that Film Centre and the IPC Film Unit were making. He was one of many uprooted by the violent creation of the State of Israel.

Little snails are seen being lifted out of the irrigation and drainage ditches. The creatures which carry bilharzia, the dread disease which causes blindness and death. Under medical supervision, copper sulphate is shown being added to the water, its green another colour in the swirling pattern of the film.

Jabra was himself the son of a carpenter, and a carpenter of Bethlehem at that. He had been educated at the Arab College of Jerusalem and Cambridge University. Before his home town had been torn in two by war between Arab and Jew, he had gone on to become Jerusalem University's College lecturer in English literature. Then followed a three-year exile in the United States, on a Rockefeller Foundation fellowship at Harvard. He painted, wrote poetry, and was at this time also engaged in a novel.

Hunters in a Narrow Street tells the story of a young Christian Arab from Palestine, whose girl is blown up by Jewish terrorists in Jerusalem, and who takes a teaching post at the University of Baghdad. The bulk of the book reports verbatim and in depth his conversations with a motley group and cross section of young Iraqi intellectuals – all contemptuous of their contemporary society, and all anxious to blow it sky high. Suicide, murder, and mayhem are discussed and put in hand against the older generation and the status quo. Jabra's hero has a hectic love life to set against all this, exchanging the clutches of someone else's rich and bored upper-class wife for an uncertain and unspecified future with a passionate and idealistic young girl, to whom he was engaged as a tutor of English.

How much of all this was autobiographical, and how much inspirational, only Jabra can say. Certainly in the Baghdad of the time of our filming he appeared to be very happily domesticated.

'... And a river flowed out of Eden ...'

A charming wife, happy children, a nice home – hung with his own paintings – all made a most pleasant background to our discussions and planning of the dialogue sequences now due to be filmed for *The Great Question*.

First and foremost was a search for characters to play the parts of Usta Rzuqi and his cronies. Iraq then possessed neither film studio and theatre, but in the Institute of Fine Arts at the Ministry of Education Jabra knew a drama group. Its leading light was one Haj Naji al Rawi. He joined us for a drink at the Sinbad Hotel. It was immediately obvious to all of us that he was a natural Usta Rzuqi. I rehearsed him, and shot a test. He was splendid, a born actor. Others of his group fitted the parts of Usta's *chaikhana* companions, and the real experts in engineering, irrigation, drainage, health and education were chosen by the Development Board. Shukri found a location which would serve as our carpenter's village. It was only an hour's drive south of Baghdad. Ctesiphon.

Ctesiphon. Once again the shades of antiquity enveloped my filming in Iraq; just behind the *chaikhana*, there rose more than a hundred feet into the sky an enormous arch – fourteen hundred

The great arch of Ctesiphon

years old, and still today the widest single-span vault of un-reinforced brickwork anywhere in the world. The banqueting hall of Chosroes the Great, the Persian king who challenged the power of Rome, and sacked Antioch before Belisarius marched his legions down this same valley of the Euphrates.

With a sound crew flown out from England, filming now went forward apace. Haj Naji al Rawi gave us a bravura per-formance as Usta Rzuki, and we lined up and shot the Development Board's experts almost on a conveyor belt of fast production. I flew back to London with *The Great Question* at last in the can, and seemingly set for a long life on the screens of its country of origin. But the pressures beneath the surface of Iraq were about to burst forth in their greatest eruption yet – and sweep this film into oblivion, along with much else besides.

Passed to and fro between scoring and recording rooms in London and cutting rooms in Baghdad, requiring approval screenings at various times and stages both in England and Iraq, it was almost summer of the following year before the first approved print of the film was ready for its premiere. But for the Iraqis time was running out: they could not wait to be persuaded by Usta Rzuqi of the virtues of patience. A generation was now of age who wanted none of Prime Minister Nun al-Said's cautious championing of a British alliance: young men, and young women, who refused to accept any longer the passive degradation of their peasantry and still, as they saw it, the largely foreign control of their country as well as an alien and enemy occupation of Palestine.

The hero of Jabra's *Hunters in a Narrow Street* had not forgotten all his 'years in Jerusalem, for they had passed through the same atmosphere of protest, defiance and anguish, under the predatory shadow of police and soldiery'. Back there we had contended with alien forces, trying to assert our will against another will that sought our destruction, until it almost succeeded. But here, in this city, the contention was within; it was the set of a city groping in the dark, stumbling upon sharp edges. It was the nightmare that had to be dreamed before awakening'.

In Baghdad a group of young army officers seized power. The Prime Minister was murdered, and his body dragged through the streets. The young King Faisal, whose portrait had first welcomed me to Iraq sixteen years before, was gunned down against the walls of his palace. It was the end of an era.

Iraq was plunged into chaos. The British Embassy was attacked and fired. *The Great Question* had been answered, in no uncertain terms; and the prints of this film languished on the shelves of a now defunct film unit, whose British technicians fled the country. IPC's monopoly was brought to an end – the company expropriated and taken over completely. Jabra remained and, while the bullets were flying around, kept his head by translating *Hamlet* into Arabic.

To be, or not to be. To attempt national development before, or after political revolution. That is indeed the great question.

What happened in Iraq was no surprise to me. A year before I started work on that film, a report was made to the Development Board of Iraq by one Lord Salter. This former Deputy Director

280

of the United Nations Relief and Rehabilitation Administration – for whom I had filmed the early days of European post-war recovery – then Chairman of the Advisory Council of the International Bank, reported that in Iraq attention had been 'to too great an extent concentrated upon dams and water schemes, while other forms of development have been neither studied nor promoted adequately... Housing, the most obvious of the Board's enterprises which can give quick results directly visible to the ordinary man, has hitherto been on a negligible scale'. He referred to popular resentment 'no less dangerous because it now obtains little expression in Parliament'. He criticised severely the Development Board's irrigation policy. 'The immediate objectives of policy, in a country with so small a population (six and a half million) should be to open up new land (i.e. by new irrigation projects) as and when it is actually needed for available settlers. It is more urgent to do this than to provide irrigation for all that is potentially cultivable'.

On being asked my opinion of the original script by John Shearman, the producer, I put my finger on this last point. (I had not filmed for the *March of Time* in China eight years before for nothing.)

'We don't say anything about what is to become of the new cultivable land which will be made available by irrigation – who is to own it and work it.'

'We can't. That's politics.'

One of the very first measures that Abdul Karim Kassem and his original group of revolutionary young army officers put into practice in Iraq was a comprehensive land reform.

And Babylon? After he had set out to settle Kurdish claims once and for all with poison gas, 'Babylon' was selected as the code word for the giant cannon with which Iraq's later dictator Saddam Hussein planned to obliterate Israel. And the place itself? To be scrubbed, cleaned, and restored to a Disneyland semblance of its former glory, and placed in its refurbished walls bricks inscribed with the name of Saddam Hussein. But for this latter-day Nebuchadnezzar the writing on the wall could well have been spelt K U W A I T, where his invasion attempts and attempts to to seize power were defeated and fought off – and *The Great Question* become not so much how best to go about the peaceful and progressive development of an *Emergent Nation* – but more how to contain the military ambitions of a resurgent Islam.

With response to such motivated assault on the twin towers of New York's World Trade Center in the autumn of 2001, the people of this area nowadays known as Iraq once again faced conflict of virtually biblical dimension. *The Great Question* remained, as always, just simply survival.

8. FILM AND RACE

'An identity is questioned only when it is menaced, as when the mighty begin to fall, or when the wretched begin to rise.'

James Baldwin

Author at recording of *African Awakening* with Wolfe Soyinka and producer James Carr

As we walked towards the main gateway of the Film and Television Institute of India one evening at the end of a hard day's work at Poona, Basil Wright and I were accosted by a group even darker than the shadows from which they emerged. Africans. Very unhappy Africans.

'Can you please help us, sir?' their spokesman asked Basil, and he then went on to tell us that they had been sent by their respective governments of Ghana, Nigeria, and Tanzania to study filmmaking here at this Indian centre of experience and excellence. But they were cold-shouldered. After classes, no one spoke with them. Socially, they were ignored, ostracised, by their lighter-coloured hosts. Could we somehow help them to get away – to rearrange study for them, but at a film school in England? Here indeed was a lesson, I thought. Colour prejudice is not just a matter of simply black-and-white.

But to someone like myself, born white in a European country at that time long the master of what it called the 'Dark' Continent – and today the uneasy home to many black Britons the sons and daughters of formerly West African slaves – this must surely now be the paramount issue of our times. Casting the very first vote to which I was ever entitled in a British General Election, in 1945 this had gone to the Labour Party, as much because of its commitment to Indian independence as anything else. Sixteen years later, I was given the chance to do something about it – at least on the screen.

'We are now beginning work on the next film operation planned for the Company. It is a most ambitious project, and it may prove, when we have dug into it more deeply, that it is not a feasible one. What we hope to do in short is to produce a film which shows pictorially the emergence of the African personality!'

The opening paragraph of the letter of introduction back in 1961 – a whole generation before Nelson Mandela was at last to be released from South American imprisonment – which transported me to Africa. To West Africa, and the former slave routes.

It was a propitious time in which to attempt something never before feasible. For hitherto, Black Africa had been almost entirely ruled by European colonial powers. There could be no free or genuine expression of an African personality within the framework and control of an alien imperialism. Now, in just four short years, the British were granting freedom to their former colonies of the Gold Coast (now the independent state of Ghana), Nigeria, and Sierra Leone. Nigeria, with then a population of more than fifty million, was the largest of all Africa's new nations. The only thing that these not so very long ago tribal areas had in common was a shared domination by the British, who had brought to them as they saw it their own sense of justice, order, and development – and the language through which these African millions now spoke to the world; and, in which, as I now hoped and planned this film, they would be enabled to express, freely, their own personality.

For as I was able to demonstrate later at Poona with Richard Cawston's BBC film *Born Chinese*, personality can be collective, as well as personal. Even racial. Certainly there can be no question that there is an Afrikaner personality. It had dreamed up, and imposed on the Africans unfortunate enough to find themselves at this moment of history in the south of their continent, A*partheid*. The Russians might not have allowed Solzhenitsyn freedom to receive his Nobel Prize for literature in 1972, but eleven years previously, just months prior to my own arrival in Africa to attempt this film, the South African Government had permitted Albert Luthuli a brief respite from captivity to receive the Nobel Peace Prize. In Oslo, this imprisoned President of African Congress had declared that: 'To remain neutral in a situation where the laws of the land virtually criticised God for having created men of colour was the sort of thing I could not, as a Christian, tolerate'.

Two years before, smuggling film shot in Johannesburg out of the country disguised as a musical, and calling it *Come Back Africa*, Lionel Rogosin had given us some idea of what it meant to be black, and suffer the indignities and injustices of Apartheid. Also set in South Africa, Alan Paton's *Cry The Beloved*

Country – the tragic tale of a white farmer and a black preacher finding friendship through linked family tragedies – was filmed by Zoltan Korda in 1951, with the African-American actor Canada Lee in the starring role, and retitled in the United States *African Fury*.

Forced to deny that he had ever been a Communist, further work was still none the less denied Canada Lee in that 'scoundrel time' of the early fifties Cold War, and he had died penniless just a few weeks after this Korda film had opened in New York. His performance as the Reverend Stephen Kumalo is one of great dignity: the black hitherto portrayed in the cinema as very much a stock figure. Incapable of self-control, if not venal when given power, as by Griffith in *The Birth of a Nation*. Singing, dancing, entertaining in musical after musical, from *St. Louis Blues* to *Carmen Jones*. Forelock-touching, devoted slave to white masters in countless films, climaxed with an Academy Award for Hattie McDaniel as Scarlett's 'black mammy' servant in *Gone with the Wind* (to the première of which in Atlanta she was denied admission). There had been some notable exceptions. Back in 1929, King Vidor made *Hallelujah*, an early 'talkie' and Hollywood's first 'all-negro' film. In 1946, at dear old Denham and on location in East Africa, Thorold Dickinson had made *Men of Two Worlds*, a sincere attempt to penetrate the clash of cultures between white and black together with the conflict within just one African personality. We were at this time still the better part of a decade away from Jules Dassin's *Up Tight*, William Klein's *Eldridge Cleaver*, Agnes Varda's *The Black Panthers*, and a black James Bond called *Shaft*. But ever a law and a prophet unto himself, and using his technique of realism based on fact, in *Lost Boundaries* Louis de Rochemont had already, as far back as 1949, made the first American feature film to tell how it was to have black blood in an America then still so confidently and complacently white.

In general, the British could not be cast as villains in the story I now set out to tell, even though they had colonized – and exploited – more of the dark continent than most. Their administrators were, with rare exception, men of good will, genuinely committed to assisting what no one could reasonably have disputed were – purely because of geographic and historic circumstance – the peoples of lesser-developed countries only some part of the way along the road to total self-discovery and ultimate self-government. The trouble was that the British attitude of paternalism ran so deep. Back in 1926 that conscientious production group which we have met before restaging the battles of World War One, British Instructional Films, came up with an extraordinarily misconceived contribution to imperial enlightenment in a film called *Palaver*, written and directed by Geoffrey Barkas and shot almost entirely on location in Nigeria. This was a full length feature film, when location filming away from studios on such a scale was unheard of. Full marks certainly for the two men, one woman unit who overcame all technical, if not sociological difficulties. The production assistant, who subsequently became the director's wife, summarised their intention as follows.

'The general idea was to show the life of a British District Officer in a remote part of the Empire, administering justice, building roads and bridges, teaching the natives to develop their country and live peaceably together'.

The reality, when finally shown on the screen of the Marble Arch Pavilion in September 1926, was somewhat different. Two actors, plus one glamorous actress, had also sailed out to play the principal parts in a story the trio concocted after their arrival in Nigeria. Criticised by their producer back home as 'not strong enough', this tale told of an upright District Officer, a devoted Nurse in the nearby hospital, and a weak and drunken tin-miner who peddled gin to the 'King of the Pagans' in return for the labour of two hundred of his subjects. This villain had of course to be given a very un-English name, Fernandez. The climax is reached when our hero orders him out of the country. In retaliation, Fernandez persuades the 'King of the Pagans' to launch an attack against his enemy, the District Officer. But let their scenario speak for itself.

'At dawn Alison, shaving outside his tent, is astonished to see an arrow flash past and bury itself in the canvas. Quickly he seizes his revolver and the Union flag which every District Officer plants in his camp, however small, and runs to cover, followed by his cook, while his bearers scatter in all directions. Arrows and spears are coming thick and fast, and he is almost surrounded when he gains the shelter of a group of rocks. A grim fight ensues. The pagans are ugly and determined. Alison fires into them again and again. A deep gash from a spear appears on his arm. Ammunition is running short, and the position looks pretty desperate when the sound (and remember this was a *silent* picture) of thundering hoofs is heard, and down the valley sweeps a splendid company of loyal Angas, armed to the teeth.'

As a reprisal, our administrator of colonial justice, as portrayed in this historical curiosity of more than seventy years ago, burned down the pagan village.

A feature film, with location material shot in Uganda as well as Nigeria ten years later, was a much more stylish affair altogether. This was *Sanders of the River*, produced by Alexander Korda before he built and moved into Denham. (As a student in England at the time Jomo Kenyatta – the future President of a free Kenya – got a day or two's pay as an extra.) The original idea for this film had come from stories by Edgar Wallace of a trader working his way along an African river which might have been the Niger, peddling his wares to the people and tribes living along its banks. But script-writer Lajos Biro built up the character of Sanders, the British Commissioner, and balanced this star part with another of equal importance for an African, Bosambo, the one chief of the local tribes who remains loyal when fighting breaks out. No great shakes as a film, although at that time a money-maker for Korda, *Sanders of the River* is significant for the presence in its cast of Paul Robeson. He played Bosambo, who might nowadays, because of the character's support of the British, been described in all-Black Panther circles as a Quisling of the River.

Robeson's grandfather had been a slave on a plantation in North Carolina. Alongside some 200,000 so-called Negroes, he fought in the Union Army during the American Civil War. Emancipated by Lincoln and victory, the way was clear – but not

288

easy – for his grandson to gain a scholarship to attend Rutgers; the State University of New Jersey. Paul became a star football-player – the first black 'All-American' – and then went on to study law, entering the theatre almost by accident on the stage of the Harlem YWCA. In its 1920 production of *Simon the Cyrenian*, Paul Robeson played the part of the African who is said to have carried Christ's cross to Golgotha. Tremendous stage presence, star quality (and the need for money with which to support a family) soon made Robeson a personality and a force to be reckoned with in the American theatre of the twenties. It was also discovered that he could sing. *Show Boat*, and his hit song *Ol' Man River*, were to haunt – if not diminish – Robeson on through the years. His first film was to be a silent production of *Body and Soul*. 1933 saw a big hit in Dudley Murphy's direction of Eugene O'Neill's *The Emperor Jones*, and two years later it was England, which took Robeson to its heart – and Bosambo in Korda's *Sanders of the River*.

In latter days, Robeson (and his admirers) did all they could to clear him of complicity in what they saw as an imperialistic conspiracy. He claimed that his part in the finally released film had been falsified from the original interpretation he had agreed to play. Be that as it may, nine months after the general release of *Sanders of the River*, Paul Robeson went on record to state that:

'During my recent tour of America, on many occasions people would come up to me in small towns, where formerly I could have walked unrecognised on the streets, congratulate me on my performance as Bosambo, and tell me that the film had given them new ideas about the African Negro. Many of them confessed that, before seeing the picture they had regarded the Negro as a violent savage, having gleaned their notions of him from such films as *Trader Horn* and the Tarzan adventures, in which the natives were depicted as paint-daubed, gibberish-mouthing, devil-worshipping creatures. But they had come to see him as a man with lucid emotions and a code and language of his own'.

Whatever Robeson did, he invested with such dignity that he never needed to apologise, to anyone. Three years later, in the company of fifteen hundred English seaside holiday-makers, I sat at his feet at a song recital. They demanded *Ol' Man River*. He obliged. Then, as an encore, he sang a song of his own choosing. It was unknown to this audience, but its message was clear. Clear enough to create a sense of unease amongst them. In that prosperous middle-class seaside resort of Folkestone, the summer of 1939, Paul Robeson sang the *Ballad of Joe Hill*. The Swedish-American union man who was 'framed' by the 'copper bosses' of Utah for attempting to organise the miners.

Five years before I had sat at his feet in that English concert hall Robeson had visited Moscow. His host had been Eisenstein. What brought them together was a project the Russian had cherished ever since he had failed to come to terms with Hollywood during that unfortunate period of his career. It was the story of a free Black Republic many years ahead of its time.

Liberté, Egalité, Fraternité – the rallying call of the French Revolution, which, two hundred years ago, set aflame the liberal conscience of its time. But in the French owned Caribbean island of St. Dominique (now Haiti) the slaves made the mistake of thinking that this applied to them too. Under the leadership of one of their own race and blood, in 1791 they overcame their alien overlords and created the first free black nation. Their leader was Toussaint L'Ouverture, under whom the *London Gazette* was pleased to report that 'the black man is treated with the most perfect respect and equality', and in whom no less than Wordsworth thought he had glimpsed an example of 'Man's unconquerable mind'. Discussing this as a film project with Marie Seton all these many years later, Eisenstein believed that a slave, only a single generation away from Africa, capable of organising such resistance and then defeating the troops of Napoleon, must have been more than just an exceptional person – that such achievement could only reflect the developing genius of his people: 'If a race is biologically and psychologically inferior in its roots, such a man could not appear in its midst'.

Toussaint was of course eventually defeated, to die imprisoned in a dungeon high in the French Alps – but what a story, what a film. No wonder Eisenstein wanted to make it, and with

Robeson in the lead. Together they discussed this in Moscow, that Christmas week of 1934, but it was not to be. The Stalinist apparatchiks demanded of Eisenstein that he hurry up and make a film about 'Socialist Creation' in the Soviet homeland – and Robeson returned to *Sanders of the River* and four more films notable only for his presence; before, on the eve of World War Two, starring in *The Proud Valley* for Michael Balcon by then at Ealing. Directed in this story of a black stoker who jumps ship in Cardiff, to be welcomed by the coal miners of a nearby Welsh pit – 'We're all black faces underground' – by Pen Tennyson who had assisted Hitchcock on *The 39 Steps*, Conway on a *Yank at Oxford* and Vidor on *The Citadel*.

The abortive black revolt in Haiti, a couple of centuries before its time, continued to fascinate Eisenstein, and was to haunt him as yet another of his never to be realised projects. In his teaching at the Moscow Film School, he would set his students the task of writing out shot lists and camera angles of a already written sequence from *Black Majesty*, when, after Toussaint's own capture, two of his lieutenants escape from a trap laid for them in turn by the French.

Now, another world and twenty-seven years later, Paul Robeson, that great fighter for civil rights, was a prisoner in his native land, his passport withdrawn. Here, in Nigeria, from whose shores his forbears had been shipped to America in chains, I stared at a blank, and white, sheet of paper, wondering how to get on film the story, the personality, of free black men.

I did not particularly want to meet administrators, politicians, traders, business men. I wanted to meet writers, painters, musicians. As soon as possible after my arrival in Lagos, that lagoon-like capital of Nigeria, I made it clear that I had to get to know African artists and their work. For if the film was to reflect the African personality, it must speak in African terms. My aim was to make a film without any externally written and spoken commentary whatsoever. (Thank you, Mr Pennebaker.) Either on screen themselves, or in quotations from their writings, Africans must contribute and speak the words and language of this, their film. Despite the great diversity of local languages and dialects, this was possible because English was the *lingua franca* of not only Nigeria, but also of the peoples in the two other countries I had to visit and incorporate in this single, cohesive interpretation. An early call was therefore scheduled to the local radio station, which commissioned such work from local Lagos-based Nigerian writers and musicians.

In a small office sat some half dozen young Nigerians: poet, dramatist, actor, composer. These were the people with whom I had to make genuine contact, achieve communication. These were the people who had to be convinced of my good faith. I knew what they must be thinking, for in their place I would have thought exactly the same. Here is another of those bloody English intellectuals, eunuch-like in his guilt complex, attempting to identify with the noble savage, while at the same time convinced of his own innate intellectual superiority. I myself would have wanted nothing of such patronage.

But from the moment I explained that in this film no word was planned to be mine, no commentary was envisaged as being grafted on afterwards, that all the words and thoughts would be their own, that I was going to impose no pre-conceived script, and would only attempt to synthesise on the screen their own happenings, dramatise their own dreams, then the tension and the reserve disappeared. I was accepted, but I must wait. There was another of their company, due at any time. He I must meet. In walked no Bosambo.

From the moment of his entry, this last arrival and personality filled the room – and enriched the film. Wole Soyinka.

Wole Soyinka had been born in Western Nigeria twenty-seven years before. He had studied at the College established by London University in what, in any atlas of fifty years before, had been marked as Yoruba, and then left this land of his fathers for the country of his tutors. After eighteen months at the University of Leeds, he had come down to London and got a job as a play reader at the Royal Court Theatre, then at the crest of the new wave of British dramatic protest. On its stage, only twelve months before, Jimmy Porter had first looked back in anger. Of the same age as John Osborne's anti-hero, Wolfe Soyinka spoke for a new African generation who, one could but assume, now looked forward in hope.

Soyinka started to write plays of his own. He returned to his homeland the year of its independence from British colonial rule, seven months before this meeting of ours, and formed his own drama group, 'The 1960 Masks'. The Sunday following our meeting he was rehearsing a play, and he asked me along. I accepted his invitation with delight, and enormous relief. I had made contact with an African, a truly articulate African: an African whose translation of Euripides' *Bacchae* was to be in the 1973 repertoire of the British National Theatre. A leading critic was then to write that 'Wole Soyinka has done for our napping language what brigand dramatists from Ireland have done for centuries: booted it awake, rifled its pockets and scattered the loot into the middle of next week'.

And what was our language? The language of Shakespeare, Shaw, and Osborne – and now of Soyinka. The language of the British sailors, soldiers and merchants who had first opened up this territory to the outside world; and the English Christian missionaries who had followed shotgun and gin bottle with crucifix and bible.

'An de Lawd, He done go work hard for make dis ting dey call um Earth. For six days de Lawd He work and He done make all ting – everyt'ing He go put for Earth. Plenty beef, plenty cassava, plenty banana, plenty yam, plenty guinea corn, plenty mango, plenty groundnut – everyt'ing. And for de wata He put plenty fish, and for de air He put plenty kinda bird. After six day de Lawd He done go sleep. An when He sleep, plenty palaver start for dis place dey call um Heaven. Dis Heaven be place where we go live after we done die, if we been so-so bad for dis Earth...

'Darkness enveloped me, but piercing through I came; night is the choice for the fox's dance, child of the moon's household am I. And the lightning made his bid, in vain. When she cooks is the cloud ever set on fire? ... Say someone comes for all the rest. Say someone asks was it for this, for this, children plagued their mothers? ... Child, there is no other choice but one of suffering.

293

And those who tread the understreams add ashes daily to the head of Forest Father. Rest awhile. The beings of the forest have been called to dance a welcome; to quiet your spirit torn so loosely by the suddenness.'

The first quotation is of *Genesis* in pidgin English; and the second, some lines of dialogue from Wole Soyinka's *Dance of the Forests*. The first, a vernacular picked up by servants from their master, and the second the purest poetry, of which an African had become a master. Between the two lay a gulf which I hoped to bridge with this film. The translation of the one into the other – in a single generation – could be described as the African Awakening.

'Red is the pit of the sun's entrails', cries Soyinka's Spirit of the Sun, and black was the colour of the cast of this film. Black were the salesmen and women in the modern department stores in downtown Lagos; black were the knees of Ghana's young pioneers, a cross between Boy Scouts and Soviet *Konsomols*; and black was the hand of Nigeria's Military Minister of State, as he clasped mine in greeting (although his Irish wife's hand was white). Black were the control consoles, gramophone records and faces of the musicians, technicians, and artistes in the Lagos Broadcasting Studios. Black were the breasts of the African women, so proudly poised in the country, and so freely for sale in the nightclubs. Black were the nipples with which they suckled their children, and black were the thighs which bore them so well. But white were their smiles. White was the milk which flowed from those breasts, and white the colour of everyone's seminal genesis. Why are we then born so many different colours? As a lone pallid pink plunged into this ocean of black I was odd man out, and my colour incongruous, insipid, absurd. But it was now my job to attempt to put on to film what it was like to be black.

Nigeria had only been a single, national entity for forty-seven years. Thrusting into this then remote and unknown arc of West Africa in the nineteenth century British, French and German had agreed frontiers amongst themselves, separating their own spheres of conquest, running north from the coast where they landed, and cutting arbitrarily across the traditional homelands of the indigenous African tribes. In 1947 the British created a Federation of Nigeria out of the three provinces they had previously ruled as colonial protectorates. These three Regions, as they were then known, were based on the predominant tribe in the particular area. Thus the Western Region, to which I now drove, was the home of the Yorubas; the Eastern Region the land of the Ibo; and the Northern Region, geographically the largest of the three, the territory of the Hausa. It was an uneasy trinity, and already there were those who wondered if this federation could survive the departure of the alien master who had brought it into being, and under whose administrative and commercial acumen it had prospered, and now found freedom.

Her Royal Highness Princess Alexandra of Kent had represented the British Crown in its surrender of sovereignty over Nigeria seven months before, and I felt not unlike royalty myself as I was swept from one show-place to another, from one handshake to another. Certainly I began to appreciate their powers of endurance as I realised what a strain it was to display interest, ask the right question, look sympathetic, however tired (or bored) one might be during a sixteen-hour day which could easily cover two hundred miles, two dozen visits, and fifty or more encounters with different people, each of whom had something to say, something to contribute – and all in temperature of more than ninety degrees Fahrenheit.

My sponsors had drawn up for me a formidable programme. I did not complain. I wanted to see all that I could, meet all that I could, read all that I could, in the four weeks scheduled for this initial tour of Nigeria. However exhausted I might be at the end of the day, after however much travel, meeting, discussion and entertainment, I also had to get all of that day down in my notebook: where I had been, what I had seen, who I had met, what they had said – and what I had thought – as well as any tentative ideas and associations which might already be forming themselves into possible filmic interpretation or potential in my mind. When this grand tour was over, this record would be the raw material out of which I had to create a film. Some might say that I would have been better advised to talk it all into a tape recorder, just as it flowed in and out of my head. But I need the written word, worked out on paper page, with which to marshal my thoughts and organise my ideas, even at this early stage of a cinematic genesis.

'*May 12*: Drive to Ibadan, Industrial Trading Estate – many light industries of recent development. Vono (West Africa) Limited. Making metal bedsteads with all African, their own trained skilled labour. (Trained in three weeks before start of production.) Plan to export throughout West Africa as no other such plant in region. Raleigh Assembly Plant assembling 75 bicycles weekly. (Manager Odobo, bright, good diction) Ewekoro, Cement factory of the West African Portland Cement Company Limited. Planned with eye to expansion as biggest cement plant in the world. Conveyor Belt from quarry over the main road with name and symbol on it. (Possible transition shot.) Blue elephant symbol fountain in courtyard. Electronic control room in kiln – possible shots of African in charge – revolving kiln through window in background. (Blasting of limestone in quarry as possible shock introduction from rural agricultural sequence to dynamism of building.) Abeokuta, Nigerian Pre-stressed Concrete Company Limited, output of pylons for electric grid and blocks for bridges and railway sleepers (Power and Communication). Learnt of railway training centre at Zaria – extension of railway 400 miles in north. No hydro-electric power in Nigeria yet – all thermal, oil. To 'The Green Springs Hotel', Ibadan. Chalets in attractive grounds – swimming pool for possible dialogue sequence young Africa at play? Ibadan – largest city in West Africa – second only in size to Johannesburg in Africa as a whole – very attractive on hills – excellent general views. (Possible shot of riveter in CU on top frame of new building with roofs of old town far below in a building sequence). Women traffic police on point-duty at intersections.'

And on the opposite page of my notebook, late that May night in 1961 Ibadan, I wrote: 'Open on breakers, coastline and forest, with evocative poetry of slaves – abruptly cut across with contemporary radio commercial ... the dilemma thus immediately set – from the formerly primitive to the currently commercial – is there going to be a purely African revolution? Party of young Africans picnicking on beach – from close-up laughing girls in party as dance music follows commercial into opening sequence of booming city life – Accra, Lagos, Freetown – and our story...'.

At the end of this intensive tour and survey of the West African scene, there were to be more than fifty such pages, filled with similar thoughts and impressions of the peoples and places that I was meeting and visiting. When production began five months later, no less than three of the locations noted in this single day of the diary were incorporated into the action; and the opening of the film itself, although somewhat adapted, also developed out of this first original idea of an abrupt jump from the elemental African past into the commercially acquisitive present.

My tour, like the film planned to result from it, was sponsored by a British production company; and my hosts, more often than not, were Englishmen. But when I reached Sapele, after ten days of travel throughout western Nigeria, I was the guest of an African.

Mani Obahiagbon was the Public Relations Officer of the African Timber and Plywood Company, which cut, sawed, and exported timber from the forest with which we were surrounded. He was in his late twenties, intense in his thinking, bearded and black, and lived in a comfortable prefabricated house provided by his employers. The living-room was lined with books, the record-player was stacked high with Mozart and Beethoven, our glasses were seldom empty, and our conversation lasted long into the night.

Mani had been eight years in England, and done the almost obligatory period of study at the London School of Economics. His socialism was now being diluted by J.K. Galbraith, and other apostles of the managerial society. But his African nationalism was as intense as I hoped mine might have been, had I been born in his place – and here in Sapele we were certainly in a very genuine and indigenous Africa.

To reach this settlement of timber trading I had flown over miles of unbroken forest, the density of its green rivalled only by the apparent impenetrability of its interior. To reach Sapele I had then had to take a boat, which had nosed its way down the river which was the only thoroughfare for those who were not on speaking terms with the denizens and spirits of the forest. Here indeed was a heart of darkness, and my jumping-off point for this descent into the real Africa was Benin.

'You must have Benin in your film', said Mani Obahiagbon. But I could not see why. Benin was a very drab and uninteresting little township; and its sole claim to fame, as far as I could see, lay in its choice as the capital of a new, and then about to be created, fourth Nigerian Region of the Mid-West. Such parochial politics in one country were certainly not the province of a film which had to unify its theme throughout three. But in Benin there was a statue. Nothing grandiose, barely life-size, and no one seemed to give it a glance. To Mani though, this stone figure was little short of a god. Here, it seemed, was a martyr, a Gandhi of the Gold Coast, a Joan of Arc of the everglades. The name was *Overami*; and thanks to my host's devotion to his memory, and my own subsequent search amongst the archives of the British Museum, I was able to piece together his story.

More than a thousand years ago, in a search for a homeland of their own, a tribe left Egypt, crossed the African continent, and settled in the security of the forest near the mouth of a great river. By the beginning of the 16th century this Kingdom of the Bibis, Benin, was unrivalled in Africa. It embraced the whole of the Niger delta, and encompassed virtually all of southern Nigeria. Lagos, the capital, was originally founded by a Benin army, and right until the end of the 19th century its citizens were forced to pay tribute to the *Oba*, the King, of Benin.

Political power in this great African medieval kingdom, sophisticated and flourishing at a time when Henry VIII had yet to break with Rome, or the Pilgrim Fathers sail to Plymouth Rock, was in the hands of the *Oba*, and three main groups of titled chiefs. Each group had ritual and administrative functions to perform, individually and collectively, and each group was directly responsible, through its leaders, to the *Oba*.

The royal domains were parcelled out between chiefs of all the three groups, and some of lower rank; each being responsible for the maintenance of order and the collection of tribute in their respective areas. Military leadership was divided between chiefs of the Usama and 'Town' groups. Thus the main power groups were neatly balanced against each other, with the *Oba* standing at the apex of a series of pyramids.

The *Oba* was the supreme political, judicial, economic and spiritual head of his people. His ancestors and he himself were the soul of the nation, and therefore the object of the principal state cults and religious observances. Human sacrifice was the core of the latter, which was focused on the *Oba* divinity as the reincarnation of his ancestors. Upon the well-being of the *Oba* the health and prosperity of the whole nation was believed to depend.

The first Europeans, Portuguese missionaries, reached Benin in the reign of the *Oba* Esigie, early in the 16th century. Esigie was tolerant of their faith and teachings, and even permitted churches to be built. Thousands of his subjects were baptised before the death of John Alfonso d'Aveire in 1514, the greatest of these Jesuit proselytisers, who brought the Cross, and the concept of Crucifixion, to Benin.

In 1651 a Father Joseph Xison reached Benin. The then *Oba*, Ahenzae, refused to grant him an audience – as an oracle had predicted that one of the kings of Benin would die at the hands of the European; although he did accept a letter from the Pope.

Such missionaries, and merchants, of the 16th, 17th and 18th centuries brought back to Europe their wonder at the splendour of this African kingdom. They were greatly impressed by the civic planning which had gone into the construction of Benin city, and by the size, distinctive style and elaborate scale of its buildings. The city was surrounded by a great wall, approached on horseback by way of formal gateways. It was a city of wide streets and boulevards, divided into halves, 'Palace' and 'Town', and subdivided into some fifty wards, each characterised by a particular craft, profession, or state function. Each ward had its own chiefs and elders, responsible for its internal affairs, and each was affiliated to one of the three palace societies.

The firearms brought by Portuguese traders, together with the trade in slaves, encouraged by the coming of the Europeans, stimulated conquest and war. The boundaries and ambitions of Benin grew greater. Exported were slaves, ivory, pepper, palm oil. Created was the mightiest kingdom in Africa – and bronze carvings that today fetch a fortune in the sale rooms of London and New York.

In 1702 Benin was rent by a disastrous civil war, and with the abolition of the slave trade – as profitable to African chieftains as it had been to European adventurers – the fortunes of Benin began to decline. In 1885 the British proclaimed their sovereignty over the coastline around Lagos, and began to push into and explore the hinterland. Three years later, in his still relatively unknown capital city one hundred and fifty miles to the north east, one Idugbowa was crowned *Oba* of Benin. He was the thirty-second of the dynasty which had led his people, like another before him, out of Egypt – and he was destined to be the last.

At his coronation Idugbowa took the name of Overami, by which be was to be known throughout his reign. He is described as tall, of a mellow complexion, and the possessor of a majestic voice; and almost immediately after the pomp and circumstance of his coronation three Europeans arrived in Benin city. They came to negotiate a treaty and trade, but made little impression. Life in Benin went on as before. The white men had come face to face with Overami, but withdrew. Meanwhile this new *Oba* had to face a much more urgent threat against his position and power within his own kingdom.

At the close of this coronation year, the Chief Ruler of Akure had caused to be cast state swords for his own use, without the sanction of the *Oba*. When Overami heard of this early in the following year, he sent a loyal chief, Okpele, to take the swords from this dissident Daji of Akure. Okpele marched on such presumption with several cannons and kegs of powder, and this show of force and threat were sufficient. The swords were surrendered. The over-ambitious chief pledged his homage, but within Benin itself Overami still faced a greater threat to this throne and inheritance.

A group of chiefs, led by Obaraye, Ohazelu, Osia, Eribo and others, were suspected of opposing Overami's accession. Uwangue Egiebo, described as the *Oba*'s favourite, advised his master to oppose these men, and they were accordingly put to death. As a result of this advice, and the jealousy resulting from the influence which he had thus come to exercise, Egiebo was murdered by members of the House of Iwebo in revenge. Overami realised that he was surrounded by intrigue, and that his own life was in danger. An enquiry was instituted, and it transpired that two of the principal chiefs of the House of Iwebo were behind the conspiracy. With their accomplices they were charged with murder and, after a summary trial, found guilty and executed. Their names were Esasoyen and Obahiagbon.

Obahiagbon? When I was confronted by this name, in this context, on the yellowing pages of an old document in the Reading Room of the British Museum, I nearly fell out of my chair in surprise. For this was of course the same as the name of my own host in Benin. No wonder he had felt so strongly about this tangled tribal history of his heritage and birthplace. No wonder the name Overami had made his eyes flash, and his fists clench. I read on, with an even greater interest and fascination.

With this execution of what I could only now surmise was my friend's grandfather, Overami secured his succession with blood, and prepared to celebrate a somewhat less sanguinary ceremony. Two years after his coronation he gave his eldest daughter Princess Evbakhavbokun in marriage to one Ologboshero. The occasion served to draw attention to his by then undisputed power and authority as *Oba* of Benin. Guests and sightseers came from near and far. The crowds in the city during the procession were so great that some were crushed to death. The streets were decorated and illuminated. Much pageantry attended this display of the ruling house in all the confidence of what was fated to be its last decade. Presents of slaves and jewellery were showered upon the bride and groom.

But scarcely had the rejoicings died away than the Oracle of the Oghene of the *Oba* made a dire prophecy. It predicted that a great calamity was coming to Benin. This warning was conveyed to Overami, who continued, however, to prepare himself confidently for the so-called Ceremony of the Coral Beads. Once in the lifetime of every *Oba*, sacrifices were made to him as the incarnation of his ancestors, and the soul of his people.

The human sacrifice to be offered was a man named Oyibodudu. Just as the executioner was about to kill him he shouted to the watching Overami, and all the surrounding priests and spectators, that the White Man was greater than all of them, and that they were coming soon to fight and conquer the *Oba* and Benin. Immediately he had uttered this prophecy, he called to the executioner to get it over with, and his head was split upon the block.

A year later the White Men did indeed come to Benin once again, but peacefully, and Overami entered into a treaty allowing the British in Lagos to trade with his people. Meanwhile, his authority was undisputed, and in the ninth year of his reign, he prepared to enlarge his realm. Overami caused to be built at the village of Obadan a great war camp; and ordered every town and village throughout the kingdom to send him soldiers. A force of over ten thousand was assembled for operations against Agbor.

But to the south a far greater power was also preparing to carry its flag further, and before Overami could launch his legions, a British political and trade mission set forth from Lagos to implement the recently negotiated treaty. On the 1st of January 1897, the acting Consul, James E. Phillips, together with eight other Europeans and more than two hundred African carriers, started out for Benin. Messengers were sent ahead to inform Overami that they were on their way. The *Oba* was however observing at this time the annual ceremony known as Ague, during which he could not, and indeed must not, be seen by strangers. He therefore sent a message in which he asked the White Men to postpone their visit for two months. Phillips refused. Overami then sent word that he would receive the mission. He sent a party led by five of his chiefs, Ologboshero, Obakhavbaye, Uso, Obadesagbon and Ugiagbe, to escort the party of British to Benin city.

Before they reached Benin, all but two of the Europeans were massacred by this reception committee.

When they returned to Overami with news of their deed, the five chiefs expected praise, believing that nothing but good would come of their action. The *Oba* knew otherwise, and told them and his court, to prepare for the inevitable reaction. The priests began an orgy of human sacrifice in an attempt to placate the spirits, and ward off the danger. Within three weeks a punitive expedition of British sailors, marines, and local levies was on its way. Benin was bombarded, and the Palace of the *Oba* destroyed. The city was taken by assault on the 17th day of February 1897. Fires spread from the palace to the buildings in the city, which burnt for five days.

When the British had begun to draw near, and while one Asoro fought a spirited rearguard action at Unu-Eru, Overami had donned his state robes and regalia, and sat within the Tower of his Palace, awaiting their arrival, and his own end. But after a while he was persuaded to flee into the surrounding forest. After six months of wandering he re-entered Benin city with an unarmed escort of eight hundred. He abased himself three times on the ground before the British Resident, a Captain Roupell, seated at a table at the opening of a small tent. Beside this new, alien ruler of Benin, stood a Captain Carter of the Royal Scots, a Lieutenant Gabbet of the Royal Welch Fusiliers, and a British Medical Officer: four white men to witness the downfall of an African dynasty and the abasement of its sovereign.

As Overami – like Toussaint L'Ouverture before him – was being led on board ship to exile, and in his case banishment at Calabar, he is said to have exclaimed: 'I appeal to the Almighty and the Spirits of the departed *Obas* of Benin, my Fathers, to judge between me and the Binis, who ill-advised and cunningly sold me into the hands of the British troops in search for their own liberty and benefit. Oh Benin! Merciless and wicked! Farewell! Farewell!'

It was hard to believe that all this had happened within a single lifetime. How many remembered Overami now, I wondered. A Nigerian nationalist, such as my host Mani Obahiagbon, revered his memory as a symbol of the white man's rape of his country. But now himself involved in commercial operations of these same white men – which he knew in his heart to be responsible for his country's development, and his own education – he suffered an almost schizophrenic conflict of loyalties. To work for white men, many of whom he knew to be his own intellectual inferiors, was humiliating. But it was these same white men who had led his country into the mainstream of the modern world. If they had not come to Benin sixty years before, the streets of that forest-girt kingdom would still be running red with the blood of human sacrifice. Now he, the grandson of one who had plotted for that same gruesome throne, read Salinger and Shaw, and played Prokofiev for his pleasure.

He also worked for a timber company, and as its launch took me down the Ethiope river on the next stage of my journey, we passed ocean-going steamships anchored in its midstream. They were loading logs. We cut under the stern of one of them, bound, as I was told, for Liverpool. It was the flagship of the recently established Nigerian National Shipping Line. As it swung above me, I looked up at its name. OBA OVERAMI.

But if the Nigerian kings of old had been humbled and bundled into banishment by alien adventurers, Ghana, the next country on my list, (and prior to independence from colonial rule known as the 'Gold Coast') had produced if not a Garibaldi, at least a Mussolini. Born on a Saturday, and therefore, according to tribal tradition first named Kwame, Nkrumah then seemed to be what he himself thought he was – the *Osagyefo*, the Redeemer, of Africa.

He had been a seventeen-year-old pupil-teacher in a village school when the Principal of the Gold Coast's Government Training College had recommended him for higher education in the capital, Accra. This official was English, the year was 1926, and Ghana was then a British colony. The future Duke of Windsor had recently visited this segment of the empire over which he was to rule for ten brief months, and, as Prince of Wales, graciously named this school founded by a Canadian-born Governor. Achimota College was to teach, train, and graduate many leaders of a future free West Africa; not least of all Kwame Nkrumah, who was later to pay his own special tribute to the assistant vice-principal, Dr. Kwegyir Aggrey:

'To me he seemed the most remarkable man that I had ever met... It was through him that my nationalism was first aroused. He was extremely proud of his colour but was strongly opposed to racial segregation in any form and, although he could understand (the) principle of "Africa for the Africans", he never hesitated to attack this principle. He believed that conditions should be such that the black-and-white races should work together ... He used to expound this by saying "You can play a tune of sorts on the white keys, and you can play a tune of sorts on the black keys, but for harmony you must use both the black and the white"'.

Above its Latin motto of *Ut Omnes Unum Sint* [So That All Might Be One], the crest of Achimota was still a shield surrounding the black-and-white keys of a piano keyboard.

'I could not', Nkrumah had written, 'accept this idea of Aggrey's as being practicable, for I maintained that such harmony can only exist when the black race is treated as equal to the white race; that only a free and independent people – a people with a government of their own – can claim equality, racial or otherwise, with another people'.

None the less, he was so fired by Aggrey's example that after graduation, and a spell of further teaching in colonial schools, he successfully applied for admission to the first institution in the United States to give higher education to Blacks, Lincoln University in the State of Pennsylvania. On borrowed money, and on one ship as a stowaway, he made his way to London.

'Mussolini invades Ethiopia' was the banner headline which greeted him in England, and as he read of white men gloatingly boasting of their bombing of his brethren, the twenty-six-year-old Kwame vowed that the tune and theme of his life would be played on the black keys alone – and by the fingers of the left hand. He met British Marxists, read Kant, Hegel, Descartes, Schopenhauer, Nietzsche, Freud, and Lenin; and graduated from Lincoln in 1939 a Bachelor of Arts with distinctions in economics and sociology. Other degrees followed: Bachelor of Theology, Master of Science, Master of Arts, but to achieve and pay for all this acquisition of the white man's knowledge, he had to work and sweat for every minute. He froze in a shipbuilding yard, sold fish on street corners, and shovelled the entrails of animals into the processing machinery of a soap factory.

Armed with all that he thought America could teach him, Kwame returned to England. The Second World War had just ended. A Labour Government was in power, committed to the freedom of colonial territories. It was a time of high hope, the heyday of the British Left. The most monstrous racist in history had just been incinerated in the ruins of Berlin; the newly-born and hopefully named United Nations held out the promise of man's now seemingly inexorable move forward into international and multi-coloured harmony; and at the London School of Economics Harold Laski had all the answers.

Nkrumah enrolled at Grays Inn, to study law, and at the LSE. He registered at University College, and studied 'Logical Positivism' under Professor Ayer. 'In spite of this, it was only a matter of weeks before I got myself tangled up with political activities in London.'

He became secretary to a Pan African Congress, held in Manchester under the chairmanship of America's Dr. W.E.B. DuBois, one of the founders of the National Association for the Advancement of Coloured Peoples, and was pleased to report that 'it adopted Marxist socialism as its philosophy'. He organised African students into agitational bodies, founded a newspaper *The New Africa*, and visited Paris, where he discussed and planned a Union of West African Socialist Republics.

Then came the opportunity, the moment for which he had been preparing himself ever since, as the only child of his mother, born on the day of his grandmother's death, he had become aware that something set him apart. He received a letter from home. It offered him the post of General Secretary to the colony's United Gold Coast Convention. He accepted, and within ten years had turned that embryonic political clubbing together of a few middle-class intellectuals into a mass party which swept aside all opposition, and himself into absolute power as Prime Minister – and soon President – of the first independent West African state.

And yet within less than another decade he had plunged his country into bankruptcy, and himself into exile.

Here was a man who once said of women that he felt they would trap him and take his freedom away, and who, as well as maintaining a wife and a family, installed a girlfriend as Head of his country's Television Programmes. Here was a man who once said of money that it should play a very minor part in a man's life and who, as Chief of State, channelled a small fortune of public money into his own private accounts. Here was a man who once said of religion that it should be a matter of a man's own conscience, and who allowed and encouraged his own deification. Seldom has there been a greater demonstration of the truth of the old adage that *all power corrupts and absolute power corrupts absolutely.*

Nkrumah has been called many things, from a Messiah to a mug. But he was essentially a tragic figure – the Trotsky of the African Revolution. He transformed his country into the base for, as he saw it, the liberation of the entire continent from neo-colonialism. His ambition was to unite crumbling colonial Africa in a vast, new black empire under his own and Ghana's leadership. Instead of working to balance his own budget, he squandered millions of Ghana's hard-earned currency in an effort to undermine and overthrow the governments of other African states not to his liking. Better by far to have been a Stalin, and have concentrated on the industrialisation and development of his own country before attempting to make the world over in his own image. Certainly he was adept in neutralising his own opposition. By the time of his overthrow, his gaols were filled with his opponents and critics. But liberation came too late for one such political prisoner. Dr. J.B. Danquah who, back in 1945, had offered Nkrumah the post of General Secretary to the United Gold Coast Convention, and first brought him back to Africa and launched him on the road to power. Outspoken in his criticism of his protégé's excesses, Danquah died in the prison to which he had been committed for his sins.

But in June 1961, when I first came to Ghana in search of my film of the African Personality, the emperor still appeared to wear clothes, the idol's feet had yet to be seen to be cast in clay. To this Land of Promise American, British and Russian aircraft of Ghana Airways brought pilgrims and disciples from all over Africa. The cocoa crop was in, and business was booming. The streets of Accra were filled with busy people and steams of traffic. Planned and built by the British, a new deep-water port was already in service at Tema, displacing the picturesque but now inadequate surf-boats of Accra, which had previously been sufficient for the limited seaborne trade of the colonial past. A vast development scheme was planned for the river Volta, aiming at nothing less than the industrialisation of a country hitherto totally dependent on the fortunes of a single agricultural crop. A 350 feet high dam was being designed, to contain a 2,500 square mile reservoir behind it, 300 miles long, feeding a hydro-electric installation planned to generate 750,000 kilowatts; which in turn would provide the power to smelt and produce more than 200,000 tons of aluminium a year. Nkrumah had obtained American support for this great project from the Eisenhower Administration; and now, as I made my first call at his headquarters alongside the old fort from which his forbears had been carried away by the slavers in chains, the black star of his fortune was at its apogee.

Kwame Nkrumah, the *Osagyefo*, had just returned from the United States and Britain. He had lectured the United Nations on what to do in the then tormented Congo, and had been received at the White House by the Kennedys. He had dined with Queen Elizabeth, and told other British Commonwealth Prime Ministers what to do about Rhodesia and South Africa. In his own patrician way his host, Harold Macmillan, had singled him out for particular attention and personal flattery. Now, back home in Ghana, he had just taken over complete control of what was now the country's one and only political party; declaring that: 'I see before my mind's eye a great monolithic party ... united and strong, spreading its protective wings over the whole of Africa from Algiers in the north to Cape Town in the south, from Cape Guardafui in the east to Dakar in the west'.

All this was very heady stuff, but in Ghana I searched in vain for any writers comparable to the Nigerians I had already met. Certainly there were poets, but no novelists of the calibre and accomplishment of Cyprian Ekwensi or Chinua Achebe had yet emerged in Nkrumah's kingdom. There was no one of the range, scale and magnitude of Wole Soyinka. I flew north, to the territory of the Ashanti, a tribe the British had been forced to fight in order to subdue; and whom Kwame was never able to bring to heel. I continued to build up my now bulging notebook. A compendium, as it were, of shots which my camera eye had not yet put on film, but only on paper; out of which would be edited – created – the 'script' which a real camera would finally be set up to shoot. Day by day, night after night, the entries grew.

'To TRADES UNION CONGRESS (GHANA). Secretary-General John K. Tettegah: very powerful personality recently setting up all African Trade Union Federation as opposed to ICFTU and WFTU. Will arrange filming of branch meeting – builders union; and seminar of 80 union leaders that he would address. To GHANA YOUNG PIONEERS. National Organiser Z.B. Shardow: a party leader of obvious dedication. Can arrange filming of young pioneers reciting their pledge, and general activity. To GHANA AIRWAYS. Chairman Mercer and General Manager Gill. Will provide all facilities including aircraft at our disposal. Viscount (Aircraft) with Ghanaian First Officer on domestic and regional services in October. To HQ BUILDERS BRIGADE. National Organiser Arabic. Passing out parade after four weeks' training of drill and discipline etc. Band and speech. Clearing some 2,000 acres of virgin bush in SOMANYA in Eastern region 11 miles from Volta River where they will settle and develop a co-operative farm. A movement basically to combat unemployment in its initial origin. Have songs of this work similar to new world spirituals. Bulldozers and heavy equipment in clearance for farm. To SIR ROBERT JACKSON Economic Adviser to the President. Thoroughly approved theme and purpose of the film; mentioned how important *land* was in any country's development. Drinks with Lemieux, Chief of Ghana Film Unit, he on loan from National Film Board of Canada. He won round and now helpful, and sympathetic to the film.'

From the Ashanti gold mines, whose once rich lode had given this coastline its original name, to the Cocoa Marketing Board, whose product was now far more valuable to Ghana's development; from Achimota College to the more recently established Ghana National College; from St. Peter's Anglican Church to the Black Star Shipping Line; from the printing presses of the about-to-be-banned *Ashanti Pioneer* to the offices of the London Daily Mirror owned *Daily Graphic* (whose editor had just returned from a visit to some of his already imprisoned colleagues); from the Pioneer Tobacco Factory to a brewery, fermenting and bottling *Star*, *Tango* and *Krola*, I plodded my way through the paradoxes of Kwame Nkrumah's Ghana. I completed my reading of Nkrumah's autobiography. One paragraph I copied out into my notebook, word for word:

'I uncovered the dish and helped myself to some of the now cold and somewhat unappetising fish stew. I noticed that the ants had already settled themselves into the pieces of bread that had been left for me and I sat and watched them as I ate. "Nothing will stop them," I thought, as I watched these minute creatures running purposefully backwards and forward to the bread. "They will always succeed in their objective because they are disciplined and organised." There was not a single slacker among them'.

Named after the Mountain of the Lion, the next country on my list, Sierra Leone, has a capital named after the civil rights which were, in essence, the theme of my film, *Freetown*. A century and a half earlier, the British were shipping 40,000 slaves out of West Africa every year, but if they had the good fortune somehow to set foot in England itself, they were then set free. A certain Granville Sharp proposed that such freed slaves should be shipped back to Africa, and settled somewhere where they could prosper in a congenial climate. This tiny state of Sierra Leone, the most western of all British West African possessions, was the choice.

For the purpose of my film, Sierra Leone had very little more to offer than this historical significance, but to preserve the balance of filming in these three English-speaking states of West Africa, I had to work in a fair amount of this pint-sized former colony, then independent for just fifty days. Dutifully I met and talked with the officials of the Government's Ministry of Information, including a fortunately about-to-be retired British Permanent Secretary, who informed me in a tired and patronising way that 'there is nothing here'. He should have read Graham Greene, who found material enough during his wartime intelligence role in Freetown to write one of his most successful studies of the human predicament, *The Heart of the Matter*. Fortunately for me there was, as I always discovered, an African in the background of the office very much on the ball, and wholly sympathetic: Bankole Timothy, busy on a life of Nkrumah, whom he seemed to view with some degree of uncommitted ambivalence.

On the top of the hill there lived a really great African, Davidson Nicol, Principal of the University College of Fourah Bay. We established an immediate rapport. (After one seizure of power after another in the years to come, he was to be appointed his country's Ambassador to Britain.) Nicol understood immediately what I was going to attempt in this film.

'You must include the Ife heads and the Benin bronzes. Don't forget we were creating works of art long before you came. There was a university at Timbuctoo a thousand years ago.'

Her African forbears transported in chains, the rage in the blood of Dr. Nicol's West Indian wife was more impatient of action:

'The opposition will win the elections here. There is already starvation in some parts of the country. A one-party type of gov-

311

ernment, such as in Ghana, is the only thing for emerging countries such as these'.

Nicol was, however, disappointed to hear that the former French territories of West Africa were not going to be included in the film, as well as the countries which, in my brief, were described as Commonwealth West Africa. He quite obviously saw himself as a West *African*, first and foremost. The artificial barriers of frontier and language imposed by conflicting colonialisms meant nothing to this genuine *savant*.

With the British, the French had been the other great imperial power in Africa. Their still associated territories interspersed these that I was now visiting like so many additional segments in a multi-decker sandwich. Unlike the British, the French had not practised a rigid social colour bar. They pampered the *evolués*, the indigenous intellectuals, but ignored the ignorant poor. The British, to their credit, treated the poorer elements fairly, but were suspicious of the educated; particularly of the politically conscious educated. One result of this is that the majority of the new African film-makers were from French-speaking Africa, where the intelligentsia and the liberal arts were encouraged, while the former British territories have concentrated more on television, which UNESCO would have us maintain at Poona is first and foremost a teaching medium.

To the colonial French, their subject peoples were, just simply, French; and so, automatically, civilised. Literature, rather than film, was the medium of their message. The President of Senegal, Leopold Senghor, was an accepted *auteur et poète* in his own right. He it was who had first coined the phrase *la personalité Africaine*. The British had been, in their own way, more messianic. Their task, as the progressive amongst them had seen it, was to teach. The Colonial Office had set up Film Units in many of its overseas and dependent territories. In Ghana, it had been the Gold Coast (now Ghana) Film Unit. Its task the making of educational and instructional films. It sent to London – to train under that same but by then much older George Pearson who had made silence speak in his silent film *Reveille* – young Africans to take over writing, direction, camerawork, sound re-

312

cording, and editing from their British tutors. Well trained too. In every one of the three countries, when the time came to shoot this film of mine, technicians from these government film units augmented the basic crew who came out with me from England.

From time to time in the colonial past the French had sent out expeditionary film units, but their interest had been more anthropological than political. Marc Allegret's 1927 *Voyage au Congo* was an early example. It was the result of his experience in using a film camera as a recording instrument in his studies of African peoples while working as an ethnologist that had led Jean Rouch into the technique of what came to be called *cinema vérité* – when he came to apply this technique to the people of Paris. Now, in 1961, at the start of my own film of the African Personality, Rouch had just completed *La Pyramide Humaine*. Shot at an integrated school in Abidjan, French West Africa, this recorded an attempt to bring together white and black pupils who outside the school hardly ever mixed at all. The more primitive ethnology which had once absorbed all his enthusiasm and energy was soon to be the subject of many successful and valuable films made by others directly for popular television: such as Adrian Cowell's award-winner for ATV, *The Tribe that Hides from Man*, and Granada's *Disappearing World*. That primitive, picturesque, but primeval Africa was indeed disappearing. There were doubtless some who would have liked to keep it that way. My task was to put on film the new Africa which was now appearing, a sleeping giant at last awakening.

If anyone spoke for Africa and the Africans in this film, it would be, I assured myself, Davidson Nicol. For had he not already written of Africa that:

'You were once just a name to me,
But now you lie before me with sombre green challenge
To that loud faith of freedom (life more abundant)
which we once professed, shouting
Into the silent, listening microphone;
Or, on a London platform, to a sea
Of white, perplexed faces, troubled

313

With secret Imperial doubt'.

After the company and conversation of such a man as this, it was harder than ever to remain polite in the face of the prejudice which passed for profundity on the part of most of my fellow-countrymen in Freetown. The Governor-General was, however, a being of different calibre, a splendid example of the very best type of British public servant. Sir Maurice Dorman shared my respect for men like Davidson Nicol, and impressed me as being very much the right man, in the right place, at the right time. In our talk together he stressed the importance of adult education in the West African situation. The gulf between the generations was wide enough, in all conscience, everywhere. Here it could well be catastrophic. The new generation all went to school and could read and write. Their fathers were wholly illiterate. The new generation took the automobile, the washing-machine, and television completely for granted. Their fathers still worshipped strange gods and demons in the depths of the forest. As we, the white man, faded from the African scene, so would the religion we brought with us. Islam was much more suited to the African character and way of life, and was making converts all the time. Independence had come to these countries at a moment when the great powers threatened to blow up the world. Nehru's philosophy of 'Positive Neutralism' was at that time the only, and inevitable policy of Ghana, Nigeria, and Sierra Leone. Sir Maurice quoted an old African proverb that 'When the bull elephants fight, the grass is trampled down'.

Before I could begin to attempt to detach myself and attempt to place in perspective all that I had learnt, felt, and experienced in three different African countries during the previous non-stop seven weeks, there was still, here in Sierra Leone, the inevitable round of schools and technical training establishments to be made. But at long, long last, having been shown and duly impressed by the two major exports of iron ore and diamonds, I settled down with a very long, and very cold beer in Freetown's Bedford Hotel; and, like Graham Greene's tormented character before me in the same place, and perhaps even at the very same table, began to ponder the Heart of the Matter.

My task now was to construct a film through which could be expressed the African Personality: to be shot in three different and even antagonistic countries, without any such national division ever becoming distinct enough to upset an essentially overall unity; and, bearing in mind that it was one such – and a very powerful one indeed – that was sponsoring its production, at the same time giving reasonable credit and prominence (without naming names) to the commercial organisations which had played, and were still playing a key role in the development of West Africa and the Africans. All these different factors had to be reconciled, in terms of cinema, in one organic unity – and I wanted no part of any commentary to be written and recorded after filming was over: the device which is so often used to paper over the cracks of inadequate construction. In any case, it was the African who had to talk in this film – not some anonymous and emasculated voice laid on afterwards.

The heart of this matter was (and is – at least to my mind) to see, somehow to conceive, the completed film as a whole, before a foot of film ever flowed through a camera – and still preserve flexibility and spontaneity when it comes to the actual filming.

Driving along in Eastern Nigeria, there had been a signpost. UDI it said. That rang a bell. *Daybreak in Udi* had received the 1949 Academy Award as the Best Feature Length Documentary of that year. (*A Chance to Live*, a release by the *March of Time* on the rehabilitation of Italy's war orphans, had received at the same time the Oscar for the best documentary short.) *Daybreak in Udi* had been produced by the British Crown Film Unit, seeking horizons wider than those domestic now that the war was over; hopefully finding them in the British Colonial Empire as it moved forward to freedom from Britannia's apron strings. World War Two had indeed been British Documentary's finest hour. Money for production existed for the asking. Exciting subjects abounded. Now, with the arrival of peace, everything suddenly seemed flat.

315

The visionary gleam (of documentary) had not, wrote John Grierson in 1951, 'fled at all. So far as such obvious social fronts as were occupied in the 'thirties are concerned, it is there, wherever the backward people – or as we now more sensitively call them the under-developed peoples – are to be found... if indeed I were facing the issue of sponsorship as a young man, content with the earlier dream of documentary, I would draw a conclusion from the appearance of *Daybreak in Udi...*'.

But in that film we are still beset by colonial circumstances, polarised by paternalism. It is what *we* are doing for *them*. Against traditional prejudices, *Daybreak in Udi* was the story of the building and acceptance of a maternity clinic by the people of a remote village, who acted with great dignity and conviction. But the central character was that old friend of ours, the District Officer. Certainly to be seen doing what *Palaver* claimed to be his mission twenty-three years before, but here, as portrayed on screen by a genuine example of the species, stiff, authoritarian, and uncertain (despite sun-helmet, walking stick, and crisply-creased short trousers).

That *Daybreak in Udi* exemplified an outmoded approach and attitude, not least of all in its style of filmmaking, was soon apparent, despite the gallery of international awards it went on to garner. The old, traditional type of documentary film was also dying a slow death. Its arteries had hardened. In attempting to repeat its early successes, it merely repeated old formulae. It had come to rely more than ever on commentary to tell its stories, against sometimes beautiful but increasingly sterile images. In the fifties a brash young infant had knocked it sideways, and off the cinema screens for good. Television.

None of the formal and mannered compositions of which Eisenstein was so fond for this new child of instant communication. None of the meandering idylls of a Flaherty for this electronic iconoclast in the living-room. Significantly and simultaneously, with the onset of television had come a dramatic development in the range and portability of sixteen millimetre cameras and recording equipment. One man with a camera in his hand, it was believed, could indeed be as unobtrusive as a fly on

316

Benin heads

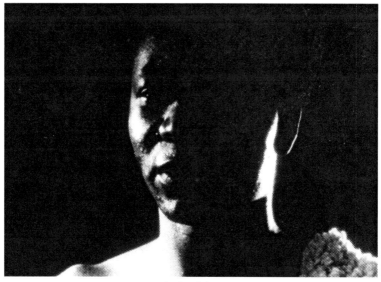

Wole Soyinka

317

the wall. Technique no longer seemed necessary to recreate reality – high-speed film (or now tape) and lightweight camera could record it, exactly as it happened.

'To catch spontaneously', is how John Schlesinger has described this new wave of personal TV documentary. But surely it is a greater challenge, resulting in a far deeper contribution to true communication, *to interpret creatively*. 'All art is a readjustment', to quote Malraux once again.

In *African Awakening* I attempted a synthesis of the two schools, exemplified by Vertov on the one hand and Eisenstein on the other: setting spontaneous, on the spot, off-the-cuff filming of Africans talking to camera, to themselves, to each other, within the framework of a creatively conceived, highly stylised, and carefully structured film. Time and place meant nothing in this concept. For if ever past, present, and future were telescoped into an instant of history for anyone, then this was indeed the case for the new, young African generation who were both its spokesmen and subject: at one and the same time the interpreters and those interpreted.

I saw the opening of the film as a prologue.

'If the nineteenth century saw no more significant development than Europe's discovery of Africa, our own twentieth century is witness to no greater fulfilment than Africa's own dramatic entry into the world.'

On screen we would watch a great airplane landing at London Airport. From it would descend Africans. But what we hear is a complete reversal – a voice reading Chinua Achebe's description of the coming of the European to Eastern Nigeria: 'Their arrival had caused a considerable stir... Stories about these strange men had grown, since one of them had been killed in Abame and his iron horse tied to the sacred silk-cotton tree...'.

Cables have meanwhile been seen connected to the aircraft, suitcases unpacked in a London hotel: 'It was the time of the year when everybody was at home … the harvest was over ... they spent the first five nights in the market place ... '.

Newly-arrived young Africans were seen talking to British students in the grounds of an English university: 'And went into

318

the village in the morning to preach the gospel ... It was not very easy getting the men of high title, and the elders, together, but they persevered ...'.

On the terrace of the Palace of Westminster, an African delegation were to be seen the guests of British Members of Parliament: 'And in the end they were received by the rulers of Mbanta'.

Africans would then be seen in Britain, at Agricultural and Technical Training Colleges, factories, shipyards, and one of the first generation of nuclear power stations then under construction. Surrounded by all the electronic paraphernalia, challenge, and threat of nuclear fission, one African would be seen to stand alone. His eyes fill the screen. The picture would then slowly become the primeval forest. Against contrasting shots of the West African landscape, the voice of Wole Soyinka speaks the film's opening statement:

'I am the African.

I am the Bantu striding hot storm over the brown whispering veldt that rides in my blood like a battle.

I am the Zulu. I stood with my spear amongst the impis of Chaka.

I am the Tuareg, witness to the faith of a prophet from Sudan to Sahara.

I am the Ashanti.1 fold my strength in the beaten gold of a stool shaped for immortals.

I am the Fulani, driving the wealth of my cattle from Lake Chad to Dahomey.

I am the Sherbro, building my home in the place of a mountain.

I am no more the man of Zambesi than I am the man of Limpopo.

I am no less the man from the mountains of Kavirondo than I am the warrior bred of the Masai.

I am as much Ibo as I am Yoruba'.

A noble sentiment, particularly in view of the massacre of the Ibos by the other tribes of Nigeria five years later. However, such a bloody failure of high hope was not to be anticipated, let alone envisaged, in my *African Awakening.* The calypso-like words and rhythm of a specially composed piece of Nigerian 'Highlife' music then accompanied a rapid impression of modern and contemporary African city life. Hands beat on a drum in a night club, and bells tolled in a church on Sunday morning.

'I do not deny that the creeds brought to us from Europe cover great truths ... but I cannot see that these European formulae, unmodified, should be imposed upon Africa.' The voice of Soyinka again, as the camera now comes upon Davidson Nicol, talking to students at Freetown's university: 'The first pupil to be enrolled here at Fourah Bay in Sierra Leone nearly a hundred and fifty years ago was a former slave, Samuel Adjai Crowther – there is no limit to the opportunities that now await his successor'.

Taken as a slave in a tribal raid on his village, the young Samuel Adjai Crowther had been born a Yoruba at the beginning of the nineteenth century. Within twenty-four hours of his capture he had known three different owners. He was swapped for a horse, a wad of tobacco, a flask of rum. His hand was chained to his neck. He was marched to Lagos, fettered to other slaves with a long chain which ran through an iron band round each of their necks; one of a hundred-and-sixty-five such unfortunates thrust aboard a Portuguese slaver. But fortunately for this future Bishop of the Anglican Church, Britannia ruled the waves and had at last outlawed slavery. The Royal Navy intercepted this cargo of African flesh, and Adjai was put ashore at Freetown, a free man. He was baptised into the Christian faith in 1825, taking as his surname the name of one of the London Committee of the Church Missionary Society – a Samuel Crowther, vicar of Christ Church, Newgate Street, in the City of London.

But although Adjai could make no more legible mark than an X when he was formally enrolled at the Church Missionary Society's School in Freetown's Fourah Bay, it is as Samuel Adjai

Crowther that this brilliant educator and evangelist is known to history. He was ordained a Priest in St. Paul's Cathedral by the Bishop of London; the first African to be admitted to Christian Holy Orders. He was received by Queen Victoria and the Prince Consort at Windsor Castle. He translated the Bible into Yoruba and, in 1841, as a missionary bearing witness to his faith, sailed up the then unknown Niger with a party of European explorers.

Crowther was one of the few to return alive, and this combination of the evangelical with the expeditional gave me the next link in the narrative.

Nearby Freetown's Bishop Crowther Memorial Church was a complex of modern automatic workshops. Here young African apprentices were taught the mysteries of the internal combustion engine.

'Describe the four-stroke cycle of a diesel engine', was to ask an examiner of these fledgling automotive engineers. 'Right, and as you know, harnessed to a propeller, the diesel engine will drive a ship.'

Immediately we were on the Niger: that great river which might have been Sanders', and which charted the original course of West African exploration. From Yola on the Benue, past Numan, Djen, Ibi, and Makurdi; from Jebba on the Niger, past Lokoja, Onitsha, Aboh and Patani, tugs towed cargoes of cotton, cocoa, timber, groundnuts, palm kernels and oil down to the sea and out to the world – and the camera sailed with them.

The export of raw materials from the seaports of Nigeria, Ghana, and Sierra Leone, and the import of the machinery of their hoped-for industrialisation, followed in a natural progression. The international trade which has always been one of the greatest carriers of new skills, new techniques; and more, new ideas and experience between nations and peoples – 'and today a mastery of words first brought to these shores from across the seas'.

Near the mouth of the Niger, the camera slid past the stern of a steamship tied up and loading at a wharf. Its black superstructure blotted out everything; the screen became, as a result, also black:

School of business management

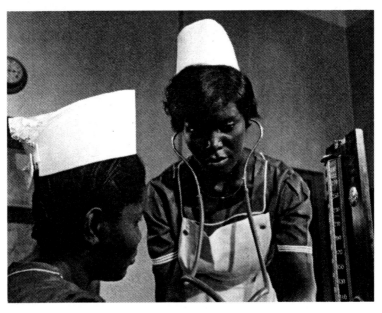

Nurses in training

'Darkness enveloped me,
But piercing through I came – '

The voice of the African spoke once again, and the rays of the sun burst through the darkness of the forest surrounding the waters of the river:

'Night is the choice for the fox's dance
Child of the moon's household am I,
And the lighting made his bid-in vain,
When she cooks is the cloud ever set on fire?
Father of the Fetish house am I'.

We were in a theatre, at a performance of Wole Soyinka's *Dance of the Forests* The audience sat quiet and still, young people. And then on the screen – as the voices of other Africans of this new generation were heard pondering the questions of forthcoming examinations – others were seen studying electronics, nursing and child-care, the literature and writing of other countries, and the tapping out on typewriters and the making of words in this strange English language. Graduates were seen with diplomas, at work on the land, at the controls of aircraft; in newspaper and advertising offices, banks, business houses, factories; and operating the cameras and directing the production of television programmes.

Discovering at Ibadan, in Western Nigeria, Africa's first television service, I planned to sit a group of young Africans in just such a studio, in just such an unscripted discussion about themselves, their hopes and their future as might – if it came off – well round off the film. But meantime, as I settled down to the construction of the 'script', it seemed to me that the film, which was planned to open with a prologue outside of Africa, might just as well close with an epilogue of Africa making her impact in the world. At the United Nations.

'At the United Nations the countries of free Africa now form the largest single block of members, and comprise virtually one third of its entire membership.' On screen we were to see a meeting of the General Assembly. African delegates, particularly those from the three countries in which the film was set, would be addressing the world forum – but we would hear the Voice of Africa speaking some lines of poetry by Nigeria's Dennis Osadebay:

> 'I'll wait no more:
> I'll lead myself towards the goal.
> On library doors
> I'll knock aloud and
> Of the strength
> Of nations past and present I will read,
> And brush the dust from ancient scrolls.
> I'll sail the seas
> And learn the might of God and man,
> Behind my name
> To tie a string of alphabets.
> I'll come back home with strong arms bared
> I'll go forward and do and dare'.

So much for the bare bones and format, on which I could graft spontaneous happenings and sayings whenever they occurred during actual filming. Filming, which, with the small, self-contained unit of documentary production, can – and should be – the greatest possible fun in the world. To shoot such a film we were a basic unit of five: myself, camera assistant, sound recordist, production manager (stuck with the often thankless task of keeping us on the right and tight rails of budget and schedule) and cameraman. For as now a 'Writer-Director' I was no longer my own cameraman; Iraq and *The Great Question* the last film that I was ever to photograph, as well as direct, myself.

Applying for my first job – any job – in a film studio soon after my sixteenth birthday, Ealing's Studio Manager had asked me what I wanted to do. 'Direct films, Sir', had been my reply. A roar of laughter – followed by 'you'd have to start as a Third Assistant Director, going round knocking on doors and getting the artistes on the set. Got a job in the Camera Department though, film loading, can't pay you any money though'. Yes please, and

324

I'd started the following day, to be put on a slightly more permanent basis as a Clapper Boy four weeks later. And so my pathway to direction led by way of the camera, to me of equal, if not greater importance in what is after all primarily a visual art than the typewriter – and any fool can shoot talking heads and call it a programme. But how might I now fare with someone else operating 'my' camera, to my direction? I need not have worried. We hit it off instinctively, each of us respecting and now sharing in the other's experience and passion – yes, passion – for the moving image and how it can be fashioned to tell a story, and serve as the instrument of the '*creative* treatment of actuality'.

Then in his fourth decade of picture-making, Ronnie Anscombe had first entered the industry as a mixer of chemicals in a film laboratory. In the days of his apprenticeship, films were still silent; but students of the camera who care to take a look at Britain's first 'talkie' – Alfred Hitchcock's *Blackmail* – can see the young Anscombe playing the part of a member of Scotland Yard's Flying Squad in that film's opening sequence. This picture, like many of Hitchcock's earliest, was made in the studios of British International Pictures at Elstree, Britain's first truly international centre of film production. As an assistant, and later camera operator, Anscombe had worked on many of BIP's epics, both silent and sound. He had learned his craft the hard way, apprenticed to such pioneers as Claude Friese-Greene, the son of the man who built Britain's first genuine motion picture camera. Anything but 'artistic', Anscombe was nonetheless a genuine artist. He could, if you wished, shoot *a la nouvelle vague* at the drop of a tripod, and set up and light the House of Lords for a seven Technirama camera coverage of a State Opening of Parliament before you could call 'cut'. He was quick, he was adaptable, but he had to be humoured. Anscombe asked little more of life than it should furnish his family with security by providing his camera with exciting subjects to film. But he did demand, daily, one creature comfort. Something he firmly believed to be not only necessary for his continued health and well-being, but, as I had soon come to recognise as his director, also essential to the true creative working of his *oeuvre*: Guinness, good Dublin stout.

The Production Manager, Bruce Sharman, and I always made certain that there was an adequate supply of this beverage wherever we might happen to be. Did a hotel or rest-house have Guinness? If so, okay. If not, the unit looked elsewhere for its accommodation. The furthest trip we ever had to make from the sources of such sustenance was our five-day journey down the Niger river. Sharman soon overcame this problem. Ten crates of Guinness were duly delivered to the quayside where we were loading camera, film, sound recording equipment and provisions.

'All aboard', and we were off. Fast and furious filming of the great confluence of the Niger and the Benue rivers slipping away behind us; the huge barge-train our tug was hauling; the tropical storm which, without warning, burst over our heads and gave us a wonderfully pictorial sequence of storm sweeping these West African waters. Drenched, but delighted with such an immediately unexpected bonus of dramatic material, we sat down to relax.

'What will you drink, Ron?'

'I think I'll have a Guinness.'

To the stern of the tug *Gongola*, on which we were travelling, and where our supplies had been stacked. Consternation. No Guinness. It had been left behind. For the one and only time in the whole thirteen weeks of our cheek-by-jowl life and work together, there were hard words between camera and production departments. But if the *Gongola* refused to heave-to and go back for the missing Guinness, full speed astern was quickly rung up on the engine room telegraph when another piece of cargo jumped overboard.

The ship was entirely African-run. The Master was African, the Chief Engineer was African, and the crew wholly African. Like us, they travelled self-contained, but carried their rations more on the hoof. Not having been yet converted to the Muslim faith of their brethren to the north, they had no inhibitions about eating pork. Breakfast, lunch and dinner had been tied up aft, squealing mightily at the prospect of the fate before it. By the time we were some twenty miles downstream the pig had succeeded in working itself loose of its halter. With a splash it was overboard.

'Stop the engine! Hard astern! Lower a boat!'

We hove-to. A boat was lowered, and a race ensued between the Africans rowing against the current in pursuit of the pig, and the poor animal itself, swimming like mad towards the freedom of the shore a good half mile away. We all rooted for the pig, but Anscombe, always the betting man, laid odds on the boatmen. The pig put on a burst of speed which would have done credit to an Olympic sprinter, and reached the bank first. Great cheers from us. But alas, the bank was steep. It floundered about, trying to find a foothold. The oarsmen stepped up the pace. One leaped ashore. A sudden distant squeal, and all was over. We had fresh bacon for breakfast.

Our Sound Recordist was Carlyle Leonard Mounteney, for short 'Ching'. He was a contemporary of Anscombe's, and we had worked together before. As Anscombe brought into focus the face of Africa with his camera, so Ching caught its sound – and sometimes its fury – with his microphone. From the throbbing of the tribal drums of the so-called primitive – which we played down (there had, after all, been so much of this in the past) – to the impeccable English of its university professors:

'I believe that here we have something to give and something to show the world. It need not be in ballistic missiles, but maybe in the moulding of the man's mind. It may be in the re-discovering of the making of the African as his contribution to the world. Behind it all we need a strong backing of African studies, African history, so that we can be fitted both internally and externally, so to speak, for the work of a modern country – a modern independent country.'

The Vice-Chancellor of Ghana's University at Kumasi.

Ching's tapes also brought back the songs of trade union rallies, and the music of *Highlife*:

Students graduate

Trade unionists applaud

'We shall unite as workers still
And work in concord, love and peace,
That we may build a nation strong
To fight the cause of workers' rights.

'Now freedom is the thing
That makes Africa sing,
Don't hesitate
To celebrate
This great awakening'.

Ching was a good sound man – but the noisiest I have ever known. You could hear him for miles. He had done a stint in the Navy during the War, was sometimes called the Commander as a result, and had developed a piercing quarter deck-like amplification to the decibels of his own delivery. A whisper from Ching was guaranteed to deafen at a distance of yards. Never did I wish that he could have kept his mouth more firmly shut than on one occasion in Northern Nigeria.

It was a typical one of our seventy-seven shooting days. We woke up at dawn in Zaria, and were on the road by 8.30. At 11 o'clock we were fifty miles south, lining up and filming an interview in Kaduna with the African General Manager of the United Africa Company – exporters of groundnuts and palm oil – having twice lost our way as we drove through the dense dust tracks of this great Nigerian Muslim north. A very serious lunch then followed, at the home of that Company's Public Relations manager and his wife. Our final destination that day was to be Ibadan, three hundred and fifty miles to the south west, where all had been arranged for our filming Wole Soyinka's *A Dance of the Forests* the following day. No problem – we were all booked on the Nigerian Airways Kaduna-Ibadan flight that same afternoon. Normally Sharman had us so scheduled that if we made an air hop like this most of our still cumbersome 35 millimetre equipment and accessories followed by road, and we shot simple silent coverage until it all caught up with us once again. This time, time itself did not permit. We had bought four extra seats

329

in the aircraft – the front four – and supervised the loading and strapping down of all our crated equipment in this forward section of the passenger cabin.

The flight was called. With the other passengers, we trooped aboard and fastened ourselves in, seated behind what appeared to be a mountainous weight of boxed-up camera and recording gear. The Captain climbed in, and made his way up the aisle. Ching, who had enjoyed his lunch enormously, called out cheerfully as he passed: 'You'll never get off the ground with that lot!'.

The Captain smiled faintly and closed the door of the flight deck behind him. The plane lurched, then settled down a few further inches into the ground. The under-carriage had given way.

All climbed out. No spare parts, and no chance of a patched-up repair getting us airborne for hours. Ibadan, our destination, was only a grass landing strip. No aircraft could land on it after dark. We had had it. Sharman battled bravely with the airport telephone, and finally got through to our man in Lagos. At whatever time we might arrive there – to which we were now diverted if we ever got off the ground that day at all – he promised to have cars waiting, and get us somehow to Ibadan in time for the next morning's filming. We finally landed near midnight, and he did. Then followed a furious drive through another tropical rain storm the eighty miles to Ibadan, which we at long last reached at two o'clock in the morning. That day's unit call was 7.30. I snatched a few hours' sleep; but Anscombe, always the ever-ready, just made a date at the local dance hall. With no sleep at all he then went straight on to shoot the most beautifully photographed sequence in the whole film.

Realism went overboard. Coloured light from any but natural sources underscored the symbolism of Soyinka's play; but not before the patience of Sharman and I had been stretched to near breaking point by a palefaced gentleman from the Arts Council of Great Britain, attached to the University where we were staging *A Dance of the Forests*, who persisted in maintaining that we would be better employed in filming his production of *The Importance of Being Earnest*.

Wole Soyinka not only wrote and produced *A Dance of the Forests*, he also played the leading part; Obaneji – Forest Head – who presides over gods, men and spirits. In spite or because of this supreme position, Forest Head is intensely human. Convinced that nothing ever changes, he finds it difficult to accept this as a fact, and persists in his secret task – his 'eternal burden' – 'to pierce the encrustations of soul-deadening habit' ... to torture awareness from man's soul. But the futility of it distresses him; his sorrow is evident; he – and not one of the humans whose fate is the subject of the story – is the chief tragic character of the play.

Six years later Soyinka's magnificent verse was being declaimed far further afield than the campus of a West African university – and he had been twice imprisoned in his own country. One by one the London School of Economics graduates were toppled from their positions of executive power, and in country after country the military took over. Colonel slew colonel, tribe slaughtered tribe, Ghana's 'Redeemer' Kwame Nkrumah died a discredited exile, Nigeria exploded into civil war and the African Awakening became a knock on the head.

And now African killed African. Black man slew black man. Just at the time Nigeria's General Gowon was marching on Biafra's Colonel Ojukwu – and Soyinka was in solitary confinement under suspended sentence of death for opposing this fratricide – that apostle of Black Power, Stokely Carmichael, was informing English intellectuals in a BBC panel discussion that: 'When the question of violence is ever brought up, I say that the Western society ought to be the ones to talk about it. They invented it, they're the ones who have ruled everyone by it, and now they are going to receive just what they've brought to the world'.

Nearly fifty years before Carmichael was born, the relief expedition was entering the city of Benin. Of Overami's capital, as the first white man set foot in it, an African has written: 'Outside, in the open space, the state of things was almost more frightful than in the Juju compounds – everywhere sacrificial trees on which were the corpses of the latest victims – everywhere, on each path, were newly-sacrificed corpses. On the principal sacrificial tree facing the main gate of the King's compound there were two crucified bodies, at the foot of the tree seventeen newly decapitated bodies, and forty-three more in various stages of decomposition. On another tree a wretched woman was found crucified, while at its foot were four more decapitated bodies. To the westward of the King's house was a large open space, about 300 yards in length, simply covered with the remains of some hundreds of human sacrifices in all stages of decomposition'.

Was the violence of this great, black African kingdom invented by the white man? Come on now, Mr Carmichael. The difference between Benin and Belsen is only one of degree. Neither you nor I can claim credit, or discredit, for the invention of violence: it is endemic in the human condition, and has been ever since the son of the father of us all murdered his brother. If Cain and Abel lived anywhere, they were Semitic desert herdsmen of what we now call the Middle East, and their colour was neither white nor black. The only hope for any of us, of whatever colour, lies in implementing the theme of Kwegyir Aggrey's faith that: 'You can play a tune of sorts on the white keys, and you can play a tune of sorts on the black keys, but for harmony you must use both the black and the white'.

But let Soyinka sum this up. In his 1965 novel, *The Inheritors*, one of his characters, a Nigerian, argues with an American Black: 'It is this cult of Black Beauty which sickens me. Are albinos supposed to go and drown themselves, for instance?'.

And, in his film scenario of *The Autobiography of Malcolm X*, James Baldwin has his convert-hero put it this way: 'The true Islam has shown me that a blanket indictment of all white people is as wrong as when whites make blanket indictments against blacks'.

African Awakening (as I called the film we made) achieved success. It was chosen by a committee which included Carol Reed, Thorold Dickinson and Edgar Anstey as the one British film produced in 1962 'judged to contribute most effectively to public appreciation of an outstanding achievement resulting from international co-operation in education, science, and culture', and thus worthy of UNESCO's Kalinga Prize. To me, its real accolade was to come in Poona, seven years later. I screened it at the Film and Television Institute of India. Amongst the audience was that small group of forlorn, lonely Africans.

'We liked that film', they came up and said to me afterwards. 'It told the truth.'

It is now forty years on from my own projection of the African Awakening: a whole generation of further struggle, which

African Awakening debated on television

has witnessed an entire new generation of African films and African film-makers like Oumarou Ganda, Sarah Maldoror, and Ousmane Sembene coming of age. In 1976 Sembene's *Xala* – an ironic allegory of male impotence among the African bourgeoisie – was the first black African feature to be shown commercially in Britain, and previously there had been sightings of this Senegalese Director's *Emitai*. The story of a village rebelling against the conscription of its menfolk by the colonial power during the Second World War. The women withhold the rice, the

French flush it out, and shoot down the men who refuse to carry it away. Like Overami before him, this latter-day African Chief dies cursing the gods and the spirits who have let such a disaster befall his people. There have been comedies, like Sembene's *Xala*, and even a wide-screen epic, *Sarrounia*, shot on location in Burkina Faso (formerly Upper Volta) by a galaxy of talent. Directed by the Mauritian writer-director Med Hondo, based on a novel by Aboulaye Mamani from Niger, edited by the Cameroonist Marie-Therese Boiche, and with a score composed and performed by musicians from Burkina Faso and Gabon, this tells of the eponymous heroine, leader of her people, who rallies them in an attempt to halt the original advance of French imperialism and take-over of their territory. A genuine *African Queen*.

Feature film production has developed in the other formerly French colonies of Mauritania, Ivory Coast, Mali. Strongly influenced by the commercial Indian cinema patronised by its Asian population, Kenya has come up with a few. As yet only derivative of Western formulae, Nigeria also and Ghana too. For a fortnight every other year, the capital of Burkina Faso, Ouagadougou, is host to a Pan-African Film Festival. Both in the United States and Britain dedicated Blacks, either as individuals or collectives, have succeeded in getting their stories on to cinema screens, but only little ones, in art house ghettoes. Notable has been *Testimony*, dedicated to James Baldwin. An elegiac meditation on a British Black's search for her roots and confrontation with her other self left behind to face the failed promise of Nkrumah's Ghana, written and directed by John Akomfrah. Only the big battalions, and white ones at that, have been able to raise the finance, arrange distribution to stake out the *profitable* film production of the dichotomy of black-and-white on big screens, world wide. And inevitably only the safe and newsworthy box office setting had to be South Africa.

Cry Freedom, Richard Attenborough's epic of the writer Donald Wood's struggle to get the true story of Steve Biko – done to death in custody – out of the country and to the world at large; *A World Apart*, Chris Menges' personalisation of the issue in a white middle class girl's resentment of her mother's absorption in the anti-Apartheid struggle; *A Dry White Summer*, the Martinique-born Euzhan Palcy's unfolding drama of family and friends attempting to discover the truth behind the disappearance of a black boy following the massacre of a peaceful demonstration in the Johannesburg suburb of Soweto. For the latter MGM, no less, dug out of retirement Marlon Brando, whose key line as a jaded civil rights lawyer is 'Justice and the law are not on speaking terms in South Africa'.

But none the less, even at a distance with Zimbabwe at that time safe shooting territory for such as MGM, Goldcrest, and Film Four International to risk their money, all of these major *international* blockbusters personalising the racial tensions of the drama suffer the inevitable consequence of mediating the horrors of Apartheid through White consciousness – not Black. The Black Experience inevitably becomes secondary to the White point of view. However sympathetic (and that very word breathes patronage) is there not possibly a whiff of cultural colonialism in these nevertheless well-intentioned films?

In the United States however Spike Lee, that so-called 'black Woody Allen', has opened up in the way of material the whole Black culture of America. But can we really say that the ethnic beat called rap is truly a dance of the forests? Urban jungles perhaps.

Of all the great films that might have been, very near the top of the list must surely be Eisenstein's *Black Majesty*, the story of Toussaint L'Ouverture and the aborted Black Republic of Haiti; and of all great films which might yet be made surely *Overami of Benin* must make some claim – particularly if brought to the screen by Wole Soyinka.

9. FILM AND THE NATIONAL IMAGE

'Even when it is conceded that a nation is not merely
what it is at a given moment but in its entire potential,
a danger remains for all who sometimes wonder, as
I often do, if the nation they know is not simply one
of their imagining.'

Wole Soyinka

Profile of Britain

As someone hoping to be a film-maker in Britain you might nowadays well set out to learn all about it at the National Film and Television School. Why so-called *National*? Presumably because it is supposed to serve the interests of the nation as much as the art and craft of the moving image.

What is this thing called a nation? As the individual personality develops it first of all discovers itself to be a member of a family, which is in turn part of a larger collective sometimes called a tribe. Many tribes, sharing racial blood and origin, can be drawn together into a still larger collective and, over the years, subordinate their particular characteristics into the larger community of self-interest called a nation.

At peaks of national endeavour, soul-searching, and rediscovery, nations have used film to demonstrate their collective purpose, analyse their angst, reassure themselves. Moreover, at any period, the films of a nation tend to reflect the current mood of that nation. Defeated and pre-Hitler Germany gave us the subjective fantasies of such monster supermen as Doctors Caligari and Mabuse. During the same period, Soviet Russia threw up a totally different style and technique of revolutionary motion picture art in *Potemkin* and *October*. During the 1930's depression-ridden but still at the time fundamentally optimistic America gave birth to Disney's cocky *Three Little Pigs* and the aggressively assertive and self-confident *March of Time*. Wartime Britain was the genesis of those particularly English and sensitive films of Humphrey Jennings, *Listen to Britain* and *A Diary for Timothy*. With rare exception, men fighting in a national cause were heroes to Hollywood, in a long catalogue of films from World War One's *Wings* to Korea's *Pork Chop Hill*. With failure to win in Vietnam, however, all wars to Hollywood became a senseless shambles. Korea was dismissed in *M.A.S.H. Catch 22* said 'so what?' to World War Two, and what was seen to be the final end to the American dream aptly entitled *Apocalypse Now*. And then along came *Rambo*, to avenge defeat in Vietnam by celluloid proxy.

The search for a national rather than a racial identity is the continuing story of the African Awakening. The collective roots of community are still more tribal than national. The struggle to maintain Nigeria as a national unity, after the attempted break-away by the Ibos of its east into the belligerence of Biafra, is evidence indeed of the fragile nature of so many claims to be individual and independent African nations, lined up at, and answering the roll-call of the United Nations. To come much nearer home, my own national identity – so my passport informs me – is British. But the United Kingdom – as this country of mine is defined and spelt out at the United Nations – has only been so for barely 300 years. That tribal (clannish if you like) people who call themselves Scots live in a country with a long and independent history of their own. Nationalists persist in their own, non-English language in Wales, fire-raising second homes owned by intruders; and Ulster, Northern Ireland, the fourth constituent part of this so-called United Kingdom, torn by civil war against the flag and crown which symbolises that union, could be said to be Britain's Biafra.

Until the advent of television (and the *March of Time* and its successors) it was only the seldom commercially shown documentary film that took a look at the state of the nation on its cinema screens. With the coming of TV, hardly a night passes without our being made all too aware of not only our personal, but also our national problems and shortcomings. The first time I filmed the face of my own land and people was for television, but for a national audience other than my own. The subject was the British voting in a General Election, and the producers, and audience, American.

For eighteen years, as part and parcel of commercial cinema programmes, the *March of Time* had reflected from American screens a more genuine image of the real United States, on British screens posed the problems facing the British, and on world screens dramatised the international dramas of the time. By the early fifties, television was taking over. TV series such as the Ed Murrow/Fred Friendly *See it Now* discussed and illuminated mid century issues in the living-room, every week. The cinemas were emptying. Executive Producer of the *March of Time* for the last ten of its valiant years was Richard de Rochemont, younger

brother of founder Louis de Rochemont, who had left to revital-
ise the feature film away from Hollywood Studios, shooting true
stories in the locations of their actual happenings. Years later, in
an endorsement of my previous writing on the period, it was
Richard who had written me of how, and why, this unique
documentary-journalistic film series finally died. 'MOT was the
baby of Roy Larsen (President of Time Incorporated) and my
brother Louis. I was nursemaid, preceptor and tried to bring it to
maturity. The final phase was flubbed, I believe, because Larsen
would not admit that TV was stealing and copying some of our
techniques without being willing to accept the whole package.
The networks wouldn't risk letting an outsider (MOT or Time
inc.) editorialise on their (really the public's) air-waves, which
they hold on a tenuous franchise, our only way out was to produce for theatrical release some sort of super-documentary of
feature length. Spyros Skouras (Head of Twentieth Century Fox
who released the MOT) was willing to guarantee their release,
and thus their basic costs. It meant a change of formula, and a
disavowal of the format that Roy and Louis had worked on so
long. Roy and I parted and the rest seems to be on the record'.

For the record, headed up by a former General Manager of
Life, there was a brief and ignominious attempt by Time Incorporated at a weekly *March of Time* series in television. I shot
three of them and then, in due course, left to work for NBC, the
network which had at first shown them, but which was now
starting up a new programme all its own.

Time Incorporated was in publishing, not broadcasting. That
was the heart of the matter. The organisation was to acquire a
handful of TV stations, but this could never be more than a drop
in the bucket compared to the nation-wide networks controlled
by the three giants; ABC, CBS and NBC.

More than twenty years later, there was a footnote to this
failure by an outsider to get a foothold in American network
television.

Towards the close of 1974, it seemed that perhaps the time
had come to drop the embargo of Castro's Cuba. Two Senators,
accompanied by a large group of pressmen, journeyed to Ha-

vana, and saw much of Fidel. A former press aide to Robert Kennedy, and a colleague who had been press secretary to Senator George McGovern during his presidential campaign of two years earlier, had joined forces and set up a company to film interviews with personalities never normally interviewed on television; Tito, Howard Hughes, Chaplin, Castro. They obtained more than twenty hours of exclusive film on Castro – the first such interview Fidel had given in fifteen years – four months before this first opening-up of Cuba to representatives of the United States Senate. They were stunned to discover that the networks would not touch it.

Finally CBS did take some of this footage, incorporated it with a fresh interview they were able to arrange with a CBS News correspondent, and then and only then did it become legal, and a CBS report: *Castro, Cuba, and the U.S.A.*

Winding up their company, and their hopes, an older and a wiser Frank Mankiewicz ruefully reflected that 'we were met with an attitude that if a network man wasn't there, it didn't happen ... For all my experience with the networks – going back to 1966 – we didn't know about the policy against freelance journalism'.

But back once more to beginnings. The *March of Time* had originated in radio. At the time of its demise, a radio programme was once again midwife to the new dimension of successful news analysis which overtook it in television. *Hear it Now* was a narrated compilation of the historic sounds and broadcasts of the 1930's and 1940's put together for CBS by Ed Murrow and Fred Friendly. They had persuaded the network to let them try their band in television. *See It Now* was the visual as well as aural counterpart they then came up with, at first as provocatively and as sensationally successful on the little screen as the *March of Time* had been in its heyday on the larger screens of once-filled cinemas. Unlike Westbrook Van Voorhis, who had narrated MOT all the way from radio into and out of television, Ed Murrow was sensational on camera, emblematic of integrity. *Christmas in Korea* was as much a milestone for *See It Now* as *Inside Nazi Germany* had been for the *March of Time*. And then there came the McCarthy programmes, with which Murrow and Friendly devastatingly demonstrated the shallow fakery and fraud of the demagogue who did so much to undermine America's mid century faith in herself.

The rival network, NBC could not afford to be outdone in this new development in mass communication. They came up with *Background*. This was the period of the mid-fifties, which some have since called the Golden Age of American Television. After shooting a film for Louis de Rochemont on the Suez Canal, I went to work for *Background*, in Europe.

For *Background* I directed and photographed reports on post-war Germany, the Italian Communist Party, and the refugees flooding into Austria from Hungary and then other 'Iron-Curtain' countries to the east. Anchorman and interviewer on this last programme had been NBC's Edwin Newman. In Munich we set up and shot a long interview with a Czech ice-skater who had defected to the West. In the summer of 1955, I went on to direct his interrogation of my own country's candidates for power, as NBC reported on the British General Election of that year.

My impression of my homeland – looked at by then through virtually American eyes – was that ten years after defeating all their enemies, life for the British seemed good. Six years of Labour Government had liquidated an empire and inaugurated the Welfare State. Buttressed by billions from American Marshall Plan aid, commercial recovery had brought the Conservatives back to power. Sir Winston Churchill, their leader, had announced his retirement. Sir Anthony Eden succeeded him. Within nine days, this heir long-apparent, announced his intention of going to the country for a mandate. The General Election was scheduled for the last week in May.

The real background to that now rather remote general election was the forthcoming meeting between Eisenhower and Khrushchev in Switzerland. For the first time since they had started to brandish nuclear weapons at each other, the Americans and the Russians were about to sit down at the same table, and see if they could agree to live in the same world together without blowing us all up.

341

Mid - century

Half way to where?

Within five weeks of Stalin's death two years before, Winston Churchill had been the first to call for such a meeting at the summit with the new Soviet leaders. Although cold-shouldered by American Secretary of State John Foster Dulles, in Britain there had been mounting pressure for such high-level talks. The need and desire for such an attempt to end the Cold War was the major issue of that 1955 election. The British did not wish to perish lamely in a nuclear holocaust for which many thought the United States might be responsible. The basic choice before the electorate was which of their two major parties they wished to see representing them at this vital American-Soviet conference to end the atomic impasse.

For the American network I decided to dramatise the political issue in Britain by going to two constituencies, one typically Conservative, one Labour.

For this I now needed three cameras: two I would train on the speakers – the first camera, with a long-focus lens, operated by myself, to hold him or her in full screen close-up; the second, always similarly loaded with its maximum thousand feet of what was then 35mm film operated by an assistant, holding them in mid-shot, so we could catch gestures as well as facial expression. The third, hand-held by former *March of Time* assistant cameraman John Peters, wandering round the crowd, catching long-shots and close-ups of the audience – argumentative or indifferent – as cut-aways and reactions to the candidates covered closer by the other two. I used two cameras for the interviews, which were conducted by Ed Newman – who was to play the same role on a much more prestigious scale many years later when he served as one of the moderators in the nationally televised firstly Ford-Carter and then the Reagan-Mondale TV debates. My own camera holding the victim under scrutiny in close-up, and the other, set up beside it with a wider angle lens, shooting a picture which included Newman as well. After the interview was over, and the candidate departed, we would play back the tape recording of its question and answer, and then shoot separate close-ups of Ed Newman once again asking his questions and reacting to the answers, to be cut into the film of the two-shot interview in order to give it a final overall variety and pace. Standard practice nowadays.

Although British born, as a non-American working for a non-British programme, I felt I might, at least just this once, on this assignment, be considered (whatever my own political inclinations) impartial, if not 'objective'.

The Labour Party believed that it was most suited to the pursuit of peace. Its election manifesto drew attention to its belief that 'The most profound challenge of our time is the gap between the highly-developed industrial nations of the West and the peasant millions of Asia and Africa. The Labour Government responded to this challenge and earned the confidence of the colonial peoples. For this reason alone no one is better fitted to represent Britain at high level talks than Clement Attlee – the man who freed India, despite Conservative jeers of socialistic scuttle'.

But in the market square of High Wycombe in Buckinghamshire my cameras recorded another point of view. 'Let's consider the matter which for many of us is probably even more important. What success have we had in trying to find a formula for peace? What success have we had in reducing the world tensions? Remember we came into power with a cry of warmonger ringing on our ears. No party that had any desire to make war could have gone about it in such a way as Sir Anthony Eden has done. No party that wanted to make war could have had as their Foreign Secretary and now their Prime Minister a man who is universally acclaimed, and praised, what is more, by socialists in the House of Commons; he has been a man who has worked harder than anyone else during the last few years for peace.'

So spoke company director and Conservative Member of Parliament John Hall, to an audience of countrymen and craftsmen in High Wycombe. One of fourteen hundred and nine candidates, he sought election from this constituency of light industry and agriculture which met, and drank, of an evening, at the 'Red Lion'. In the campaign of 1832, Disraeli had declared from the balcony of this former coaching inn that if elected he would guarantee 'to rouse the dormant energies of the country, to liberate our shackled industry, and re-instate our expiring credit'. Sounds familiar.

A clarion call echoed by more than one latter-day and aspirant prime minister, hopefully following in his footsteps. A hundred-and-twenty-three years after Disraeli, I stood Ed Newman on this same vantage point to introduce the programme to our American audience. For myself, I knew this Thames Valley well. Before the Second World War I had spent many a happy day along the river banks. Now, from Marlow, through Cookham, Beaconsfield and Gerrards Cross, we drove to Uxbridge, for an appointment with Anthony Eden at the pinnacle of his long-suffering and patient political career. Past the village of Denham.

Denham. The studios were still there, but they no longer conjured up Oxford colleges, oriental palaces, Imperial Russian ballrooms. The original British Hollywood had become another casualty in television's conquest of the cinema. The vast area of sound stages which had seen Dietrich in flight from the Bolsheviks, Taylor disarmed by Oxonian tradition, Donat demanding justice for medicine, were then stacked high with the stores and supplies of the United States nuclear-armed Air Force, to whom they had been leased for this purpose by the inheritor of the property, the man with the gong – the Rank Organisation. Korda himself had now less than a year to live. But he had been true to the end to his original pledge to 'encourage the people who really matter to the screen ... (that) they shall not be forced to shelve all their best ideas to satisfy the whims of a commercially-minded board of directors'.

Back in Britain after the war, and availing himself this time of substantial government funding, Korda had indeed still been able to maintain this original commitment. By then the major talents of the recent British feature film renaissance had all begun to feel restricted by the Rank Organisation for which they had made most of their recently outstanding work. These talents had all then joined forces with Korda, no longer at Denham but at Shepperton Studios where, twelve years before, he had shot some of the exteriors for *Sanders of the River*. Amongst them were David Lean, for such as *The Sound Barrier* and *Hobson's*

Choice; Powell and Pressberger for *The Small Back Room* and *Gone to Earth*; Carol Reed for *The Fallen Idol* and his Korda-Selznick masterpiece *The Third Man.*

The pleas, and charms, and ambitions of actors Korda could never refuse. As Orson 'Third Man' Welles has told us, he loved them. Robert Donat wanted to direct and star in his own film version of *The Cure for Love*, Walter Greenwood's play of the trials and tribulations of a soldier returning to civilian life. Go ahead, said he. Ralph Richardson had long wanted to direct. No problem – so he was soon in the director's chair filming himself and others in an adaption of R.C. Sherriff's *Home at Seven*. Emlyn Williams (that Caligula to Laughton's Claudius) likewise. He had an original story he wanted to film, set in the valleys of his beloved Wales. Korda gave him the means, all the facilities that he needed and, if nothing else, *The Last Days of Dolwyn* introduced a young Welsh actor called Richard Burton to the screen. (That not one of these films was a *commercial* success does not, surely, in any way diminish Korda.)

After *Henry V* and *Hamlet*, the Rank Organisation refused any further financing to Laurence Olivier in his filming of Shakespeare. The actor-knight-producer-director turned to his old boss, Korda. The only producer – as Graham Greene has told us – 'with whom (he) could spend days and nights of conversation without so much as mentioning the cinema'. That *grand seigneur* of celluloid didn't even hesitate. Made in British Lion's Shepperton Studios, *Richard III* was the penultimate film to be produced and released under the banner of London Film Productions, this General Election year of 1955.

Outside Uxbridge Station, from which I had commuted daily to Denham in the distant days of Korda's glory, Britain's latest Prime Minister now enjoyed the uncritical attention of a largely middle-class audience. The adoring look in the eyes of some of its matrons testified clearly enough to the irresistible appeal of Eden's impeccably cut clothes and upper-class accent. Accompanied by a new wife, and making very much the same speech at every half hour halt in this the first and last campaign which he would ever wage and win as Prime Minister, Anthony Eden ass-

Political adversaries
in the 1955
British
General Election

Aneurin Bevan

Anthony Eden

'Every man in
politics is a
failure'

says 'Nye' Bevan

ured his listeners (and my NBC camera) that: 'There are now prospects of meeting with the Russians at various levels, including the highest level. Last summer, about this time – my wife was with me – we were at Geneva. Trying very hard to get a settlement to the Indo-China war, which at times looked uncomfortably like becoming a world war'.

That had been indeed Eden's finest hour. France had been defeated in Indo-China. Eden, as Britain's Foreign Secretary, had been the prime mover in a settlement between Molotov, Mendes-France, Chou En-lai and a somewhat recalcitrant John Foster Dulles. Armistice agreements had been made for Laos, Cambodia and Vietnam. A somewhat shaky patchwork peace which presumed the neutrality of two of these former kingdoms of Indo-China, and divided the third. It didn't last long.

Forever famed for his dramatic resignation from the government of Neville Chamberlain's pre-war appeasement (a gesture which the commentary of this election film was to rather unkindly describe as achieving more for the homburg than for peace) undoubtedly Eden's great talent for diplomatic compromise had just recently averted – if only postponed – the threat of world war in South East Asia.

And the tragedy of this man was that it was war which was to destroy him. A war of his own making, less than two years ahead of those days so full of promise. Suez. Word of which was to reach me while filming a petroleum pipeline in Iraq, soon to be blown up as a consequence by the irate locals who were then to go on to set fire to the British Embassy; all of which combining to delay the final completion (and almost instantaneous shelving) of *The Great Question* for another year.

'If you listen to what Sir Anthony Eden has been telling us he merely intends to go on for the next five years as he's been going on for the last three-and-a-half years. So you have neither a new government nor a new policy. All you have got is a new Prime Minister. And so we want to know, and I think the country wants to know, why it is that this particular moment has been selected for the general election?'

The great town hall of Huddersfield rang that week of May 1955 not to the choruses of Handel's *Messiah*, but to the emotional oratory of Aneurin Bevan. 'What is the biggest contribution that can be made towards the pacification of the tensions in the world?' this former Labour Minister went on to demand of his devoted audience (and of the cameras I had trained on him). 'The biggest single contribution we can make against pushing back the horrors of a nuclear war is that we should have men and women in the House of Commons who are naturally sympathetic to what ordinary men and women elsewhere are hoping to accomplish. We have therefore been hoping for some time that we should have the opportunity of putting in the House of Commons people who are naturally sympathetic; because the Tories, with all the good will in the world, cannot speak the language of the modern world at all – they're speaking the language of a world which is now dead'.

Certainly the abortive invasion and assault with which Eden chose to change Egypt's government and policy seventeen months later were to be more reminiscent of the methods of his nineteenth century predecessor Palmerston.

We came to Bevan's speech in the West Riding of Yorkshire by way of a Lancashire faced with a slump in the cotton trade. In former days, the fellahin along the banks of the Nile had provided the foundation for the cotton fortunes of Lancashire. Now other markets existed, and other machinery, tended by the cheaper and more productive labour of an increasingly industrialised world for which Britain was no longer the workshop. To an 'objective' observer/reporter of my native land such as I now presumed to be, it seemed that the cold logic of their diminished status had not then yet been recognised by the British. Massive American aid had so far made up for the loss of the more than four thousand million pounds of their overseas assets liquidated during the war. The reality of national insolvency and international impotence was still being obscured, let alone faced. More than a century of industrial and commercial pre-eminence had led to a complacency in which the old-fashioned virtues of self-reliance and thrift were being increasingly obscured by the facile

349

rewards of an instalment plan affluence. Eden's successor would soon be telling the British that 'they had never had it so good'.

That the British had done more than any other nation to lead the world into the twentieth century was an historic fact. From Khartoum to Canton their railways had linked and developed peoples and countries. From Buenos Aires to Basra their industry had transformed continents. Their own admirable system of domestic government had provided a sound and honest system of administration for vast areas of the globe which had previously known only tribal autocracy or feudal corruption. But their sense of, and belief in their own therefore apparently inherent superiority had led all but a few notable eccentrics to live lives apart from the peoples they ruled. In the clubs which they founded, from Nairobi to Accra, from Calcutta to Kuala Lumpur, the only 'natives' permitted to enter were their servants. To a clap of hands and a shout of 'boy', gentlemen old enough to be their fathers would run to do their bidding. The words 'please' and 'thank you' were conspicuously absent from their already somewhat limited vocabularies. But by now, in 1955, there really was little for them to be arrogant about. For these fifty million people in a tight little island unable to support itself, the problem of survival in an infinitely more competitive and less subservient world had still to be faced – let alone solved.

In the cockney constituency of Southwark the price of tea was a major issue. Balancing what the Washington correspondent of the London *Times* would be pleased to report as 'an objective and discerning survey of the campaign', I had brought our cameras from the fields of Buckinghamshire to this Labour stronghold in south-east London; while, at Blackburn, I followed Barbara Castle as she toured the cotton mills and appealed for the votes of their dispossessed operatives. At street corners in this drab Lancashire town she lambasted the Conservative government's record at home, and its subservience to American interests abroad. Then a member of Labour's National Executive (and future Cabinet Minister) this fiery feminist already stood well to the left of her party on many issues, not least of all foreign policy. But no one spoke more eloquently in the true British radical tradition than Aneurin Bevan. After we had recorded his speech to the great gathering at Huddersfield, we attempted to penetrate the philosophy of the most controversial political personality of those days.

The vast hall was empty. The last supporter had sung *The Red Flag* and gone home. Midnight had chimed from above our heads when Ed Newman sat down with Aneurin Bevan, and with my two eager sound cameras I followed every cut and thrust of the almost Shavian dialogue that ensued – and which, as it has never been seen or heard in Britain, I think is worth quoting in full.

Newman: Mr Bevan, you said in your speech in this hall tonight that millions of people overseas are anxious for a Labour Government. Do you think that any of these anxious people are in the United States?

Bevan: I think there are. I think there are large numbers of people in the United States who would like to see a British Government asserting itself more, and having more influence in the formation of American policy.

Newman: You seem to feel it's your mission in life to civilise the United States.

Bevan: I wouldn't say civilise the United States. That would be far too offensive a term to use. But I think we have something to contribute, and that our contribution has not been made from here with enough energy, and has not been received by America with sufficient receptiveness.

Newman: Why do you think that the United States might be more receptive to greater pressure from a Labour Government?

Bevan: I didn't say it would be more receptive, but the energy from this side might be a little greater.

Newman: Do you expect to have office in another Labour Government?

Bevan: can't answer that question. It's in the lap of the gods.

Newman: Mr Bevan, let's talk about you for a minute. I think you'll agree that a good many people in the United States, and quite possibly in Britain too, lie awake nights thinking about you as a Prime Minister some day, or at any rate in a position of great influence again. Do you think that the sleeplessness that these people suffer from is justified?

Bevan: I don't quite know what causes it. I could answer the question more effectively if I knew what their fears were. I doubt whether there are very many in Great Britain. I know there might be large numbers in the United States, but there I think their fears are artificially fostered, by people who think that my point of view is hostile to their own interests.

Newman: Mr Bevan, you're not anti-American you would say?

Bevan: I would say it's very foolish to call me anti-American. I'm anti no nation at all. I am no more anti-American than I'm anti-Russian or anti-French or anti-German. There are very large numbers of Americans who share my point of view, therefore it's quite silly to talk about individuals being anti this country or that.

Newman: Would you agree that some people might think that because it often seems that you're far more critical of the United States, and perhaps even of your own country, than you are, let's say, of Communist China?

Bevan: You might sometimes form that impression, but that is very largely because if I'm to be quite frank about it, my point of view is selected very carefully by people who want to present me from a particular angle, and if I say something which is friendly to the United States it's very rarely published.

Newman: Well if you said something friendly now I imagine it would be heard. Is there anything friendly you would care to say?

Bevan: Well, I'm very fond of a very large number of Americans and have a great admiration for America. For example, I think that the United States made a very considerable contribution to European recovery immediately after the War by Marshall Aid, and I've always regretted that that has been substituted for military aid. I think that has been a futile contribution, because I believe that the answer to communism in the world is not a military answer, but an economic and political answer.

Newman: Mr Bevan, some people, and you may no doubt call them misguided, get the impression that you think the world has much more to fear from the United States than it does from Communist China or Russia. Is that the case?

Bevan: America is much more powerful. It's the mightiest nation the world has ever seen, and its impact upon world policy is so much greater as a consequence. And we're always afraid that the power might be used by misguided or irresponsible people. And there has been some justification for it because we have heard American statesmen – if they can be called statesmen – always talking about preventive war and things of that sort. And therefore lesser breeds like us are afraid that you might run amok.

Newman: The hydrogen bomb?

Bevan: We think that the tests of the hydrogen bomb should stop. We are just frightened, as I said in my speech tonight, about the rise in the radioactive background to the world at the present time.

353

Newman: Suppose the Conservatives do win. What sort of Prime Minister to you think Anthony Eden will make?

Bevan: In my view not a very good one. In my view he's too tepid. In my view he has exhausted his potentiality for effectiveness before he has taken office. He's been made to wait too long.

Newman: Mr Bevan, you once told me in which I suppose was an unguarded moment, possibly in jest, that you thought of yourself as a kind of political Robin Hood. Do you really consider yourself that?

Bevan: It's obviously very foolish for me to have an unguarded moment with you, and I don't propose to have another.

Newman: Having been in politics this long time do you think you have been a success or a failure?

Bevan: Every man in politics is a failure.

Aneurin Bevan shared one thing in common with Anthony Eden. Both had resigned from the Cabinet on an issue of principle. As Minister of Health in the post-war Labour government, Bevan had made the theme and the argument of *The Citadel* seem to come true. He had been responsible for creating the National Health Service: that essential pillar of the Welfare State which guaranteed free medical care to all and every one of its citizens. But, faced with the rising costs of re-armament forced upon Britain by the Korean War, Chancellor of the Exchequer Hugh Gaitskell had determined to balance his 1951 budget by restoring certain charges.

'It would be dishonourable for me', Bevan (then Minister of Labour) had declared, 'to allow my name to be associated in the carrying out of policies which are repugnant to my conscience and contrary to my expressed opinion'. Thereupon, along with Harold Wilson and John Freeman, he had resigned from the

354

Government. His action had split the Labour movement, and Bevan himself had only been saved from expulsion from the Labour Party itself by one vote. Wilson stayed with it, to become the next Labour Prime Minister, making Freeman British Ambassador in India and Washington. With the return of the Tories to power once again in 1970, Wilson wrote the story of his first administration, and Freeman became Chairman and Chief Executive of London Weekend Television. At the time of this 1955 interview, Bevan was already a dying man.

At two o'clock in the morning of our interview, Nye Bevan had to catch a train to his next speaking assignment. We offered to drive him to Leeds in order that he might be on time, despite a connection missed on our behalf.

As we drove onwards through the deserted darkness, Bevan talked to Newman and me of his life, tempering an unexpected admiration for Churchill with a loathing of the party he had led since the war. Born fifty-eight years before a miner's son in the foothills of the Black Mountains of South Wales, the young Nye had helped to found the Tredegar Medical Aid Society. To finance this fledging health cooperative, the miners paid three pence out of the few weekly pounds in their pockets – and were able, as a collective, to employ six doctors. Just such a self-financed group practice as advocated by Doctor Ralph Richardson/Denny to Doctor Robert Donat/Manson in *The Citadel*. In one of his last speeches in the House of Commons three years after our interview, Bevan was to claim this to have been the origin and the model for all that he later tried to achieve.

In Paris, three years before our encounter, and while waiting to be launched into the making of a series of films for the United States Mutual Security Agency – which Bevan believed had so mistakenly and unfortunately replaced the original Marshall Plan – I had read in his book *In Place of Fear* his description of struggle in the starving coalfields during the economic depression between the two world wars.

From Tredegar, Ebbw Vale, Nantyglo, and Blaina he had marched at the head of the unemployed miners, demanding Poor Law Relief. (For the release entitled *Black Areas*, Edgar Anstey

355

had directed a *March of Time* camera covering this famous demo of the thirties.) In a work house yard, a friend urged Bevan to quit Britain.

'This country is finished. Come with me to Australia ... There is no hope for us here. You and I between us can do better for ourselves in a new country.'

But Nye Bevan stayed on to fight; and, as I watched his solitary figure disappearing into the gloom of Leeds station, I pondered on the closing words of his statement to my camera. 'Every man in politics is a failure.'

Within five years untimely death was to rob Aneurin Bevan of any further chance to serve Wales, and Britain. Driving back through the industrial heartland of a still sleeping country, I recalled a saying of that earlier candidate to stand as a prospective Member of Parliament for High Wycombe. Disraeli once said that 'A statesman is the creature of his age, the child of circumstances, the creation of his times'.

National identity must be some sort of conglomerate and multiple of individual personality. We are all, every single one of us – and always have been – creatures of our age, children of circumstances, creations of our time. Statistically, at that particular pinpoint of history, I was just one of the 53,755,000 inhabitants of the United Kingdom. And then, eight years later, at the same time as personal circumstances forced me to take a hard look at myself and my origins, I was asked to focus a camera on the past, present, and future of this land of my birth. Britain.

For by then the national penny seemed at last to have dropped. The British had finally been forced to face the facts of life. Suez had been the watershed – the traumatic turning point. Once again, just like in those good old days in the desert, soldiers had gone ashore into Egypt. Here, just fourteen years before, had been fought and won Britain's last great solo feat of arms, the great battle and victory of El Alamein. Now our warriors were only up against *wogs*. It should have been a pushover. It was of course a fiasco. America's threat to cease support of the pound, and Russia's to rain down her rocketry, had forced on the British the most ignominious withdrawal in their history. No one could pretend any longer that the pound stood high, or that the country was still in the big league. Britain was broke, the people adrift. Harold Macmillan, who succeeded Eden in the shambles of Suez, had gambled in getting into the European Common Market as the panacea for all ills. The French then vetoed that.

On January 30th, 1963, Macmillan spoke on television. 'We must be ready to accept change, to modernise, to adapt, to get rid of obsolete plant, and perhaps more important, obsolete ideas.' The following day, on behalf of the Labour Party in opposition, George Brown had his say. 'We simply cannot afford any longer to hang about. We must take decisive action, and take it now.'

Decisive action, so far as the Government's official image-making machinery was concerned, was to make a film. A film which would demonstrate to all the world that Britain was not yet down and out. I was asked to make it.

A government of both Conservative and Labour Parties had once sponsored some of the finest, and most successful, documentary films ever made. Churchill's war-time coalition gave virtual *carte-blanche* to a Ministry of Information which, under the direction of Jack Beddington, produced a series of films that mirrored magnificently Britain, and the British, during 'their finest hour'. But such as *Target for Tonight, Fires were Started, Listen to Britain*, and *A Diary for Timothy* were now little more than curiosities, a source of material more often than not for the satirists of the sixties and the makers of TV's everlasting compilations.

After the War, this British Ministry of Information had become the Central Office of Information. What had been a major producer and promoter of national propaganda, answerable, if at all, to a single inspired and professional Director-General, became a common service department acting only at the behest – and under the control – of particular government departments.

Announcing the death of the MOI in 1945, Prime Minister Clement Attlee had declared that 'in the view of the government, the responsibility of the information policy of a department must rest with its Minister, but there are various technical functions, notably on the production side, which it would be uneconomical to organise departmentally and which could best be performed centrally as a common service'.

In other words, each and every Minister knew best, but needed the *services* of film technicians, centrally organised, to help him put across his policies.

At once a cry of anguish had been heard in the land. The British documentary group met as a whole, and sent a manifesto to Herbert Morrison, then Lord President of the Council and responsible for the Cental Office of Information in the House of Commons. As Paul Rotha has recorded it, this document stated that 'Since the Central Office of Information took over certain functions of the Ministry of Information... experience indicates that, as far as film production is concerned, the new machinery is not working with the smoothness and speed which is required by an efficient information service. The documentary film-makers have been as anxious to contribute to the successful operation of the new Government information services in peace-time as they were during the war. The record of Government film production ... does not (now) measure up to past achievements nor to the demands of the moment. No major film, comparable with those produced during the war, has been completed. Delays and obstructions have been increasingly characteristic of the commissions which the documentary units have received. This decline can be attributed to a number of causes, which in our opinion require urgent investigation'.

'Let us be fair', Rotha went on to write, 'The COI (has) sponsored many films but, lacking the powers of initiative itself, they became more and more little films cautiously required by departments. Safe, well-made but dull, non-theatricals at ever-increasing cost, but totally without the imagination and drama and faith that made British wartime and pre-war documentary the world's envy'.

Now, seventeen years after that original criticism of the COI, it was still true to say that, so far as Government film production was concerned, 'no major film comparable with those produced during the war had been made'. As I walked into the Central Office of Information's glittering glasshouse one morning in the early spring of 1963, I was assured that the time – and the opportunity – had finally arrived.

'I've been against making this film from the start' were the opening words from the head of the table.

'We shall never be able to please all the ministries and departments involved.'

My heart sank.

'But, pressures from embassies and high commissioners abroad cannot be put off any longer.'

I held my breath.

'No. The only thing to do is for us to give you an absolutely free hand – and guarantee, for our part, to keep them off your back until you have something to show us.'

I could hardly believe my ears.

'What we want is a film that will show the world that Britain is not only a land of tradition, thatched cottages and all that, but also a country which is still a pace-setter in many fields...'

This seemed fair enough.

'And don't forget that we are talking about a country of which the correct name is the United Kingdom – we must strike a fair balance between England, Scotland, Wales and Northern Ireland.'

As a Londoner, and moreover one who had been so long abroad, I needed to be reminded that Britain had only been one, single united nation for barely two hundred and fifty years.

'Obviously you've got ideas of your own. You know your way round England. We suggest you go off and meet and talk with our people in Cardiff, Belfast, Edinburgh – and the best of British luck to you!'

The front of the locomotive that drew me into Cardiff station a few days later was emblazoned by a dragon, the mythological beast which bestrides the green and white flag of Wales. Wales, the land of Henry Tudor and Lloyd George, of tally-men and tenors. A small country whose iron, steel and sweat had once made Britain great; a proud people who were beginning to fear the loss of their own national identity under the onslaught of twentieth century admass. Southern Wales was now little more than an extension of English industry. Like so much space-age warehousing, the most fully automated steel plant in Europe then spread itself across the landscape near Newport. But in the Rhondda valley, great slag heaps still loomed over the back-to-back cottages of miners. Here was the true and original setting of *The Citadel*.

Edgar Anstey had not been quite alone with his *March of Time* camera, down there in the Rhondda during the hungry thirties. At that same time, pursuing his own personal and independent path in documentary film, with direction by Ralph Bond and Ruby Grierson, in 1936 Paul Rotha had produced one of British documentary's most notable early successes in this same part of Wales. *Today We Live* has an opening prologue in approach and style admittedly modelled after the *March of Time*, mirroring the hunger and the hopelessness that was so much the true image of the thirties – and something of the fury which had formed men like Aneurin Bevan. Stuart Legg wrote its narration. People were still unemployed 'unless it was to break up factories where they had once worked; streets which were once filled with people with money to spend are now empty except for those who try to kill time. Men who once hewed coal in the mines, coal to send great ships to sea, coal to fire the furnaces of industry, now snatch fragments from slag heaps to keep a fire in their own grates'.

In visual counterpoint, directors Ralph Bond and Ruby Grierson focused their cameras. Through Pentre, Treorchy, Cymmer and Tylorstown. At every street corner abandoned and idle men, their only contact with coal the slag heaps where we see them – with their wives, scrambling for enough to keep a small fire burning in the shacks which served as their homes.

Today We Live focused its story on three unemployed coalminers who, with other workless men, were building an occupational centre paid for by the National Council of Social Service and Land Settlement Association which sponsored the making of that earlier film. Now their sons and daughters made washing machines and watches, and lived in neat little houses heated by the flick of a switch.

Only in its wild centre and rugged coastline did Wales still seem to be Wales. But Scotland still spoke to me with an accent all its own – in the voice and person of Forsyth Hardy.

Film correspondent for *The Scotsman*, friend, amanuensis, biographer of John Grierson – the Scot who started it all – Forsyth Hardy had championed the documentary film in general, the films of Scotland in particular, for more than a quarter of a century. A Films of Scotland Committee had in fact been set up by the Scottish Development Council before the War; and Grierson had sent up, over the border, such as Basil Wright, Donald Alexander, and Mary Field to make a series of films of his homeland's character and tradition, industry and development.

The Films of Scotland Committee still existed, still sponsoring films from local units, and Forsyth Hardy viewed the London-based and national Central Office of Information with a singular lack of enthusiasm. We had lunch together. The Edinburgh Film Festival – of which he was then very much a moving spirit – had previously awarded a Diploma of Merit to my film of the Suez Canal. Now he was busy viewing films for the next of these annual occasions. He had just seen *African Awakening*. He approved. I was alright.

I have been thought shy; and yet, in order to capture the world with a camera, I have continually to force myself upon other people, impose myself on Prime Ministers and peasants, thrust my ideas down often unwilling throats, never take 'no' for an answer. Why is it people are prepared to let me poke my nose into their affairs, disorganise their lives, turn their homes upside down? Decent, ordinary human beings who would never normally dream of pushing themselves into the limelight, or get any sort of kick out of being 'in the pictures' or 'on the telly'? Perhaps, and during moments of sometimes awful despair, I like to think they sense in me something of the sincerity with which I first picked up a camera, and of which I hope sufficient remains to make it somehow still seem worthwhile.

Thomas Adam was a farmer. He bred Aberdeen Angus, those magnificent beasts whose flesh has made all the world Scots beefeaters. Here was a real man, a real occupation, his name as elemental as his calling. What had a film-maker, living always at second-hand, to set against this? I sat in his home, drank his whisky, and met his son. Could I film him, and the life of his family and farm?

Of course, any time. No, wait a minute. Not the first week of September. 'Then', said Thomas Adam, 'I shall be on Uist'.

'Uist – what's that?'

'An island in the Outer Hebrides. I go there every year to buy cattle.'

I sat bolt upright. 'Can we come with you and film the sales?'

'Of course.'

All my life I had dreamed of sailing to the Hebrides, those island outposts of the United Kingdom's northern perimeter. Now at last I would be able to do so. It all seemed too good to be true.

Lower Greenyards was the name of Thomas Adam's farm. As I walked his acres, I remembered that on this site, six hundred years before, there had been put to rout an English army besieging nearby Stirling.

The Battle of Bannockburn – and the Battle of the Boyne. In every factory I visited in the six counties that make up Northern Ireland, little Union flags were proudly perched on work-bench and lathe, and hanging from the roof. Here in Unionist territory it seemed then that no one dreamed of denigrating the national flag. No one had yet turned it into a mini-skirt or waste-paper basket. Home Rule had come to Ireland and, as a result, Protestant Ulstermen, and women, were the most diehard of British. And in a few short years, the most belligerent. To maintain that union, linchpin of the *United Kingdom*, blood would flow in the streets of Londonderry and Belfast. Civil war come to Britain.

From the remote and mysterious Mountains of Mourne, by way of the supersonic and screaming wind tunnels of the Royal Aircraft Establishment, the giant radio telescope at Jodrell Bank, gin and tonic in a nuclear power station and lunch at Lloyds of London, I made my way, pursued my pilgrimage.

And what of the sound of Britain in the 'sixties? Was it all power stations and pop, endless and inconclusive debate, property wheeling and dealing, the jingle of pollution and protest?

Did anything reach further back, into an older tradition, creatively, producing a new dimension, a fresh inspiration?

The recent consecration of Coventry's new cathedral, alongside the charred shell of the blitzed original, had been the occasion and setting of the first performance of a new masterwork of English music, Benjamin Britten's *War Requiem*.

In what is Europe's oldest music festival, the choirs of Hereford, Gloucester and Worcester had been meeting annually to make music in each other's cathedrals since 1713. This year of 1963 it was the turn of Worcester to be host, and Britten's *War Requiem* was to be the highlight of that year's Three Choirs Festival. Happy indeed was I to realise that this would be taking place during the scheduled period of our filming.

I travelled. down to that ancient city, on the banks of the Severn. I lunched with the master of the choristers, organist, and conductor of the forthcoming festival. He was as enthusiastic as I at this opportunity to incorporate something of the Requiem in the profile of Britain that I was planning to film. He gave his blessing, and promised all assistance and every facility. I travelled back to London feeling very pleased with myself. On that Western Region of British Railways some trains were then still being drawn by old Castle-class steam locomotives. One such hauled me up from Worcester. As I walked up the platform on arrival in London, I glanced at the name which it had been given when first it puffed its way out of the workshops at Swindon. It was Sir Edward Elgar. Was it still, I wondered, a land of hope and glory?

If statesmen are creatures of their age, children of circumstance, creations of their time, then so are film-makers. Certainly I was a child of circumstance – the circumstances of a century-and-a-half before, which had driven a farmer's son south from the West Riding of Yorkshire. Down to Stony Stratford in Buckinghamshire, where on the 4th of June 1843, Thomas Hopkinson married Jane Sutherland, the daughter of a dyer.

The Industrial Revolution was under way. Thomas Hopkinson was only one of many being drawn off the land and into the factories erupting all over the countryside. He became a pattern-maker in an early iron foundry. His first-born son, my grandfather, went further. He established his own business, invented new processes, built his own factory; became a Justice of the Peace, sat on the Uxbridge Bench, acquired a stately home, begat eight children – and went bankrupt.

My father was his first-born son, and, while he was being educated at the City of London School, his eldest sister was learning whatever they taught young ladies in those days at Princess Helena's College, Ealing. There she met, and became the best friend of Grace Gunton, the daughter of a retired army officer. Apprenticed to a printer, in 1859 the future Colonel Gunton had run away and enlisted as a drummer in the Grenadier Guards. Rare indeed for those days, he had been commissioned from the ranks, and fought in the battle of Tel el Kebir, which won Egypt, and Suez, for Britain. His only daughter was my mother.

Certainly I was a creation of my time – and my time was witness to a crisis of capitalism and a collapse of empire. I grew up on a diet of *Today We Live*, the early *March of Time* and *The Left Book Club*. 'Conscript the Wealth and not the Youth' was the banner I helped to carry, May Day 1938. Nonetheless, like everyone else, I was of course conscripted; and, once they put a camera in my hands, with orders to 'shoot' both friend and foe, I have to confess that up to a point I enjoyed – as well as survived – that war.

But in my own nature there still raged a far from pleasant private war, or two elements, continually in conflict: the traditional and the radical, the conformist and the rebel. Certainly I was a creature of my age – and my age was one of instant and immediate electronic communication. Driven by some deep-rooted desire to express myself and my age, what other medium could I possibly have chosen but the motion picture? And now I had to make a *British* film, set in, and all about Britain. Would the experience be comic, serious, or tragic? The outcome merely transitory or lasting?

No more deliberately *British* films have ever been made than those produced by Michael Balcon at Ealing Studios in the late

1940's and early 1950's. Seeing them now today, as we so often do on television, what in actual fact do we see? Apart from the macabre diversions of Cavalcanti and Alexander Mackendrick, in the main a people nostalgic for past glories and violently opposed to change. From *Passport to Pimlico* to *The Titfield Thunderbolt* the quaint, the cosy, the eccentric, the old-fashioned are made much of, and those who attempt change cast as the villains of the piece. At this same time Ealing also made what could well be defined as the most truly *English* film ever made, Robert Hamer's *Kind Hearts and Coronets*. Its subject is that unique and always with us national institution called class, and only by multiple assassination does our hero break out of it. Moreover the manner of its telling relies very much on the form with which the British are least ill at ease, the literary; and set as it is in the costumes of an earlier epoch, *Kind Hearts* once again insulates us from the realities and the pressures of the present. We had to wait a few more years for Jack Clayton's *Room at the Top* and Karel Reisz's *Saturday Night and Sunday Morning* for British screen heroes who didn't give a damn and who were determined to get there their way; even if both were forced to surrender to social conformity in the end.

Now it was my turn – and for me this assignment was something of a role reversal too. For had I not all that long ago written Britain off and decided to throw in my lot with the United States? But that dream had faded. To be subsumed in the intellectual anguish of Lillian Hellman's *Scoundrel Time*. In order to work at all, eminent Hollywood film-makers like Carl Foreman and Joseph Losey had had to come to Britain, their screen credits at first rendered into other names. To discover the whereabouts of the director of *From Here to Eternity* and *High Noon*, you only had to look in the London phone book under Z – and there was Fred Zinnemann. Nothing like as wounding or traumatic, my own final experience with the *March of Time* had, in its way, also left a very bitter taste.

They had put me on the payroll as a result of material that I had shot for a United Nations Relief Agency of international aid to the Soviet Republics of Byelorussia and the Ukraine in the shattered aftermath of World War Two. Devastation on a dreadful scale, but in the care and support of the tens of thousands of orphaned children an inspiring example of the will to survive even the most appalling catastrophe. Rightly anxious that as many people as possible – particularly in the United States – should see what the international community was doing about this, and that certainly in this filming of mine the Soviet people appeared to be quite normal and indeed harmless enough human beings, the UN offered it all to the *March of Time*; and in order as I believed to be able to stay with this film of mine through the edit, I had gone along with it to thereupon join the *March of Time* as its roving Director-Cameraman in the turbulent post-war world. For the most part a tremendous opportunity and experience. But then, along for screening in London came the 10th issue of the series' Fifteenth Year *The Fight for Better Schools*, a report on the inadequacies (already then) of American education. But not to worry too much was the message; we're still much better off than those slaves in the enemy camp of the Soviet Union – their educational curriculum is just one long political indoctrination. Well, up to a point true enough in those pre-Gorbachev days. But how did they illustrate this? At a Polytechnic in Kiev, capital of the Ukraine, I had filmed in 1947 young men and women recently discharged from the armed forces studying to become scientists and engineers. In the library I had shot a scene of one of them requesting a technical journal. As this was taken down from the shelf in close-up, we were able to see that this was a copy of the English automotive magazine *The Autocar*. This struck me at the time as a splendid example of what many years later we came to call *Glasnost*.

The deal between the United Nations and the *March of Time* had given the latter *exclusive* use of this material of mine for just six months. And now, in this very different political climate of just a few years later, to my horrified surprise this same sequence reappeared in the American story of *The Fight for Better Schools*. But substituted for the close-up of the English automotive magazine was the cover of a bogus Marxist text book shot in the New York studios. That did it. Film can be all too easily manipulated, and with the Cold War by then well under way, this breach of faith and fake was very hard to stomach. I announced my intention to quit; and in due course, for good or ill, it was back to dear old Blighty for me.

Is it possible to be really objective? Could I now look at my own country, the land which had made me, objectively? Could I bring to this task of filming Britain an Olympian detachment? The Current Affairs documentary programmes on television were supposed to do just that – and got into terrible trouble if they didn't. This same year that I was now setting out to do my country proud, the BBC's *Panorama*, concerned that all was not well in the land, also decided to take a close look at the state of the nation. The Assistant Editor of the programme has described how they went about it.

'We would take a critical look at Britain, her achievements, her shortcomings and, above all, her mood. So, in the middle of Friday afternoon, the decision was taken. The cutting rooms were emptied of their half-completed stories, and the BBC's film library was combed for whatever material might be of value to us. A live outside broadcast unit was sent to one to the biggest steelworks in South Wales, for we had decided to open the programme there, and to catch, live, the frank opinions of a group of steel-workers. At the same time we began to select a team of distinguished national figures who might debate the issue in the studio on Monday night. Cutting rooms and dubbing theatres worked throughout the weekend, producing what in the end became a twenty-minute pictorial survey of Britain ... John Morgan, as the reporter assigned to this part of the programme, also spent his weekend in the cutting rooms. On the Monday morning he wrote the whole of his commentary, and in the afternoon and early evening he recorded it. The job was finished within minutes of the programme going on the air – looking at the *Panorama* diary for that day I see that the live OB from South Wales ran for nine and a half minutes, and that the studio discussion – including Sir George Pollock (Director of the British Employers' Confederation), George Woodcock (General Secretary of the TUC), the Rt. Hon. Harold Watkinson (former Minister of Defence), Denis Healey M.P., and Mark Bonham-Carter – ran for over fifteen minutes. This was Monday evening, and not a single minute of this final programme was even thought of before the previous Friday afternoon...'

A crash programme if ever there was one, and full marks to Norman Swallow and his associates for mounting it so speedily and so well. But this type of television documentary can afford to be forgotten almost as quickly as it can be made. It is a one shot show, seen immediately and simultaneously by an audience of millions. Within minutes, hours, days, it will have been swamped and overtaken not only by events, but also by the stream of entertainment and comment pouring forth non-stop from that same little screen in the living-room. Within a week *Panorama* would itself be replacing it with yet another immediate look at life, another instant recipe for recovery.

I had to make something which would last a little longer than a few minutes' conversation the morning after. I had to make a film that not only faced up to the facts of life in contemporary Britain, but also one which could be shown throughout the world, over a period of years. On a park bench in Ealing, less than a mile away from my suburban birthplace, and only a few yards from the studio where I had first started in the film industry at the age of sixteen, I pondered myself, my country, my assignment. I went home. I sat down at my desk; and, through the night, I wrote my film *Profile of Britain*.

To Norman Swallow, and others working in television today, the word 'write' will bring them up short. For television programmes and documentaries of current affairs are not 'written', they are 'reported', devised, shot, edited – staged even, if you like – but not written. To go out with a previously conceived and written script is considered old-fashioned, inhibiting, even dishonest. Flexibility, spontaneity, are the keynotes. When I was setting up with Basil Wright the course of *Documentary Script-Writing* at the Film Institute of India, I was loaned many examples of the best work in television. As well as Elgar and *Born Chinese*, the BBC made available Peter Watkins' *Culloden*. Produced for, but never shown for years by the BBC, the same film propagandist's *The War Game* was lent to us by the British Film Institute. Granada came up willingly with Norman Swallow and Denis Mitchell's *A Wedding on Saturday*, and World in Action's *War on Ice* (the state of affairs in Korea). Lord Lew Grade's Associated Television was less forthcoming. His Head of Factual

Author, with NBC's Frank Bourgholtzer, films report on the Italian Communist Party for NBC *Background*

Programming wrote to me that 'the best of British documentaries are no longer scripted or written'.

This was hardly news to me. For years I had shot not only award-winning television documentaries without benefit of script, but similarly believed a direct confrontation between the camera and the immediacy of the moment to be the heart of the matter. Throughout my years with the *March of Time* and American television series such as NBC's *Background*, I had never seen such a thing as a script. For the sole purpose of record, such documents only came into being after the programme had gone out on the air. A few pages of background, dug up by a researcher, stuffed into a pocket alongside airline tickets and, camera in hand, off I used to go. Now and then, once underway and the film flowing back, there would come cables. 'Let's see how an average Japanese now lives and works.' 'Let's have a take-out on the life of an Untouchable and a high-caste Brahmin.' Just a couple of the cables I received as I had plodded on my way through Asia for the *March of Time.*

So, in *MacArthur's Japan*, I went to live for a while with Takeshi Saito, in his little house outside Kyoto, following and filming him at work on the Toyota assembly line. With clockwork camera, and suitcase of portable photoflood light, I moved in on an untouchable and his family in their hut on the outskirts of Madras, and a Brahmin priest in prayer and scholarship in Trivandrum. They, their actions and behaviour, their way of life, 'wrote' the sequence of images I shot, singlehanded. (And no mention of something called *cinéma-vérité* yet in those days.)

For *Background* it was much the same. With the reporters Frank Bourgholtzer or Ed Newman, I would work out the general line of approach. We evolved the story-lines we worked along on it together. From time to time we would go into a basement room in the BBC's headquarters building, nearby the NBC office, in Langham Place. Over a specially set up and direct radio link, we would talk with the producer in New York. This was the only sort of 'script' conference we ever had.

But *Profile of Britain* had to be first worked out and cast on paper, for the approval of the COI and the various government sponsoring departments. A daunting prospect, you might think. But one which did not at first alarm or even inhibit me as much as might be supposed.

I had evolved a method, an approach which would have been impossible if I had not previously spent years shooting film, satisfactorily but scriptless, a Director-Cameraman on my own.

This instinctively visual conceptualising worked with *African Awakening*. Set within a framework which is in the first place a creatively conceived *visual* interpretation, it allowed full scope for unstaged spontaneity during filming.

Essential is a first stage of going over, and covering, the ground, exhaustively. As extensively, and as thoroughly as if I was, TV-wise, shooting the whole thing and scene, there and then, as it presents itself, direct and unfiltered, to my camera-eye. At the end of each day, every impression, every image, thought, association, idea, is transferred from the immediate retina of that exposure to paper. (Words, dialogue, interviews can be carried in that now so providently-sized pocket tape recorder.) At the end of that first stage of investigation which, in the case of *African Awakening* was to last two months, *Profile of Britain* seven weeks, I have a dossier which is, to all intents and purposes, an enormous accumulation of images and impressions – just as if I had in fact used a camera to shoot and record them all as they occurred and presented themselves, and just as it would be if an uncoordinated camera had actually shot them. But instead of existing as then just a mountain of unedited strips of film and tape which, in time, could be edited into some sort of coherent and cohesive programme – with interviews shot and cut into a subsequently written narration – they are on paper. And my *scriptwriting* is now this next stage of editing, this accumulated catalogue, but on paper. My *script* is therefore an already edited film, edited out of all the images and their associated ideas formed in that visually energised camera-eye of my survey.

So, I do believe in scriptwriting, not as a *writer*, but as a *film-maker* who scripts out of his already researched (and paper-shot) images. And this does not mean that the shooting document/plan which results needs to remain something sacred. It is still only a framework, a guideline. One must always be on the look-out for, and respond to the unexpected during actual filming – even in fact continually attempting to precipitate it.

Confronted by the sheets of paper on what is in fact an intellectual editing bench rather than a script-writer's desk, I search first for a theme.

371

What was – is – the theme for a Profile of Britain? Not just an immediate report of contemporary unrest, protest, confusion; the long view of both past and future obscured by the dust of yet another bit of olde England going down under a property developer's bulldozer. In outline first of all, this film had to attempt an image of Britain not only present, but also future (as well as past).

It was Aneurin Bevan who once said that only the most gross incompetence could produce a shortage of food and energy in an island built on coal and surrounded by fish. Be that as it may, the coal couldn't last forever and neither would the oil soon to start flowing in from the North Sea. In Cumbria the British had just built and switched on the world's first nuclear power station, and were suitably proud of what seemed at the time a technological achievement of their own as important and far reaching as the steam engine with which they had pioneered the previous century. A second Industrial Revolution, and we did it, was the refrain. *Three Mile Island* and *Chernobyl* were as yet very distant clouds on the horizon. So in a film which had to hail the achievements of British invention, discovery, and technology as much as art, culture, and history, an immediate audience-grabber in those more innocent pre-nuclear days seemed to me to be just this.

An alarm bell clanged. To the sound of a rising crescendo of high-pitched electronics, strange and distorted shapes emerged, and moved ponderously across the screen. Into focus came the head of the tall tower of the Charge Machine, moving over the top of the reactor core at a nuclear power station. Dials flickered, indicators flashed, and the Plant Operator in the Machine Control room gazed through his observation window, a hundred feet above the atomic fission now about to take place beneath his feet. At other panels, other technicians were at their stations in the Central Control Room. The camera zoomed its way the length of the main Turbine Hall – and the voice of a commentator was to speak the film's introduction: 'This is the sound and the moment of atomic fission. This is a Nuclear Power Station. One of many built, and building in this country. Berkeley, Bradwell, Trawsfynydd, Dungeness, and Oldbury, Sizewell, Wylfa and Hinkley Point.

The exteriors of Bradwell and Berkeley gave way to an impressionistic sequence of other nuclear power stations already in preparation and under construction. In a series of swift close-ups, radioactive isotopes were seen testing seed grain for bacteria, searching for flaws in metals, tracing the course of the currents in a river estuary, and actuating equipment on a laboratory bench.

'In this country the vast power of the atom is used for peace. To generate power for the national grid ... to control the temperature and mechanics of industrial process ... to chart the ebb and flow of tides around an island shore ... to kill the germs and parasites that would deny man the food he grows ... to purify and sterilise the instruments on which his life depends ... to enlarge in fact his knowledge of what he himself is.'

Punched tape flowed out of a computer. The picture zoomed into a close-up of a drop of blood held in the beam of an electron microscope – and seemed to lose its way amongst the maze of coloured globes making up a complex molecular structure. In the Molecular Biology Laboratory at Cambridge, Nobel Prize winning Doctors Perutz and Kendrew shown to be framed and surrounded by these representative symbols of their discoveries and analysis: 'In this laboratory molecular biologists have made a revolutionary discovery: that there is an acid contained in the chromosomes of the human cell which is, in fact, the substance that transmits the characteristics of heredity from one generation to the other'.

The spiral model of the DNA Code became the scanning tube of the huge radio telescope at Jodrell Bank.

'The solution of the mystery of life on this planet near at hand, at the same time as the search for life goes on in other worlds.'

From the enormous bowl of the radio telescope, squatting like a vast, upturned saucer in the middle of a field, the picture zoomed out to a general view of the surrounding countryside – the first time that any landscape has yet been seen.

Profile of Britain – Nobel Prizewinners John Kendrew (top) and Max
Perutz with molecular models of DNA

Waves pound a rocky coastline. The shadows of clouds move over neat little fields and across a ripening harvest. A shepherd follows his flock, almost submerged in the greenness of a Welsh valley. A great English stately home spreads its facade across a still eighteenth-century setting, followed by a Scottish crofter's cottage, and a semi-detached suburban house. The morning milk is delivered.

'It is a small country. Its area is little more than that of a single American state or one Indian province. The home of a cosmopolitan people who have welcomed many to their shores since they absorbed the Norman conquest of nine hundred years ago. A land of tradition and tolerance. A nation of poets, craftsmen, and shopkeepers. Here Shakespeare wrote his sonnets, Milton of a Paradise Lost, and Marx of his theories of social change.'

A pit-head winding gear. Slagheaps. Flame and smoke above the cramped streets of a Welsh valley no longer green. (In this film, I need hardly say, there had to be my private and personal homage to *The Citadel*.) The chimes of Big Ben; and, with each chime, a cut to the capital of each of our four countries which make up Britain: the Palace of Westminster, Cardiff's Civic Centre, Edinburgh's Princes Street, and Belfast's Stormont.

'The United Kingdom of England, Wales, Scotland and Northern Ireland. A nation now at yet another crossroads of a long and crowded history.'

There have been seen statues outside these centres of government: medieval with outstretched sword, municipal with proudly clutched documents. At Westminster the picture zooms into the head of the statue of Palmerston – and mixes to that of a lion. Opening out, we now see that this is the centrepiece of a *Punch* cartoon of 1882, Tenniel's 'The Lion's Just Share'. To the accompaniment of the Victorian music hall song, 'We don't want to fight, but by jingo if we do...', the whole of the original cartoon is now reproduced on the screen, in its entirety. At that pinnacle of nineteenth-century British imperial power – immediately after the battle of Tel el Kebir – the British lion is shown standing in the centre, astride a prostrate crocodile representing Egypt. On the sidelines are a fawning Russian bear, an obsequious Spanish donkey, German and Austrian vultures and, at the Lion's feet, French, Italian, and Turkish dogs. (An attitude of mind still it seems persisting to the present day).

Again in a cartoon, dark and ominous clouds. The sky above England in Low's famous 1940 Dunkirk cartoon 'Very Well, Alone'. The whole of this Battle of Britain cartoon now fills the screen to show a single British soldier, standing on the cliffs of his homeland, defying the onslaught about to be launched on it from the mainland of Europe.

'The British', continued the commentator, 'have often been dismissed as played out by their enemies, and despaired of by their friends'.

Now a contemporary cartoon from the Russian satirical weekly *Krokodil*, or a European newspaper: an impoverished John Bull is odd man out amongst an arrogant Uncle Sam, a proudly helmeted German, and a contemptuous Marianne. On the screen, a succession of cartoon images of John Bull takes over. Down at heel, he lugubriously surveys his empty pockets. Absorbed in his own affluent image on a television screen, he smokes a cigar. Shabby and poor, he holds his hand outstretched for alms. Beside an ancient machine covered with cobwebs he slumbers. All these different pictures are then shown to be reflections – as in the various adjacent mirrors of a tailors' fitting room – of the one original John Bull, who stands and stares at this confusion of his own reflected image. At his feet, his bulldog looks up at him, devoted but bewildered.

I now set out to continue the story of contemporary Britain within the compass of a single day – a notion not entirely original. Just prior to their invasion by Germany in 1941, from an original idea by Maxim Gorki, the Russians had newsreel cameramen all over the Soviet Union record just what happened in their own assigned territory over a period of the same and simultaneous twenty-four hours. They did the same thing again in *One Day of War* (subsequently re-edited into two reels and released in this way throughout the world by the *March of Time*). Dziga

Vertov had earlier sent his camera whirling all over the place to give us a jigsaw picture of life in a younger Soviet Union back in 1928. But this had been more how it seemed to *The Man With The Movie Camera* than it actually was. Walter Ruttman had already anticipated him by swinging a kaleidoscopic camera around Berlin; with *Rien Que Les Heures* Cavalcanti had done this in a more contrived way for Paris in 1926; later on, and for *All in a Day*, Mike Wooller's ten camera units were to do this for Sheffield.

Four years after I made my *Profile of Britain* in this way, the Indian film-maker Sukhdev was similarly commissioned to make a full-length film of his country as a central feature at the Canadian International Exhibition EXPO '67. We saw this film *India 67*, at Poona. It deserved a very much wider showing. Sukhdev faced an infinitely more difficult task – there were then ten times as many Indians as British – but solved it by involving his audience not in argument, but in a scintillating and stunning orgy of images shot all over the face of that vast and contradictory subcontinent. The visual abundance, and the paradox in juxtaposition, was mind-bending, almost psychedelic. But we are not involved. The film, like many a commercial, was shot almost entirely with a zoom lens employed as a long distance telephoto. Everything is estranged from its surroundings, divorced from cohesion, alienated from association.

Profile of Britain had to present an argument. In the hands of an Anglo-Saxon Sukhdev or Pennebaker, it might have been a *Britain 63*, perhaps to some more effective that way, in that super candyfloss style of non-format filmmaking. For myself I could not conceive this round the clock *Today in Britain* as I then saw and felt it, other than as set within the gut question-mark of national survival.

'Today the British are examining themselves and their institutions more closely than ever before. Let us', says the film – ending its introduction – 'take a look at them'. And that was to be all the commentary there was. For half an hour we were then just to take a look at, and listen to Britain. Into the next thirty minutes I telescoped a day. A day which I had to devise in such a way that it put on the screen a balanced and contemporary picture of the country, and its people as a whole.

Like so many mobile mushrooms lashed with rain, the tops of umbrellas move across the screen. Underneath their shelter, city workers dodge rush-hour traffic at the start of a typically rainy day. Out of an underground railway station, down the length of a suburban train at a main-line terminus, in a stream of cars from an underpass, the British go to work. Abruptly there falls across the screen the word STOP, and the sign CHILDREN CROSSING. A white-uniformed and elderly guardian halts the traffic as little children scurry over a road into school. Children of all ages enter a variety of modern schools. On his own, the inevitable late-comer is last in. He is a little black boy. A new Briton. The first-born of parents attracted to this country – let it not be forgotten – by advertisements then only recently placed in Caribbean newspapers offering job opportunities in the United Kingdom.

Red to green, and an automatic signal flashes on a railway. In air-conditioned inter-cities, business-men drink and discuss deals. Inside a London bus, an English blonde pays her fare to a black conductor. Seen from the interior of a moving car, city streets flash past. At the wheel is a young executive. He switches on his car radio: 'And that concludes the weather report for the next forty-eight hours. And now the news in Welsh...' To the accompaniment of news of a rugby football match in the Welsh language, the driver and his car are swallowed up in the immensity of an enormous steel plant (one of the few plants so far to be spared the savage cutbacks to come.) For if a country cannot be shown to possess an up-to-date steel industry – however slimmed down and threatening to the environment – then it seems that along with nuclear power it cannot be taken seriously as nowadays industrial at all. Which is why a steel plant of its own is a first priority in a developing country such as Korea, and why there is therefore now so much competition for older producing countries like Britain.

And then the name on the facade of a building, *Belfast News-letter*; a blueprint under the eye of an electronic scanner; the flame of an oxy-acetylene jet cutting metal – and we are building a giant super-tanker in the then active and busy shipyards of Harland and Wolff. Huge pre-fabricated sections are swung into place, supervised by an Ulster shipbuilder of similar age and appearance to the Welsh steelmaker.

Big Ben chimes eleven o'clock, and a famous ship's bell comes into close-up, the Lutine Bell at Lloyds; the Underwriting Room of what was still the centre of the world's insurance, and a group of brokers and underwriters seen in conference. One broker leaves the group, called to an automatic telephone by the flashing of his code. An old cannon looms over the parapet of Edinburgh Castle. Sheep graze on nearby Arthur's Seat. At Stoneybridge, on an island in the Outer Hebrides, the rugged faces of farmers bid for cattle at an open-air auction. The cattle are driven aboard a boat for the mainland. One of our Scots farmers boards an airplane. The plane takes off, the cattle set sail; and the camera accompanies them on a voyage through a panorama of the kingdom's outer islands, its Celtic perimeter. With canvas and easel on the foreshore, a painter seen to be translating this seascape onto canvas.

In Edinburgh I had for once in my life been poleaxed in an art gallery. An exhibition of paintings by a woman artist, Joan Eardley, in two completely different and contrasting styles. The one, seascapes of magic and mystery the like of which I had never encountered before; the other, and almost as if by another artist altogether, portraits of urchins from the Glasgow slums. For me, this was a real discovery, and if anything went into the film at all I was determined that something of this feminist Scottish vision just had to be part of the multi-layered imagery of my Profile of Britain in these early 1960's.

It had been said that they had 'never had it so good'. Art then, on the cheap, to join the flying ducks on the walls of new homes replacing the back-to-back tenements of old. Reproductions of Rembrandts seen to be sold in a department store, plastic cups and washing-machines stamped out *en masse* in a modern factory. White-hot steel is poured – and our steelmaker controls its pressing by electronic pulse from a 'pulpit' high in the roof on a rolling-mill. His finger presses a button. A carton drops into place to be automatically filled with tea, drunk by a thirsty mechanic on a tractor assembly line. New automobiles and electronic hardware take shape on other assembly lines in other factories – and it is lunchtime.

High above the Firth of Forth, a riveter unwraps his lunch from the crumpled pages of *The Scotsman*. His wig pushed to the back of his head, a barrister munches a sandwich. The shipbuilder serves himself in the shipyard canteen. The Lloyds broker tastes and approves his choice of wine. A band plays in a park. In a traditional London club dignified gentlemen digest their meal to the ticking of a clock. On a bench in a park a young woman munches a sandwich while reading a paperback, Richard Hoggart's *The Uses of Literacy*.

In a completely automated Highland farm, cattle chew contentedly, and have their milk extracted from them automatically. Canned, it is purchased in a supermarket, and placed by one housewife, with the rest of her packaged shopping, in a pram with the baby. Six-year-olds draw pictures of their world in the classroom of a school. In another school a Shakespearean drama class is in progress. Boys and girls listen as a teenager reads from a textbook of *Henry V*:

> 'Now all the youth of England are on fire,
> And silken dalliance in the wardrobe lies:
> Now thrive the armourers and Honour's thought
> Reigns solely in the breast of every man.
> They sell the pasture now, to buy the horse;
> Following the Mirror of all Christian Kings,
> With winged heels, as English Mercuries,
> For now sits Expectation in the air...'.

Factory and office workers crowd beaches, transistor radios blare, and a candid camera catches Mr and Mrs John Bull letting their hair down in uninhibited holiday enjoyment. Meanwhile the voice of the schoolboy is still heard, reading Shakespeare:

> 'The poor condemned English,

Like sacrifices, by their watchful fires
Sit patiently, and idly ruminate the morning's danger:
And their gesture sad...'.

At Ascot, top-hats and horrors crown the heads of those still thronging an exclusive Royal Enclosure:

'Investing lank-lean shanks, and war-worn coats,
Presenting them unto the gazing moon
So many horrid ghosts...'.

By the paddock rails, less exalted Britons place and lose bets. In Trafalgar Square, a meeting of political protest is under way. The faces of the crowd, listening to the speaker:

'O now, who will behold
The Royal Captain of this ruin'd band
Walking from watch to watch, from tent to tent;
Let him cry. Praise and glory on his head...'.

A golden coach appears, drawn by horses through an archway. The Queen is seen to be inside, acknowledging the cheering of the crowd through which she drives:

'For forth he goes, And visits all his host, Bids them good morrow with a modest smile, And calls them brothers, friends, and countrymen'.

Outside the Palace of Westminster guards present arms, and the coach drives up. (An official film of the State Opening of Parliament had recently been made, and I knew that I could use and cut in this, and the following scene.) Accompanied by the Duke of Edinburgh, Her Majesty Queen Elizabeth II, Sovereign Lady of the United Kingdom of England, Wales, Scotland, and Northern Ireland is seen, and heard to speak:
'Throughout the coming session my Government will continue to give resolute support to the work of the United Nations... The improvement of relations between East and West remains a primary object of their policy'.

A great burst of choral and orchestral music – *Hosanna in Excelsis* and the vaulted ceiling of a great cathedral, from which the camera slowly tilts down. Through the magnificence of a medieval altar screen, down the length of the nave, the camera to continue its move; to come upon and finally frame the pyramid of the massed Three Choirs of Worcester, Hereford and Gloucester cathedrals. The climactic peak of the *Sanctus* reached in their festival performance of Britten's *War Requiem*.

The soprano sings the Latin text of the Mass. The tenor and baritone sing the verse of Wilfred Owen, while the camera moves over the faces of some amongst the audience – coming to rest on a single soldier, sitting alone.

'Oh Death was never enemy of ours!
We laughed at him, we leagued with him, old chum.
No soldier's paid to kick against his powers.
We laughed, knowing that better men would come,
And greater wars; when each proud fighter brags
He wars on Death – for Life; not men – for flags.'

The eyes of long-dead knights stared in effigy, carved on memorials and monuments within the cathedral. Tattered and torn, the banners and battle-honours of old military regiments hung from the roof. Hardly a breath of air disturbed the dust of their old D-days; but, as the music of the *Requiem* swelled even higher, the picture to become that of the interior of another, more modern cathedral, reborn from the ashes of war. Coventry. The transparent designs of John Piper which filtered its light, the rich mosaics that made up its floor, and Graham Sutherland's huge *Christ in Majesty*, which hung over its altar, to be filmed and edited into a purely abstract visual counterpoint to the climax of Britten's *Sanctus*.

Another flag fell. It was the start of a motor race. Britten's majestic music made way for the roar and scream of internal combustion engines driven at full throttle. A driver, at his wheel, helmeted; and, under another sort of helmet, a girl at a hairdresser, having her hair dried. In her hands she is seen to be holding a copy of a magazine that she is reading, *Honey*. Now a

Royal enclosure

Fully comprehensive

line of books on a shelf *Time of Hope, Science and Government, Corridors of Power, The New Men*; all to be seen to be by the same author, C.P. Snow.

Somewhere in this film which I planned virtually without commentary, on its subject of Britain in transition there had to be, none the less, effective comment. I had recently read the text of a lecture given at Cambridge by Sir Charles, later Lord Snow. I proposed that he now spoke the essence of the same lecture directly to our own, wider audience.

'It is fashionable to say that our class divisions have got less during my own lifetime. In a sense this is true. We have seen, just as all advanced countries have seen a whole great band of the working class become far more prosperous and take a new appearance, something like that of a new middle class. In most respects the country is a better one than that I knew as a child. We were born in an advanced country at a time when the majority of our fellow human beings are struggling not to be hungry and not to die before their time. If there is one thing our education should have taught us, it is that we are morally compelled to help, at least for a couple of generations. But I believe we do know that; and I believe we have the will and the daring to remould our education to the needs of a living society.'

Complex nuclear formulae now projected on the screen. A black African student seated at the Bubble Chamber Film Analysis Apparatus in the Cavendish Laboratory at Cambridge. On their way to classes in the entrance hall, other students pass the profile of Rutherford, set in a niche in the wall. His features, carved in stone, become a line drawing; and the picture now to turn into an animated cartoon film which humorously and sometimes ironically, would illustrate the following text which, in order to counter-balance the hard sell of its conceit, I planned to record almost as a parody of the more obvious type of industrial and business film (of which I was to have to make more than my own fair share).

'In 1919 the atom was first split by Lord Rutherford at the Cavendish Laboratory in Cambridge. A century before, James Watt, of Greenock, discovered the principle of the steam power that similarly transformed the face of the world a hundred years ago. Britain led the world into the industrial revolution of the nineteenth century, and into (what seemed then) the great promise that the peaceful uses of atomic power offer mankind today. The British are heirs to a long tradition of inventive ingenuity. For the Stockton and Darlington Railway Robert Stephenson built the world's first locomotive. The British invented the bicycle, and put the world on wheels. They invented the pneumatic tyre, and made their progress smoother. They invented the sandwich, and have been suffering from indigestion ever since. They invented the electric light bulb, to make sure they could see in the dark. They gave the world steel, steamships, radar, and television. They built and flew the world's first passenger-carrying jet plane. They discovered the neutron that is the key to nuclear fission, and their molecular biologists have discovered the genetic clue to the nature of our own identity.'

African faces again – and Asian – seen to be watching this little inset film of British invention, now revealed to be showing on a demonstration stand at an industrial exhibition. Overseas visitors look at and examine the latest machinery and equipment on display; while, in a high-speed wind tunnel the model of a supersonic airliner seen under test. A bottle of champagne bursting over a ship's bows, the super-tanker launched at Belfast, and in Glasgow other ships load cargoes. It is the end of the day.

A dock-worker walks home. The camera following him through Glasgow streets and into the Gorbals, typical of the rat-infested slums and homes of Eardley's urchins which linger on and even multiply in this land busily building an airplane to fly at more than twice the speed of sound. Decaying brick and pest-ridden plaster crash to the ground as a bulldozer drives its way forward. To a modern home, in a Welsh new town, the steel-maker drives home. Like so many moles, London commuters dive back into the Underground. They attempt to read their evening newspapers, jammed in like cattle. But not like the cattle at Lower Greenyards, who amble amiably home in the wide open spaces of the Scots Lowlands. The sun sets behind combine harvesters bringing in the harvest. Lights blaze at petrol-chemical and steel plants, flash on the runways of London Airport, dance in the waters of the Thames at Westminster. A patrol boat passes. In Wapping, a blaze of light and laughter bursts out of the door of the 'Ironbridge Tavern'. Another song is sung. But this is no requiem, no Heather Harper in Worcester Cathedral. This to be popular blues, belted out by a cockney landlady, Queenie Watts.

A beat of drum and a swirl of pipes. Edinburgh Castle and its floodlit tattoo. The massed pipes of the Scots Regiments march and countermarch, followed and focused by the television cameras of the BBC. Around their TV sets, with their families in their various homes, sit the Welsh steelmaker, the Ulster shipbuilder, the English insurance broker, the Scots farmer, all finally brought together by a British electronic invention in this one collective sequence, and linked together by a single happening, seen to be controlled from a small room at Television Centre.

The end of television's day brings the British to their favourite topic of conversation, the weather. The TV weatherman appears on screen; behind him, and now seen for the first time in the film, the map and outline of its subject, Britain, comes back for the conclusion. The voice that earlier set the scene:

'Not very big on the map. But a handful of people once sailed to the New World from these shores, to found, with their language and love of liberty, a great new nation. It was a group of British rebels that wrote the American Declaration of Independence. An Atlantic community, but a global involvement. An island people who have exported more than the machinery of the world's first *industrial* revolution – and the nuclear capacity of its second – but also a way of life...'.

The map has become Plymouth Sound, the Mayflower Steps, the New York skyline, the United States, and the plaque *Royaume Uni* at an international conference. As the commentary continues, a London policeman is seen listening to a crowd arguing with a speaker in Hyde Park, and judges and barristers walking in bewigged procession at the opening of an Assizes:

'... their belief that the law is made for man, and not that man is made for the law. That the state serves the people, and not that the people exist to serve the state. A concept of the essential dignity of individual man which they take so much for granted themselves that they have never bothered to write it into any formal constitution of their own'.

Coloured Commonwealth students now seen to work and play alongside young Britons at universities and training centres throughout the country; together with the faces of a new British generation, voluntarily serving overseas in African and Asian village schools.

'In a fit of absent-mindedness, so it was once said, they created an empire, today transformed by their instinctive capacity for service and survival into a Commonwealth of free peoples embracing nearly a quarter of humanity.'

The film had begun in a nuclear power station. Now it moved into the international environment of the universal atom. At the European Organisation for Molecular Research, on the borders of Switzerland and France, British nuclear physicists were seen working alongside their opposite numbers of thirteen other nations. In a London language laboratory, young Britons were shown learning French, German, Spanish, Italian, Russian, and in this way I hoped the film would reflect a nation seen now to be looking outward, discovering a new role for itself beyond its own limited and insular borders. With certainly historic ties across the Atlantic; aware of its responsibility to its former colonial subjects; but that on any world atlas seen to be European.

All very well and good. But how to bring all this into an effective conclusion on screen? On what sort of note? Certainly not in a self-satisfied burst of Elgarian Pomp and Circumstance.

Before it had become caught up in its own Cold War rhetoric, the *March of Time* had faced just such a dilemma. The current release the month I joined, *Storm Over Britain*, had reported on war's end Britain. A nation bankrupt, unable in that grim winter of 1946/47 to shift diminishing supplies of coal to run-down power stations; overseas investments all sold off to pay for six long years of total war; food rationed; industrial plant worn out and obsolete. A pre-Marshall Plan catalogue of the gloomy plight of a former superpower now down on its luck and unable to pay its way in the world. For a final comment MOT's answer was to put up on screen a London based American news reporter. Not from the parent company's *Time* or *Life* magazines, but CBS News.

'I can think of no natural way in which Britain can get out of its present crisis', said Howard Smith. 'But I'll bet anything she does.' TIME MARCHES ON!

I thought that I could do just as well, if not better, than CBS News. As young Britons were to be seen sharing in the search for knowledge with their Third World counterparts, abreast of tomorrow's technology in' the main European centre for nuclear research, and learning the languages of their neighbours across the Channel, the final words of the ultimate voiceover were to pose a question to the audience, to leave them hopefully pondering if not indeed impressed:

'Is all this but a discreet transition to an honourable but inevitable decline? Or is the current re-assessment that history has forced upon (the British) but the prelude to a new, more vital contribution? It would be a rash man, and a foolish one, that undertook to write their epitaph so soon'.

The outcome of this attempt to project my own national origin and its image on the screen was, in the eyes of the world, successful. My film of Britain received a Special Award from the Council of Europe '*pour la simplicité avec laquelle est realisee une sympathetique synthesese de la vie en Grande-Bretange*' (for the simplicity with which a sensitive general picture of life in Great Britain is presented). It was also selected as 'An outstanding film of the year' for presentation at the London Film Festival.

But to me, that film was nightmare and heartbreak. The script-treatment had been accepted, with enthusiasm, to all intents and purposes as I had written it. But when it was costed, it was found that the three sponsoring government departments – Foreign Office, Commonwealth Relations, Board of Trade – had not enough money between them to finance the film as outlined, and all that was needed was the amount already being spent at that time on quite a few ninety-second TV commercials. Rotha's original strictures on the shortcomings and inadequacy of a Central Office of Information setup were proven to be all too true.

To his everlasting credit, James Carr, the Producer and Chairman of World Wide Pictures (the contracted company) offered to make up the difference with what the COI proposed to pay him to make another film on how spies pinched government secrets. But no, I was forced to jettison much of that vision, and most of its concept, before we could afford to turn a camera at all (and it was a German camera at that). On to what remained, a commentary was wished. As commentaries go, it was good. Augmented as it came to be by James Cameron's artful alliteration. The British Government, through its official information service, could not even find sufficient money to pay the musicians for just three minutes filming of Britten's *War Requiem.* We finished up with sharing lighting costs and coverage with the BBC, at the last night of the Proms, that popular and annual music festival sponsored by the BBC, at which all join in and sing – yes, you guessed it – 'Land of Hope and Glory'. And we didn't even get Joan Eardley – very soon alas to die. No, I was told, the budget couldn't afford the side trip of the crew to Catterline, the fishing village where she lived and worked south of Aberdeen. Never mind, I suppose some might now say, there's barrels of North Sea oil coming ashore there now.

This was a very bitter lesson. And one that you can never learn at film school. That it is not you out there with the movie camera who make the film or TV programme. Don't kid yourself. It is those who put up the money who have them made; who employ you; use you; utilise and manipulate your idealism, your enthusiasm for their own, all too often, petty little time-serving, ambitious, and mercenary ends.

As his creditors are closing in on him, this is what Korda's *Rembrandt* has to say to Titus, his son: 'You're too young to know the world. You think it's a free place where you can do as you choose. Well, you're wrong. The world is a narrow cage enclosed on four sides by iron bars. Beat your head against those bars until you're sick. But you'll never get out. Never as long as you live'.

And so, what then is the answer? It has to be revolutionary. Somehow to acquire – in Marx's phrase – the ownership of the means of production. Either to have the money in the first place yourself, as well as access to the means of the distribution of your product, or acquire some revolutionary new and inexpensive method of motion picture communication outside of the system.

10. NEW PATHWAYS FROM POONA

'It may be that the present system... can survive. Perhaps
the money-making machine has some kind of built-in
perpetual motion, but I do not think so... Unless we get up
off our fat surpluses and recognise that television is being
issued to distract, delude, amuse, and insulate us, then
television and those who finance it, those who look at it
and those who work at it, may see a different picture too late.'

Edward R. Murrow

Jagat Murari, Basil Wright and author at the Film Institute of India (Picture of Eisenstein on wall behind Basil Wright)

To have by now survived more than half a century of the swings and roundabouts of the movie business, and still to be in there up and running is, I guess, something of an achievement in itself.

When I first entered the film industry, the twentieth century had two-thirds of its time still to run. It was only a little over thirty years old. This was the time, and the era, of the heyday of film as entertainment. The week I started work at Ealing Studios, the main general release was David O. Selznick's production of Dickens' *A Tale of Two Cities*, directed by Jack Conway (with Val Lewton handling the storming of the Bastille). Some months before, the seven-year-old Shirley Temple had sung in five different languages in *Captain January* while Errol Flynn bounded into stardom as *Captain Blood*. But already there flickered the threat which was eventually to empty, and in many cases demolish, those giant 'picture palaces', those super-cinemas where we went once, twice, thrice a week for excitement, entertainment, escape, and even, sometimes, inspiration. On November 2nd, that year of 1936, the BBC commenced the world's first regularly scheduled daily television service.

The motion picture film, now itself a hundred years old, is at a crossroads and turning-point of its development. In its physical form of a series of optically-recorded images, stored on a perforated and transparent band, it has changed hardly at all. Now this method and means of motion picture recording and retrieval is challenged and is being superseded by electronic tape. The huge cinemas, with their weekly or bi-weekly change of programme backed up by monolithic studios which were its backbone throughout its history and heyday, have made way for much smaller theatres (sometimes a dozen or more in a single multiplex) showing independently-financed films for indefinite periods. Above all, on the electronic tube which is the catalyst of this revolution, the cinema's former millions now watch more motion pictures than ever before – but in the form of television.

One mid-century attempt to jerk the documentary film out of its by then middle-aged rut was called 'Free Cinema', its practitioners Lindsay Anderson, Karel Reisz, Tony Richardson. Even if films like *Momma Don't Allow* and *We Are The Lambeth Boys* failed to win very wide distribution, they did serve as spring-boards for the feature films their directors really wished to make – and then went on to make during the 'boom' of the so-called 'Swinging Sixties'. But for all the Saturday Nights and Sunday Mornings, all the Loneliness of Long Distance Runners, and all those ringing declarations of working class identification, the one great *commercial* as well as critical success – and only British feature film of this period from this group which really attracted international audiences, was the John Osborne/Tony Richardson adaptation of an 18th century novel, *Tom Jones*, played to the swashbuckling and heart-breaking hilt by the young Albert Finney. It was in fact television, energised in Britain at just that same time by the competition of a commercial channel and the appointment of Hugh Greene as Director-General of the BBC, which gave new film-makers a creative environment of free cinema. Only a non profit-orientated BBC could have given the young Peter Watkins both finance and free hand to make *Culloden* and *The War Game* – even if it did take them twenty years to pluck up the courage to show the latter.

In the feature film industry today, creativity is now more a matter of putting together the deal, apportioning the percentages.

What magic did a *Clash of the Titans* have for us that Korda's *Thief of Bagdad* failed to produce forty years before? Not even as good a flying horse. Despite the thirty-four years which separated them, was the Chayefsky-Hiller *The Hospital* all that much of an advance, except in cynicism, on the Cronin-Vidor *The Citadel*? What did the later Hitchcock do other than in essence make over again, in more trendy ways, his master works of more than thirty years before? In conversations with Truffaut during the sixties he all but admitted this himself:

'The work in Britain served to develop my natural instinct, and later it enabled me to apply new, off-beat ideas. But the technical know-how, in my opinion, dates back to *The Lodger* (1926). As a matter of fact, the techniques and camera precepts that I learned then have continued to serve me ever since...'.

To Penelope Gilliat in August 1976 the old master murmured 'Self-plagiarism is style'.

393

What is the answer? Remake *Lost Horizon* as a musical and reshoot *All Quiet on the Western Front* for television? Have *King Kong* re-scale the New York skyline and re-jig *The Front Page* for the third time? Parade Underground film as something more than erotic self-indulgence? Elevate the pornography of violence into an intellectual cult? Hail Wim Wenders as a new *Wunderkind*; look to Jean-Luc Godard as a one-time *Guru*? Turn to Agatha Christie and sign up fourteen stars ancient and modern for a *Murder in the Orient Express*? Hitchcock did this one, much better, more than sixty years ago, with *The Lady Vanishes*. And, oh yes, now they've remade that too (and *The 39 Steps* – twice). It took television, with the 1980 'Time-Life' BBC Co-Production of Stephen Poliakoff's *Caught On A Train* to get us back on the rails in that genre.

For the nine month period ended 28th February 1975, Metro-Goldwyn-Mayer was able to announce its highest earnings for several years. This was not, however, the outcome of any current motion picture production. Shareholders had to thank a prospering Grand Hotel operation into which MGM had diversified, and the film *That's Entertainment* – a compilation of clips from Metro's musicals of bygone days. Four years later Metro's shareholders were even happier. Income was up still higher. And what were the company's largest grossers in 1979? *The Champ*, a remake of a King Vidor tearjerker of 1931 (already remade once before as *The Clown* in 1951), plus a 35 million dollar licence fee from CBS to show dear old *Gone With The Wind* on television. By 1995, in the centenary year of the cinema, MGM not only no longer owned any part of its seemingly everlasting gold mine, but was reduced to little more than a share-manipulated shell of its own former glory.

In this time of its apocalypse, not surprisingly what was left of Hollywood discovered that in catastrophe and gore there was still money to be made. Protesting the spate of so-called disaster movies, one disenchanted film-goer sounded off in *Time* magazine (by now well past its own mid century) that 'after *Poseidon Adventure* I fear cruising on an ocean liner. After *Airport* and its follow-up, I cringe at the thought of flight. *Towering Inferno*

394

gives me indigestion before I arrive for dinner at my favourite restaurant on the 62nd floor of the U.S. Steel Building. *Jaws* now forces me to abandon my vacation spot on Cape Hatteras in favour of the safety of the Allegheny River. Ah, the brilliance of Hollywood! In one short year it has transformed Americans into cowering paranoids whose only security is found in the tenth row of a darkened cinema'.

And then what? An ultimate cycle of films about the people who made the movies when they were people and there were movies. A film of *Gable and Lombard*, cast with a couple of un-knowns and Allen Garfield performing as Louis B. Mayer; Rod Steiger impersonating the incomparable in a production of *W.C. Fields and Me*; Robert De Niro signed up to play Irving Thal-berg in *The Last Tycoon*. A necromantic revival reaching a nadir of sorts in a 1980 TV Trilogy based on Garson Kanin's *Moviola*, with someone playing Garbo in *The Silent Lovers*, someone else Marilyn Monroe in *This Year's Blonde* – plus an entire parade of look-alike Joan Crawfords, Paulette Goddards, Tallulah Bank-heads, Carole Lombards (and of course a Vivien Leigh) assem-bled for a re-enactment of *The Scarlett O'Hara War*. While hop-ing that filming comic strips on a cosmic scale would still bring in the kids: *Superman*, *Flash Gordon*, *Popeye*, *Annie*, *Dick Tracy* … and praying for salvation from outer space and other worlds: *Star Wars*, *Close Encounters*, *Aliens*, *Star Trek*, *ET*, *Gremlins*, *Total Recall*, *Teenage Mutant Ninja Turtles*, Dino-saurs... Yes, Dinosaurs. Sixty Million Years in the Making – so the hype of *Jurassic Park* would have us believe. What better comment on all this than Langford Wilson's in *Burn This*? 'Mov-ies are (nowadays) some banker's speculation on what adolescent fantasies happen to be that week.' The four times Oscar-winner Writer-Director of such as *A Letter to Three Wives* and *All About Eve*, Joseph Mankiewicz, put it even more bluntly: 'The Mayers, the Thalbergs, the Schencks, the Goldwyns, the Cohns ... they were like the Medici compared to the money-grabbers we have today. They were picture-makers, not deal-makers. The flesh peddlers, the agents, are now in charge and never before has the

The cinema today - whatever happened to people?
Chewbacca of *Star Wars*

film industry been such a con-game. The pimps have taken over the whorehouse'.

By the mid 1960s this new breed had already taken over what was left of the old Hollywood. Studios no longer returned phone calls from old-timers like King Vidor, the director of *The Citadel* and fifty-five other feature films who had made nothing since the 1959 *Solomon and Sheba*. But although now over seventy, Vidor was nevertheless determined to show them that he was still out there and running. He thought he knew just the story with which to prove it.

In early February 1922 the Hollywood of those early silent days had been rocked by the murder of one of its leading directors. Already established himself as the director of such top stars of the time as Laurette Taylor and Colleen Moore, the young Vidor had personally known the principals in this steamy drama: William Desmond Taylor the director found shot in the back in the living room of his Los Angeles home and, a prime suspect of the crime, Mary Miles Minter, Paramount's answer to Mary Pickford and cameraman Jimmy Wong Howe's first beautiful face. No one was ever charged with the crime, but Minter's career was ruined.

Reviving his memories and still surviving contacts of the time, Vidor now set out to solve the forty-four year old mystery. By uncovering a web of corruption, establishing that the killer had been Minter's appallingly possessive and infatuated mother – who had then gone on to bribe a succession of the so-called law enforcement officers – and with a clincher to the whole bizarre scenario the discovery that Taylor had been a thorough-going and active homosexual, Vidor certainly had all the ingredients for a contemporary blockbuster. But after contact with a still alive but gross and senile Mary Miles Minter – a scene straight out of Pip's encounter with Miss Havisham in *Great Expectations*, and indifference on the part of the latter-day tycoons – Vidor completely abandoned the entire project. All this giant of the old Hollywood was able to accomplish in the remaining fifteen years of his life were two personal documentary essays.

But soon after Vidor's death at the age of eighty-seven, all the data, documentation, and materials for this attempt of his at a comeback was unearthed by Sidney Kirkpatrick, who published the whole story as *A Cast of Killers*.

To me, the saddest part of all in this woebegone scenario is the picture drawn of his wife, the so very attractive Elizabeth Hill who had sat alongside Vidor on the set of *The Citadel*, sharing his every thought and every direction, including a shared screen credit for script – and always ready with a sweet smile for that adoring eighteen-year-old clapper boy. In *A Cast of Killers* all the wear and tear of those many years since have combined to transform her into the character of the completely estranged and embittered wife, refusing to talk or share anything with him, until finally not even the same roof over their heads.

Nothing demonstrates the bankruptcy and collapse of the old-style filmmaking more than the closure, takeover by television or, in many cases, demolition of those once thriving factories of illusion, the film studios. Metro-Goldwyn-Mayer, Gaumont-British, Gainsborough, Warner Bros, First National, Fox, Columbia... the catalogue is as endless as the call-sheets once seemed everlasting. And Denham. After continuing to survive as a warehouse for Rank Xerox copying machines and a film recording facility, to be finally razed to the ground in 1980, and on this same site that Monty Marks had originally bought for London Film Productions for £15,000 in 1934, replaced by the glass and concrete headquarters of a pharmaceutical conglomerate.

Thirty-five years on since the days of Denham's glory and a booming British film industry had seemed to be such a threat that it even posed a challenge to Hollywood, a natural successor to the *March of Time* on British screens, Thames Television's *This Week*, came up with a similar overview of movie-making in Britain. This time it proved to be a very different story, which they chose to call that week of July 5th 1990 'The Last Picture Show'. Said in interview David (*Chariots of Fire*) Puttnam:

'The level of production is dropping like a stone. (Barely a couple of dozen features that year.) Something's got to be done to correct that'; and Richard (*Gandhi*) Attenborough: 'There have been ten film ministers in the present administration and I think I've seen about eight of them over the years, and one of them that we went in to see had a most marvellous opening in that he said "Well hello, I'm delighted to see you all, I think I ought to tell you straight away that going to the movies gives me a headache so of course I don't go very often"'.

Having by then twice received a fare-thee-well himself from Hollywood, for his latest blockbuster attempt to restore bankability, Puttnam had just turned back to World War Two. *The Memphis Belle* had been William Wyler's outstanding documentary of a B-17 Flying Fortress and its crew on a real life bombing mission over Germany. Their fictionalised adventures restaged in mock-ups of the veteran aircraft would, it was hoped, amply repay Puttnam's latest American investors. As he has said, 'It could have been made about a British Lancaster bomber, but we couldn't raise more than a third of the money here. The film is only commercially viable because it's about Americans'.

'The British are coming' had been the clarion call of Colin Welland on receiving his 1982 Oscar for the screenplay of Puttnam's *Chariots of Fire*. Since then however it has not been all that much of a stampede.

Individual Brits have been coming, such as recently Sam Mendes to direct *American Beauty*, and American investment has made possible such other Oscar winners as *The English Patient*. But the patient itself still languishes. The National Lottery seen as the latest shot in the arm. In recent years over £105,000,000 from this source has been invested in the production of more than two hundred British feature films. Subsequently few have even recovered their costs. Many have failed even to get a screening. The Millennium year 2000 saw a real professional brought in to sort it all out. Alan Parker. Director of such box office hits as *Bugsy Malone*, *The Commitments*, *Evita*, and *Angela's Ashes*. Appointed Chairman of a new Film Council, he now has some £25,000,000 a year to invest in production. It is his belief that in the past too many first-time film-makers were let loose on inadequately developed projects, with scripts that had barely got beyond a first draft. This echoes Hitchcock who, on being asked the most important element in the making of a film, replied 'The script, the script, the script...'.

But with all the inroads of television was there still a real audience out there? By 1984 cinema attendance in Britain had dropped to a mere 54,000,000. Increased now nearly threefold. By the Millennium year of 2000 to now more than 140,000,000. The explanation is twofold. On the one hand a whole new generation of young people identifying with the motion picture. Flocking to such attractions as *Chicken Run*, *Mission Impossible 2*, and *Gladiator*. In a radio interview soon after his appointment, Alan Parker defined this as the age group sixteen to twenty five. On the other hand the cinema industry has simultaneously transformed itself and its structure. No longer two or three in the high street, but paralleling the development of supermarkets killing off the same high street's individual single product shops, out of town multiplexes with ten, fifteen, twenty screens showing as many different films at one and the same time, under the same roof. In July 2000, just outside Birmingham, there opened the 'Star City Warner Village'. Village is right. Inside this single complex thirty individual and separate screens with a total seating capacity of 5800. Contemporary cinematic royalty performed the ceremony. George Clooney and other members of the cast of *The Perfect Storm*. The latest and aptly named blockbuster from Hollywood.

In intellectual circles this is sometimes seen as a process of 'dumbing down'. So far as the British Film Institute was concerned more an opportunity. Having for years screened classics at the National Film Theatre, and commencing with the 1946 Powell-Pressburger *A Matter of Life and Death* and John McKenzie's 1981 *The Long Good Friday* arrangements were made with Odeon Cinemas to screen classic and international films, subtitled if necessary, on a single one of the many screens in eight of its multiplexes. If the scheme proved successful, to be extended to all forty of its mammoth showcases and other groups as well. The BFI to feed in more of the quarter million titles it has in safe keeping and preservation at the National Film Archive. In the words of Joan Bakewell, then chief executive of the BFI, this would offer 'movies for grown ups of all ages'.

One audience, however, ignored by and even ignorant of all this, has remained not only constant but is, in fact, now increasing more and more. That is the audience never reached – or sought – by either commercial cinema or commercial television: the billions in the developing world thirsting for information in the race to catch up. At Poona I was in the very midst of this multitude, surrounded by just such a situation – and one solution – in miniature.

History seems to rejoice in ironies. These former studios of Shantaram's Prabhat Film Company had ceased production in 1953, at just the same time as Denham went dark, also never to

Fozzie Bear and Kermit the Frog from *The Muppet Show*

see another film shot in any one of its seven sound stages ever again. And here I now was, at this old film studio in India, also once upon a time producing its own brand of glamorous and escapist entertainment, and now converted into a training school for young film-makers of another age and a very different commitment.

Between classes at Poona, and not just to prepare for the next session, the latest script, the new student, I stole away to a quiet corner on the lot of these old studios, now transformed into the Film Institute of India. A bullfrog eyed me quizzically as I sat beside the pool, the old studio tank, long deserted by movie make-believe and now the breeding ground of kingfishers and memories.

Whatever it may or may not have meant to the students, Poona gave me a chance to reassess the motion picture over the then three-quarters of a century or more of its existence – and the part I have played in it myself. My own involvement encom-

401

passed virtually the entire spectrum of cinema. In my own successes and failures, there might be lessons.

Work in a major studio of the thirties taught me respect for the tools of my trade, and the basic tool in the making of a motion picture is the camera. As a camera assistant in the tightly-disciplined crews of those days, I was brought up to treat and regard the camera as something as precious and demanding as the Holy Grail. To me, the machine which produces the magic of a motion picture (whether photographic or electronic) is still, and always will be, something magic. No craftsman can do good work if he does not respect the tools of his trade. And there is no such thing as a good artist who is not first and foremost a good craftsman. The very first shot, the very first scene, the very first sequence of Korda's *Rembrandt* has the painter buying his paints, testing them against his knowledge of what he can make them do for him. Without fuss.

His nephew Michael has recalled visiting Korda in hospital after the second of the coronaries which were soon to kill him. By the bedside was an easel. On it, a Boudin miniature. Said Alex to brother Vincent, also visiting: 'It's so wonderful to put so much of the world into such a small space, without any bright colours or tricks. That's the way we should make films. We did it like that when we made *Rembrandt* – remember?'.

'If we don't end war, war will end us', says the protagonist of the Wells-Korda *Things to Come*; but that one then prophesied put a camera in my hand, and I was able to work out how to use it myself, to tell a story, make a statement, on my own, in that bloody training school.

The pictorial journalism of the *March of Time* brought me face to face with politics on the screen; and, as the motion picture evolved into television, the nature of personality, the projection of which is so very basic to audience identification on any screen.

Caught up in both political and personal conflicts of my own, feeling in my bones that I was American but in my blood British, I attempted identification with other races through my camera; while seeking all the time for alternative sources of sponsorship

– of money with which to make films. For long a distressingly negative experience in my own birthplace. On the other side of the Atlantic, at least for a while, government encouraged independent filmmaking – thanks to President Kennedy, who broke with established procedure and appointed Ed Murrow an unhappy head of the United States Information Agency. A filmmaker such as James Blue was given official support and encouragement to make *The March* (on Washington August 29, 1963) when civil rights demonstrators in their hundreds of thousands – and as a result of this film – audiences throughout the world heard, and saw, Martin Luther King vow that 'we shall overcome'.

As we screened *The March* at Poona, I was reminded of something that I had come across during the making of *African Awakening*: the inter-related black-and-white keys of a piano keyboard which were represented in the crest of Ghana's Achimota College, and the admonition of its vice-principal Dr. Kwegyir Aggrey that 'you can play a tune of sorts on the white keys, and you can play a tune of sorts on the black keys, but for harmony you must use both the black and the white'.

'Black-and-white together now -
Oh deep in my heart, I do believe,
We shall overcome some day.'

Ed Murrow had gone to Washington disillusioned with television – television that is sponsored and programmed as slots in, of, or between segments of entertainment. More and more the integrity of his electronic platform had been whittled away. His partner, and successor at CBS, Fred Friendly, was to resign in his turn when the network refused to replace *I Love Lucy* with the Senate Committee's hearings on Vietnam. (Nothing could have kept Watergate and its drive towards the threatened impeachment of a President off the screen.) And don't let's think the British can really adopt too great a 'holier than thou' attitude over this. Certainly Public Affairs and Documentary Programming in British Television is still – at the moment – ahead of the United

403

States. But are we really getting across to the uncommitted and hitherto uninterested majority? One would like to think so. Have our reports on Ulster, housing problems, pollution, really changed any attitudes, produced any effect, than would have been otherwise the case, inevitably sandwiched as they must be for a mass audience between chunks of pop? Would Thames Television's *This Week* have achieved its high ratings if it had not been scheduled between popular sagas of cops and legal eagles like *The Bill* and *LA Law*?

With so-called 'Public Service' broadcast nowadays virtually an anachronism, and television in Britain increasingly becoming a commercial battle for ratings, unless presented on screen by a popular and telegenic personality and structured more and more along the lines of a soap, documentary-factual programmes end up in the tail end of the schedules late at night, where their impact and influence can be at best little more than marginal.

There have been exceptions, of course. Ken Loach's *Law and Order*, and Adrian Cowell's *Decade of Destruction* at once come to mind. But the more television there is and there's more and more coming from up there in the sky and along the cables – the less impact any single programme will ever be able to achieve, elbowed out into the grey small hours of the night as would any minority programme inevitably be, under the market-led restructuring of British broadcasting proposed for the 21st century.

At the time of Britain's original application to join the European Common Market, what shocked the pundits much more than the blue language in the BBC's 1974 verité saga of *The Family* was its blithe indifference to national affairs. The government? Mrs Wilkins did once refer to 'that ponce Heath'. Inflation? 'That extra penny-ha'penny – some guy's copping for himself.' Sadly producer Paul Watson reflected that what his series showed was that 'decisions on things like the Common Market have been made by a small number of people, and most of the rest of the country just did not give a damn'. In that first national referendum one might therefore wonder if the Wilkins family were amongst the large majority of British who then voted to remain with Europe, or the more than thirty-five per cent who did not even bother.

Like a great many, when I first moved into television with the *March of Time* and NBC fifty years ago, I believed that here was the new revolution. With this, we could change the world. I still do believe this. But not on screens in drawing-rooms or sets back of bartenders. Whatever the intrinsic merit of a programme, slotted into a now virtually everlasting twenty-four hour a day deluge of mass entertainment trivia, its effect cannot be more than merely marginal.

The inevitable trivialisation of whatever it may be before it goes out on these channels, which depend basically upon entertainment for their audiences (and hence survival) is pointed up, like so much, by the Vietnam experience.

It is arguable how much the non-stop nightly presentation of battle scenes from Vietnam had to do with the unpopularity of that war. But on American screens it was undoubtedly trivialised by making it a part of the ordinarily superficial treatment of news, sandwiched between commercials. On no less than the CBS special *Christmas in Vietnam*, the scene of an American child praying for her soldier father was followed by commercials for a mouthwash and a brassiere.

Once upon a time a commercial enterprise such as the Gas Light and Coke Company would pay for Edgar Anstey's making *Enough to Eat*, enabling him back in 1935 to get on to the screens the first face-to-face confrontation of how it was to exist in London's pre-war slums. Once upon a time the Ford Motor Company let Lindsay Anderson loose amongst the fruit and vegetables of Covent Garden market, enabling him to let us share the experience of working *Every Day Except Christmas*. Once upon a time, in order to sell tea, a marketing board paid for Basil Wright's passage to the Indies, enabling him to create, in *Song of Ceylon* an enduring and symphonic masterpiece. Once upon a time, a consortium of soap and margarine manufacturers sent Peter Hopkinson to Africa, enabling him to provide Wole Soyinka with an audience of millions, and himself a national nomination for a United Nations Award.

Unilever paid for that film of the Black awakening, in the belief that its sponsorship would enhance its image and assist in its survival in Africa. An attitude to the use of film which was not held by the next Chairman of the Company. With group profits down, he could not see how such an investment could help to sell either his soap or his margarine. Unilever thereupon ceased, and ceases, to sponsor such socially concerned and committed films. The Shell Petroleum Company, whose prestigious unit produced such an array of outstanding educational and instructional films over the years has similarly followed suit, for the same hard-sell reasons. In industry, it is now the time of the accountant and the computer, no longer the era of the artist-activator with the movie camera.

This development in industry is of great significance to all of us who aspire to communicate, claim to be communicators.

At the time Unilever made possible my *African Awakening*, film was the only available solution to many of the complex communication problems of the time. In one form or another, film-trained worker and technician wooed the customer, explained technical products, attempted to change public attitudes. But now, closed circuit television has become a commonplace tool in internal company training; television advertising sells not only to the market place but technical purchasers as well, and TV's tiny screen has to all intents and purposes completely taken over the attempted persuasion of general attitudes. (Whether successfully or not is beside the point so far as the hardware of technical transmission is concerned.) What is available to industry now is a choice between a whole range of audio-visual tools, mostly electronic, some still film-based; not any longer just the traditional and formally made thousand feet of l6mm film on a spool, but videotapes, 8mm loops, close-circuit, DVDs, TV, videocassettes... And this same choice now faces everyone who has something he needs to communicate to whatever sort of an audience, anywhere. Particularly those in the developing world, who have somehow to get across to billions of people – and involve them in – a multiplicity of plans and policies and programmes for human betterment.

It was not enough that I came to be at Poona, trailing those turbulent years of filmmaking behind me. It was not enough that I had survived; to reach, by what seemed some inevitable process of my own development, this period of re-assessment at the Film Institute of India. For my students, as much as for myself, I had to come up with an answer, advise a future course of action. All paths, it seemed, led to Poona.

Today there are two Indias. On the one hand now a world leader in current information technology. The most prestigious international financial conglomerates manipulating their investments by the press of buttons to and from call centres in such as Bangalore and Hyderabad. Alongside a booming entertainment film industry somewhat sardonically described as 'Bollywood'. On the other side of the coin, as you might say, a traditional India where most of an ever increasing population find themselves – just like their ancestors – born into lifetimes of rural poverty. It is to this hitherto abiding division that international organizations such as UNESCO have to focus their attention.

With a population of then already more than five hundred million, it had been no surprise to discover that the Government of India then maintained an official documentary film production unit, second only in size and output to the former Soviet Union. Many of our young film-makerat the Film Institute of India came from this Films Division in Bombay. They were as staggered as Basil Wright and I to be told by a visiting lecturer that in this land where three-quarters of its enormous population lived in villages, the average village received a visit from a mobile film projector – and hence enjoyed a film show – only once in three years.

And this was the problem. The great enormous problem. What sort of motion picture, how to make it, *how to show it* to help this vast illiterate, and multiplying audience, most of whom lived in quite literal darkness without the electricity to run a film projector, let alone activate a television set.

Whatever happened to people - author finds out in India

At Poona we didn't just sit back and look at our own and other people's films on the screen. We didn't just endlessly analyse and debate why they had been made this way, and why not that way. We didn't just write together a score or more of scripts, as examples of how we thought it might be done. We also made films.

Basil Wright and I had originally suggested that we each make a short film from scripts which we would evolve collectively with our own group of students. This was agreed. A memorandum had accordingly been prepared for us by the Film Institute which set out two areas of choice: innovation in agricultural practices in villages around Poona, and maternity and child health services including family planning services in the rural areas. Under these headings were seven separate and possible films. Our final choice was made easy for us by the fact that only two could be shot in three days apiece, which was all the time either of us could be spared from teaching. (And only two could be at all adequately covered in the eight minutes of screen time which was all we were permitted by the Institute's grave shortage

408

of negative and positive film stock.) So we spun a coin. Basil drew the rural health centre. This left me irrigation.

Water. Too much – flooding. Too little – famine. People have gone to war for it. Vital to the barely subsistence survival of India's rural multitude.

Loud were the groans when I informed my group that we were going to write, and then shoot, a film on irrigation. 'Oh, can't we make an experimental film?' was the cry. 'Every film is an experiment' was my answer; and we all piled into a decrepit old bus and drove off into the countryside near Poona. In this fabled land of the Marathas, we were in a land haunted by perennial famine and starvation. The introduction of new American engendered high-yielding varieties of seeds would increase food production by as much as five hundred per cent per acre. But planted in this way those acres needed much more fertiliser, which in turn called for two or three times as much water flowing into their roots in the first place – and this was a land of terrible drought.

How to get water there was our story. For our little film was to be more than just a demonstration of how a script worked – or failed to work on the screen. With Basil Wright's on how a village health centre can serve a rural community, it was planned to be shown to farmers and their families throughout Mahashtra. For them it had a lesson too. The most important lesson of all. How to get enough to eat.

My group took as our hero one of them. A local farmer. A farmer whose land was dry and barren. On a nearby river bank he sits and ponders his misfortune. The voice of water tells him to get up, and take a look at what others are doing about it. He visits his uncle's and other villages. In one they have diverted the water from a stream into their fields by means of a simple earth dam. In another, a stone and concrete dam made the same system solid. But both were only seasonal. During the dry months of summer the streams ran dry. Other villagers, elsewhere, had clubbed together, and bought pumps to raise water from wells all

Author with Film Institute of India students on location.
Who needs a studio?

the year round; and to lift it, where possible, up from a river flowing at a level lower than their own areas of cultivation. Each and every method was simple, practical, and cheap. For the purchase of pumping equipment, farmers to form co-operatives, the government to lend money; which, in turn, could be repaid out of the sale of the additional foodstuffs produced. After seeing the film any rural audience could get up and apply one or other method, whichever suited, themselves. Self-help. Gandhi's golden rule for the countryside – and India.

But of course there was a catch in it. However much she may be able to increase the production of food, like the world at large, there is no hope for India unless she can reduce the production of people.

In 1947 Paul Rotha sent me to Germany to shoot scenes of starving coal-miners giving their extra pithead rations to their children. This was for his film *The World is Rich*, which I showed at Poona alongside *A Few Notes On Our Food Problem*, made by James Blue for the United States Information Service twenty or more years later. *The World is Rich* presumed that if all peoples and governments gave unqualified support to the Food and Agriculture Organisation of the United Nations – FAO – then the problem could be solved, no one need go hungry. Now we know better, or worse. James Blue's film – despite its off-putting title – put forward no solutions. It just let us hear from African and Indian farmers, took us to South America, and ended with yet another unwanted child being born into an overcrowded shanty slum intercut with crowds and crowds of people pouring across a road junction, advancing towards and enveloping the camera.

The population explosion.

When I first filmed in India her population was 300 million. Then, twenty years later, it was already more than 500 million. By the turn of the century it is estimated that, unchecked, it will have doubled again. Every village we visited had the pictorial ideograms of family planning painted on the wall of one or another house: two happy parents with just two happy children.

411

Alongside always the red triangle which was India's national symbol of her drive to halve this explosion of her own population. One of the best scripts our course produced, Sai Paranjpye's '...*bass*' ('...enough'), dramatised this most fearsome priority facing the nation. Her protagonist was a professional wrestler who had accepted and undergone a vasectomy. If someone whose job and livelihood depended upon exceptional strength and virility could come through unscathed then, after two children, go thou and do likewise was the message that this film aimed to put across to its audience. And if anyone thinks that Indian women are shy and reticent creatures, then they should take a look at the Films Division's *Actual Experience*. In this series of films women from every walk and condition of Indian life talk freely about and discuss their own methods of family planning. Without a trace of self-consciousness, uterine loops, menstrual reactions, husbands' attitudes, all were shared with the audience, directly.

Uncontrolled population growth and an exhausted soil is a double headed hydra threatening India – and potentially all of us – with hunger.

This dominated the discussions at a two-day seminar on film and television in national development, which somehow we found time to fit into our twelve hours a day, six days a week of seeing films, writing films, making films.

In a very real sense all our efforts at Poona led up to this UNESCO organised seminar; for there, around a table, it was all thrashed out. Just how could the screen media help India?

First and foremost by using the most simple approach, the most unsophisticated technique. Much to the dismay and displeasure of some – who hoped to find fame and fortune in festival displays of dazzling and complicated techniques – speaker after speaker, film user after film user, health worker after demographic expert, all stressed this point.

Forget the cities. India lives in villages. Even though your name on the film may mean so much to you, why even bother about titles when your real audience is illiterate in all fourteen of our different languages. When they are lucky enough to get one of those rare visits from a mobile film projector unit, what you might think of as your masterpiece has to compete with the noise of the generator, the barkings of dogs, the crying of babies – and the indifference of an audience free to wander about and come and go as it pleases. Personalise. Tell them a story, in a straight-forward manner, in terms of reference which they understand and with which they can identify.

With all the disadvantages of the not really so very mobile film projector units – the infrequency of their visits, the ineffi-ciency of their operators – the transfer of power to the hundreds of thousands of fragmented and isolated villages, which must be the basis of the Indian revolution, can only be effectively chan-nelled and communicated by television. Properly utilised, televi-sion can integrate, unify, and propel India forward as nothing else in her long history. These were my parting words to the as-sembly at Poona; and this was clearly understood, appreciated, and supported in this final summing up seminar.

It had been to the Film Institute of India that Basil Wright and I had been summoned by UNESCO back in 1969, but before very long it was to be renamed the Film and *Television* Institute of India – although as I wrote in my report to UNESCO (April 19th 1970) 'it will be another twenty years before television can become a truly mass medium in India'. And that therefore brings us up to the 1990s, when now it is, thanks to satellite transmis-sion.

Poona is a long way from Florida. Or is it? Cape Kennedy, May 31st, 1974. Fired into orbit, 'Applications Technology Sat-ellite – F'. After a year of transmitting educational and medical advice programmes to remote communities in the United States, out there in space 22,300 miles away, then to be shifted into an-other synchronous equatorial orbit with its thirty feet parabolic antenna aimed at the centre of India. Down there on the ground an integrated task force feeding it programmes for relay back in reverse to at first 5,000 villages. Half of these villages, in six different parts of the subcontinent, taking the feedback pro-grammes directly into specially equipped community owned TV receivers. The other half receiving the programmes by rediffusion through ground relay to conventional sets, equipped with ten feet antennae made out of chicken mesh. To overcome India's problem of her multiplicity of languages, two regions at first to share one common picture with their own dialects on the audio channels, another two areas carrying the same visual with again their own languages on the sound channel; and programmes into Bihar (on the north east) and Rajasthan (on the north west) originating separately.

SITE, the Indians called it, *Satellite Instructional Television.* The stated objective to discover if satellite TV can be used as an agent for social change and development; the programmes shot by film field units in each of the areas where direct receivers have been established, assembled back at Base Production Units in three regional centres. On a much larger and more ambitious scale, just such a system, and solution, proposed by Fred Friendly after he quit CBS, as could beam a continuous and effective non-commercial television programme, free of the networks, into homes and institutions throughout the United States. The pressure of vested commercial interests, plus a business-orientated administration in Washington, brought that inspired plan to naught. But until India placed her own home-made and self-launched satellite up there in the sky from her southernmost tip in 1986, American rocketry was pleased to serve.

The United States has had a Public Broadcasting Act since 1967. By the time of the 1976 Bicentennial Celebration of the original Declaration of Independence, there were already more than two hundred and fifty public (that is non-commercial) TV stations on the air. True, the highlights of their programmes were as often as not imports from Britain, particularly the BBC, but the home-grown *Sesame Street* was an outstanding example of audio-visual conceptual imagination. Very funny too, and snapped up by other countries as far afield as Singapore – but not, ironically, by Britain. Not, that is, until Jim Henson, their creator, brought his cast of zany puppets to England, and there – thanks to British commercial sponsorship – transformed them into international stars in the Made-in-Britain *Muppet Show.* Meantime, the American Corporation for Public Broadcasting had to go cap in hand to Congress for funds. This put non-commercial broadcasting in the United States at the mercy of political interest. A new Public Broadcasting Act provided for secure funding for an uninterrupted five-year period. In the context of the American system, this was revolutionary, but with hard-pressed educational institutions cutting back on teachers as well as learning aids, a Declaration of Independence from the commercial networks not a moment too soon. For it was the non-commercial Public Broadcasting System which had carried the original Watergate hearings in full in the first place.

And what of Britain? After endless debate and the contrary recommendations of an official committee, the Conservative Government announced in November 1979 that the then hitherto unallocated fourth terrestrial television channel would go on the air in 1982.

Soon after this announcement, a distinguished group of people numbering amongst them Richard Hoggart, Bernard Braine, Jack Jones, Judith Hart and the then Archbishop of Canterbury, wrote a letter to *The Times*. 'Amongst other things', they said, 'the fourth channel should offer a real opportunity to focus attention on issues that the other channels can treat only briefly or irregularly. Not least amongst these is the relationship between the rich and the poor countries ... a significant amount of time on the fourth channel (should) be allocated to programmes promoting an understanding of the interdependence of the developed and the developing world'.

If British Television's Channel 4 has not altogether fulfilled these pious hopes that it should serve to help bridge the gulf between North and South – the 'heads' and 'tails' of the world's rich and the world's poor – it has however breathed a kiss of life of some sort into the near moribund British film industry. By the time of its twelfth birthday, Channel 4 had caused to be made or helped to make more than two hundred and sixty feature films, including even some modest transatlantic successes like *The Draughtsman's Contract* and *Letter to Brezhnev*. *The Ploughman's Lunch*, for example, focused with deadly accuracy on the impotence of the new intelligentsia, faced with the hue and cry

415

of the Falklands War. But the overall viewpoint of these frequently quite brilliant little films was narrow, parochial: that of the new generation of a post-imperial, post-industrial country, diminished and diminishing, narcissistic. There was little, if any, choice of subject or theme outside the disenchantment of discovering that this was now no longer a land of hope and glory. Fifty years before, Korda had all of the Sudan and India as playgrounds for his Technicolored spectaculars. Sabu – that cute little *Elephant Boy* – had now been transformed into Saeed Jaffrey, the wily Asian entrepreneur of *My Beautiful Laundrette*; and almost nightly, or so it seemed to dispirited viewers, television news brought into British homes pictures of turmoil in their own inner cities. Black protest, Muslim mayhem, alongside the faces of famine in Africa. Ebbing back as the tide of history had now turned, and far too close for comfort as many now saw it, were the problems of the developing world. On the other hand it must however be said that Channel 4 has struck a balance by helping to finance *Four Weddings And A Funeral*, hailed as 'the most successful British film ever'.

At the Film and Television Institute of India we were up to our necks in the problems of the developing world, and a major aspect of the job Basil Wright and I were called upon to do was to promote an understanding of the interdependence of the developed and developing world – and if this means anything at all, it means participation.

Participation has by now become a cliché word. But it is the clue to true communication. Not we and them – but US. This is the first great lesson that I learned at Poona. And the other is that a motion picture communicator nowadays needs to be just as familiar with electronics as he is with optics. He needs to be practised in both film and television. There already existed an electronic camera no larger than an eight millimetre film camera, coupled to a videotape recorder no larger than and just as portable as the average sound tape recorder with which a great many people were by then familiar. Used as the motion picture recorder in developing countries this could, I argued, revolutionise

416

the whole practise and method of filmmaking as hitherto and traditionally undertaken.

Portable VTR (video tape recording) equipment now makes it possible for people to participate in the production of their own motion pictures about themselves; with simple, image-making and image-storing equipment, immediately played back on a screen, subsequently mixed and edited and transferred to film as may be required. This will mean a shared experience in instant visual creation and awareness, a revolutionary step forward to be able to show people immediately, on the playback television screen, what has been 'filmed', and solicit their active and conscious collaboration.

Motion picture production in this manner can restore film and audience participation. Film-maker, film user, and audience would become, at last, one collective unity. Hence would be both access and accountability; with participation, of most concern to broadcasters and communicators who see their calling as something more than merely immediate and mercenary – and a complete solution to Pennebaker's strictures of 'documentary' as a drag-like thing just 'shouting on the wall about how you don't know something'.

Film can now, and must, become an *act*. This is the third great lesson that I learned at Poona.

As a result of the ditches and dams we constructed to demonstrate the principles of irrigation to the people of the countryside around Poona, water really did flow into their fields as well as across our screen. As a result of the shared participation and experience together in their making of a film of his life as dockworker in Abidjan, the illiterate and previously inarticulate subject of Jean Rouch's *Moi Un Noir* became himself a film-maker, screening a film of his own eleven years later at the Moscow Film Festival. And long before all this Malraux did not only make his film about the España Squadron in the Spanish Civil War – he flew and fought the planes as well.

From our own marathon festival of re-appraisal at Poona, I came away more than ever convinced that the motion picture in the 21st Century needs to be used no longer as merely entertainment or even a teaching medium built around dramatic effects, but rather as a medium for direct dialogue.

Where was the dialogue in the old-style cinema, except between much larger than life-size actors up there high above us on the screen? Where is the dialogue in television, its pre-recorded image chattering away out there whether the set is switched on or not?

How can one individual, or a group, establish the mechanics of this dialogue? The tools are expensive, the major outlets owned and controlled either by monopoly conglomerates in the case of theatres or broadcasting networks in the case of television. Free as they may be from commercial direction, public service broadcasting systems and corporations soon tend to develop an inherent elitism in their structure and commissioning. Peter Davis, who was 'put on ice' by CBS following the controversy over his *The Selling of the Pentagon*, had to go outside television to make *Hearts and Minds*, an attempt to come to terms with the American disaster of the Vietnam war. At its 1975 annual Hollywood jamboree, the Academy of Motion Picture Arts and Sciences somewhat desperately awarded his enterprise an 'Oscar'.

When the movies were still in their infancy, innovators like King Vidor and Louis de Rochemont could film with homemade cameras, and their local cinemas would screen their chronicling of events and happenings in their own communities, to audiences of that same local community. But this was simple, silent filming; in a pre-monopolistic age of innocent experiment.

How then can an individual, or a group, now utilise the motion picture screen for the analysis and self-expression of its identity and needs – as a necessary and effective instrument of change?

The answer just has to be in VTR. What first made this possible was the Portapack, an electronic image recorder little larger than an average-size audio tape recorder, slung over the shoulder, and not all that much weightier; from it a cable, connected to a hand-held and miniature television camera, smaller even than many a l6mm film camera. Battery-operated, non-mechanical, noiseless, this combination gave half an hour's continuous shooting, recording extremely precise images on half-inch or wider videotape. Now a single integrated Video 8 or digital easily hand held camcorder is able to do it all, sound and picture, on a single easily slipped in tape cassette, just like at home. Your own home movie.

With such a breakthrough which makes it possible instantaneously to reproduce from life any event as it happens – an 'electronic ball-point pen' as it has been called – video enthusiasts like myself now see the opportunity to remove the barriers which exist between producers and consumers, programme originators and audience – 'developed' and 'developing'.

Unlike conventional television, what is recorded can immediately be seen and discussed. Each individual view can participate in the process. What counts is no longer mass response but individual exchanges and interactions. Recordings are seen and discussed by people in a group. At the same time another recording can be made of the discussion, so that viewers themselves become participants, at merely one remove. In this way, instead of there being only one-way communication, there is multi-dimensional communication and feedback. And in situation after situation, confrontation after confrontation, the process can be continued ad infinitum, in a multiplying creative involvement. An extension – now available to everyone – of the *direct* cinema pioneered by Jean Rouch with *Chronicle of a Summer*.

In India, in Asia, in the developing countries – where most of mankind will be living and born during the new millennium, the motion picture unit of the future will have to be a combination of film and digital videotape, with one or several operators expert in the whole electronic motivational information process, able to go into a village and shoot material during the day for instant playback or screening in an edited form that same evening. My report to UNESCO on the role of film in development went on to argue that for extension workers and trainers in all fields of development this will provide tremendously valuable support material that would otherwise be unobtainable so quickly – or so effectively.

419

Direct and actual experience of 'film' creation and audience reaction in this way, made possible by a combination of electronics and optics, will be 'film schools' in themselves. Not remote institutions teaching primarily 'film art' in three-year courses, but mobile and genuine miniature motion picture universities in which teachers and students, audience and creators, are all so thoroughly and indistinguishably participants in the entire subjective as well as objective process that the fatal division between town and country, academic and illiterate, teacher and student, could melt completely away.

Joined by teaching and communication specialists from both national and state governments, the final Poona seminar summed up the lessons of the six week course, and made its recommendations. Re-reading this official report of the time, I note that Peter Hopkinson is quoted as saying that:

'There has always been a disparity between the intellectual background of the film-maker and the people whom he filmed. To reduce the distance between the film-maker and the people in the emerging situation in the country of India, was it possible to develop a new kind of film-maker who had closer roots with the rural people? With the new mobile and portable equipment would it be possible to train even ordinary village people in the use of simple cameras and tape recorder? The films made by such people might have a certain kind of interest which the city trained film-maker might not be able to get on the film'.

A forecast of what video and digital camcorder would very soon make possible – and not just for India.

Possibly the last 'great' documentary of the old, traditional school is Robert Flaherty's *Louisiana Story*. Originally released in 1948, it dramatises this conflict between town and country, innocence and technology, in the story of a small Cajun boy's reactions to the arrival of an oil drilling team in the swamplands that are his playground – and which Flaherty's vision succeeds in rendering a veritable arcadia. Twenty-seven years later, an American video group calling itself 'TVTV' taped ninety hours of raw material on the lives and music of this same Cajun community. Transferred to film, fine-cut to an hour, entitled *The*

Good Times Are Killing Me and televised in the United States midsummer 1975, here was in every way a very different Louisiana Story. Different in approach, different in intention, different in techniques. Flaherty spent more than a couple of years and over a quarter of a million dollars: TVTV seven weeks and little more than the cost of their own board and lodging.

Shooting a documentary on tape was not all that new. At Poona I was able to show Norman Swallow's *A Wedding On Saturday*, in which he and Denis Mitchell utilised Granada TV electronic cameras to tape – then edit – the recording of such a family occasion. Never, I am certain, could an Indian audience have witnessed such uninhibited behaviour on the part of a people who had once appeared remote and distant rulers. The working class Yorkshire coal-miners of this happening, with their strange accent and carryings on, were as foreign – and as exciting – to them as astronauts. And I pointed out that film had had nothing whatsoever to do with it: except to transfer to the print we screened made from the original master videotape. What is now new is the refinement of technique, the portability and the flexibility of the equipment.

Radical Software, an aptly named New York originated magazine, reported in the 1970's on the rise in the use of videotape by community groups throughout the United States. By this means, local groups were already getting programmes into the cable television system. Of how, on the West Coast, a group set out to buy the franchises for television stations, beginning with KVST – TV Los Angeles. 'Fully 80 per cent of our air time will consist of locally-orientated, hard issue public affairs programming' stated their intention. A Canadian counterpart was *Challenge for Change*. All over the country pools of portable VTR equipment were made available for community use. In one project, a mining village in Alberta without water, sewers, gas, or even local government, a group committed to change this state of affairs – and operating this lightweight electronic hardware – talked with people in streets, shops, pubs, about what they thought should be done. Their answers, on tape, were edited and shown to a large local gathering. As a result, action committees were formed, and the provincial government forced to face up to change.

Videotape leading to action in a disaffected Canadian coalmining village in the 1970s – and a clockwork camera shooting thirty-five millimetre optical film in the depressed Rhondda Valley of the thirties: *Today We Live*. At a 1974 screening of this film, director Ralph Bond told how its sequences were scripted and filmed, thirty-eight years before, there and then, as a community project.

One of the arguments used nowadays to demolish the Griersonian ethic, and justify the subjective 'please yourself, express yourself, internal revelation' approach to film is that the world we live in today is too complex, too impersonal, almost too much out of any one person's control for any one person to do anything about it, outside of him or herself. Electronics, on the one hand the cause of so much contemporary alienation can also, like most things, be made to serve the threatened individual – through the group.

Shot on tape, a moving picture with its accompanying sound can now be transferred easily to film. Shot on film, a moving picture is just as simply – and cheaply – transferred to tape. You can record, edit, mix, project, broadcast what you want to say, any which way you like, to one, two, three or a million viewers at a time. Community video is essentially the low-cost application of television – or film – to the communication needs of community groups.

Starting to Happen was the title, the title of a 'film' made up of transfers from videotape, shot by local people on the problems concerning them, in the very unfashionable South London working class suburb of Balham. Hoping to bring young people together by starting a playground, a young woman believed that it was important for people to come somehow together, because nowadays 'people just shut doors … don't communicate any more'. Housewives went out into the streets and interviewed their fellow citizens about what they thought was wrong with the place. During the 'filming' a child, crossing a street, was actually knocked down. This turned *Starting to Happen* into a blueprint for community action, as it then went on to document the movement to get a safe pedestrian crossing evolving into an organised campaign, with growing pains and disagreements about strategy and strained relations with the local establishment.

Starting to Happen was shown in a BBC programme. 'Why', one of its presenters was asked, 'Balham?' Why not? We all of us have to start somewhere.

And a starting point may even be the classics. Audiences at the 1977 Berlin Film Festival saw a new screen version of *Hamlet*, produced by Celestino Coronado for less than five thousand dollars – because he shot it in the first place on videotape. At the 1979 London Film Festival – for reasons economic as much as aesthetic – *The Song of the Shirt* was seen effectively to employ video in its re-enactment of the degradation of women in the sweatshops of the previous century. More recently – and with the onset of home video creating that magical margin of profit so desperately needed by producers – for his own screen version of Cocteau's *The Eagle Has Two Heads*. Antonioni also turned to video.

Broadcast television soon saw in this not only a source of cheap programming, but also an opportunity to demonstrate its own concern at the hitherto lack of wider access to its screens. In 1990 the BBC came up with *Video Diaries*, in which it was claimed documentary tradition was turned on its head when the subjects of the programmes pointed the cameras at themselves. Each 'diarist' was given a simple-to-operate video camera, and told to use it to tell us about their lives. An exile in England for six years, one Robert Wilson returned to report on his hometown of Belfast. Another of these video diarists went back to Philadelphia, in an attempt to lay the ghost of the demons she had suffered ever since physical abuse in childhood. Yet another, further afield, to Calcutta, and the daunting task of a family planning centre trying to cope with the explosion of births.

When the American film-maker Tom Joslin was diagnosed as HIV Positive, assisted by his lover, he began a video-film diary. In *Silverlake Life: The View From Here*, we see him being chanted over by a nature healer, arguing over his treatment, and

423

with his conventional parents back home for Christmas. As his condition gets worse first his lover, and then a colleague take over the filming. We witness his death. The zipping up of his corpse in a body bag. The funeral and the delivery of the ashes.

In Britain video has also brought us in an intensely personal way the death of a once proud and vital industry. When the closures of most of what little remained of Britain's coal pits became all too clearly a government objective, one miner's wife decided to do something about it. With a video camera. Brenda Nixon. We join her at home, with her family, and with the close-knit local mining community – all faced with the loss of their livelihood and no prospect of anything else. Share with her the struggle of 'Women Against Pit Closures'. Their occupation of collieries, and, in this 1993 BBC *Video Diary*, their chaining themselves in protest to the doors of the faceless government authority responsible. Back in 1938 King Vidor, and MGM, gave us a picture of the miner's world when it mattered. Now that it no longer seemed to count any more, Brenda Nixon – and video – gave us another.

Pushing the limits of the screen of change in Poland 1979-81, Andrzej Wajda gave us two masterworks, *Man of Marble* and *Man of Iron*. The first a Citizen Kane-like telling of the destruction of a legendary national hero by local Stalinism, the second the carrying on of a struggle by his son in the ranks of *Solidarity* in the Gdansk shipyard. During the crackdown that followed, Wajda had this to say about video:

'It ruins what cinema is for me: an audience and a communal experience. But video can also be a form of freedom: for instance, where television is state controlled and regulated, as it is in socialist countries. By putting a cassette into his VCR, someone can destroy the official programme; he is not forced to take what is shown to him. I think this is the main reason for the striking increase of video in Poland. There are no official figures, but it is estimated that there are already about 100,000 VCRs in the country and that the number is doubling each year. As filmmakers, we must take this into account and begin to think of making our films independently on video'.

How right he was. For in this way video came to play a key role not only in the success of *Solidarity* in Poland but, in the form of *samizdat* cassettes, throughout the revolution which finally flung Stalinism off the backs of Eastern Europe. Made in this way surreptitiously on Video 8, hundreds of copies of the massacre of Christian Armenians by Muslim extremists in Nagorno Karabakh were distributed unofficially throughout the Soviet Union, with a copy delivered to Mikhail Gorbachev in the Kremlin. In Rumania the revolution headquartered itself at the National TV Centre in Bucharest. Instant communication throughout the country for the Interim Government which followed the downfall of the dictator Ceauşescu. Nearer home, video even went to the aid of the beleaguered Salman Rushdie. Cassettes of Channel 4's *Hullaballoo Over The Satanic Verses* – which included a television interview with the threatened author – circulated widely in Pakistan, thanks to producer Tariq Ali.

Even so, in Britain, that pioneer of so much worthwhile factual film and television, the outlook is bleak. Bleak that is for someone trying to beat the system, hoping to get a story on to regular broadcast TV, even if inexpensively shot on video. Not only is there the inevitable obstacle of getting to and then persuading a sympathetic commissioning editor. Very soon, if the worse case scenario is realised, there could be very few if any of these left in this field at all; certainly not so far as 'market forces' are concerned and with the BBC's own future as purely licensefee funded also under threat. With the many new broadcasters terrestrial as well as satellite in competition the one with the other they will need to maximise viewers, and 'quality television' – by which is really meant documentary as opposed to admass – will almost inevitably be downgraded as of minority interest, if not to a very large degree jettisoned. But in our own hands, and amongst ourselves, we can still do it; and, as recent events in Eastern Europe have demonstrated, given the chance will even change history.

And in today's multi-channel digital technology there is now of course the INTERNET.

In probably his last interview – to Elizabeth Sussex – John Grierson tells how de Sica's scriptwriter Cesar Zavattini once made a speech in which he thought it would be wonderful if all the villages in Italy were armed with cameras so that they could make films by themselves and write film letters to each other, and that this was supposed to be a great joke, and everyone laughed and laughed.

Everyone, that is, except Grierson: 'Because I think that is the next stage'.

In India - students set up a shot. Author ponders the future

Revised April – June 2001 Peter Hopkinson.
Note: Poona is now spelled Pune but still pronounced 'Poona'.
Bombay is now 'Mumbai'.

Appendix:

Peter Hopkinson – Production Record (1936 - 1995)

1936   Entered film industry as clapper loader, Ealing Studios.

1937-   Camera Assistant with Alexander Korda and Metro-
1940   Goldwyn-Mayer British Productions on such pre-war feature films as *A Yank at Oxford*, *The Citadel*, *Good bye Mr Chips*, and *The Thief of Bagdad*.

1942   British Army Film and Photographic Unit.
Directed and photographed film of allied aid and Lend-Lease to the Soviet Union *Via Persia*.
With British Eighth Army contributed to the filming and production of *Desert Victory*.
Covered landings in Sicily and Italy. In charge of film and photographic coverage of special operations in the enemy occupied Balkans. Accompanied and filmed raids on Albania and Yugoslavia. With small party of paratroops landed in Greece, and two days before arrival of regular troops filmed liberation of Athens.
Organised coverage of Japanese surrender in Siam and Indo-China.

1946   Director-Cameraman United Nations Relief and Rehabilitation Administration. Covered UNRRA activities in Austria and Italy. Made film of former Polish slave labour returning home from Germany. Travelled and filmed throughout Poland, including the former German Territories then being resettled.

Obtained visa to enter the Soviet Union, and filmed UNRRA operations and life in Soviet Ukraine and Bye- lorussia. Released by the *March of Time* as *The Rus- sians Nobody Knows*.

1947   Joined the American documentary series the *March of Time*. Directed and photographed: *Battle for Greece*, the background to the Greek civil war

1948   *Asia's New Voice– The Promise of Pakistan*. The com- prehensive story of Indian independence and future trends and developments in the subcontinent.
Battle for Bread. Film of FAO operations in China, sponsored by the United Nations and produced by the *March of Time*. Sequences in China of American aid and support to Chiang Kai-shek and the eclipse of his support on the mainland.

1949   *New India's People*. Built around the lives of four Indians: a young Bengali journalist, a Mahara- jah, a Brahmin priest, and an Untouchable.
MacArthur's Japan. MOT release and report on post-war and occupied Japan.

1950   Sequences of MOT releases in Europe. *My Trip Abroad*, with Mrs. Eleanor Roosevelt as she travelled through Norway, Sweden, Finland, Denmark, Holland, Luxembourg, France, and England, reporting on post war recovery. Produced by MOT for the United States Economic Cooperation Administration, the administra- tors of the Marshall Plan in Europe.
Updating sequences and material for this MOT Holy Year reissue of *The Story of the Vatican*.

1951   *Flight Plan for Freedom*. Coverage of the UK based operations of the United States Strategic Air Command.

Formosa – Island of Promise. Arranged, researched, directed, and photographed this final MOT theatrical release.

1952   Assigned by the United States Government, Mutual Security Agency, to the production of a series of films for television on the general theme of European recovery. Released through the American Broadcasting Company. Directed and photographed: *North Sea Harbour*, the recovery of Hamburg, Germany's most energetic and liberal city. Told around the life of a shipyard worker.
The Ruhr. Germany's great industrial heartland, and the life of a refugee miner from the east zone.
Keep Them Flying. Life on an American air base in central France. The reactions of the Americans to the French, and vice-versa.
The Other Paris. Report on the French working class, and the development of the non-Communist trade unions. Centred around two railroad workers.
The Smiths of London. Post war Britain. Its recovery and contribution to western defence, told through the life of an average family.
Rejoined the *March of Time* in New York for a television series released by NBC.
Germany Today. Survey and report on post-war Germany. The struggle for re-unification against the background of economic revival.
Vienna Today. The contrast between the traditional life and culture in this then occupied city behind the 'Iron Curtain', and the centre of international espionage and intrigue which it had become as a result.
The Middle East. Report and survey from this key and turbulent area. Interviews with General Naguib, Persian Prime Minister Mossadeq, and the Lebanon's Charles Malik. Coverage ranging from Egypt, through the Lebanon, Jordan, Kuwait, Iran, and Israel.

1953   Left the *March of Time* to join Louis de Rochemont Associates as European Representative and Director of a proposed TV series: *Our Times*.
Researched, prepared, and wrote scripts on the then British bid for civil air supremacy, the British Monarchy and the Duke of Windsor, anti-Americanism in Britain, the French worker-priests, Berlin, NATO, India, Hong Kong, and many other subjects.

1954   Nominated by the Overseas Press Club of America for its annual award for The Best Photographic Reporting from Abroad on Foreign Affairs.
For Louis de Rochemont: directed and photographed a film of the Suez Canal, which received a Diploma of Merit in the 1955 Edinburgh Film Festival, titled *To Open the World to the Nations – Suez*.
Joined the National Broadcasting Company of America as European director of the series *Background*. Directed and photographed *Duel for Germany*: the struggle for re-unification set against the background of the booming city and port of Hamburg.
Italy on the Brink. A report on the strength of the Italian Communist Party, Europe's largest, analysed through a look at two communities, the city of Bologna in the prosperous north, and the village of Lavello in the impoverished south. Presenter Frank Bourgholtzer.

1955   NBC *Background*. *Escape*: the great exodus across the frontiers of Hungary and other eastern European satellite countries into the freedom of Austria. The particular story of one such refugee, her escape, and subsequent struggle for an American visa.
British General Election. The election of 1955 focused on a crosssection of constituencies.
An exclusive interview with Aneurin Bevan, in which he propounded his political philosophy. Presenter of both programmes Edwin Newman. *Meeting at the*

Summit. The background story to the Geneva conference and meeting between Eisenhower, Krushchev, Eden, and Faure. The apparatus and mechanics leading up to this historic rendezvous in Switzerland.
Youth Wants to Know. Directed two filmed programmes in this NBC series, the first to be mounted outside the United States, on the occasion of the first International Conference on the Peaceful Uses of Atomic Energy at Geneva, Switzerland. Admiral Lewis Strauss, Chairman of the United States Atomic Energy Commission as the central figure of the first, India's Dr. Homy Bhabha, Chairman of the Conference, the second.
Call to Freedom. For NBC *Project 20*. Directed and photographed special feature film of the reopening of the Vienna State Opera, and its historical production of Beethoven's *Fidelio*. Returned to England.

1956   For Film Centre. Directed and photographed *The Great Question*. The impact of oil on Iraq, and the transformation being attempted in every aspect of the social, agricultural, and industrial life of that ancient land by the then most comprehensive development plan in the Middle East.

1957-   Travelled and filmed in Malaya, Australia, Kenya,
1960   the Sudan and Britain, writing and directing a series of films sponsored by British industry and the Central Office of Information, Shell International Petroleum Company & Unilever.
For Ford Motor company *Bandwagon*, Premier Award British Industrial Film Festival, 1959.

1961-   Sponsored by Unilever. Wrote and directed *African*
1962   *Awakening*. The new African generation now in charge of its own affairs in the independent states of Ghana, Nigeria, and Sierra Leone. The thoughts, hopes,

fears, background, commerce, and culture of the African personality. Official British choice for UNESCO's Kalinga Prize for the film 'Judged to contribute most effectively to public appreciation of an outstanding achievement resulting from international cooperation in education, science, and culture'. Featuring the presence and poetry of the Nigerian Nobel Laureate Wole Soyinka.

1963   *Asian Crescent*. Malaya and Malaysia. The struggle to weld together into a single nation people of different racial origin, language, and culture. Malay, Chinese, and Indian. A new Federation caught at that time between the vast mass of hostile Chinese to its north and the armed belligerence of Indonesia to its south. Commonwealth Film Festival 1965.

1964   Wrote and directed *Today in Britain*. A close look at Britain and the British at this point of their history. Narrated by James Cameron. 'An Outstanding Film of the Year' London Film Festival. 'Special Award' Council of Europe.
For the Port of London Authority; researched and wrote the script of a film on the *Port of London*. Its social history and development, and the problems it then faced in adapting to the changed pattern of trade and transhipment.

1965-
1966   Wrote and directed three films for Ministry of Defence: *School is Everywhere*. The story of soldiers' children constantly moved around from Hong Kong, Malaya, Singapore, Aden, Malta, and Germany - and how their education was none the less maintained and even enhanced.
Official British entry 3rd Festival International Film Militaire 1967.

Home is the Soldier. A light-hearted look at the problems confronting a soldier's return to civilian life, and how he could be helped to get himself a house of his own. Bronze Award British Industrial and Scientific Film Association Festival 1968.

Three Hundred Years On. A not unaffectionate history of the British Army and the times it has lived and fought through. From the Civil to the Boer War. Recreated by creative camerawork of the details of paintings and relics preserved in the National Army Museum. Royal Command Film Performance 1968.

1967 *Flame in the Desert.* A study of what it means to be precipitated into the nuclear age from a tent in the desert in less than a lifetime. The story of the Arabian Gulf State of Qatar. The original nomadic life of the Bedouin, now suddenly revolutionised by the discovery of oil. In microcosm the pressures and progress of the Arab world. directed in association with Near East Sound Studios, Beirut, with music by Toufic el Bacha.

1968 *Ghana – A Report.* A documentary TV report on the first colony in Africa to achieve independence after the second world war, two years after its change of direction – following the downfall of Kwame Nkrumah.

1969 For the Decimal Currency Board devised and wrote the script of *All Change.* The background to the decimalisation of Britain's currency, and the revolution in financial trading practice that this brought about. Dramatised through the experiences of two adjacent and competitive shopkeepers.

Published *Split Focus*, the personal story of this career up to the filming of *Fidelio* in 1955.
Appointed by UNESCO as Consultant to the Film Institute of India's second regional training course on docu-

mentary short-film script writing, to provide guidance and teaching support in the field of documentary and short-film production for use by television.

1970   Wrote and directed *Partnership for Prosperity*. Three major conglomerates coming together to manufacture aluminium on an industrial scale in a rural area of Wales. Including the shipment of the raw material from Ghana, from the ground up to the creation, the construction and the coming on stream of an industry new to Britain. The reaction of the local mainly farming community to this development. Concern expressed regarding possible pollution and environmental damage, balanced by the argument for its overall and lasting economic advantage to an area in hitherto economic decline.
Also commissioned by the Rio Tinto global mining group, scripted and directed *Better Then The South* at Palabora in South Africa, the largest scale mining of copper in the world. This immense industrial complex framed within a challenge to the system of Apartheid prevailing at the time.

1971   For the Department of Trade and Industry, through the Central Office of Information, wrote and directed *Physics and Engineering*, In which physics is related to modern technology arising from the work of the engineer and his collaboration with the physicist in aspects of electricity, the structure of matter, light, temperature/pressure, humidity and heat. The results of this collaboration seen to be wide-ranging. Magnetic levitation, economic power-generation using super conductivity, electronic miniaturisation, laser-beam transmission of telephone traffic along fibreglass cables, weather control and computerised meteorology, and thermography's many applications, from detection of pollution to diagnosis in preventive medicine.

434

1972   For the Tin Industry Research and Development Board produced, wrote, and directed *Timah* and *Time for Tin*. The first film illustrating the background, nature, and contribution that the Tin Industry makes to the progress and development of Malaysia, its largest producer. The second also in German, French, Italian and Japanese versions for international release, demonstrating the metal's contribution to contemporary technology. Gold Camera 'First Award' United States Industrial Film Festival, Chicago, 1973.

1973   Wrote, produced, and directed for UNESCO a series of films on the subject of Family Planning Communication. Demonstrating the methods of producing low cost visual aids in Kenya, the utilisation of folk media in India, the coordination of a multimedia campaign with field workers in Iran, and a programme of research and evaluation into results undertaken in Venezuela. Title of single combined version of all four films: *A Matter of Families*.

1974-   UNESCO appointed Chief Training Adviser to a
1975   newly established factual television production unit in Costa Rica. A UN supported aid project to this Central American social democracy, whose president was to receive a Nobel Peace Prize for his success in ending civil war in the region. Subjects ranged from the conservation of the flora and fauna of the rain forest to the plight of immigrant blacks on the Caribbean seaboard, rural cooperatives, and the culture of the pre-Colombian past.

1976   Also for UNESCO, with facilities and support from the British Museum, *Coin Collections*. The preservation, analysis, calibration, and lessons to be learnt from this aspect of historical heritage.

1977- 1978	In Scotland, wrote and directed documentary features on the construction of two major infrastructures for the petroleum industry. A storage terminal for North Sea oil on the Moray Firth, and the offshore platform for the Magnus field. From the delivery of material to be assembled in the dry dock of Highland Fabricators on the Dornock Firth, to completion and float out.
1979- 1980	Formed a Joint-Venture Company in Kuala Lumpur to develop and produce Malaysian based factual and drama TV series. Wrote, produced and directed two films on the theme of racial integration, essential to Malaysia's survival as a single unitary state. *Settling the Future*, the national scheme to resettle the primarily rural Malays in economically more productive areas and environments, in an attempt to counterbalance the advantages enjoyed by the city based and commercially more orientated Chinese. *Malaysia Outward Bound*, a young Malay, a young Chinese, and a young Indian brought together in the shared bonding experience and challenges of the Outward Bound School at Lumut, on the country's west coast. Narrated by Andrew Faulds.
1981	Researched, wrote, and directed retrospective accounts of two key actions of world war two, told by original participants backed up by archival combat filming of the time and fresh filming at the actual sites. General Montgomery's failed airborne action at *Arnhem* in northern Holland, September 1944, and in particular how the regimental medical units did their best to care for casualties cut off as they were from main army support, and finally accompanying them into captivity. Camera returning with at that time a young medical officer to the actual site and area, where he tells how it was to set up aid posts and do what they could for the

wounded under such conditions. The result of failure to secure the original objective of that bridge across the Rhine too far. Hundreds of miles down river, and six months later, advancing American units discovered just one bridge intact across the Rhine. They were just in time to prevent it being blown, as all the other such crossings into the heart of Germany already had been. Here, at *Remagen*, they seized the opportunity, and General Patton was able to build up a substantial bridgehead on the eastern bank in southern Germany. Filmed at the Pentagon in Washington, original participants tell of this experience, and how it really was. An outstanding military lesson of don't hesitate, and seize the opportunity. The programme supplemented with US Army filming of the original crossing, plus further interviews and contemporary filming at Remagen and its approaches. Both productions for the SSVC.

1982- 1984	In association with Al Khair of Amman, Production consultant for factual film making in Jordan. Over this same three year period also wrote and directed *The Dead Sea Lives*. The rendering of its high degree of salt into a source of fertiliser on an industrial scale. The integrated construction of an evaporation system, refinery, and township in this remote and barren environment. A major project in the development of Jordan, supplemented with further filming in Aqaba, Jerash, and Petra. Narrated by Sarah Kennedy and Geoffrey Palmer. Bronze Award British Industrial Scientific Association 1984.
1985- 1986	Wrote, compiled and directed *A Quality of Life;* a three part history of Britain 1930-1960. 'Industry and Technology'. 'Transport and Communication', 'Social Developments'. Narrated by Robert Powell. British Film Institute Award for Archival Achievement 1986.

1987-   Based on the Ironbridge Gorge Museum in Shropshire,
1988   wrote, co-produced, and directed *A Bridge in Time*. The
         origins of the Industrial Revolution here on the banks of
         the river Severn in 1779, and its lessons for our own
         time today. Presenter: John Craven. Award of Creative
         Excellence United States Industrial Film and Video
         Festival 1989.

1989-   The ending of the Cold War opened the way for this
1990   film-maker's return to Minsk, capital of Belarus.
         Where, more than forty years before, he had filmed
         United Nations aid to the war shattered city and its sur-
         viving people. Now, and with the support of Russian
         TV and a Moscow based crew, he films its recovery.
         They track down a cross section of its citizens he origi-
         nally met and filmed as war-orphaned children in UN
         assisted care. In this very personal testament they wel-
         come him and camera to their homes and workplace,
         telling of how it has been for them during this interven
         ing period of history - and their hopes now for the fu-
         ture. With his original UNRRA/*March of Time* filming
         of them counterpointed and integrated with this new
         material and rediscovery, the survival and example of
         these *Orphans of Minsk*.
         Produced, presented, and personally reported for the
         Channel 4 Season *Soviet Spring*.

1991   Granada supported development of production projects
         in Costa Rica. The history of the region dramatised in
         music, mime, and dance by a young group, the 'Cantata
         Centro Americana'. Also the lives and works of two
         painters the muralist Cesar Valverde, and the expres-
         sionist Francisco Amighetti.

1992   In recent years there has been no more spectacular de-
         velopment of British industry than North Sea oil. That

438

there are risks involved was brought home to TV viewers one night in July 1988. Occidental's offshore 'Piper Alpha' rig was ablaze. Helicopters winching survivors to safety above the flames. The industry realised that it still needed to know more about the nature of hydrocarbon fire. The opportunity soon came, and on an immense scale.

The Gulf War. The defeated and retreating Iraqis set ablaze over six hundred of the oil fields in Kuwait. The Steel Construction Institute, British Petroleum Research, and British Gas Reserve and Technology despatched a team to the area, and *Kuwait – Scientific Fire Mission* was the result. Written, compiled and assembled from the video and radiometer material they shot amidst the flames, and supplemented with further filming back in Britain of computerised analysis and data based animation. Set within the context of North Sea operations and the construction of the Magnus structure previously filmed.

National Film Theatre Lindgren Lecture on 'The Use and Abuse of Archive Film'. Illustrated by examples of his own work and its utilisation over the years.

1993-1995   For the BBC Centenary Season of Cinema in 1995, Wrote, produced Compiled and directed an archival programme of *Power Behind the Image*. From the original Lumière film of that train arriving at a country station to examples of contemporary video diaries. Focused in the main on how Britain has used the moving image to tell its own story this century while, as it draws to its close, how the parallel development of electronic technology has now made it possible for everyone to express something of their power behind the image. Presenter Siân Phillips.

Onscreen Contributor

1952   NBC. *March of Time* TV Series. *New India's People*. Studio discussion prior to network transmission.

1985   CHANNEL 4. Representation the *March of Time* cinema series 1935-51. Personal recollections and anecdotes of filming post war international subjects, including complete screening of *Asia's New Voice* and *MacArthur's Japan*. Flashback Television.

1995   BBC. Photoplay Productions *Cinema Europe – the Other Hollywood*. The silent cinema and the coming of sound. Childhood recollections.

1997   Tangrams Productions, Munich. French-German ARTE Channel. *A New Dawn for Europe*. Retrospective programme on film production for the post war Marshall Plan. At first hand how it was to be so commissioned, with selected extracts from his own productions in France and Germany.

1998   History Channel. Flashback Television: *I, Witness*. Telling how it really was to film combat in World War Two, illustrated with examples of his own original filming made available by the Imperial War Museum.

Index

441

442

443

445

446

447

448

449

450

451

453

455

458

459

Lightning Source UK Ltd.
Milton Keynes UK
UKOW020610011211

183017UK00012B/98/A